ASANTE BEFORE THE BRITISH

Asante

BEFORE THE BRITISH

The Prempean Years, 1875-1900

THOMAS J. LEWIN

THE REGENTS PRESS OF KANSAS
Lawrence

Library of Congress Cataloging in Publication Data
Lewin, Thomas J., 1944-
Asante before the British.
Bibliography: p.
Includes index.
1. Ashanti—History. 2. Prempeh, King of
Ashanti. 3. Ghana—Colonization. I. Title.
DT507.L48   966.7   78-8003
ISBN 0-7006-0180-5

*Publication of this book was assisted
by the American Council of Learned Societies
under a grant from the Andrew W. Mellon Foundation*

To

Phyllis, Sharyn, my mother,
and the memory of my father

CONTENTS

LIST OF ILLUSTRATIONS

ACKNOWLEDGMENTS

Generous financial support from several institutions made this study possible. I am grateful to the United States Department of Health, Education and Welfare for a grant allowing my participation in the Interdisciplinary Seminar in Field Methods organized by the Institute of African Studies of the University of Ghana and the Program of African Studies at Northwestern University in 1968. The Program of African Studies, at the recommendation of the National Unity Fellowship Committee, awarded me a fellowship to carry out my research abroad in 1970–71. Grants from the Graduate School and the Department of History of Northwestern helped defray the costs of preparing field materials for public deposit. The Graduate Research Fund and the Department of History of the University of Kansas supported part of the research and writing and also provided funds for clerical assistance enabling me to systematize my remaining oral sources of information.

I owe a special debt of gratitude to my doctoral thesis adviser, Ivor Wilks of Northwestern University, for his initial suggestions encouraging me to embark upon this project. His continuing counsel, astute criticism, and willingness to share his unrivaled wealth of knowledge and materials during the past six years has lightened the burdens of completing this study. I am also indebted to his own pioneering inquiries into Asante history and the many rich and enlightening discussions which took place as we both simultaneously labored over our manuscripts.

My two stays in Asante were made deeply meaningful through the kindness and friendship extended to me by its people. Appreciation extends to the many extraordinarily patient Asantes who devoted so much of their time and energies to assist me in sorting the complexities of their late nineteenth-century political life. The auspices of the Asantehene Nana Opoku Ware II facilitated my investigations with officeholders in Kumase, Bekwae, Dwaben, Edweso, Kokofu, Mampon, Mamponten, and Nsuta. Adu Gyamera, al-Hajj Sulāyman, al-Hajj Sumalar, Domfe Kyere, H. Owusu Ansa, I. K. Agyeman, Issa Kilishi, Kwabena Baako, Kwadwo Afodo, Malam Gariba, Malam Haruna, Mamunatu, and Owusu Nkwantabisa were among those who encouraged me frequently to consult them and were particularly supportive of my research. Although at times it was extremely painful to recall episodes in the Prempean years, they willingly shared their experiences and permitted me to quote their accounts in the text. Their vivid recollections enabled me to perceive the diffusion of British imperial power through their eyes. I hope that I have adequately conveyed their account of the final days of the Asante kingdom. Any expression of gratitude to these individuals and the numerous other Asantes who assisted me cannot but be inadequate. This study represents but a small return of my obligation to them.

I am equally grateful to my Research Associate, the late Seth Kwasi Dwamena, for his lively and unfailing interest in my research. The intensive schedule of field interviews followed in 1970–71 would have been impossible without his historical acumen, keen memory, and remarkable judgment. From Kwasi I learned the special crafts necessary for collecting oral testimony, and to a considerable extent he is responsible for the success of my field endeavors. While in Kumase the hospitality extended to me by Edmund Bannerman made many extra hours available for research. Residing with his family enriched my life and work in Asante.

It also gives me great pleasure to express my indebtedness to other friends and colleagues who have in one way or another contributed to this study. To Louise Love goes thanks for her incisive comments, encouragement, and editorial assistance which have clarified my views on several points. Clifford Griffin's insightful suggestions and tireless guidance brought perspective and coherence to this work. Our ongoing dialogue and warm friendship have been of significant benefit to this undertaking. I should like to thank John Alexander for his critical reading under the pressures of time and his useful commentary on the final draft. At various earlier stages in the work, I profited from interchanges with Francis Agbodeka, Robert Garfield, Robert Hamilton, Thomas McCaskie, John Rowe, and Joseph Agyeman-Duah. H. A. Lamb and Adu Boahen kindly sponsored my research affiliation in the Department of History of the University of Ghana. Norman Carpenter is to be commended for his help in the preparation of the maps.

I am obliged also for the efficient and essential service rendered by the staffs of the Africana Library at Northwestern University, the Balme Library at the University of Ghana, the Public Record Office, the British Museum, and the Institute of Commonwealth Studies in London, and by the archivists at the Methodist Mission in London and the Basel Mission in Switzerland. I have benefited from access to the translation of sources made by Paul Jenkins of the Basel Mission, and I thank Kurt Ninck of the Basel Mission for elucidating several obscure passages in the F. Ramseyer correspondence.

And, finally, my greatest debt is to my wife, Phyllis. At every stage she has been my foremost critic and sustainer. But, most of all, I thank her for her love and companionship.

1

THE SETTING

Asante was changing. The leaders and people knew it could never be the same. The elders faced many problems, so many new and different things. Chiefs fought each other. Chiefs that the Asantehene ruled for a long time rebelled. They began to look elsewhere for their lord. . . . Trading was hard in the north and in the coastal towns. Even trade in Kumase stopped for a time. How were Asante men and women to live their lives? And the whites were also coming closer to our lands. Every Asante—men, women, and children—looked to the young Agyeman Prempe to help the nation of our ancestors. But he too came to know that the whites were ambitious. They came to trade, to change our customs, to conquer, to rule. They would not allow Nana Asantehene's successes to continue. We waited. We watched. We heard the elders talk far into the night, every night. We wanted to live our lives. . . . It was a short, glorious time when Nana Prempe ruled our nation.—Domfe Kyere

The last twenty-five years of the nineteenth century—the quarter-century that preceded the Yaa Asantewaa War of 1900 and the extension of British colonial jurisdiction over the Asante nation—framed a decisive and sometimes painful period in the history of the Asante people. This turbulent era witnessed a series of administrations, some of them unprecedented, that culminated in the return to legitimate monarchy in the person of Agyeman Prempe who assumed caretakership of the Golden Stool in 1888. Prempe's road to office was not, however, an easy one nor was he without rivals. A long and bitter campaign, which to a considerable extent polarized the nation into ideologically opposed camps, preceded the eventual acceptance of Prempe's leadership. The constituencies of these rival factions emerged from the opinions and loyalties that had been forming over issues and administrations that had dominated the four-year interregnum between 1884 and 1887.

The disparity of opinion on the manner in which power should be distributed among the districts of Asante and the capital in Kumase was one of the primary sources of conflict throughout the interregnum. Resistance was offered in a variety of forms by outlying district heads to the accumulation of power in the central seat of government, and, when possible, these leaders applied economic, political, public relations, and diplomatic leverage to advance their interests. During the four-year vacancy in the nation's highest office between the reigns of the Asantehene Kwaku Dua II and the Asantehene Agyeman Prempe, provisional and self-styled governors led the nation. Thus, when Prempe came to office in 1888, he assumed executive responsibilities in a political system that had been headed for four years by leaders who had ruled without the legitimate consent of the nation, a system that had been the battlefield of opportunistic maneuverings for individual and local advantage.

With the advice of leaders in the councils of government, Prempe attempted in the years between 1888 and 1896 to reunify Asante after the divisive partisan strife and to restore political order through lenient and conciliatory programs of action. His administration reactivated the tradition of strong central government in Kumase but did not seek the strict reduction of power in the outlying districts as a necessary concomitant of the increase of power at the center. Furthermore, Prempe's supporters did not conduct a "purge" of opposition loyalists, such as had been common under previous rulers. Indeed, overtures of reconciliation were graciously proffered to these dissidents after a time. Prempe's programs of reunification were for the most part well-received and had met with substantial success when the British abruptly terminated his rule by his arrest and deportation.

Understanding the working of the British hand in Asante politics in this period, as the British became more and more purposeful in their dealings with the central government in Kumase and with leaders in the outlying districts, is critical to an accurate grasp of the complicated interactions within Asante and between Asante and the neighboring Gold Coast Colony government. While the British presence in the Gold Coast Colony had been a significant factor in Asante political calculations throughout the nineteenth century, after 1894 the British instituted a major strategy aimed at the seizure of authority in Asante. Prior to 1894 and the inauguration of the British "forward policy," British diplomatic contacts ostensibly supported the central government in Kumase and at the same time negotiated with local leaders on grounds of economic and diplomatic expediency. The British decision in 1896 to extend protection over Asante at the very moment in Asante's history when a great measure of political order and stability was being regained is one of the inescapable ironies of the Asante position in the closing years of the nineteenth century. Asante leaders failed to appreciate the true nature of British desires and goals, and of British strategy and tactics in the metropolitan region. And Prempe and his advisers never seemed to recognize the futility of their diplomatic missions to alter the course of British ambition in Asante. While leaders in the Asante capital tirelessly labored to consolidate national strength within their borders, they suddenly confronted Asante's impotence to resist the superior force of European military technology. The sudden and unexpected British takeover of the reins of government in Kumase administered a shock for which the people of Asante were ill-prepared.

In order to set the stage for the Prempe administration and for the problems and issues that it faced, it is necessary to review the relationships among several of the outlying districts of metropolitan Asante and between those districts and Kumase subsequent to the British invasion of Kumase in 1874. That invasion, the first by a European power, traumatized Asante society and profoundly altered the attitudes and decisions of all Asante politicians. In the aftermath of the hostilities, leaders of many of the outlying districts formulated policies of local supremacy and worked to establish the right to initiate actions and negotiations independent of the central government. The traditional relationships among the districts in the Asante political structure became strained after 1874, and the ambitions and aspirations of several individual local leaders became significant for the nation as a whole.

Late nineteenth-century Asante politicians grappled with one of the oldest politicocultural problems, that is, the relation, the proper relation, between the core and the periphery. This debate was not merely a question of how people should be governed or what the form of government should be, though these points were clearly part of the larger issue. For Asantes it was a question of what should be the relations between the imperial or national-state center and local interests, local power, local pride, and local lives. What types of diversity within the political community should exist? What "rights"—though they often took the form of custom, tradition, religious principles, and economic interests and desires —do the people of the local political units have as against the "rights" or wishes of the center? Controversy over this fundamental problem colored the political culture in which Prempe and Asante statesmen operated.

The complex problems of dissent in the localities offered an enormous challenge to the Prempean government's goal of national reconstruction. Prempe attempted to realize this goal with a policy of permissiveness— granting far-reaching prerogatives to leaders in the districts while strengthening the government at the center of Kumase. In reviewing the actions and decisions that took place in the leading districts of Asante prior to and during the regime of Agyeman Prempe, it becomes apparent that the two-hundred-year-old Asante political system was vastly complex and flexible. It was capable of experimenting with trial modes of governing and with changes in the major seats of political power without destroying the state's ability to return to traditional forms of rule when the collective wish of the nation dictated. The conflict and intense competition for political power that occurred intermittently between 1874 and 1900 were as much indicative of tremendous energy and interest in the political system as they were harbingers of division and breakdown of law and order. One must temper the negative view that might at first glance be taken of such an unpredictable and unstable period by the more positive recognition that such a period is often the mark of vitality and resiliency in a system that is in the process of establishing a new equilibrium.

In addition to the complicated and sensitive issues internal to Asante, Prempe and his councillors faced problems and tensions arising from Asante's economic participation in the expanding rubber trade and its world-wide market implications. Participation in this international market meant the exposure to norms and customs that were alien to Asante. The inevitable conflicts between European and Asante traditions, values, and modes of thought resulted in various forms of misunderstanding and hostility that rendered economic and diplomatic contacts less than mutually satisfying. The intrusion of the Wesleyan and Basel missionaries within Asante borders intensified the anxieties generated in Asante by its entry into an economy that was dominated by powers whose aims and methods were not thoroughly understood. These missionaries, far from limiting their activities to the spiritual and religious domains, attempted to modify Asante social and economic institutions and became involved in political and diplomatic maneuvers aimed at achieving these ends. The British and missionary views of "human sacrifice" in Asante is a case in point to illustrate the way in which partial information and naïve interpretation by members of one culture concerning the activities of another can lead to a severe and unwarranted judgment that becomes part of a rationale for aggressive and punitive policies. Indeed, the vexing topic of ritualized killing, murder, and terror in Asante political culture must be approached with special caution and self-awareness in order to avoid cultural biases and hasty judgments based on irrelevant values.

Asante views of political and judicial violence, slavery, and diplomacy, like most of the issues that comprised late nineteenth-century Asante history, were often bewilderingly complicated and were subject to misleading coverage in public documents. Thus the reign of the Asantehene Agyeman Prempe and the prolonged and confused interregnum which preceded it have long been neglected by historians. The standard histories narrate the schema of political events and dates, discussing briefly the role of very few prominent personages, and delineate the broad outlines of British policy towards Asante in the closing decades of the century. Interestingly, these works have had little access to the Asante perspective on late nineteenth-century political affairs and are characterized by a distinct British viewpoint, seemingly a consequence of the reliance on official British source materials.[1] By contrast, Ivor Wilks' research on Asante history has attempted to correct this imbalance for the first three-quarters of the nineteenth century. Through the use of written source materials, his recent massive study provides a much needed cultural perspective and frame of reference for this treatment of the Prempean years and Asante society on the eve of the British take-over.[2]

A great deal of information concerning Asante attitudes, feelings, and interpretations of the problems that occurred between 1874 and 1900 was gathered by the author in interviews conducted with survivors of Prempe's reign. These firsthand accounts contribute superbly toward elucidating the private motives, public sentiments, and behind-the-scenes maneuverings that surrounded the events of the twenty-five years. They are of inestimable value for portraying the personal context in which politicians moved and convey a remarkable flavor for comprehending the varying nature of Asante political life. For this reason, the accounts compiled from these interviews, carried out in 1968 and 1970–71, are quoted at length in the text to augment and inform the narrative.[3] Obviously, there are certain kinds of information that do not find their way into official records and that are lost with the deaths of the individuals within whose memory they remain. The picture of a period that can be compounded from the testimony of survivors is a mosaic of detailed, personal, and sometimes contradictory pieces of information. This information will not allow a simplistic view of the operations of government. It becomes clear that policies were not arrived at by easy consensus, unanimity did not exist over which course would best assure the welfare of the nation, and agreement was reached with difficulty in selecting leaders deemed wise, capable, and fair. There is, as one learns from listening to Asantes speak about their own past, a welter of personal feelings, private ambitions, family loyalties, and district pride that is as much a part of the impetus for the backing of one candidate or platform over another as are the seemingly objective rationales that are put forth for public consumption. The words of the Asantes themselves provide insights into "the way it was" that could never have been discovered in written sources alone.[4]

In addition to the contribution made by oral data to the scope of our information about nineteenth-century Asante, making it both deeper and more complete, the Asante accounts carry with them an emotional dimension, a sense of personal relevance to a nation of individuals, that is often of necessity lacking from the recitation of historical events. This emotional dimension is, of course, an integral part of the historical moments as they happen, but a reconstruction of this dimension must ordinarily be a matter of educated guesswork. The firsthand accounts of events and feelings in the last quarter of the nineteenth century in Asante, which is so distant from us in both time and space, provide the emotional and dramatic backdrop that actualize the historical period and put it into a human perspective. The intensity of feeling that can be part and parcel of a specific historical moment is especially poignant in the eyewitness accounts offered by Asantes who were present at the arrest of Prempe in 1896. Even after the palliating effect of the passage of almost seventy-five years, the wide-ranging and deep emotion expressed by the Asantes over the sudden and shocking loss of this leader enables the reader of those accounts to enter into the period with greater understanding and compassion than is possible when the intellectual faculty alone is exercised.

The amount and complexity of the data provided by Asante informants forbid the comfortable adoption of a simplistic, unqualified, and definitive stance on the state of Asante in the closing decades of the century. Although there was a great deal of consistency in the oral accounts, the interviews did not render identical versions of the historical happenings that were within the memories of the informants. Each citizen, no doubt, had an individual and somewhat unique perspective on political events, and some were inevitably privy to information that only reached others through propaganda or hearsay. Even so, it is important to know what was believed to be happening whether rightly or wrongly because, as becomes clear in reviewing Anglo-Asante diplomacy in this period, misapprehensions and flawed communication can be prime and pivotal factors in determining the course of events. The view that emerges of Asante through the use of oral materials is complex, emotional, and sometimes difficult to reconcile.

The hindsight that the elderly Asantes bring to bear in their accounts of the last years of Asante sovereignty is frequently marked by pathos and irony, as time has shown that some of the noblest and most majestic acts, particularly on the part of the young ruler Agyeman Prempe, were often exercises in futility. Acts of bad faith and manipulations of the European powers in their dealings with Asante are just cause for bitterness and regret to those who remember Asante in the fullness of power and autonomy. The impact of a ruler like Prempe and the significance of

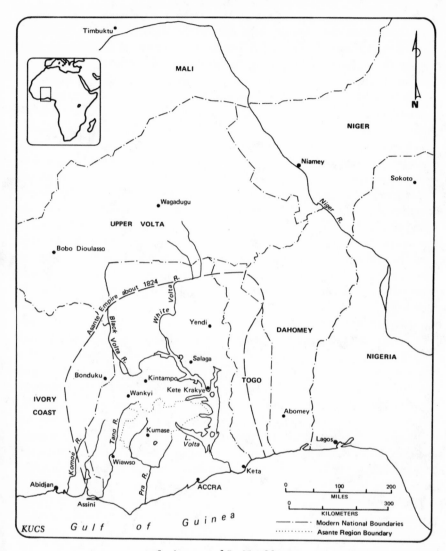

1. Asante and Its Neighbors

the complex interactions among the components of the vast political, economic, and diplomatic Asante state structure cannot be fully understood without the penetrating and revealing data supplied by the men and women in Ghana who generously assisted the author in the reconstruction of the sunset of Asante's independence.

2

THE LATE NINETEENTH-CENTURY ASANTEMAN

Nana Asantehene ruled over the nation of our ancestors. He was our lord.
Kumase was the center for all Asantes.—Adu Gyamera

POLITICS AND SOCIETY IN HISTORICAL PERSPECTIVE

The nineteenth-century kingdom of Asante was one of the most elaborate
social and political organizations to flourish in the West African forest
zone. This was an inevitable outcome of two hundred years of intricate
political and socioeconomic developments. In the later part of the seventeenth century, the Asante state structure consisted of a loosely knit
federation of small chiefdoms located in the central part of the modern
Republic of Ghana. The Kumase *oman*, or territorial division, and the
amanto, or outlying districts, of Bekwae, Dwaben, Kokofu, Mampon, and
Nsuta were the original founding members of the kingdom. These polities shared the common language of Twi (or Akan) and a social system
based on scattered *mmusua kese*, or matriclans.* Ruling families of the
amanto, except Mampon, were Oyoko clan members, and a segment of
that clan provided the rulers of Kumase. The *amanto* capitals lay within
a thirty-five mile radius of Kumase. This area of four thousand square
miles constituted the metropolitan region, the home of the Asante *paa*,
the "true" Asante chiefdoms and people.[1]

Under the leadership of Osei Tutu, an Oyoko royal from Kumase,
the *amanto* forged an informal military alliance employing administrative
procedures and imported firearms from the coastal states of Denkyira and
Akwamu. They conquered the surrounding indigenous Akan communities whose forefathers had migrated from regions south of the Pra River
over the preceding two centuries and incorporated these hunting, fishing,

---

* The English meaning of a Twi common noun is given when it is first used in
the text. A glossary of Twi terms appears at the back of the book.

9

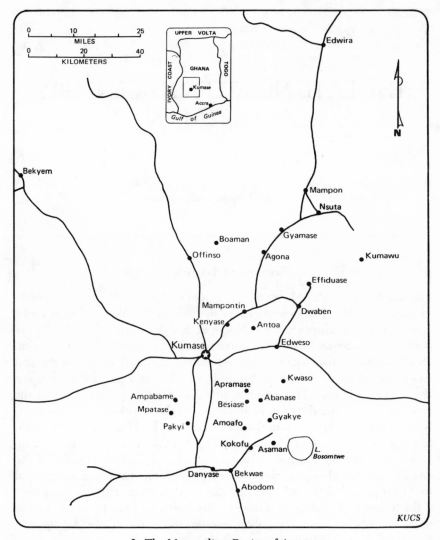

2. The Metropolitan Region of Asante

and gold-mining settlements into the political structure. Osei Tutu and his companions founded the town of Kumase, two miles from Tafo, a prosperous city-state on an important gold trade route between the Niger bend and the Guinea coast.[2] Surrounded by the Nsuben rivers and situated on a rocky hill, Kumase had a natural defense amid lush, fertile soils and a relatively mosquito-free, healthful environment. The heavy forest cover and the plateau of Kumase and its environs markedly contrasted with the more open, drier, forest-savanna country of northern Asante, the region situated north of Mampon scarp, a line of hills running thirty-three miles north of Kumase in a northwest to southeast direction.[3]

Following the defeat of Denkyira in 1698–1701, Osei Tutu, the *ohene*, or chief, of Kumase, became the Asantehene, his capital became the seat of central government and the center of the Asanteman or Asante

Dense rainforest vegetation in the Atwema region

Nation, and his rule gradually extended over the newly evolved state. All preexisting Akan stools and symbols of political authority were banished. National unity was expressed through the institution of the Sika Dwa, or Golden Stool, the sacred embodiment of the Asante people. New national oaths and festivals centered around the supremacy and glorification of the Asantehene's ancestors, and Akan deities symbolized the creation of the novel political order.[4]

During the eighteenth century, the kingdom expanded beyond the forested heartland of the metropolitan region. In the northern savannas, Asante controlled both settled and thinly populated territories extending from Bonduku, capital of Gyaman (Ivory Coast) in the northwest, through the northcentral-northeastern kingdoms of Gonja, Dagomba, and Mamprussi and as far east as the town of Krakye on the Volta River, where the inhabitants spoke Guang. Within this hegemony administrative power was concentrated in the hands of Asante officials whose main bases were the market towns of Banda, Daboya, Yendi, and Salaga. From these centers, state functionaries supervised commerce in centralized and acephalous societies whose inhabitants had varying social organizations and spoke an array of different languages. In some areas, the Asantes permitted the existence of local dynasties as long as they accepted the tax and tributary requirements fixed by the central government in Kumase. In the Gonja kingdom, for example, indigenous ruling houses remained. Elsewhere, as in the Banda region, the pre-Asante dynasties were destroyed, with much bloodshed and ruin. In the humid, mosquito-infested south, Asante control extended over the Guinea coast from Little Popo (Togo) in the east to Cape Lahu (Ivory Coast) in the west. The polities of Akwamu, Assin, Denkyira, Akuapem, and the Fante lands, long-standing middlemen in the trade with agents of Danish, Dutch, English, and French companies dotting the coastline, were within the imperial ambit.[5]

The empire's far-reaching expanse yielded exciting and bountiful markets. Commerce flourished. Forest products and gold and kola nuts flowed through the ancient distributive network of Western Sudanic trade routes to the towns of Timbuktu, Jenne, Segu, and Gao on the Niger, to Hausaland (Northern Nigeria) in the northeast, and ultimately over the Sahara to the immense markets of North Africa. From the north, slaves, leather goods, sheep, silks, blankets, and manufactured goods crossed into the towns of the metropolitan region. Southwards Asante traded palm-oil, ivory, and gold dust with European representatives in the towns of Cape Coast, Elmina, Winneba, Saltpond, and Accra, and brought back iron implements, salt, rum, guns, and gunpowder.

Asante's vast political and economic expansion posed unprecedented problems. The imperial system spread over a hundred thousand square miles and contained some three million multiethnic inhabitants living in communities with enormous cultural diversity. Greater Asante, the area encompassed by the empire, had boundaries approaching those of modern-day Ghana. Eight great-roads, four northern and four southern, linked Kumase to the Muslim north and the European traffic on the Atlantic seaboard.[6] By the end of the eighteenth century Kumase had become the metropolis of the far-flung empire, and Asantehene Osei Kwadwo (1764–77) and his immediate successors, Osei Kwame (1777–98), Opoku Fofie (1798–99), and Osei Bonsu (1800–23), concentrated administrative power in the city by constructing a revolutionary governmental machine designed to cope with the demands of imperial status.[7]

A tightly controlled, bureaucratic system of government evolved. Administrative functions were assigned to specific groups belonging to different departments headed by senior Kumase officeholders with large

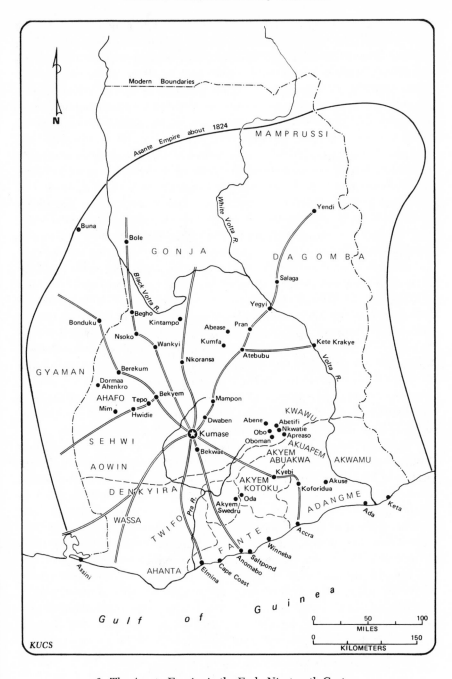

3. The Asante Empire in the Early Nineteenth Century

staffs of lesser-ranked officials. Appointed officials took charge of state trade in kola and ivory and state-owned mining in the rich gold fields at Sankore (in Bron Ahafo), Manso, Nkawie, and Osino (in Akyem Abuakwa). Other groups conducted state trade in the northern and southern markets. An accounting system, staffed by literate Muslims, was created. All parts of Greater Asante were subject to an essentially uniform system of taxes and levies. Skilled, experienced functionaries negotiated foreign affairs in distant West African capitals and within the confines of the empire. Almost every aspect of social and political activity in Kumase had a corresponding department and officials presided over by the Asantehene and his councillors. As Kumase became the center of government, the original outlying *amanto* and other districts and towns of the metropolitan region were reduced to the position of senior units with limited powers in the kingdom. During the first three-quarters of the nineteenth century, Kumase became the apex of an extensive political and military hierarchy and the focal point of legal, economic, and religious life for the one-half million residents of the metropolitan region.[8]

The city of Kumase, housing a resident population of some twenty thousand, was the nerve center of the imperial system. It bustled with active and attentively engaged citizens who were always conscious that their town was the center from which all power and authority flowed. Nineteenth-century Kumase, a vibrant, ordered capital, was populated by those involved in governmental business characterized by mobility, careerism, and intense competition. The affairs of state attracted sons and daughters from the best families in the nation and offered avenues for rapid advancement regardless of geographical or ancestral origins.

Demand for prestigious positions in the Asantehene's household and departments produced an electric environment in which individuals and groups jockeyed for favors, patrons, and loyalties. As with all political life in nineteenth-century Asante, the essence of politics in Kumase was power and money, a world of rivalry and resistance, maneuvers and chicanery, threats and violence, successes and failures, and deviance from custom and precedent.[9] Shifting and fluid alliances of power and authority usually took precedence over relationships based on kinship (or clan) ties and vague allusions to perceived traditions and ancestral codes. Above all, imaginative Asante men and women, whether on the national, regional, or local level, employing wit and guile, strove to mobilize support and out-maneuver each other so that complex responses and choices, some rational and some biased, could be made.

> People from outside Kumase stayed with a person in his ward. In every ward there was a chief with his subjects. My father worked in the palace. He stayed with one of the ward chiefs.

14

Asantes in the wards always talked politics. They talked outside the palace, in the courtyard and on the streets. Often they talked into the night. More people would come late at night. They discussed who had a case at court, who was fined, and what the chiefs said. They always talked about who did what things in Asante, and where and how things were done. They seemed to know everything. Some told Nana Asantehene what was discussed. Some kept it to themselves. Some day, if these people served in the palace, they could use this knowledge.[10]

A cosmopolitan metropolis, Kumase was the magnet that drew delegations from every reach of the empire and diplomats from neighboring states. The city fascinated and bedeviled converts to Christianity and nineteenth-century Europeans seeking commercial treaties, consultation, and assistance. The patronage of the Asantehene encouraged the finest craftsmen to settle in the town's environs. Specialists in goldsmithing, weaving, pottery, woodcarving, and smithing, who worked in separate suburbs, were joined by other skilled craftsmen brought in as captives from the conquered territories. The highest skills in various handicrafts were found in the city. Muslim settlers, serving as scribes and physicians at the Asantehene's court, and itinerant traders from the northern entrepôts mixed with Fante artisans and refugees from the coastal states. At the time of national festivals the city swelled to a hundred thousand as villagers packed the noisy streets for the occasions.[11]

Kumase's spatial organization, architectural design, and indeed every physical detail reflected the paramount authority of the Asantehene and his councillors.[12] Dominated by the rambling, massive Aban, or palace, official residence of the Asantehene, the town divided into seventy-seven *abrono*, or wards, separated by twenty-seven streets. The houses of the palace, the town's only stone building, lay along a wide street running through the center of the city, enclosed on three sides by a high wooden fence, and bounded on the fourth by marshes of the Nsuben rivers. Within the courtyards of the palace, the councils of state and the Asantehene's court convened. In adjacent areas, functionaries of various departments maintained separate living quarters and carefully maintained *adampan*, or offices, sized according to their rank and the volume of daily business they transacted.[13] Three contiguous streets served as the Asantehene's private recreational quarters when national political (and religious) observances—the annual Odwira and the Adae ceremonies—confined him to the palace.

Outside the royal dwellings, the Asantehene's agents carefully monitored all traffic in the city and its environs. Illegal entry was prevented, Asante and foreign visitors supervised, and aliens detained for

Sideview of Manhyia, the Asantehene's Palace, Kumase

days. Officialdom demanded proper protocol, especially in the way an official was addressed. House size and kind of construction were pre-determined, unauthorized embellishment was proscribed. Even leisure time was scrutinized. Casual evening strolls, for example, were forbidden. Dress codes were strictly enforced.[14] Underpinning the authoritarian ethic was the enormous influence of custom and spiritualism symbolized by the shrine priest Anokye's legal code which set standards for ethical conduct and pervaded most aspects of urban culture and political life.

> People were not allowed to farm in the capital. This was the priest Okomfo Anokye's decree when he felt the need to create a large capital for the Asantes. . . . Anokye decreed many important historical laws. If one held a bottle of palm wine, and it fell and broke, the person was in trouble for this. Anokye received his own instructions from his shrine. If a man had sexual intercourse with his niece, it was an offense and was punishable by death for both the niece and the man. If a pregnant woman was found guilty after a trial and was to be killed, the executioners had to wait until after she delivered the child. Then the mother was killed. The baby was offered to the Asrampon shrine. If a girl menstruates and does not declare this openly to her parents for the puberty rites to be performed, and later she's found to be pregnant, she and her parent would have to slaughter sheep. This is to purify her. Anokye also said that

eggs should not be broken on Kumase streets and that the dumb and deaf should not be killed. A madman also should not be killed. He himself is not aware of what he is doing. Asantes did not kill without reason.[15]

The dignified Opanin Domfe Kyere, about 98 years of age, Kumase

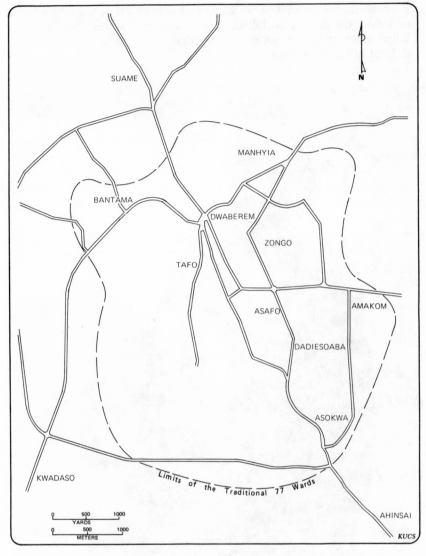

SUAME

MANHYIA

BANTAMA

DWABEREM

ZONGO

TAFO

ASAFO

AMAKOM

DADIESOABA

ASOKWA

KWADASO

Limits of the Traditional 77 Wards

500   1000
YARDS
500   1000
METERS

AHINSAI

KUCS

4. Late Nineteenth-Century Kumase and Its Environs

Kumase's wards were small, rarely consisting of more than three thatched houses, and, according to Domfe Kyere, were "not grouped according to clan but rather people serving the same stool lived in the same ward."[16] Prominent military and civilian personnel resided in separate areas. Other wards received their names from noteworthy historical events or the functions they performed. Apremoso, or the place of cannons, reminded Asantes of the trophy captured in the war with Denkyira. Members of the Oyoko royal family lived in Akanase. The Asafohene and Bantamahene, senior commanders of the town's defensive organizations, lodged in Asafo and Bantama, respectively. The Adumhene, or chief of police, and his people stayed in Adum nearby the public execution grounds. Foreign laborers and nonofficeholding Asantes segregated themselves. The Muslim community, for example, occupied Dominase and Serebosakyi *abrono*. Court craftsmen worked in Kete and Boagyawe. Royal cooks, drummers, and other minor functionaries stayed in Soodo and Ntuom, close to the palace.[17]

The city's two markets were held daily from seven in the morning until sunset. The larger, Dwaberem, had numerous rows of merchandise varying from locally produced crops and craft articles to rare imported delicacies. Plantations surrounding Kumase, on which Kumase officials' slaves worked, supplied foodstuffs, vegetables, and fruits: yams, cocoyams, corn, cassava, millet, plantains, rice, bananas, sugar cane, oranges,

Bustling Kegyetia marketplace, Kumase

pawpaws, pineapples, pepper, okra, and eggs. For the thirsty there were local beers, palm wine, rum, and gin. Calabashes, sandals, pipes, and wooden stools were in the craftsmen's stalls and sheds. Women and men vendors hawked imports from the northern and southern trade centers, including cottons, silks, beads, gunpowder and firearms, lead, tobacco, and iron farming implements. And always sliced beef, mutton, fowls, dried fish, smoked snails, deer, and wild hog were available for the culinary delight of Kumase families at the one large evening meal.[18]

Governmental service, business, festivals, and the constant bustle of urban life in Kumase were always subjects of lengthy discussions in the Asanteman.

Woman marketing plantains in Kokofu marketplace, southern Asante

Kumase was a trading center. Not the biggest in the Asanteman, but still a trading center. Foodstuffs, meat, everything the people of Kumase needed. The market was not as big as now but still was quite large. People also gathered in Kumase for the Asantehene's festivals—Odwira and Adae—which may at times last a week. These days were very important to all Asantes. Nana poured libations to the ancestors and so that our crops would grow. After the ceremonies people left for the villages. Kumase was not one place at that time. There was bush between the Amakom and Adum areas. The town ran from Adum to the palace area. People crossed the Subin valley through the bush to Amakom. . . . Another reason Asantes came to Kumase was to visit or stay with chiefs or for trials at the chiefs' courts. The chiefs of Tafo, Amakom, Sepe, Buokrom, Bantama, Gyaase, and others permanently lived in Kumase. The movement of people to Kumase depended on their purpose. The prices were always higher in Kumase than elsewhere. People were always busy. The Asantehene's *nhenkwaa* were all over. They watched all that went on. I myself stayed with my father. He was an *ahenkwaa* from Sepe. He worked in the palace. My father owned a house here in Kumase and visited his wife in Sepe at times. Many from the villages put up houses in Kumase. This was so they had a place to stay when they worked in the capital. Those without houses slept where their *ohene* slept. Or they slept in the village and left for Kumase early in the day and returned to the village on the same day.[19]

Competition in Kumase's markets epitomized the most intense level of commercial exchange in the nation. The highest prices and the widest selection of trading items were in the capital. A substantial proportion, perhaps all, of the city's population obtained their daily sustenance in the marketplace. Actively involved in this and similar trading opportunities, the people of wealth, or *asikafo* (sing. *sikani*, from *sika*, "gold" or "money"), capitalized on Kumase's market potentialities.

During the nineteenth century, the *asikafo* in governmental service ranged from senior officeholders in the civilian and military establishments of the capital to minor functionaries in the Asantehene's household

Bread merchant traveling to Bekwae market, southern Asante

21

and administrative departments. They possessed regalia—elaborate stools, silk and cloth umbrellas, wooden and metal chairs—that indicated varying degrees of high social and political status in the official hierarchy. On state occasions these officeholders ostentatiously displayed their rank and recognizable positions for the Asantehene and the public at large. They were always preceded by a procession of *nhenkwaa* who waved elephant tails, blew elaborate horns, and drummed continuously.[20] Rich commoners—those *asikafo* without office—chose to remain outside the public limelight. Instead, they financed electoral candidates, influenced public opinion, and advised national and local politicians. All Asante *asikafo* were defined as:

> rich men who own large estates, and are capable of granting large loans; in ancient times they owned many slaves. All Sikafo are highly respected, so long as it is known in the community that they obtained their riches by honest means and hard work. They are well-to-do people, on whom the state relies for pecuniary assistance, especially in granting loans.[21]

Private entrepreneurs accumulated their wealth through trade. Several types of commoner *abatafo*, or traders, operated in nineteenth-century Asante. They differed in the scale and organization of their operations and utilized differing financial resources to underwrite their activities.[22] Some *abatafo*, residing in Kumase, in the *amanto*, or in the kola-producing towns and villages of the metropolitan region, exchanged kola for slaves in the northern markets. Their *abusua*, or matrilineage, provided the requisite capital for their marketing sojourns. Slave labor, in turn, increased farming and plantation productivity for the *abusua* on the local level. Such an *abatafo* usually did not make a trading journey two years in succession. The *abusua* financed another individual in subsequent marketing seasons, and the slaves benefited the entire *abusua's* production efforts.

By contrast, the *abatafo* known as the *adwadifo* (sing. *odwani*) primarily concentrated their efforts on the metropolitan region markets. In Asante various kinds of markets existed, depending on the sorts of goods sold and the number of people in the surrounding towns and villages. *Adwadifo* watched the market schedule closely: it determined their movements during the week. The *odwani* traveled outside his or her town to retail the merchandise.

> Such a person could go from Kumase to the town of Nkawie where a market was held every Wednesday and then to the market at Edweso which was held every Sunday. This same person would also go to the market held on Friday near Dwa-

ben. This was called the Oyoko market. This type of trader would return to Kumase or his starting point on the same day. He would always look for places where there were local markets and find out on which days they operated and where they were held. He had to dispose of his goods in a relatively short time in order that the goods he bought in bulk would not spoil. Such a trader was often helped by his children, or he would employ people to help him with the trade.[23]

A third type of *abatafo* moved his base of operations to the kola-producing areas of the metropolitan region. These *akwantufo* (sing. *kwantufo*) were full-time trading specialists. They operated between central Asante and all external markets. *Akwantufo* made extensive preparations for hiring large numbers of laborers and carriers, prepared the kola in the wet season for trading ventures in the dry season, and were continuously involved in all aspects of the long-distance trade. Much of their *mpaso*, or profits, derived from a carefully nurtured credit system extended to other Asante *abatafo*.

> Before the borrower took the gold, it was weighed. The value of the gold was learned in this way. Then the borrower knew how much to bring back after six months. The borrower added gold when he returned the loan. Gold was weighed when it was returned to find out the true value. The Asantes did not write agreement notes. There was a third person—the *okigyinani*—to guarantee the loan. He said he would pay if the borrower did not pay back the loan.[24]

Other *abatafo* concentrated their efforts on quite specialized items with relatively limited markets. They exchanged, for example, *fonwoma*, or black monkey skins, for foodstuffs in Kumase, or sold *nkoo*, or parrots, for rum in the coastal ports. As a group, they relied on the *akwantufo* for the capital necessary to start their ventures. All private traders used their profits to continue trading or to farm and buy slaves. In Asante it was well-known that "if you worked hard, had many laborers, and a good season for your farms or trade, then you would become wealthy."[25] Nevertheless, private traders were restricted by the advantages the state gave to its own trading personnel. The Asantehene's *abatafo* under the supervision of the Batahene of Kumase, a chief in the Gyaase Fekuo, received the best prices for their annual kola crops, never paid for the use of roads in central Asante, and were entirely subsidized by the national treasury.[26]

State regulations further inhibited the number of wealthy commoners and the ease with which large amounts of capital could be concentrated in private hands. During the first three-quarters of the nineteenth century, the Asante government's stringent fiscal policies permitted private traders and farmers to maintain their livelihood but prohibited them from accumulating inheritable wealth. Asantehenes and their councillors, moreover, frequently fined commoners who had made too much money and deprived them of their gold resources.

> If a *sikani* had a case at court, either a chief's or at the Asantehene's, he was fined heavily because he was regarded as a rich man. But a *sikani* frequently was set free and took all his property in the form of gold dust to the palace. Then the Asantehene would start to take the capital from him. The court said that he would surrender his gold or face execution. He had little choice, especially if he or his family had displeased the Asantehene. Thus many rich men pretended to be poor in Asante. This was to avoid these legal fines if they were found guilty at court. The fines were scaled: more for the *asikafo*, less for the poor man.[27]

The majority of *asikafo* in governmental service were Kumase *nhwesofo*, or overseers (literally, "caretakers"), charged with administrative responsibility of towns and villages in Metropolitan and Greater Asante. As the Asantehene "owned" *all* the land and people in the kingdom, they supervised his realm and represented him at various levels of the political hierarchy. Their office-estates—that is, the lands and *nkoa*, or subjects, attached to their stools—contained population centers ranging from fifty to five thousand persons in the metropolitan region and twenty to a thousand in the adjacent areas of Kumase Ahafo, Ahafo Ano, Asante Akyem, and Manso Nkwanta.[28]

The Kumase chiefs' office-estates were acquired, enlarged, and reduced in several ways. The Asantehene distributed lands of defeated chiefs to distinguished Kumase military commanders and rewarded others for renowned sociopolitical services to the state. The monarch and his councillors promoted chiefs by selling towns and villages on the real-estate market, thereby increasing an office-estate's expanse and influence. The government in Kumase resettled prisoners of war, slaves obtained through tribute, and free immigrants which augmented the laboring and military potential of an office-estate. Finally, on rare occasions Asantehenes marketed towns in the metropolitan region to increase revenues in the national treasury.[29] These monies could be used to reward Asante officials with property or income.

Kumase *nhwesofo* had councils composed of subchiefs of their office-estate, and these subchiefs in turn had councils consisting of the *mpaninfo*, or heads of families, representative of the various matriclans in their jurisdiction. Council members at each level represented their

The main street in the town of Edweso on a sultry afternoon

constituents. As additional towns and villages were added to the office-estate, they were assigned a place in the hierarchy, while the main demands upon them were military levies in time of war, service to the Asantehene, plus a loyalty, expressed in taxes and tributes to the *nhwesofo* and through them to the Asantehene.

Landholding and juridical patterns within the office-estate were very convoluted. Kumase *nhwesofo* supervised just land units, just people, or, as was most common, various divisions and combinations of land and people within a designated geopolitical unit. Lesser ranked *ahene*, or chiefs, subordinate to the *nhwesofo*, often supervised single towns or villages. Some had responsibility for only quarters of localities. Junior officials, however, could oversee twenty or thirty towns within their administration. Still others by-passed the intermediate hierarchical levels and served the Asantehene directly. *Nhwesofo* seldom had responsibility for *all* the land and people within their office-estates, which were scattered throughout the metropolitan region and rarely formed cohesive, discrete spatial units. Their influence and rank were primarily determined by the number of people they supervised and the wealth of the office-estate in taxable minerals (e.g., gold), kola, palm-oil trees, and rural plantation production (e.g., yams, corn, cocoyams, plantains, and cassava output).[30]

The *odekuro*, or local chief or headman, was the official whose

The Mampontenhene with his district *ahene*, Mamponten, Asante

responsibilities actually touched upon most nineteenth-century Asantes who lived and worked in a village environment. Every Asante has a village, and the village was the home of the Asante in the nineteenth century regardless of whether a citizen was born in Kumase, Bekwae, Dwaben, or any other center of local administration. Supervised by the *odekuro*, the village constituted the basic political and economic unit in Asante. It was composed of localized matrilineages, subdivisions of dispersed Akan clans, whose members usually occupied specific wards. Matrilineages, headed by the *ofiepanin*, or lineage elder, had rights to that portion of the village land which belonged to the matrilineage. *Ahoho*, or strangers, received farming rights from members of the matrilineage, subject to the approval of the *odekuro* and his council of elders.[31]

In the village the *odekuro* initiated the annual agricultural cycle when he formally requested the men to begin work on his *afuo*, a farm or plantation. All the villagers assisted him through the stages of food production: weeding, planting, harvesting, and transporting the crops home or to the local market. On individual farms the women performed most of the daily work, while the men felled heavy trees, burned dried wood, enclosed fields, and prepared the ground for cultivation. Shifting cultivation was the prevailing method of land use, and manured fields lay fallow for two or three years. During the dry season from late December to early April, men and women fished or gathered snails to supplement their farming activities. In some villages hunting by the men constituted another economic pursuit. Most villages manufactured their own compound utensils, stools, clothes, tools, and gold products which were exchanged throughout the district.[32]

For villagers the *odekuro* exercised profound economic, legal, and religious authority in addition to his integral place in the political hier-

A compound house in a typical Asante village

archy. Village institutions centered around his activities. The *odekuro* appointed tax collectors or collected taxes himself. He gathered the *nto*, or yearly rental fees, paid by farmers who were not subjects of the stool and assembled produce from slaves who farmed the plantations and paid their taxes in yams, eggs, fowls, goats, and plantains. Two-thirds of the village taxes and other monies accruing from the farms and plantations went directly to the *nhwesofo* who, subsequently, returned one-half of his portion to the *odekuro*. The *odekuro* used half of his share for personal expenses and the remainder for subsidizing local road improvements, maintenance of the local court and council, and provisioning the village's forces for warfare.[33] The *odekuro* made military assignments, and, in the late nineteenth century, he and his contemporaries in the district could organize and supply three thousand men in only three days.

The *odekuro* also led the local Odwira festival, celebrated at the end of the Asante year in late September, following the harvest of the yam crop. During these festivities the ancestors, the gods, and the omnipresent spirits of the trees and rivers ceremonially devoured the yearly yam crop. As he poured libations to local shrines in the memory of departed ancestors, the *odekuro* ritually demonstrated the paramount importance that all Asantes attached to the fruits of their cultivation.[34]

> Every Asante knows from where he comes. The *odekuro* of a place knows the history of the place and the families. The people go to him with their problems. His court settles disputes over land. The elders respect him. Nana Asantehene knows him and respects him. He sees Nana in Kumase. He knows when there are good prices in the market. He tells his people this. He tells them when the crops are ready. He protects them and knows where everybody lives and what they are doing. For the village the *odekuro* is the world.[35]

Nineteenth-century Asantes identified their origins with reference to their birthplace in the village as well as the region in which that locality existed.[36] Asantes often conceived of their political and socioeconomic status in terms of the historic function of their specific "home" district,

The venerable Adu Gyamera, about 110 years of age, and great-grandsons, Kwadaso, Kumase

and, consequently, pointed to that district as a frame of reference for their status within the community, in Kumase politics, and also in the context of wider Asante political life. Citizens from the Atwema towns of Abuakwa, Agogo, and Boko, for example, always noted that the Atwema district to the west and southwest of Kumase, by contrast to other metropolitan regions, had a distinct service function in late nineteenth-century Asante political culture. The name Atwema, so it was claimed, literally meant "to draw people" to the Asantehene's palace.[37] As the Atwema people were among the first to become minor functionaries in the government and served as the Asantehene's goldsmiths, pipe fillers, cooks, drummers, and traders, citizens from that district took particular pride in their long association with the civil arm of the bureaucratic apparatus.

Along with Atwema the Kwabre district to the east and northeast of Kumase was perceived as the major economic hinterland of the Asante capital. Amansie to the south and southeast had politicoreligious significance: it was the place of "origin of the nation," the area from which the earliest Oyoko royals migrated, and the region in which the Golden Stool "descended from the sky."[38] Asante Akyem inhabitants to the east of Kumase stressed their military identification as their district was considered a vital "buffer" territory for the defense of the Asante capital. Kumase Ahafo, the region to the northwest of the capital, was distinguished by its hunting, gold mining, and economic contribution to the welfare of the Asanteman.[39] Clearly, then, Asantes possessed a definite and specific concept of regional—and individual, household, and village —political space with well-defined boundaries. Regional "mental maps" thus served to fulfill Asante needs of physical and social orientation, to disseminate verbal information, and, on another level, to clarify the Asante understanding of their position in relation to their environment.

THE ORGANIZATION OF THE ASANTE STATE

The trend towards the progressive accumulation of power and authority in the central government in Kumase dominated Asante political life throughout the first three-quarters of the nineteenth century. The centralizing policies of the Asantehenes—Osei Kwadwo (1764–77), Osei Kwame (1777–98), Opoku Fofie (1798–99), Osei Bonsu (1800–23), Osei Yaw Akoto (1823–33), Kwaku Dua I (1834–67), and Kofi Kakari (1867–74)—and the increasing extension of the authority of Kumase over the spheres of politics, economics, religion, justice, and warfare resulted in major changes in the national political structure. Nineteenth-century Asantehenes and their councils in Kumase, comprising representatives of

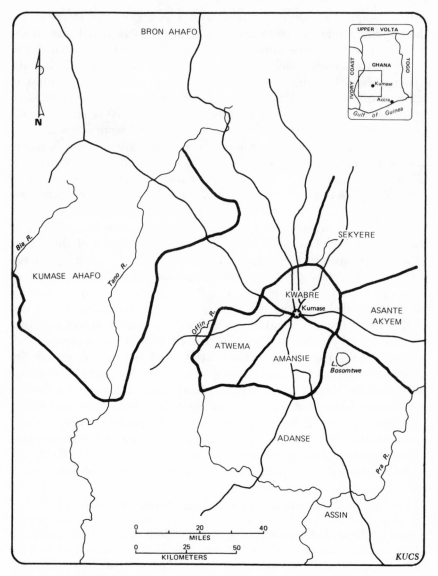

5. The Major Regions of Late Nineteenth-Century Asante

the interlocking bureaucratic, military, and princely elites of the capital, directed the affairs of state to the virtual, and at times total, exclusion of the other main components of national political life, notably, the *amanhene*, the rulers of the founding *amanto*. Kumase's ascendancy in national politics derived in part from the growth of an innovative bureau-

Suburban Kumase

cratic structure, and in part from the social changes which permitted Kumase society to develop a far greater degree of social freedom and economic success than the *amanto*. These social changes were, in turn, consequent upon the practice in Kumase of awarding governmental offices on the basis of achievement rather than ascription. Careers in government and business, which were highly competitive and prestigious, were thus open to talent in the *amanto* and the capital: the Asantehene and his councillors were able to utilize the full resources of Asante skill and enterprise at their command.[40]

At the head of the Asante state stood the Asantehene, custodian of the Sika Dwa. He was the guardian of the temporal and spiritual unity of the kingdom and was also the chief executive, commander-in-chief of the army, and head of the highest court. Although his enormous powers clearly gave him the potentiality of becoming an autocrat, his exercise of these powers and his independence in decision-making were, in fact, closely circumscribed by the legal and customary norms of the polity; blatant violations of these norms could result in public and formal charges leading to deposition. Furthermore, Asantehenes attained power under the aegis of a dominant political faction and were expected to pursue the programs and policies of that faction. Failure to keep faith with the interest group that brought him to office could also mean the monarch's destoolment. In theory, the Asantehene could not, therefore, establish an autarchical administration but had to be aware of and responsive to the needs of the nation and the demands of leading political groups at all times. Yet, the Asante political system did not function in "machine-like" fashion without the influence of the character, personality, strength, or will of the monarch.[41] At times an Asantehene ignored or defied the faction (or "party") that brought him to power and would then employ his vast, if circumscribed, authority to implement policies of his own choosing, relying on the inherent powers of the kingship to overcome faction and tradition alike.[42]

Asantehenes in the nineteenth century presided over the decision-making councils of the Asanteman. The highest council in the nation was de jure the Asantemanhyiamu, or the Assembly of the Asante Nation.[43] The origins of this body presumably date from the formation of the Asante kingdom in the late seventeenth century. Originally, the Asantemanhyiamu was intended to function as the supreme legislative and judicial body of the Asanteman. Its membership was determined on a territorial basis. In the late eighteenth century it probably had some two hundred members. The amanhene, other heads of outlying territorial districts of the metropolitan region, and certain prominent ahene from Kumase had seats on this council. Occasionally, provincial rulers from areas within the imperial ambit but outside the metropolitan region—for example, Dagomba, Nkoransa, and Takyiman—might also be represented. The Asantemanhyiamu routinely convened only once a year at the time of the Odwira, the festival when subordinate rulers reaffirmed their allegiance to the Asantehene in Kumase. Participants at the regular annual sessions debated matters of political, judicial, and financial importance on both the district and national levels. The Asantehene convened extraordinary meetings of the Asantemanhyiamu in situations of crisis, such as debate over war and peace in foreign affairs, the ratification of treaties, or the implementation of force against rebellious leaders in the metropolitan region, or for major policy innovations, such as the relocation of the empire's principal economic centers. Further, the mandate of the Asantemanhyiamu was, in theory, necessary for decisions involving substantial outlays of men and money. Considerations of time, distance, and expense and the need to maintain continuous leadership on the local level frequently forced the heads of outlying districts to send representatives to these meetings in Kumase, rather than attending in person.[44]

Because of the unwieldiness of the convocations of the Asantemanhyiamu and its obvious insufficiency for the management of the complex day-to-day affairs of government, which required constant attention because of the size of the Asante dominion and the scope of governmental involvement in Asante life, a second body, the Council of Kumase, developed in the early nineteenth century. It gradually assumed, de facto, the powers of the Asantemanhyiamu and dealt in an *ad hoc* manner with various governmental matters which could not be postponed for the Asantemanhyiamu's decision.[45] Presided over by the Asantehene, the council operated as the highest court of justice and the chief advisory body of the monarch; it thus performed functions not unlike the English Privy Council. During the middle of the nineteenth century, it extended its influence over domestic administration, conducted foreign policy, taxed, and levied tribute. By the late 1870s the Council of Kumase had become, along with the Asantehene, the actual central government of the Asante Nation.

The council's membership varied over time and according to the type of business under discussion. Usually, senior officeholders of the Kumase district occupied seats on the council. These politicians were representatives of the main *fekuo*, or groupings of administrative offices, which constituted the principal divisions of central government. Regular members with voting rights included the Bantamahene and the Asafohene (two senior military commanders and leaders of the Kumase forces), the Anantahene (another important military leader), four or perhaps more of the eight *akyeame*, or counselors and spokesmen of the Asantehene; and the Adumhene, the Gyaasewahene, and the Manwerehene (chief of the Asantehene's personal servants and household), and other heads of civil and administrative organizations of the state; and the Akyempemhene, Atipinhene, and Atene Akotenhene, the representatives of the princes or sons and grandsons of past Asantehenes or the reigning monarch. These mostly appointive bureaucratic, military, and princely offices constituted a majority in the council and had been created by late eighteenth- and nineteenth-century Asantehenes to counter the power of the more traditional or wholly hereditary offices.[46]

A second group in attendance comprised the occupants of certain important offices in Kumase who sat by virtue of their stool's historic and demographic importance in the formation of the kingdom. This group included, for example, the Tafohene, Amakomhene, Adontenhene, Kyidomhene, and Oyokohene of Kumase, all of whose offices antedated the creation of the Asante political order. The first occupants of these ancestral offices had claimed descent from Twi-speaking families inhabiting Adanse, Bekwae, Kokofu, and regions south of the Pra River. The founders of the kingdom had "come to find" these matrilineal, hereditary stools in the metropolitan region. Thus the Asantehene Osei Tutu and his associates had depended heavily on the manpower and counsel of this original political elite in the early days of the kingdom.[47] Finally, the council's coopted members brought outside expertise and specialized skill and knowledge for specific issues—for example, Muslims and other north-

ern dignitaries who frequently advised the Asantehene on imperial relations with the North and had crucial diplomatic and economic links
in Asante's savanna hinterlands.[48] These officials were adjunct members
without voting rights in the deliberations. Developed in response to the
exigencies of government business and changing in composition according to the nature and requirements of that business, the Council of
Kumase was the principal arena of administrative power under successive

The Asantehene's Imam, al-Hajj Sumalar, and his Asante Nkramo advisers,
Suame, Kumase

nineteenth-century Asantehenes. Nevertheless, the Asantemanhyiamu retained its fictional traditional role as the supreme decision-making organ;
and in the crises of the late nineteenth century, several of its members
attempted to reassert its nominal power, including the right to approve
the selection of a new Asantehene.

The Council of Kumase's arrogation of the powers of the Asantemanhyiamu and the concentration of power under the Asantehene and
his Kumase councillors evoked strong antagonisms in the outlying districts in the late 1870s and 1880s. Various powerful politicians in the
amanto of the metropolitan region and in the *amansin* and *mantiase*, the
tributary provinces and towns of Kwawu, Nkoransa, Asante Akyem, and
the Bron area, questioned and challenged the highly centralized, bureaucratic system of government that had developed in *ad hoc* fashion in

Kumase.[49] They agitated for major changes in the organization of the political system, to circumscribe the intensity, depth, and scope of the power-complex known as the "central government." The dissenters argued for new or restored political status for their respective units within the Asanteman and sought to effect a fundamental redistribution of political power in the system as a whole. Their demands were a challenge to Kumase's supremacy but were apparently not indicative of disenchantment with the idea of central government as such. It was fundamentally the primacy and legitimacy of the Council of Kumase as the supreme decision-making body of Asante that was in question in the final two decades of the nineteenth century.

The Asantehene and the two conciliar bodies formed the decision-making parts of the Asante political system. However, the actual tasks of administration and control were carried out by a bureaucratic apparatus which developed as a consequence of a series of radical political changes in the late eighteenth and early nineteenth centuries. These changes, developed in the Kumase context, undermined the power and authority of the Kumase traditional chiefs. Most of the functions of these chiefs, who occupied ancestral and thus hereditary stools which had existed prior to the formation of the kingdom and had been incorporated within the newly formed state, were transferred to a new class of officials appointed and controlled by the Asantehene. These functionaries administered the complex affairs of the expanded Asante empire in the nineteenth century. The new offices held by these appointed officials were created as patricentric stools known as *mmammadwa*; that is, they were usually occupied by the sons and grandsons of the previous occupants or of the Asantehene himself.[50] This mode of succession contrasted sharply with the matrilineal succession of the traditional hereditary stools and the subsidiary offices associated with them. One of the foremost groupings of patricentric stools thus created in the early nineteenth century was that of the Ankobea, a *fekuo* which consisted of the Asantehene's personal paramilitary bodyguard.[51] Owing in large part to the existence of the Ankobeahene and his fellow officeholders, Asantehenes in the late eighteenth and early nineteenth centuries could effect major structural alterations in the Asante central government.

One result of these changes was the emergence of several major arms of bureaucratic administration. The Gyaasewahene, occupant of the Pinanko stool, had general responsibility for the financial affairs of the state. As treasurer the Gyaasewahene, assisted by the Sanaahene, supervised income and expenditure and could, by means of his financial court, increase revenue from the metropolitan region and the provinces of the empire by adjusting the overall level of taxation in the form of tribute, poll taxes, death duties *(awunyadie)*, and tolls. Officials in the Gyaasewa organization, with the assistance of the *odekuro*, personally collected revenue in every village of the empire. Within the Gyaasewa, the Batahene —also appointed by the Asantehene—was responsible for the organization of state trading. His office recruited its functionaries from groups of lesser officials in Kumase, notably the *asokwafo*, or hornblowers, and the *akyeremadefo*, or state drummers. In addition, the *nkwansifo*, or highway police, who regulated immigration and trade on most of the major roads of Asante, and the functionaries of the public works department, charged with sanitation in the environs of Kumase and road maintenance in the metropolitan region, worked within the Gyaasewa organization.[52]

The second major arm of the bureaucratic infrastructure consisted of the officials in the political service who conducted diplomatic negotiations in the nineteenth century with the Danes, British, Dutch, Dahomey, Gyaman, Krakye, and other neighboring colonies and countries. This organization recruited its members from the *akyeame*, the *afenasoafo*, or swordbearers, and from other lesser-ranked chiefs in Kumase. Concerned with arbitration, conciliation, and the resolution of possible military disputes in the conquered territories and provinces administered from Kumase, these officials often set up their own courts to administer justice and to settle specific local litigation and could, if necessary, call upon military resources for settlement.[53]

The provincial administration constituted the third principal division of the bureaucratic apparatus. To administer and regulate provincial affairs, Asante resident commissioners were stationed in tributary territories of the empire and supervised local political and economic matters along with subject rulers and their lesser chiefs. In many regions this structure replaced the older system whereby each conquered area had been relegated to the administrative supervision of caretaker chiefs *(nhwesofo)* in Kumase who acted as the subject's ruler's patron *(adamfo)* at the Asantehene's court and were officially responsible for the management of affairs in the outlying region.[54]

The three sections of the bureaucracy and the *esomdwa*, or patricentric service stools within each division, functioned in close cooperation with each other and with the Asantehene and his councils. Royal appointees performed *esomdwuma*, or service work, for the Asantehene and their juridical status was that of *asomfo* or *nhenkwaa*, that is, people in service in a department of the civilian and military establishment of Kumase.[55] The concept of service *(esom)* recognized by these personnel and their administrative agencies which were created by the nineteenth-century revolution in government was a distinctive component of the ethos of Asante political consciousness, and the power of nineteenth-century Asantehenes and their councillors in Kumase expanded greatly with the emergence of this new bureaucratic structure. Unlike some contemporary European states, notably France before 1789, the Asante bureaucracy never escaped from royal control. The property of Asante bureaucrats remained always at the disposal of the Asantehene, and these functionaries could not become an independent propertied class. The Asantehene retained at all times the right to remove (as well as appoint) bureaucratic functionaries for incompetence, disobedience, or inefficiency, which guaranteed his power over the bureaucracy and its continued functioning as an arm of royal authority. In addition, the appointive character of these offices and the importance of merit in the recruitment process reflected the achieved status attained by this administrative class of officials in the Asante government and the significance of the appointive principle, which was an assault on hereditary succession to both office and property.[56]

The principle of succession by appointment from Kumase was extended in the mid nineteenth century and especially after 1875 to the outlying districts of the metropolitan region, thereby further increasing power in Kumase at the expense of the *amanto*. As the original and founding members of the Asante kingdom, along with Kumase, these districts enjoyed special rights and privileges in the government of the nation. Internally, each *amanto* was basically organized much like the district of Kumase, with its own organs of administration, treasury, law courts, and armed forces.[57] Each held an Odwira at which subordinate chiefs and village leaders of the district reaffirmed their allegiance to the *omanhene*, or head of the district, a process similar to the *amanhenes'* periodically swearing the oath of allegiance to the Asantehene in Kumase. Originally, Kumase had occupied a position of *primus inter pares* among the founding units of the Asanteman. By the middle of the nineteenth century, however, Kumase had emerged as far more than the "first among equals," as the real powers of the *amanto* had been systematically curtailed in the councils of government.

Despite the retention by the *amanhene* of most of their rights and powers in regard to local jurisdiction within their compact and concentric stool lands, they lost their decision-making leverage on the national level to the elite in the capital who dominated the Council of Kumase. During the middle of the nineteenth century, no *amanhene* could hold an Odwira until he had attended the one held by the Asantehene in Kumase. The Asantehene and his councillors in Kumase could demand funds from the district treasuries, and appeals from the courts of the *amanhene* could be taken to the Asantehene's court in Kumase. Finally, the troops of an outlying district could be called into the service of the Asantehene, thus depriving the *amanhene* of their means to defy the wishes of the central authority. Yet, the ability of the Asantehene to appoint and remove rulers of the outlying districts was the most significant factor in the progressive reduction of the influence of the *amanhene* in nineteenth-century Asante politics.[58] Asantehenes selected and ousted several *amanhene* even though the senior stools of the *amanto* were in theory hereditary, matrilineal offices descending in the same line from the formative period of the Asante polity. By making these rulers—the founding authorities of the kingdom—merely another category of Kumase appointees, the Asantehene and his councillors in Kumase maximized their ability to concentrate all effective power in the central government.[59]

Leaders in Kumase and the outlying districts who stood behind or challenged the centralizing policies of the nineteenth-century Asantehenes had to take into account in designing their programs the influence of the *asikafo*, the men and women of wealth in Asante, and various other unofficial groups whose presence formed a constant backdrop to all Asante calculations. Among these influential interest groups in the nineteenth century were the *nkwankwaa*, commoners or young men without office.[60] This group consisted of the politically, and often socially, disadvantaged of Asante society: minor government functionaries, the discontented among the *mmamma*, those barred from promotion and from office within the departments of government, ambitious and opportunistic *nhenkwaa* seeking greater political and social mobility, and some of the disfranchised, underprivileged, and dispossessed members of society with political aspirations for a career in government service or a place in the ranks of the *asikafo*.

The Asante Nkramo, or Asante Muslims, who were under the administrative supervision of the Nsumankwaahene of Kumase and served as scribes, physicians, and spiritual advisers to the Asantehene, constituted another pressure group in Asante political life. Although the power of the Asante Nkramo community was not constant in the nineteenth century and its number never exceeded seventy-five or a hundred, these descendants of the noted and influential scholar Kramoteaa, who was brought to the capital during the reign of the Asantehene Kwaku Dua Panin (1834–67), were influential participants in economic matters and intermittently criticized national and local administrations. The Nkramo's ability to write took on magical and occult properties and had obvious practical political advantages. These Muslims sold Koranic quotations as charms, and the Asantes respected the scraps of paper for their literary value, while the quotations further reinforced the Asante regard for the Koran as sacred.[61]

Concomitant with his responsibility for the Asante Nkramo community in the capital, the Nsumankwaahene of Kumase, whose office had been created so that the priests of foreign shrines could be enlisted to

The vigorous Mamunatu, around 97 years old, and her grandchildren,
Kwadaso, Kumase

promote the well-being and success of the Asanteman, supervised the practicing Asante shrine priests *(akomfo)* and priestesses *(akomfo mma)* of important deities in the metropolitan region. As guardians of the traditional religious order and the sacrosanct prophecies which colored Asante political behavior, the collective wishes of the shrine authorities had to be reckoned with by national and local politicians. Shrine personnel, numbering in the hundreds, were the protectors of the spiritual world in which Asante politicians acted, deliberated, decided, and solved problems. They performed variegated functions in the daily lives of Asante leaders and people, and their cults, besides preserving the status quo, embodied Asante beliefs in the spirits of the gods and the powers of nature. Possessing charms, amulets, and talismans, these *nhenkwaa* of the deities which filled the metropolitan region were consulted for their predictions on the outcome of military campaigns and national disasters, the prosperity of the new season's crops, the workings of the Asante penal and civil code, and the activities of national festivals. Hundreds of metropolitan shrines constituted the new abodes of ancestral spirits, the *abosomon*, or higher gods of the Sky and Earth, and the more minor spiritual deities considered to be of vital interest to the nation.[62] Each district, town, village, matriclan, and officeholder in Asante had its own shrine and caretakers, while the Asantehene's special priests resided within the confines of the royal palace. Counseling with administrators in Kumase and the centers of local administration, the shrine personnel advised on matters of war, civil disputes, land litigation, and foreigners' motives and ancestry. In the rural communities, shrines protected Asante farmers, traders, hunters, and craftsmen by appeasing the malevolent spirits of the wild forests, rivers, plants, and animals.[63] Thus, depending on the issue at hand and the Asantehene in power, the shrine authorities could play a significant role in decision-making. Whether significant or not, their views were always solicited and contemplated.

All of these segments of nineteenth-century Asante society were sensitive to political issues affecting their vested interests and lobbied, at times violently and disruptively, for decisions that promoted their special causes. All drew their strength from constituencies on the district and village level and remained in close contact with the *adekurofo* who in turn communicated their concerns to national leaders in Kumase.

While proud and passionate Asante leaders grappled with the complex, far-reaching, and momentous issues on which the internal political dynamics of the nation hinged, Europeans encroached more and more on Asante's autonomy.[64] During the late nineteenth century, European, notably British, expansionism and imperialism deeply affected Asante political culture. In this era Asante history became inextricably linked to the wider world. The diffusion of British and other European agents as officials, soldiers, entrepreneurs, and missionaries and the relentless spread of their politics, commerce, and values served as catalysts for socioeconomic changes in Asante and dramatically altered the complexion of the Asante body politic. As the scope and intensity of European activity and involvement increased in the closing decades of the century, Asantes contended with the first sustained threats to their nation's independence and political sovereignty.

3

FOREIGN FACTORS
IN ASANTE POLITICS

The whites never supported Nana Asantehene. The rubber traders resisted him. Things were changing in our nation.—Kwadwo Afodo

The British Intervention in Asante Politics

The power, presence, and commitment of the British based in the adjacent Gold Coast Colony affected the actions and policies of late nineteenth-century Asante leaders. British involvement in Asante domestic politics was a significant feature in all political calculations and in the relations between constituent parts of the Asanteman. Yet the ever-increasing British influence in the Asante political system had a historical legacy far antedating the final decades of the century. Since the early nineteenth century, officials in Kumase had continually confronted difficult diplomatic problems arising from British activities in regions south of the Pra River.

Commercial contacts between the Akan communities of central Asante and the British began in 1645 when British merchants commenced trading operations on the southern Gold Coast. By the beginning of the nineteenth century, British entrepreneurs operated from ten well-equipped forts or trading stations along the coast. Under a charter granted by Parliament in 1750, the London-based Company of Merchants administered these stations and their forty to fifty residents who reaped high, private trading profits from the palm products, gold, and slave trades.[1] The company rented the land upon which the forts were situated from local rulers who had fallen under Asante imperial control during the late eighteenth-century wars of expansion. Its restricted legal jurisdiction, exercised by the governor residing at Cape Coast Castle, only extended to those in the company's pay. To provide for the security of their forts and to develop local trading opportunities, the British had formed alliances with leaders of the coastal and hinterland polities. These pacts aided the company in maintaining a potent military position in order to safeguard its mercantile activities and, if possible, expand them at the expense of its Dutch and Danish coastal rivals.[2]

The company's endeavors to extend and reorient its trade with the interior coincided with the Asante government's reassertion of its imperial sway over the Fante lands in 1807. In that year the British first committed their forts' resources to defend their Fante trading allies. The British also believed that the Asante incursion presented an excellent opportunity for establishing alternative sources of trade with merchants north of the Pra River. This new commerce would offset mounting administrative expenditures on the coast, especially following the abolition of the trans-Atlantic slave trade, and would ease the burden of large annual grants from Parliament.[3] Henceforth, British authorities became inextricably involved in Asante political relations with its rebellious coastal subjects, a pattern that continued after Parliament annexed the forts to the Crown Colony of Sierra Leone in 1821 and placed them under the administration of the governor in Freetown, and when the British Crown more permanently took over direct responsibility for the forts and their administration in 1843.[4] Between 1811 and 1826, Fante revolts against their Asante overlords precipitated three separate military engagements between Asante forces and British troops.

The Anglo-Asante treaty of 1831, which officially ended the hostilities of 1824 and 1826, provided the legal charter for the structure of diplomatic relations between the two powers until the early 1870s. Under the terms of this accord, the Asante government abrogated administrative responsibility over its former southern provinces: Accra, Adangme, Ahanta, Akuapem, Akwamu, Akyem, Aowin, Denkyira, Fante, Sehwi, Twifo, and Wassa. The British, in turn, guaranteed to Asante direct and unrestricted commercial access to the Gold Coast coastal ports. At the same time, the pact allowed the southern provinces an ambiguous independence under the British aegis. Henceforth, the former southern provinces became known as the British Protected Territory.[5] Decision-makers in Asante, during the period when this treaty was in force, interpreted the terms of the agreement only as stipulating surrender of Asante's right to exact "tribute and homage" from the southern provinces; they did not believe that Asante had relinquished ultimate sovereignty over this region. The provisions of this treaty were, in fact, vague and allowed for varying interpretations. This uncertainty created a situation of latent conflict between the British and Asante over the southern provinces that could be forestalled only by an overriding spirit of compromise and negotiation.[6] The vexed issue of sovereignty in the Protectorate was obscured by the power vacuum in the south where both the British and the Asantes failed to exercise decisive responsibility. Furthermore, in such polities as Akuapem, Akyem, and Assin, "pro-Asante" interests emerged that were committed to a revival of close political union with Asante. This, then, further complicated questions of legal jurisdiction, administrative responsibility, and economic activities in British controlled areas.

Asante diplomatic contacts with British officials on the Gold Coast progressively deteriorated in the middle decades of the nineteenth century. Throughout the 1840s and 1850s the British administration, with its headquarters at Cape Coast, competed with Kumase for its own sphere of influence over the southern region, and, after purchasing the Danish settlements on the Gold Coast in 1850, expanded its own commitment. During that period controversies intermittently arose between Asante and the British over the closure and maintenance of the southern trade routes, the extradition of Asante citizens from British administered territory, the restitution of fugitives and criminals, and the Asante government's policies of maintaining political influence over its southern domains.[7]

With respect to these difficulties a series of protracted and unresolved incidents prompted the Asante government to commence preliminary military operations in the British Protected Territory during the first half of 1863. Asante forces secured the release of their fugitive subjects, and, by the middle of May 1863, all troops returned to the metropolitan region. The British governor, Benjamin Pine, immediately pressed for an attack on Asante and initially received permission from the home government to launch a full-scale invasion provided he could secure the active participation of Britain's Gold Coast allies. Although Pine could not enlist coastal cooperation, he ordered two thousand British and colonial troops to invade Asante. The expedition advanced to the Pra River, the southern boundary of the metropolitan region, and retreated on orders from the home government, ostensibly because of the high incidence of disease among the non-African soldiers. In accordance with its general policy in West Africa, Britain opposed the expansion of its political and military commitments and the acquisition of new territories.[8] British troops did not engage the Asante army in a major battle and stopped short of invading the Asanteman. Nevertheless, the hostilities between Asante and British "protected" forces in 1863 underscored the developing conflict between the Asante government and the British administration on the Gold Coast.

Asante politicians throughout the greater part of the nineteenth century were all of one mind as to the goals of foreign policy. They wanted, in general, to maximize the power and authority of the Asante state and, specifically, to maintain and exploit Asante sovereignty over the southern provinces. Controversy existed, however, as to what means would best achieve these ends. Participants in this controversy divided themselves between two interest groups whose political philosophies were alternately mercantilistic and imperialistic in orientation. The two factions, labeled "peace" and "war" parties, determined the nature of political debate in the field of foreign relations for most of the nineteenth century.[9] The peace party regarded the state as essentially organized for the generation of wealth through the promotion of trade and saw wealth as the most significant instrument for the maximization of the power and authority of the Asante polity. Peaceful solutions to the problems of government in the field of foreign affairs held, for this faction, the surest guarantee of continued Asante power and empire through its trading wealth and economic leverage. The opposing party, influenced by the heritage of eighteenth-century Asante military expansion, rejected this mercantilistic view of nationhood and argued that the state was fundamentally organized for the control of territory and the exaction of tribute. Thus, the "war" interest held the belief that the subjects of the Asante empire should be kept in line by military means.[10] For most of the nineteenth century, the debate between the peace and the war interests affected all participants in the decision-making process, including the Asantehene, and the views of the dominant interest group prevailed in the government of the day. The British and other Europeans active on the Gold Coast, who kept a keen eye on the changing political climate in Asante, tended to misinterpret the dichotomy in political philosophies of the leaders of Asante as an indication of division and debilitation in the councils of government. Clearly, for the greater part of the nineteenth century, the existence of rival factions signaled a vital and fluid political system that possessed the strength necessary to debate options in political ideologies and loyalties. The British, however, always carefully observed the debate between the war and peace interests in Asante, primarily because of the series of armed conflicts that had occurred between British and Asante forces.

Diplomatic relations between Asante and the British rapidly worsened after 1863. In late 1866 the Asante government began a phased program of intervention in the south designed primarily to reoccupy and reassert Asante political control over the provinces of Assin, Akyem, Denkyira, Wassa, and Elmina. The war, or expansionist, councillors, who constituted a majority in the councils of government, formulated and implemented this plan. Their outlook had prevailed in the sphere of foreign policy during the last years of the tenure of the Asantehene Kwaku Dua I (Panin). The installation of a new Asantehene, Kofi Kakari, brought to office by the majority war interest in May 1867, did not change the government's policies.[11] Kakari's election in 1867 was uncontested, and his accession signified the continued dominance of militant councillors in the Asante government. Lacking a base of political support outside the war leaders who brought him to power and relying on their support to remain in office, Kakari had to back publicly the government's imperial program. For "the war had been decided on much before his installation, not by the king, but by his great men whose influence he could not resist."[12] Consequently, the new monarch allegedly swore upon his installation that "my business shall be war."[13]

The Asante government's war program culminated in a full-scale invasion of the British Protected Territory during the last half of 1873. Following a massive mobilization lasting from January to June 1873, three large Asante armies crossed the Pra River and invaded and reoccupied most of the southern region. The main Asante force defeated the Assin, the Fante, and the Denkyira and encamped some fifteen miles north of Cape Coast in June 1873. The second column penetrated the Wassa region, while the third army moved into the Akyem country. By the middle of 1873, the three armies had accomplished the government's political goal: the Asante forces of reoccupation enjoyed virtually undisturbed control over the British Protected Territory. In late October 1873, authorities in Kumase ordered the recall of the Asante armies from the south and suspended mobilization. By December 1873, all Asante troops had returned from the south, and demobilization was well under way.[14]

Although the troops returned home, the severe social and economic strains created by the war program were still apparent in the nation. During the early 1870s the homefront economy suffered from the government's emphasis on wartime measures, which caused food shortages, manpower deficits, closure of trade routes, and heavy taxation. The prospect that popular agitation against the government would result in social and political upheaval alarmed Asante officials during 1873. In response, Kakari's administration applied governmental power to the rising social unrest in Asante. Stringent methods of political and social control were implemented to suppress internal dissent. From early 1873 until the army's recall later that year, the government strove to maintain a blackout over news concerning the operations in the south. News censorship took a drastic form: all citizens found discussing military matters were subject to death. Further, deaths among rank and file combatants were suppressed by governmental order, which was a departure from military procedure that had been followed in the nineteenth century.[15]

Elaborate measures to insure internal security and political surveillance in the capital complemented the Asante government's control over news from the war zone. The exigencies of war forced Kofi Kakari to resort to methods of political violence to maintain the operations of the political system and to control an increasingly restive civilian population. The Asantehene executed leading commoners who allegedly opposed his policies and often denied citizens their rights under due process of law. During the "reign of terror," reported in Kumase from 6 August to 10 September 1873, the government ruthlessly suppressed political dissent in the capital. Observers remarked of the occasion that "no one could understand whether it was an outburst of ungoverned passion, or an intimidation of absolute power."[16] The Asantehene, however, maintained that the increase of violence in the capital would deter both personal (e.g., banditry and rape) and political (e.g., assassination of officials of the Council of Kumase) criminal acts. Yet at least one contemporary particularly noticed that heightened police control and the application of terroristic procedures appeared to stimulate more popular agitation against governmental policies.[17]

The socioeconomic and political strains caused by the government's war program had a profound impact on most Asante politicians, including the Asantehene Kofi Kakari himself. Kakari clearly perceived the wartime difficulties and its detrimental effects. Although he publicly supported the militants in his administration and the invasion of the south, he at times sought by private and confidential means to find a peaceful solution to the problems of government in the field of foreign affairs. Amidst intensive council meetings over the southern problems in September and October 1872, Kakari sent personal emissaries to assure British authorities that he would argue for peace during the deliberations, and again privately urged caution during the mobilization of early 1873.[18]

Despite several private efforts for moderation and conciliation, Kofi Kakari did not formally oppose or challenge the war councillors who dominated his administration. The Asantehene's traditional and legal role as head of the Asanteman meant that his public pronouncements had to conform with the guidelines set by decision-makers in the councils of government. His executive responsibility and, more importantly, his reliance on the war leaders, who had brought him to power, seriously thwarted Kakari's ability to assume independent diplomatic initiatives.

The Asante government's war program incited the imperial government in London to send a large expeditionary force into Asante. The Asantehene and his councillors were unaware of the British decision before their own move to withdraw Asante armies from the south. And from 1866 to 1873 Asante troops had been ordered to refrain from operations against the British as such. Nevertheless, in late December 1873 and early January 1874, British columns advanced north of the Pra River for the first time in Asante history. Kofi Kakari's last-minute overtures to deter the invasion failed. British columns marched northwards, encountering fierce resistance at the town of Amoafo (near Bekwae) on 31 January and at Odaso (several miles from Kumase) on 3 February 1874. Kofi Kakari, who personally led the resistance at Odaso, responded positively to the challenge of the intrusion and rallied Asante morale during the fighting of early 1874.[19]

Regiments under the command of Sir Garnet Wolseley, commander of the British Expeditionary Force on the Gold Coast, looted Kumase on 4 February 1874. Strangely, no additional Asante resistance occurred while British contingents briefly encamped in Kumase and burned the capital. Asante troops also did not attack Wolseley's forces as they hastily returned to Cape Coast in mid February 1874. Following the invasion Kumase envoys, acting on instructions from Asantehene Kofi Kakari, made a peace settlement with the British. By the terms of the treaty negotiated at Fomena on 13 February 1874 and ratified the following March, the Asante government agreed to pay a war indemnity and relinquished all political claims to the southern provinces. A British Order in Council of 6 August 1874 incorporated most of these southern domains within the newly created Gold Coast Colony.[20]

In the confused aftermath of the British invasion, Kofi Kakari and his councillors in Kumase strove to rebuild a foundation for future Anglo-Asante diplomacy and for the revival of Asante trade to the coastal ports. After the ratification of the peace agreement the Asantehene took initiatives primarily designed to assuage British concern over the Asante government's adherence to the provisions of the Fomena treaty. Hence, starting in June 1874, the Asantehene's *nhenkwaa*, or envoys, began to make regular indemnity payments (in gold dust) to British officials in Cape Coast and to hold regular meetings with British administrators on the coast. During these discussions the Asante diplomats stressed (as they were to do throughout the 1870s and 1880s) that the British should assume administrative responsibility over all territories within British legal protection, that is, particularly over the Protectorate, the area directly south of the Pra River.[21]

The Anglo-Asante confrontation of 1873–74 altered the course of foreign relations between the two nations for the remainder of the nineteenth century and materially influenced all Asante forethoughts in subsequent years. Aside from the immediate traumatic effect on the Asante political and socioeconomic structure of the war years, the proven superiority and devastating examples of modern British weaponry and technology left a residue of collective fear among Asante officialdom. For the rest of the nineteenth century the political elite of Kumase and the outlying districts never forgot the devastations of British Martini-Henri

47

rifles and cannons.[22] Remembrance of these horrors influenced all future decisions with British officials and made dissident Asante politicians very eager to have British assistance in their opposition to authorities in Kumase.

After experiencing the tragedies of warfare with Britain, most Asante politicians were psychologically overwhelmed by the thought of a new confrontation. Asante leaders soon recognized the bankruptcy of war government plans and, with the permanent loss of the southern provinces, adjusted to the changes in national geopolitical thinking. Officials in Kumase concentrated their efforts on promoting national reconstruction, modernizing the structure of central administration, and implementing governmental reforms designed to respond to the rapid political and socioeconomic changes occurring in the metropolitan region in the aftermath of the stunning war years. Under the new Asantehene, Mensa Bonsu, who came to power in late 1874, Kumase politicians also sought to strengthen governmental control over the remaining provinces and tributaries, notably those in the north, northwest, and northeast.[23] Thus the seventy-five-year-old debate between peace and war interests lapsed temporarily.

Seven years later, however, the revival of the war interest in the councils of government once again brought Asante to the brink of war with the British. War party views dominated the diplomatic conference held on 19 January 1881. On that occasion the Kumase envoys, Asabi Antwi, Bosommuru Dwira, and Anani, formally announced to the British governor, Samuel Rowe, that the Asante government would attack Assin (which was under British protection) unless the Gyaman prince, Owusu Taseamandi, was immediately surrendered. Owusu Taseamandi had been groomed by Kumase to occupy the Gyaman stool and had allegedly been abducted from the capital on 10 January 1881 with the complicity of British officials in the Colony.[24] British actions on this controversial issue infuriated authorities in Kumase. The increase in British intelligence operations in the late 1870s and the widespread Asante belief that agents from the Gold Coast government encouraged the refugee Dwabenhene Asafo Agyei to launch an invasion of Asante from the eastern parts of the Colony, further enabled the war councillors to extend their platform and briefly to enlarge their constituency.

Governor Rowe considered the Asante envoys' statements "virtually a declaration of war." He ordered full-scale military preparations in the Colony, requested reinforcements from Britain and the West Indies, and alerted the navy to prepare for an invasion.[25] Accordingly, the dormant struggle between peace and war advocates for control of the Asante government sharply intensified following this British response. One contemporary, for example, observed that the Asantemanhyiamu's deliberations at Bantama in early February 1881 took place "amid a great deal of war talk, and that it was intended to put all the Assin traders and other British subjects in Coomassie in irons."[26] Mensa Bonsu himself briefly assumed a militant stance, while the Bantamahene and the Bekwaehene started to mobilize their districts. The intervention of the Asantehemaa Afua Kobi and of the Kokofuhemaa in the interest of peace at this critical stage, and the skillful delaying tactics of the Asantehene during the month of January evidently persuaded many of the more recent converts to the war party to change sides once again.[27] The popular furor over the prospects of war also convinced several prominent politicians to reconsider and to support peace initiatives. The Basel missionaries Buck and Huppenbauer, who visited Kumase on 5 February 1881, maintained that the Asante populace would resist an invasion north of the Pra but also observed:

> The people do not like war at all, but it is said that the Englishmen are coming against them. They expect war, as they have heard something of soldiers stationed at Prahsue, but they will certainly not begin. Perhaps, if they are attacked, they will defend themselves, but they are also quite displeased with their government and some speak of running away.[28]

The triumph of the leadership in Kumase over the war interest thus averted the outbreak of hostilities in early 1881. "More peaceable councils," it was reported, "have probably prevailed at Coomassie."[29] In the middle of February, the Bonsu administration again sought to reestablish cordial relations with the government of the Gold Coast Colony. Another mission to the coast, led by the experienced Kumase diplomat Benni, allayed British fears by providing assurances of the government's intention to maintain the peace. The new national consensus in favor of peace policies gained further momentum at the diplomatic talks of April and May 1881. The Kumase envoy, Boakye Tenten, occupant of the Boakye Yam Panin *okyeame* stool and husband of the Asantehemaa Afua Kobi, who had come to office in the administration of the Asantehene Kwaku Dua Panin and had held the senior post of co-governor of Salaga, headed a large delegation of over four hundred. Representatives from the Bantamahene and Asafohene of Kumase and from the Mamponhene, Kokofuhene, Bekwaehene, Nsutahene, Asumegyahene, and Amoafohene, along with two sons of Asantehene Kwaku Dua I and a host of functionaries of the central government, joined the embassy. The delegation met with Governor Rowe at Praso on 16–17 April, consulted with various Colony chiefs at Elmina on 28 May, and subsequently held more talks with Rowe on 30 May.[30] Thus, overt hostilities with the British were averted in 1881 by the timely application of diplomacy. This war scare had, however, brought to light the reversal that had taken place in popular sentiments and the ascendancy of peace interests in the field of foreign affairs. The year 1881 saw the final gasp of the long-lived war interest in Asante. "Peace, open roads, and trade," the motto of nineteenth-century peace governments, once again became the national refrain that expressed the tenor of Asante foreign policy.[31]

Although the problem of sovereignty in the southern region was resolved in 1874 and the oscillations between war and peace parties were put to rest in 1881, the British progressively assumed a more active and purposeful role in Asante affairs throughout the 1880s. The economic policy of the British during the 1870s and early 1880s was relatively consistent. Administrators in the Gold Coast Colony officially promoted the diversion of trade originating in the northeast and northwest away from Kumase and encouraged northern, Asante, Hausa, and other traders to use routes circumventing the eight-trunk radial pattern of the Asante great-roads system.[32] Thus, British officials tested the notion that, with their encouragement, a grid pattern could be created which would deprive the Asante government of its profits gained through state monopoly of the public sector and strict regulation of private entrepreneurial activities. The British also strove to preserve and acquire existing and potentially strategic markets outside the metropolitan region, which was an aspect of their larger West African plan to counter the rising costs of administrative posts by expanding their customs jurisdiction and taking key coastal and river ports under their authority. British support for the rebellious leaders in the Bron coalition in the late 1870s and early 1880s, as well as British assistance to the "anti-Kumase" factions in Gyaman in the mid-1880s, resulted directly from the economic manipulations of administrators in the Gold Coast Colony, and had the approval of European and African mercantile interests in Accra, Ada, Axim, Cape Coast, Elmina, Saltpond, and Winneba.[33] In spite of widespread enthusiasm outside of Asante for the plan, attempts to create a grid pattern for the conduct of trade failed, and the long-standing radial pattern was not substantially altered and is still evident in the road network of modern Ghana. British efforts to superimpose a grid-pattern trade route over the familiar radial pattern failed in large part because of the habitation of traders to the older routes. Elderly Muslim traders, who had in fact used the radial route pattern to obtain Asante kola in exchange for cloth, slaves, and goods in the late nineteenth century, gave accounts of which the following is typical.

Many of the people from Hausaland came to Salaga to trade. Some also came to Bole, Yendi, and Kintampo. This was the time before Nana Prempe was taken away by the whites. All these traders knew the old trade routes to follow. Even our *bayi*, or slaves, knew these routes. We knew where to stop for the night and where to get our food. We knew how much to travel everyday. We knew who was friendly and where the robbers stayed. We knew how to get water and who sold the donkeys. We were never fearful, like the Dagombas and Gonjas, because we traders from Hausaland were strong. The Asantes liked us for this quality. Even to this day we follow the same routes to trade. The routes serve the trade—nothing could make us change and take other routes.[34]

On the political level British policy in the late 1870s and early 1880s was more random than their well-defined economic strategy. Governors of the Gold Coast, not the Colonial Office in London, formulated plans and directed their agents to develop on the spot policies concerning the outlying districts of the metropolitan region and the Protectorate based on expediency alone. British actions were tactical and predicated on the sixfold nature of Anglo-Asante relations. Interactions between members of the Asanteman and representatives of the British invariably had ramifications affecting the view that the British took of Kumase and the districts, the stance Kumase adopted towards the British and the divisions, and the perspectives that the districts assumed in their relations with the British and Kumase. The multiplicity of viewpoints brought to bear on foreign policy, coupled with the lack of an overall unifying British strategy in Asante, complicated the events and issues of the period.[35]

Following the invasion of 1874, the British supported the existence of the central government in Kumase, worked towards the restoration of a unified Asanteman, and upheld the position of the Asantehene. Gold Coast governors recognized Kumase as the proper diplomatic seat to discuss the familiar problems of trade, open roads, and refugees. The colonial government thus backed the authority and policies of the Mensa Bonsu administration (1874–83) in the metropolitan region. For similar reasons the British supported centralists in Kumase and the movement to restore the monarchy in the mid-1880s. British envoys, concurrently, sided with localists and separatist politicians in various electoral contests in Adanse, Bekwae, and Kokofu. Furthermore, the British consistently aided "anti-Kumase" politicians in the Protectorate because they desired loose, informal connections with Kumase and wished to keep the Asante connection more-or-less severed. Colonial administrations, in addition, permitted partisans of unsuccessful Kumase contenders to operate in the

Protectorate and the Colony following their candidates' defeat.[36] The British, therefore, strove to maintain the integrity of the Asante Nation and keep the central government strong but intended to make absolutely certain that it never regained its earlier nineteenth-century power. The Asante government should remain potent; it should never again assert its power to threaten the welfare of the colonial administration in the Colony. Underlying the British tactics of expediency was the continuous desire to keep the commercial conduits open in order to placate British and African mercantile interests on the coast and, of course, the ever-present fear of Asante military action.

After 1875, authorities in Kumase frequently used the services of British agents dispatched by their superiors in Cape Coast and later in Accra. Leaders in the Council of Kumase and the districts routinely resorted to British advice, mediation, and arbitration to settle intra-Asante political disputes when a third party was necessary. The rebellious Dwabenhene Asafo Agyei and his adversary, the Asantehene Kofi Kakari, for example, requested British mediation in August 1874 in an effort to avert civil war. Similarly, in 1886 the Bekwae and Adanse looked for British support to shore up their separate causes in their mounting confrontation.[37] By utilizing envoys from the Gold Coast administration and by relying on the constant possibility of British military intervention, dissident local Asante politicians in the post-1874 era attempted to gain a greater voice in national decision-making and to participate more in governmental discussions. Further, they could embrace viable political and economic alternatives that were at variance with the aims of the Asantehene and his Kumase councillors. If they wished, localists could threaten to secede by seeking British protection in the event Kumase officials implemented policies that conflicted with their own aspirations. Thus, the British were involved on all levels of Asante political interactions in the late 1870s and 1880s.

While British officials in the Gold Coast Colony engaged in these diplomatic machinations, their presence south of the Pra River had another stirring, yet intangible, impact on Asante collective consciousness. Increasingly in the years after 1874, several Asante leaders recognized that new factors of change, especially the close proximity of the British and the inroads of European culture in general, would modify the quality of Asante life and substantially alter long-standing political and socioeconomic institutions. Asantes, in and out of government, pressed for changes in the political process and viewed the administration of the Colony and aspects of its government as a model for change.[38] The Colony's system of justice that local chiefs came to depend on for confirmation of their judicial authority was one main attraction. British officials had implemented conscription policies based on voluntary service that were applied in a nondiscriminatory way to all societal segments. Indeed, this offered advantages over the Asante military system whereby the *odekuro*, under orders from authorities in Kumase, drafted men into the army, and the burden of fighting rested mainly upon poor Asante commoners and foreign-born slaves. Reformers in Asante politics strove to promote literacy through English-style education and seemingly admired the growing role of the Colony's free press that criticized arbitrary tax and bureaucratic decisions of colonial officials in the capital of Accra. They also apparently considered agitation for looser state economic policies that offered viable alternatives to the Asante government's semi-nationalization of the Asanteman's economy.[39] The constant political and commercial interchange between Asante and the Colony also roused the reformers' thoughts on the British political vision: theories of parliamentary democracy and elective representation at the center, liberty of the individual and suffrage for the masses, national self-determination, and alterations in the monarchical system. The exposure of the Asante government and its people to alternative political philosophies through contact with Europeans exercised a radical and profound impact on the mentality of late nineteenth-century Asante leaders.

ECONOMIC CHANGE: THE EMERGENCE OF NEW INTEREST GROUPS

The British sphere of influence on the Gold Coast stimulated the assimilation of ideologies and value systems alien to Asante economic traditions and thought. During the late 1870s and 1880s, entrepreneurs within the social category defined as *asikafo* responded to the expansion of the export-oriented British commodities trade and the growth of overseas markets for new Asante products. Asante's increasing participation in the world market and the development of new commercial activities in the metropolitan region constituted a major threat to the centralized economic power and control of the Asantehene's government in Kumase.

Rubber entrepreneurs, joined by gold, kola, and palm-oil traders, challenged the state's ability to regulate the economy of the Asanteman through the Bata Fekuo, or State Trading Company. In effect, these economic interest groups believed that areas of private economic life should exist entirely beyond the purview of the political system and should hence be free of the crippling burden of government taxation and interference in the profit-making ability of the private sector of the community. Thus these groups attacked the high degree of state control over the patterns of economic organization in the first three-quarters of the nineteenth century and, thereby, called into question the entire complex mechanisms of governmental taxation which existed in the nineteenth century as well as the tight state regulation over the means of production, distribution, and exchange in the Asante Nation.[40] By questioning the traditional restrictions upon private entrepreneurial activity, Asante traders attempted to modify the government's regulation of the economy.

The attitudes of these entrepreneurs were reminiscent of those held by exponents of laissez-faire principles in Britain at that time. They sided with the politicians, private citizens, and Asante commoners who agitated for a restriction or diminution of the power of Kumase to regulate and manage the Asante economy in such enterprises as mining, trading, and ivory collection. Later, members of this group sided with the British in their attempts to extend "protection" to the Asanteman because of the promise held out by the British of open roads and free trade. By demanding that their economic activities remain outside the political system—particularly the rubber trade, which originated in the early 1880s in Asante and rapidly expanded in the early 1890s—these new and influential interest groups posed a serious challenge to authorities in Kumase and to local officials who favored continued state domination over the economy of the nation.

One of the more noticeable governmental controls over the economic activities of Asante citizens throughout the nineteenth century was the extensive and high rate of taxation which inhibited the accumulation of capital and stifled the development of independent financial houses.[41] Tributes, usually paid in gold, cloth, livestock, or slaves, were levied by the Gyaasewa organization (Exchequer) on the provinces, conquered towns, and markets of the Asante empire and from European merchant establishments in the coastal ports. Poll or census taxes, levied directly by the central government on heads of households in the towns and villages within the Kumase district, were similarly collected in gold dust through the agency of the Gyaasewa with the assistance of the *odekuro*, while tolls were exacted for road-use by functionaries in the *nkwansrafo* organization under the supervision of the Batahene in Kumase. In the metropolitan region these taxes usually amounted to one-half or more of a private individual's yearly income. Slaves who worked on village plantations paid three-quarters of their annual income to the *odekuro*. Private Asante traders paid tolls which nearly always were 10 percent of the estimated value of the merchandise they transported. Most significant for the restriction of private entrepreneurial activity was the heavy *ayibuadie* and *awunyadie*, or death duties, imposed on personal estates and liquid assets at death. Informants noted, for example, that the inheritance taxes frequently were equivalent to the total worth of the estate.[42] Linked closely to the impact of these taxes was the imposition of exceedingly high interest rates—up to 33.5 percent per month—on capital loans that might otherwise have been used to finance independent wholesale and retail business ventures. The state often arbitrarily refused to grant loans to private traders and farmers, especially in times of war, and always insisted that all loans be paid back within six months. The Asantehene and his councillors in the nineteenth century insisted that private creditors charge exorbitant interest rates, which averaged as high as 50 percent per month, and had quickly to be repaid in gold dust. The Asantehene, moreover, had rights to all gold nuggets found in mines and alluvial deposits throughout Asante. The Gyaasewa organization returned two-thirds of the value of the nuggets in gold dust to the finder and the *odekuro* who supervised his village.[43]

The main segment of the state's very complicated and little researched organizational and financial structure was the Bata Fekuo. As one of the dominant agencies of nineteenth-century Asante government, the Bata Fekuo, consisting of numerous officials (*asokwafo* and *akyeremadefo*), traders and distributive agents, enjoyed special economic and political privileges in the regional and long-distance kola and palm products trade. Throughout the first three-quarters of the century, its public traders had primary responsibility for the promotion, maintenance, and growth of state profits from commerce. Working in concert with the other major departments of the Exchequer, the Bata Fekuo adjusted to the economic vicissitudes created by altered commercial potentialities in the patterns of supply and demand, product application, and distribution.[44] This arm of government effectively ordered and regulated the conduct of trade between Kumase and the Asante-dominated markets of the northern hinterlands, and between Kumase and the European and African merchant establishments on the coast. The design of the Asante economic system was calculated to keep most of the profits generated by the marketing of Asante natural resources within the control of the central government and its agents and at the same time to maintain Asante's traditional role as middleman in all commercial transactions between the southern and northern entrepôts. Immigration regulation was part and parcel of the state's control over the economy of the Asanteman. From mid century onwards, the Asante government prohibited the influx of Muslim, Fante, and other foreign traders and their agents into the metropolitan region. Although the government in Kumase successfully curtailed the competition of foreign traders from the 1840s through the 1860s,[45] the Mensa Bonsu administration, in the aftermath of the war of 1873–74, apparently once again permitted a limited and controlled infusion of outside entrepreneurs, particularly those with needed skills and capital from the Gold Coast Colony.[46]

The Bonsu government's economic program had several other innovative features designed to expand the extensive system of commercial intercourse on the principle of reciprocal exchange and to maintain the control of the state over its peripheral markets. The government, for example, established a new mart at Kintampo, located in the inner province of Nkoransa, to safeguard commercial interests in the northern hinterlands from the threat presented by the rebel northeastern Bron coalition and from the loss of the market of Salaga after 1875. By the early 1880s Kintampo served as the primary outlet for the nation's kola resources and linked Asante via trade arteries with Timbuktu, Mossi, and Hausaland.[47]

Mensa Bonsu and his councillors carried out a similar trade policy in the southern part of the metropolitan region. Responding to the measures taken by local leaders to achieve economic self-sufficiency in Adanse, the administration rerouted the trade from Edubiase (the main market in Adanse) to a new exchange center established at Ankase some thirty miles from Kumase. The importance of Ankase for the exchange of coastal goods rapidly increased in the postwar era. Lonsdale in November 1881 attested to the "large number of people" assembled in the mart held every Friday and noted the presence of officials from the central government who decided legal cases and "reported all of importance to Coomassie."[48] Ankase in fact became the new price-fixing center of the southern metropolitan region: merchandise—especially spirits and manufactured articles—sold there by traders from the Colony increased in value by 25 to 50 percent upon arrival in the capital.[49] Thus, paying tribute to the Asante government's commercial policies in the south and applying doctrines about the role of "middlemen states" which he had formed elsewhere in West Africa, Governor Rowe in October 1881 wrote:

> Coomassie has been a centre through which alone tribes east, north, and west of it have been able to obtain the European merchandise imported on this part of the coast. The policy of Ashanti has been one of firm resistance to any effort on the part of these tribes to bring on their produce beyond Coomassie, and the Ashantis have thus monopolised the trade with those districts in such articles as they required from the seaboard.[50]

Concomitant with the relocation of the principal exchange centers in the north and south, the Bonsu government took steps to increase trade with French merchants at the free ports of Grand Bassam and Assini and thus to decrease dependence on the British for war materials. In these two ports Asante merchants could also carry on trade directly with ships from Bristol. British accounts of February 1881, for example, noted that

Asante traders, besides making large purchases of war materials in the British forts, obtained "immense quantities" from merchants at Assini.[51] The Bonsu administration, however, also sought new trade possibilities in the trans-Volta region and recruited foreign entrepreneurs to assist in the economic development of that area. In August 1875, the Asantehene formally commissioned M. J. Bonnat to establish factories along the Upper Volta and to receive a monopoly of the Volta trade for six years. In return for this privilege and for promised protection, Bonnat and his associate, C. de Cardi, a Liverpool merchant, guaranteed the government a percentage of the profits from all goods passing through their depots.[52] To augment further its trading sphere, the government became interested in the construction of a railway to Kumase and frequently consulted with the French and Dutch consular agent, Arthur Brun, as to the potentialities of such an enterprise.[53]

Besides trade, the Bonsu administration's economic program included monetary policies formulated to cope with conditions in the postwar era. Stringent controls on currency, the gold-mining industry, and the circulation of impure gold, as well as the periodic detention of Assin, Fante, Akyem, and other entrepreneurs from the Colony who attempted to alter the rates of exchange and thus to inflate the price of consumer goods in the metropolitan region, were facets of the new financial policies.[54] The central government also strove to maintain tighter supervision over operations in new gold-mining areas such as in Adanse, where a particularly rich mine was discovered in 1881, and over activities in older mines located in the Manso, Bibiani, and Sankore districts.[55] The state's increased control over the gold resources of the nation was essential for the improvement and development of the extractive industries—gold and rubber—which occurred in the late 1870s and early 1880s.

During the early 1880s, the rubber trade in Asante began to assume significant dimensions. Because of the near collapse of the central government in this period, the rubber *asikafo* who first worked in Ahafo, Nkoransa, Sehwi, Wam, and Wankyi had an opportunity to design the new industry in such a way as to circumvent government restrictions and to minimize the government's share in the profits. As their interests benefited from the dissipation of central authority, these merchants and middlemen tended to support politicians who were identified with localist policies and who resisted the accumulation of power, especially economic power, in Kumase. The spread of rubber tapping and trading foreshadowed major economic changes in the metropolitan region and was intrinsically linked with village producers, their middlemen, and the *adekuro* who presided over local buying centers and the economic gains of entrepreneurs in their districts.[56] An informant, who at the age of thirty had been a rubber tapper and owner of land and slaves, who had accumulated limited capital from kola and other trade, and who had established broker connections in Asante in the early days of the rubber trade, offered the following telescoped perspective on the beginnings of this new industry in the metropolitan region.

> The rubber trade started just before Prempe's time. That was the time the whites introduced the trade. The Asantes had trees in the forest but did not know how to make money from these trees. People at the coast knew how to get the rubber first. When rubber collection started in Asante, the people were informed by their chiefs who beat the gong-gong in the towns and villages. The chiefs told the people to start trading in rubber. So Asantes who had not been traders before started to trade in rubber. At the same time, these Asantes also traded in *hye*, or local incense, gotten from trees. The Asantes sold the incense along with the rubber to the whites on the coast. It is impossible to say which of the *asikafo* first joined the rubber trade. Many different people joined in. The one who owned the land had to get one-third of the profits whether a chief owned the land or not. There was much rubber in the Bron area. In this area the owners of the land had people to go around to find out how much rubber the traders had collected. Then these people took their one-third. The rubber in the Bron area was far greater than that which existed in Asante. Rubber traders went from Kumase to Ahafo, stayed there for some time moving from place to place collecting rubber, and then passed through Kumase to the coast. They stayed in Ahafo for two or three months, or sometimes forty days. Asante traders had slaves to carry the rubber. Some Asantes moved to the Bron areas. Some settled there. Traders came to them to get the rubber for the coast. Anyone who founded a new settlement took the lands immediately around it to be their property. The Asantes at that time did not bother much about the size of a person's land. Only chiefs and *asikafo* counted for much in the olden days. When the whites came to Asante, they demarcated and made boundaries. Then the value of land became important.[57]

The influence of this rising commercial elite in the political process and especially in the field of foreign affairs became manifest and prominent throughout the 1880s and early 1890s. The rubber *asikafo* resisted any new governmental controls and continually supported national and local politicians who agitated for limited central government power and authority. At the same time, many rubber traders favored far greater British influence in the metropolitan region for the guarantee of open roads, free trade, and middlemen profits. The inevitable tension with this interest group, whose power was coextensive with the wealth at their command, presented significant problems for the Prempean administration in its efforts to design programs for national unity in the aftermath of the political and economic turmoil of the interregnum.

The Missionary Presence: Cultural Conflict in Asante

As with other problems facing late nineteenth-century Asante leaders, the issue of whether or not to allow European missionaries to proselytize in Kumase and the outlying districts had been a heated and controversial topic for the greater part of the century. The elements that comprised the debate over the missionary question disclose a great deal about the value structure underlying the operations of the Asante social and political system under the pressure of European expansion. The Wesleyan Methodist and Basel missionaries, for their part, saw as their vocation the propagation of the Gospel and the promotion of Western literacy among the "pagans" and sought to foster the social and moral institutions that conformed to Christian doctrine. Missionary activity in the metropolitan region and the Colony thus raised realistic fears among many Asante politicians who believed that the values contained in their foreign religious dogma would prove detrimental to the continued functioning of customary Asante social, political, and economic life.

European missionary programs began on the Gold Coast in the seventeenth century. The initial efforts of single or small groups of missionaries to establish schools were unsuccessful primarily because their foreign language instruction had little relevance to daily village concerns and their religious beliefs and self-sufficient economic communities sharply clashed with traditional social patterns and undermined coastal authorities' religious and secular powers.[58] During the first half of the nineteenth century, the expansion of European trade, administration, and related Western influences encouraged personnel from the Wesleyan Methodist Society and the Basel Mission to create permanent inroads into various Gold Coast communities. In their schools the Wesleyans, who first came to Cape Coast in 1835, and the Basel missionaries, whose first school was started in Danish Christiansborg in 1828, placed a far greater emphasis on the appreciation of local customs and vernacular and the study of indigenous belief systems and institutions. Stressing the value of Western literacy for enlarging commercial opportunities and employment in the expanding ranks of the colonial civil service, the missionaries also fostered indigenous economic enterprise. They established several agricultural training centers, which were early experiments in commercial agriculture, and industrial workshops for training locksmiths, carpenters, blacksmiths, shoemakers, wheelwrights, and other artisans, who rapidly found gainful work in the coastal and inland towns.[59] By the late 1850s the Wesleyan and Basel missionaries were the principal forces for Western education in the Colony, and some one thousand students studied in their primary schools. Their graduates, imbued with a background in Western political and religious thinking, formed the corpus of clerks, interpreters, and civil servants for the colonial regime or became teachers, catechists, and local preachers in the growing mission field.[60]

European missionaries, however, encountered an entirely different reaction in Asante from that which occurred in the coastal towns. Considerable debate in the councils of the Asante government took place over Wesleyan and Basel desires to reside and open schools in Kumase and the metropolitan centers of local administration. From the 1830s to the 1860s a number of Asante leaders recognized that the missionaries offered certain tangible benefits for the Asanteman. Among these benefits were the political advantages of Western literacy for treaties and letters, exposure to Western cultural styles, improved communication with Europeans on the coast, and increased trade possibilities. Missionaries were seen as a beneficial diplomatic link between Kumase and European administrators in the Colony, and their schools could educate and provide skilled training for privileged young Asante royals which would (and had) served to modernize the economic and military structures of the kingdom. As McCaskie has observed, to the Asante perhaps most important among the positive values of the missionary presence was the introduction of modern medicine. European medical techniques were highly respected for their efficacy. Frequently, a person who had a disease that was considered incurable by the shrine priests or the Asante Nkramo was saved by the missionaries' superior medical expertise.[61] The advantages of European medicine and literacy prompted several leading Asante politicians, who had trading connections with Western-educated Fantes, Ewes, and Akuapems in the southern areas, to persuade the Asantehene Kwaku Dua Panin to allow the Wesleyans in 1843 to open a school in Kumase.[62]

> In the days before Nana Prempe I became the Asantehene, there definitely were "conservative" chiefs who were opposed to anything that was not "pure Asante." They were against, for example, schools and missions. They were against education. Christianity followed education. But other chiefs opposed this group and wanted to bring in British ideas, especially schools and education. These British ideas could be blended with

Asante values. But the Asantehene must be in control of the change.[63]

The Wesleyan station in Kumase failed to attract a sufficient number of students, and the missionaries' conversion efforts were short-lived. Within ten years the Wesleyans had returned to the coast, leaving an abandoned school in the Asante capital. Their egress delighted the spokesmen in the councils of the Asante government who had continually viewed the European schools as agents of "creeping imperialism"[64] and believed that the spread of literacy to the Asante populace would be accompanied by the introduction of Christian values and sweeping social changes with unmanageable political and economic ramifications.[65] At the official level Western education was, therefore, discouraged because it was seen as conflicting with Asante culture and the Asante belief in ancestral spirits. Missionary doctrine promoted the abolition of polygamy, slavery, and traditional modes of ritualized killing; it was feared such changes, if enacted, would undermine the social fabric of the nation and introduce an unwanted mood of egalitarianism among the people.

> The whites wanted to establish education and Christianity in Asante. The Asantes had their own forms of juju, fetish, and talismans. The Asante chiefs and elders felt that Christianity would destroy this form of religion. It was against Asante traditions and customs. For instance, Christians do not marry more than one wife. Christians teach that slaves should be freed. Slaves become stubborn and do not obey their masters. Then everything changes. Slaves rob and kill traders. No one works the farms. The chiefs have no servants. So the fetish people were against Christianity. The Nkramo were against it. The Asante chiefs and elders said "no" to the Christians and the whites.[66]

The missionaries' opposition to slavery in the metropolitan region and the distinct probability that they intended to work towards the eventual emancipation of slaves, as they had done in the Colony, was an unthinkable proposition for most of the Asantehene's nineteenth-century councillors. Slaves, whether foreign-born captives of war, or obtained through tribute from northern polities or from debt repayments, were involved in every aspect of nineteenth-century Asante economic and social activity.[67] A large amount of the *asikafo's* wealth and surplus capital for investment in agriculture and commerce was converted into slave ownership. Along with free commoners, slaves constituted the bulk of the labor force to clear dense forests and to plant and raise crops on the plantations and farms which supplied the food needs of metropolitan towns and villages. The Asantehene's own slaves cultivated his plantations, the largest in the kingdom, in the environs of Kumase and thereby fed the numerous functionaries who served in the royal household and the bureaucratic departments of government.[68] Nearly all prominent families in Kumase and the outlying districts owned scores of slaves who lived on, protected, and worked their plantations scattered throughout the Atwema, Kwabre, Manso, and Sekyere regions. In the household, slaves were used extensively as personal and domestic servants and bodyguards for district heads, *adekuro* and their advisers, and the leaders of Asante matriclans. At state gatherings their numbers symbolized the wealth and social status of officeholders and families.[69] And the descendants of slaves often occupied a number of the major offices in the kingdom and were among some of the wealthiest private traders in the metropolitan region.[70]

Aside from their food producing value in Asante agriculture, slaves played a crucial role in the exchange economy and other domestic economic pursuits. They were employed in all state-directed commercial activities such as mining in the royal gold fields, ivory collection, and the constant search during the rainy season for new alluvial deposits in central Asante, Akyem Abuakwa, and areas as distant as the Gyaman mines. The organization of slave labor as headloading carriers in trading parties underpinned the lucrative palm products, kola, and European merchandise trade within Asante and between Asante and its northern and southern markets.[71] Slaves were likewise involved in all Asante small-scale industries; they were employed by skilled artisans and shared in the field of house construction, design, and ornamentation in Kumase and most local communities.[72]

Slaves in the nineteenth century were economically and hence politically indispensable to Asante society. Their vital auxiliary functions were also essential for the well-being of the Asanteman. The Asante army in the first three-quarters of the century frequently included between one-fourth and one-fifth of the total population in the metropolitan region, while the lower ranks of this widely acclaimed fighting force were composed entirely of slaves either recruited locally or from the northern hinterlands.[73] This manpower was mobilized in the eighteenth- and nineteenth-century wars of expansion, in punitive expeditions to crush rebellion against Asante authority, and in feuds between local officials. Indeed, slaves were at times forced to assume an active role in Asante customary and religious life. An unfree individual in the community was much more likely to fall victim to outbursts of ritualized killing in times of national disaster, the death of Asantehenes, or during particularly important military campaigns.[74] But most Asante citizens recognized and appreciated their slaves' key involvement in every facet of Asante life.

We build a nation with strangers and slaves. A stranger marries in a town. He gives birth to children. He does not go back. Strangers helped the Asantes to become strong in the olden days. The Asantehene owned the savanna and the Asante land. There was no difference between the two lands. The Asantes were the Asantehene's *nkoa*. Slaves became *nkoa* to Asantes. After all *nkoa* stayed here for a time, married and had children, they became Asantes.[75]

Most nineteenth-century Asante politicians thus feared that the missionaries and their European counterparts would interfere with the institution of slavery in the metropolitan region. A closely related concern was the missionaries' ethnocentricity and intolerance of Muslim and polytheistic beliefs which tended to produce distorted perceptions of Asante culture and forced many outsiders to offer misleading generalizations about Asante legal practices and customs. Frequent reference can be found in the nineteenth-century missionary (and other European) literature to indiscriminate, brutal "human sacrifice," rampant slaughter of innocent victims, and bloodthirsty Asante savagery which brought forth outcries of horror and indignation from the Christian teachers and Gold Coast administrators.[76]

During the first three-quarters of the nineteenth century, many killings which the Europeans called "human sacrifice" were judicial executions sanctioned by the Asante penal code. The Asante government's recourse throughout the century to the periodic public execution in the capital of criminals for a wide range of offenses was a manifestation of state power and a form of social control. These highly formalized and ritualized mass executions, occurring on restricted occasions, were clear expressions of royal power. Trials for capital offenses such as murder and adultery with prominent officials' wives were heard in public before the Asantehene in state. The Asantehene's official department, headed by the Adumhene and his *nhenkwaa*, carried out the executions in specific, well-defined ceremonial locations in the wards of the capital.[77] The punishments preceding decapitation were scaled according to the severity of the crime and the position of the aggrieved person. Different violations resulted in differing sorts of executions. But individuals who were executed almost always had been sentenced to death, and years often passed without a single murder or execution.[78] Most homicide cases were in fact punishable by heavy fines.

The Asante judicial process thus demonstrated the deterrent power of the Asantehene, accentuated the distance between officialdom and the masses, and publicized the penalties for violating the kingdom's widely construed penal code which clearly indicated what transgressions were illegal. Powers of pardon and execution resided solely with the Asante-hene. No officeholder or private citizen, regardless of rank or wealth, could legally inflict the death penalty because royal assent was required for all capital punishment.[79] The interpretation and judgments of the Asantehene's court were literally life and death decisions, and the populace always was aware of the penalties for violating the Asantehene's laws.

Public executions in the capital emphasized the centralized power of authorities in Kumase, and the implementation of judicial violence, widely accepted by the mass of the Asante population in the nineteenth century, reflected the Asantehene's power. It also created an aura of fear around his office. Furthermore, the public nature of political violence was often justified as necessary to maintain the operations and existence of the political system itself. Informant accounts indicate, for example, that governmental use of Mossi, Hausa, and northern slaves to murder discredited, banished, or unsuccessful political rivals, which commonly occurred at prescribed locations, constituted another way in which Kumase officials maintained their control over the political system and eliminated future foci of political conflict. Such murders also received public approval.[80]

Other forms of public violence, although greatly exaggerated by nineteenth-century European visitors to the Asante capital, had a cultural foundation in Asante society. Yet ritualized killing without trials was not an Asante characteristic but a characteristic of *some* Asantes at *some* times. For the most part it was accepted by *both* the Asante leadership and the Asante people in the greater part of the nineteenth century. Such killings, according to one informant, were

> carried on. But not nearly as often as people outside felt. They depended on how severe the situation was here in Asante at any time. For example, if no rains came, the shrine priests and the Muslims prayed. Later they told the Asantehene that if you want rains, we must get somebody to be killed. They made the choice of the type of human to kill. The choice depended on how tense the situation was here. If the priests called for a pregnant women, the executioners went around and looked for one. Any pregnant woman in this case would be killed. The executioners put the woman on a stool against a tree with biting ants. Then they placed a rod through her head down into the stool. Before the woman died she felt the pain of the rod and the ants. This was one kind of killing that the Asantehene did not decide. The executioners did not catch people at random. They first asked if the person was a royal, connected with a chief, or serving in the palace. If a person was none of these, he was killed. . . . "A person who is entirely new to a place is

one with whom we end our funerals." When the Asantehene was sick, it would have to be done. This was our custom and tradition. I never saw sacrifice as such. I did see people with rods through their mouths, or eyes cut out, or lips removed. But this was for violating the Asantehene's laws. It was a different thing. If the Asantehene was coming, the ordinary people were not to look at him. If a person was bold enough to look at the Asantehene, he would be caught and killed. No one decided such a case. This all created an air of fear around the Asantehene.[81]

The periodic slaying of other innocents, particularly the *ntafo*, or people from the northern savanna hinterlands of the Asante empire who had no protection and were not connected with political authorities or matriclans, was vividly described by one *ahenkwaa* whose father worked for the Adumhene of the Asantehene Kwaku Dua Panin in the 1860s.

The *ntafo* knew that some Asantes were killing people here in Kumase. When an Asantehene died, he was buried with *ntafo*. Divisional chiefs would sell *ntafo* for Twi-speakers and then kill them at the Asantehene's burial. Or the divisional chiefs would steal a person for the burial. Royals were the only Asantes safe from this. Also Nkramo [Muslims] were not killed. An Asante would often run to the Nkramo's house. He was safe there. He became a subject of the Kramo [Muslim]. Asantes who were to be killed rushed to the houses of the Nkramo for protection and came out after the burial of the Asantehene. When an Asantehene is buried, one of his wives and one of his sons were killed. Also the different groups in the Gyaase gave one person to be killed. All these would go to serve the Asantehene after his death. The *ntafo* feared because they could be killed by other Asante men when the Asantehene died. But the *ntafo* were not needed for the Asantehene's burial. Nobody could find out that a *ntafo* had been killed. He went out of the house and never came back.[82]

Because of the close relationship between the public nature of violence and the punishments of the Asante penal code, a great potential always existed for the Asantehene to use the judicial process for unrestrained political violence to exert the prerogatives of royal power and control over state policy. In times of protracted competition for office, political upheaval, or when Asantehenes strove to augment their authority, political violence often became an acceptable official means to settle controversial issues. Then, after a spurious trial, politicians, *asikafo*, or *nhenkwaa* were likely to be eliminated for holding differing political views; opinions were often interpreted as a challenge to the entire political system.[83] Still other executions occurred under the guise of legitimate political behavior and, thereby, contributed to growing polarization and radicalization of political positions. This also suggests that at these turbulent periods in early and mid nineteenth-century Asante history the political system did *not* tolerate differing opinions and options very well or effectively.

In spite of the frequent resort to assassination in late nineteenth-century Asante politics, it is apparent that this device and ritualized killing without due process of law were not always fully sanctioned and at times generated discomfort (but usually not fear or opposition) among the Asante people. Thus, much of the political violence—especially the assassinations—that occurred was carried out by Asante leaders in an underground fashion, and information concerning these matters was systematically distorted or suppressed. This accounts for the bewildering array of "sudden illnesses" (e.g., smallpox, dysentery, and the like) to which Asante politicians seemed to fall victim.[84] General popular disapproval of the unrestrained use of political violence may be inferred from the secrecy that surrounded the events. This secrecy and the purposeful distortion of information, however, makes it difficult to discover exactly what motivated these crimes, and how they were carried out and by whom. The effect of this secrecy has carried over into modern times as evidenced by the frustrating reluctance of elderly informants to discuss these matters.

The majority of the Asantehene's councillors apparently believed that missionary work among the metropolitan populace would intrude upon their clandestine activities and thereby interfere with what they considered an integral part of the legitimate structure of Asante political life. There were enormous, and probably insuperable, barriers to mutual understanding between the Asante leadership and the missionaries with respect to their separate goals and values. The missionaries, however, persisted in trying to bestow the "blessings" of an imported civilization on the Asante Nation and insisted that all killing was a moral crime, while the Asantehene's councillors, for their part, kept a practical eye on the missionaries to see what useful purposes the foreigners might serve.[85] Conflict remained in the Asante government throughout the nineteenth century over the twin European concepts of literacy and education.

During the years 1863 to 1874, the Asante government increasingly took a dim view of the missionaries within its border because the growing likelihood of a confrontation with the British "protected" allies on the coast brought all Europeans under suspicion. These suspicions were justified as it became apparent that the missionaries in Akyem and Kwawu informed the Gold Coast government about Asante military preparations.[86] After the hostilities of 1874, the Asantehene Kofi Kakari again indicated a willingness to allow the Wesleyans to reestablish a station in Kumase;[87] but, when Mensa Bonsu assumed leadership of the nation, the question was debated among the ruler's councillors. Following the arrival of the Reverend Thomas Picot in the capital on 10 April 1876, the matter required a firm decision. Consequently, the issue as to whether the missionaries would be permitted to return to Kumase was brought for discussion before the Council of Kumase on 21 April. Led by the aged, ailing, and semiretired Gyaasewahene Adu Bofo and the Bantamahene Kwabena Awua, who had been leading war advocates in Kakari's government, the Asantehene's more conservative councillors stressed the dangers to the established socioeconomic and political order. They argued that Asante needed to cultivate only commercial, not religious or cultural, relations with Europeans in the Colony. During the deliberations the Asantehene Mensa Bonsu, supported by several Adanse chiefs, at first embraced the opposing position. He indicated that the Wesleyans were welcome if, like Thomas B. Freeman during the reign of Kwaku Dua Panin, they "helped the peace of the nation and the prosperity of trade."[88] Yet the Asantehene, aware of the strength of conservative feeling on this issue, later asserted that his government would not select children for schooling, would not permit freedom of conscience in Asante, and would enforce the nation's laws regardless of the presence of Europeans in the capital. An informant explained the conservative sentiment in the councils of government.

> In the reign of Bonsu Kumaa [Mensa Bonsu] the elders and other chiefs advised the Asantehene. They must have been against the introduction of education in Asante. They felt education was a new thing. It would make the people too proud. The Asantes were not used to it. Education was against the Asantes. The Asantes did not know how it would affect their traditions and customs.[89]

The result of the debate of 21 April 1876 was a clear victory for the Asantehene's more conservative advisers: Picot's proposal was rejected. Yet the missionary issue continued to polarize political opinion throughout the remainder of the nineteenth century. In March 1881, for example, the Asantehene bowed again to his more liberal councillors and expressed his desire for the reestablishment of schools and a station in Kumase. Although Mensa Bonsu did not specify a time for the recommencement of the mission, he convinced the Wesleyan missionary Fletcher "that he was in earnest" about the invitation.[90]

The Basel missionaries during the 1880s usually chose to establish stations in areas where there was opposition to Kumase's control such as Kumawu, Agogo, Akyem, and the trans-Volta Twi-speaking provinces. Although, as part of their strategy, the missionary Fritz Ramseyer and his cohorts had insisted that they would take no part in Asante politics, their stake in local and national decision-making became more and more obvious to Asante leaders in the closing decades of the nineteenth century. For example, Ramseyer and his fellow Basel workers in 1883 supported Kofi Kakari's efforts to regain the throne primarily because they thought Kakari would permit missions and schools in Kumase and the metropolitan region. In addition to playing an unsolicited role in late nineteenth-century Asante politics, the Basel missionaries upset the Asanteman's economic equilibrium by sponsoring apprentice centers and training people on the borders of the metropolitan region in skills such as carpentry and lockmaking.[91]

During the middle of the 1880s, the Basel and Wesleyan missionaries were operating in several of the outlying districts and provinces which had a limited commitment to a close political union with Kumase. In their efforts to spread their Christian principles, the missionaries' doctrine opposed Asante ways, especially the vital Asante distinction between ritualized killing, judicial violence and capital punishment, and political executions. Yet the provocative new ideas embodied in their education, medical expertise, and life styles continued to be debated and closely examined by the Asante government. By the late 1880s, when Agyeman Prempe took over the leadership of the Asanteman, the missionaries had become increasingly associated with the policies of intrusive European powers and as such they incurred the enmity of many of the Asantehene's councillors who suspiciously watched the growing involvement of European powers in the metropolitan region and struggled at a particularly crucial time in Asante history with the clash of cultures.

4
DYNAMICS OF THE INTERREGNUM, 1884-1887

Asantes worried and wondered. The nation was troubled with changes. We looked to the chiefs and elders to end the unrest, the killings, the bloodshed.
—Owusu Nkwantabisa

THE CONTEST OF 1883–1884: KOFI KAKARI AND KWAKU DUA II

In 1884, for the first time in the nineteenth century, no candidate was put forward to occupy the Golden Stool of Asante. The unprecedented four-year vacancy that ensued in the nation's highest office commenced with the death of the Asantehene Kwaku Dua II in June 1884 and lasted until the election of Agyeman Prempe in March 1888. The interregnum period was a time of intense competition for power and deep concern over the political and socioeconomic issues of the day. Usual electoral procedures were by-passed during the hiatus in normal state functioning, and various leaders experimented with new modes of governing that were without warrant or precedent. The shifting alliances and general political instability of the period climaxed in bloody internecine struggles for possession of Kumase.

The deaths in June 1884 of the newly elected Asantehene Kwaku Dua II (Kumaa) and the former monarch Kofi Kakari, who had been rival candidates in the election of 1883–84, created a vacuum at the top of the major Asante political factions and gave rise to provisional forms of government in the Asanteman. During the contest of 1883–84, Kwaku Dua's candidacy had had the full support of those politicians who advocated the continued concentration of administrative power in the central government in Kumase and desired to continue close ties of political union with the center. Kakari's candidacy, on the other hand, had primarily received the backing of the outlying district heads who challenged the Council of Kumase's exclusive right to nominate Kwaku Dua for the office of Asantehene without consulting all prominent Asante authorities.[1]

Certain of the chiefs from outside Kumase championed Kakari's cause so that they could regain their eighteenth-century rights in the councils of government and coerce authorities in Kumase to convene the Asanteman-hyiamu before selecting the occupant of the Golden Stool. The dispute over which of the two main governing bodies of the Asanteman, that is, the Council of Kumase and the Asantemanhyiamu, was to be recognized as the supreme decision-making council of Asante became emblematic of the entire power struggle between leaders in Kumase and the outlying districts and provinces.

Kwaku Dua's victory over Kofi Kakari in 1884 was engineered by his uncle, the elderly and influential Akyempemhene of Kumase, Owusu Koko, who had lived in forced exile from the capital since his abortive efforts to bring his protégé, Kwaku Dua Kumaa, to office amidst the political turmoil surrounding the death of the Asantehene Kwaku Dua Panin in April 1867. Owusu Koko, born about 1820, the son of the Asantehene Osei Bonsu, had been a key adviser and decision-maker in the administration of the Asantehene Kwaku Dua Panin during the 1850s and 1860s and had gained a widespread reputation as the prime spokesman for pacific policies in the field of foreign affairs.[2] The Akyempemhene, in backing Kwaku Dua Kumaa again in 1883, brought to his nephew's cause all the fervid commitment of one whose own reinstatement in the councils of government depended on the outcome of the election. Owusu Koko's connection with Kwaku Dua II gave the latter's candidacy the further advantage of British support in his bid for the Golden Stool. British endorsement of one candidate over another was instrumental in determining the outcome of the election.

In the contest of 1883–84, the British favored Kwaku Dua over Kakari because they identified Kakari's candidacy with the war government that he had headed from 1867 to 1874. Gold Coast officials feared that Kakari's election would signal a return to war policies. While Kakari's personal political philosophy was not militaristic, he was not able to rid his name of the association with the war interest that had brought him to power in 1867. Kakari himself had sought to correct this stigma both in his policy statements and in his conversation with British agents in the town of Akuropon during May 1883.[3] By contrast, the British viewed Owusu Koko's long political career as commendable from the standpoint of foreign policy. Since it appeared that Owusu Koko backed Kwaku Dua in order to run the government himself in the capacity of regent, the British were ready to support his efforts and thus insure a peace government and diplomatic relations compatible with open trade roads and mutually profitable commerce.[4]

So eager were the British to destroy Kakari's bid for power that they did more than merely endorse his opponent. In May 1883, when the supporters of Kwaku Dua and Kofi Kakari prepared to resolve the election by a trial of arms, a British political agent, Knapp Barrow, intervened in the military preparations and informed Kakari that if he were to ascend to the Golden Stool, the British would demand a sum of 49,000 ounces of gold still outstanding under the Fomena Treaty of 1874.[5] This agreement, which officially terminated the Anglo-Asante conflict of 1873–74, had been signed while Kofi Kakari was head of state. Although the previous administration of the Asantehene Mensa Bonsu (1874–83) had renegotiated the terms of the indemnity payments, Barrow, acting without the sanction of his superiors in the Colony, ignored the more recent settlement. The Colonial Office formally approved of his independent actions four months later.

Throughout the second half of 1883, British authorities continued to see in Kakari's candidacy a potential threat to the Gold Coast. Barrow's attempt to thwart Kakari's election hopes was temporarily successful. Kakari's supporters dispersed and returned to their respective towns. By August of 1883, however, both sides again began mobilizing their constituencies. Armed actions took place in Breman, and later on a larger scale in Kenyase, six miles northeast of Kumase. A nonagenarian informant whose father, the Mamponhene Kwame Adwetewa, was killed at Kenyase on 10 August 1883, provided the following account illustrative of the complex and personal variables operating around the conflict.

Kwaku Dua contested with Kofi Kakari who went to stay at Breman sometime after he left the Golden Stool. Some people in Asante felt that Kakari should be made Asantehene because in his first reign he gave money freely to people. Yaa Akyaa [the Asantehemaa] supported her own son, Kwaku Dua, and the two sides fought at Breman and later at Kenyase. Agonahene Atuahene and Nsutahene Yaw Akroma at first supported Kakari. Mamponhene Adwetewa first backed Kakari but then changed his mind. The Mamponhene went to Kumase to intercede between the two parties. He did this through the Kenyase *ohemaa*, Kaneku. Mamponhene told her to tell Yaa Akyaa and the chiefs in Kumase that Mamponhene did not support any party but rather had come to intercede in this dispute. Yaa Akyaa sent several messages that the Mamponhene should keep away from Kakari's side because they were going to fight. Yaa Akyaa added that the Mamponhene should withdraw all his guns from Kenyase back to Mampon, which the Mamponhene did. Then the Kumase people defeated Kakari. Agonahene and Nsutahene burned themselves with fired gunpowder and also burned their stools. The Kumase troops caught and cut off many heads of the Nsuta and Agona troops. [One] could see blood in the streets of Kenyase. Kwaku Dua's forces returned to Kumase. They surrounded the Sekyere towns of Agona, Nsuta, and Mampon. Mamponhene said he did not support Kakari and was not involved in this war. Mamponhene had changed his mind. He first supported Kakari because Kakari had married two of the Mamponhene's sisters, Amma Mmaaboa and Akua Kyem, and treated them well. Mamponhene wanted his two sisters [same mother, same father] to enjoy the privileges they had when Kakari was on the stool first. Mamponhene Kwame Adwetewa was advised to change his mind by his father, Kwame Agyei, who was one of the *nhenkwaa* [servants] of the Baamuhene of Kumase. But the Kumase troops did not believe the Mamponhene. He was taken to Kumase by Asamoa Kyekye, a Kumase *asafohene*, who had defeated Safo Anwona at Kenyase.[6]

Kumase forces prevailed in the important Kenyase battle, but a clear-cut victory still eluded Kwaku Dua's side. It seemed by the end of August that partisans from both camps wished to avoid a repetition of the hostilities. Owusu Koko accordingly took the initiative to propose a peace conference. Kofi Kakari's main allies misconstrued the Akyempemhene's true intention and agreed to the proposal. During the ensuing proceedings Owusu Koko's followers treacherously massacred as many as two thousand of Kakari's supporters in Kumase and its environs. Further, Owusu Koko initiated a "reign of terror" against individuals who were believed to favor Kakari's cause in the metropolitan region. Reports indicated that over a thousand more people were executed on orders from Owusu Koko by late September 1883.[7] Kakari himself was captured by Kumase forces in the town of Bekyem on the Gyaman road in the first week of September 1883. Following Kofi Kakari's imprisonment in the capital, Owusu Koko and his Kumase councillors formally confirmed Kwaku Dua as Asantehene-elect and began to prepare for his full enstoolment. By April 1884 Owusu Koko and the councillors in the capital had achieved a measure of national unity, economic restoration, and public acceptance for Kwaku Dua's enstoolment. Kakari's most vocal champions in Asante were either dead, imprisoned, or losing power in their territories. Kwaku Dua Kumaa, at the age of twenty-four, was installed on the Golden Stool on 28 April 1884.[8] The new Asantehene's forty-four-day reign offered a brief respite from the enmities of the electoral campaign.

During the administration of the Asantehene Kwaku Dua, then, the Akyempemhene Owusu Koko and his advisers attempted to consolidate the gains they had made towards economic recovery and political stabilization in the metropolitan region. Leaders in the Council of Kumase sought to resolve the significant issues of the day within the familiar peace party rubric of a "good king, peace, open roads, and trade."[9] Inherent within the political position of Kwaku Dua Kumaa's reign was the axiomatic assumption that legitimate administration resided with the officeholders constituting the Council of Kumase. Significantly, advocates of the Kakarian cause continued, even after his defeat, to challenge that assumption. On 11 June 1884 the Asantehene died, allegedly of smallpox. Although British sources rely on this explanation for Kwaku Dua's death, Asantes from outside Kumase who saw the monarch's body lying in state maintained that he was poisoned by Kakari's followers.[10] Thirteen days later Owusu Koko executed Kakari.[11] The sudden deaths of Kwaku Dua

Nhenkwaa patiently awaiting the start of funeral services for the Asantehene Osei Agyeman Prempe II, d. 1970, Kumase

and Kofi Kakari, both politically motivated, ended the brief period of stability and legitimate rule and ushered in an unprecedented era when no monarch was nominated for the nation's highest office and new self-styled rulers contested the authority and leadership of the Asanteman.

THE COUNCIL OF KUMASE UNDER OWUSU KOKO

By late 1884 the consensus on which the power of the Council of Kumase rested was exceedingly fragile. Most contemporary reports concur on one central theme characteristic of Asante public life following the demise of both contenders for the Golden Stool: a state of lawlessness and anarchy prevailed in Kumase and its neighboring towns.[12] Initially, however, there were signs that the Akyempemhene and authorities in Kumase might organize a new administration to restore order. Indeed, some observers thought that Owusu Koko himself might ascend to the throne or appoint a successor to Kwaku Dua Kumaa. Throughout the second half of 1884 the Akyempemhene and his supporters in the council took steps designed to achieve two goals: the nomination and enstoolment of a new Asantehene, and the effective use of force to arrest secessionist activity in the Manso towns. Politicians in Kumase apparently believed that political order would be restored if both of these aims were attained.

Official British sources indicate that Owusu Koko and his councillors and the Asantehemaa (or Queen Mother) Afua Kobi put forth the name of one Kwasi Kisi as a candidate for the Golden Stool in October 1884.[13] Seemingly, this individual was a member of the Kumase royal family named Kyeretwe who had not been allowed to compete for the Golden Stool in March 1883. Although he possessed the right genealogical qualifications, Kumase officials considered him unduly arrogant and ill-tempered. These aspects of his personality had disqualified him.[14] Thus, if indeed this Kyeretwe was nominated for the office of Asantehene in 1884, Owusu Koko and the councillors in Kumase knew prior to the nomination that he would be unacceptable to the *ahenesifo*, or kingmakers. It seems, therefore, that Kyeretwe's nomination was merely a gesture to win British assistance and to bring outlying district and provincial rulers into the capital once again for council deliberations. The specter of the "reign of terror" that had resulted from a similar Owusu Koko initiative prevented most of the district chiefs from coming to Kumase in 1884. They preferred to call on British arbitration to settle the election proceedings. Furthermore, the unilateral decision once again to nominate a candidate for the Golden Stool without first consulting the *amanhene* and provincial rulers served to alienate local officeholders who believed that this problem had been resolved, at least in part, by the electoral contest of 1883–84.

The Council of Kumase's second goal—winning political control of the Manso district—was implemented militarily in late November 1884. This resort to arms was designed to arrest the independent course of action that had been adopted by the leaders in Manso as well as other southern districts during the Asantehene Mensa Bonsu's administration. Rebellions had occurred throughout 1883 in the southern districts of Manso Nkwanta, Bekwae, Dadiase, Danyase, Amoafo, and Kuntanase. *Asikafo* and *nkwankwaa* elements in these districts had revolted against the central government's policies to increase the level of taxation throughout the metropolitan region. In 1882 the Bonsu regime had introduced

74

new rates of taxation on the southern gold-mining industries and harshly enforced violations with heavy fines. In addition, the Asantehene had taken measures to despoil numerous trading *asikafo* in the southern region. Mensa Bonsu's weak personal position during his last year in office had merely compounded the popular demands for economic reform and the social protest in the capital over his unlawful executions. Although southern leaders lacked an overall unity of goals, several had aspired to secede from the Asanteman.[15] Kumase's desire under the leadership of Owusu Koko to regain control of the Manso district stemmed from specific knowledge of that geopolitical area.

Authorities in the capital anticipated that they could regain control over the gold mines in the Manso district by means of a show of force in 1884. In the early 1880s several Manso chiefs who supervised the state's gold-mining operations had come increasingly under the influence of entrepreneurs from Cape Coast, Elmina, Anomabo, Accra, and the Akyem region. These merchants had been instrumental in fomenting secessionism during the administration of the Asantehene Mensa Bonsu. The continuing economic competition with coastal entrepreneurs over the gold resources of the Manso district became a recurrent irritant for officials in the central government. Furthermore, several of the largest Manso towns were under the nominal administrative supervision of the Asafohene, Asafo Boakye, an outspoken advocate of a military solution to the Manso problem who had argued his case during the council deliberations following the deposition of the Asantehene Mensa Bonsu in early March 1883.[16] Asafo Boakye undoubtedly again pressed for his own financial interests in the Manso region which were intrinsically linked with the central government's desire to control the Manso gold resources. The Bantamahene of Kumase, Kwabena Awua, probably supported Asafo Boakye's arguments for an invasion of the district. While in exile in Manso Nkwanta in 1882–83, Kwabena Awua had persuaded several dissident Manso chiefs to return their allegiance to Kumase and thus believed that a significant faction in the district would agitate for the restoration of close political ties between the Manso towns and Kumase. In addition, officials in the central government had several specific grievances against Kwasi Kasa, one of the most prominent separatist leaders in the Manso district. Kwasi Kasa was one of the first Manso *ahene* to secede in early 1883 and also was one of the most militant of the Manso rebels. His followers, according to the Kumase envoys on the coast in October 1884, had robbed and imprisoned several Asante chiefs—Nkawiekumaahene Antwi Agyei, Besiasehene Kukoro, Mpatasehene Adu Kwaku, Atwemahene Kwame Antwi Agyei, and the Edwesohene Kwamo Wuo—allegedly while these *ahene* were en route to Kumase to attend the enstoolment ceremonies for Kwaku Dua in April 1884.[17] Kwasi Kasa's actions disrupted the proceedings in Kumase and also prevented other Asante *ahene* from traveling to the capital to swear the oath of allegiance to Asantehene Kwaku Dua.

Finally, and most significantly, the Manso Nkwantahene Yaw Amponsa, besides indicating that he would secede in February 1883 and that he might support Kofi Kakari's restoration, had in 1884 encouraged the Atwema farmers to the west and southwest of the capital to boycott Kumase and not market their produce there.[18] Yaw Amponsa supported this boycott, which was clearly detrimental to the authorities in Kumase, and he also sought to enlarge his own constituency in the adjacent Manso towns which were under the administrative purview of senior Kumase *nhwesofo*. This last move prompted Owusu Koko and his advisers to launch attacks on several Manso and Atwema towns in late November 1884.

In order to smash the boycott originating in Atwema and to regain political control over all the Manso towns, Kumase forces led by the Ankobeahene of Kumase, Ata Gyamfi, and Boakye Tenten, occupant of the Boakye Yam Panin stool, invaded several strategic areas in the Atwema and Manso districts. The Kumase officials who led this offensive apparently believed that they had great influence in these areas. Instead they miscalculated their attempt to pacify the districts, and the invasion alienated the local population. At the outset the Kumase column fell into an ambush and met defeat at the hands of the Manso Nkwantahene Yaw Amponsa near Nkwanta. Following this initial setback, the forces from Kumase were again defeated in engagements at the Atwema towns of Trede and Tarbuom.[19] The defeats at Trede and Tarbuom were largely a result of the military assistance given to the local forces by Saamanhene Akyampon Panin, who was the Gyaasehene of Kumase and the chief of the rural town of Saawua, about eight miles from Kumase. Reports indicated that the Council of Kumase's casualties in these encounters were heavy: eleven senior *ahene* including the Sanaahene (or Treasurer) Opoku, the Ankobeahene Ata Gyamfi, and the Domakwaehene Amankwa were allegedly killed; and eleven Kumase chiefs were captured, including Boakye Tenten and Owusu Koko, who were both executed.[20] These murders, then, eliminated many of the old guard elite in Kumase whose military, civilian, and diplomatic careers stretched back into the reign of the Asantehene Kwaku Dua Panin (1834–67).

AKYAMPON PANIN'S MILITARY TAKE-OVER AND ADMINISTRATION

The engagements of November 1884 also revealed the precarious political position of Owusu Koko and the councillors in Kumase. No Asante leaders from outside Kumase, for example, supported the offensive. Further, the sparse population of the Manso district indicates that the defeat of the Kumase column was engineered by Akyampon Panin with assistance from dissident chiefs in Saawua, Atwema, Manso, and perhaps Edweso. This suggests that the five district heads mentioned by the Kumase envoys on the coast had not intended to renew their allegiance to the Asantehene. Rather the evidence shows that they were planning, along with Akyampon Panin, to topple Owusu Koko's regime. Because the offensive of November left the capital defenseless, the dissidents could implement their plan to seize power. In late November or early December 1884, Akyampon Panin left Kaase, some three miles from the capital, and led a force into Kumase that ousted Owusu Koko's supporters. The Saamanhene, maintaining constant communication with the network of Kakarian partisans in Akyem and the Colony, rapidly informed British officials that they should back the new military leadership in Kumase.[21]

The primary motives for the coup were dissatisfaction with Owusu Koko's policies and the desire to restore political order in the metropolitan region. Several secondary considerations also prompted Akyampon Panin to seize power in late 1884. Akyampon Panin had a long and distinguished career, had widespread political connections throughout Asante, and undoubtedly had accumulated numerous favors over the years. Thus, the Saamanhene was able to support Kakari's restoration in 1883 (one of the few Kumase officials to do so) without endangering his position.[22] But it seems that Akyampon Panin participated in few, if any, council deliberations during the reign of Asantehene Kwaku Dua Kumaa. His dissatisfaction with the regime in Kumase and his support for Kofi Kakari forced him to take action. On the ideological level, however, Akyampon Panin was a centralist of the older generation who believed in a strong central government with an Asantehene who would listen to counsel but at the same time work to maintain Kumase's dominant power in internal political affairs.

Akyampon Panin relied on the financial support of wealthy private traders in the town of Saawua. Several prominent *asikafo* in Saawua— Kofi Kwakye, Osei Kwabena, Adusei, Poku Saawua, Kwabena Nkatia, Banahene, and Kwadwo Bi—prospered from the rubber and gold trade and subsidiary commercial pursuits in the early 1880s. These entrepreneurs and others in Kokofu, Bekwae, Kuntanase, and Berekum favored cordial relations with European and African mercantile interests in the Gold Coast Colony and required political stability to pursue their trading and distributive operations.[23] Owusu Koko's regime had failed to provide the requisite order which would enable traders based in Saawua and other districts to prosper. The *asikafo*, therefore, exerted pressure on Akyampon Panin to seize power in the capital. In circumstances that are unclear, the deposed Asantehene Mensa Bonsu had deposited 3,200 ounces of gold in Saawua on 10 March 1883.[24] Perhaps the disgraced Mensa Bonsu attempted to finance his own political comeback, or strove to recruit Akyampon Panin for his cause, or simply bribed the Saamanhene to intervene to save his life amidst the rumors that Owusu Koko intended to execute him. Nevertheless, part of this money capitalized the Saawua rubber trade and purchased modern Snider rifles and ammunition from coastal merchants. Saawua troops equipped with Sniders made Akyampon Panin one of the most formidable leaders in Asante in 1884. The British agent Donald Stewart, for example, remarked that the "mere possession of these arms seems to give him [Akyampon Panin] a political importance which would be hardly due to him considering the inferior number of his forces."[25] It is doubtful that this calculus alone was a sufficient reason for the Saamanhene of Kumase to make a personal bid for power, especially in light of his concern with political trends in the capital.

Forces loyal to Akyampon Panin secured Kumase and temporarily stabilized affairs in the urban area in December 1884. The change in leadership affected the composition and operation of the Council of Kumase. Although the council continued to function at least nominally as the executive institution, its membership was restricted both in prominence and size. In the late 1870s, the Council of Kumase probably had some 120 members. According to the missionary W. Terry Coppin, who entered the capital on 28 April 1885, the council consisted of only a few noteworthy officeholders. Among these were Asafo Boakye (born about 1830), a son of the Asantehene Kwaku Dua Panin who came to office in 1863. He was married to a prominent Kumase woman, Akua Afriyie. Others present included several senior Kumase functionaries, such as Kwaku Bosommuru Dwira, who was a son *(oheneba)* of the Asantehene Osei Yaw Akoto and began his civilian and diplomatic career in the 1860s, and Owusu Koko Kumaa, who was a son of Akyampon Panin and had had a distinguished diplomatic career in the lower echelons of governmental service.[26] But political power lay with the Saamanhene's rural supporters who resided in the villages outside Kumase. Coppin remarked that it took only five minutes, rather than the usual five hours, for him to greet the assembled chiefs in Kumase and noted: "Many of its principal people having been killed or poisoned, the Council is represented for the most part by men of little note, and represents the capital only, which stands alone and deserted, not as the voice of the Ashantee people that they would be glad to be thought."[27] Following Akyampon Panin's entry into Kumase, several prominent officeholders who had survived the military operations of November retired to the safety of their towns and villages. Other leading officials had been killed during the engagements in Manso and Atwema. Still others were apparently murdered after the Saamanhene's forces secured Kumase. Asantes believed even the exiled Asantehene Mensa Bonsu and the former Asantehemaa Afua Kobi had been executed.

One consequence of Akyampon Panin's coup was a reduction in the political influence of the Council of Kumase; it no longer exercised the functions of central government. Coppin learned that "*not one* of all the vassal states now pays tribute or in any way submits or refers any of its affairs to the capital."[28] Accordingly, economic and social life in the urban area suffered. In marked contrast to the first three-quarters of the nineteenth century, Coppin commented on Kumase's wretched poverty and filth, and the decline in the quality of life in the capital in 1885.

The city is being gradually forsaken by its inhabitants, because there is nothing to sustain them. This explains the disappearance of rows of houses which once lined the streets, the dilapidated state of most that remain, the thoroughfares overgrown with grass in most places from 12 to 15 feet high, the encroachments of the bush on all sides, and the general ruinous appearance which the place presents. Gold digging and earth washing, once so strictly forbidden in the capital, is now extensively carried on. The poverty of the people forces them to do this. All that Kumasi now possesses and can control is a few villages. These are insufficient to furnish subsistence to all its inhabitants.[29]

Although economic prosperity in the urban area declined in the aftermath of the military coup of December 1884, the situation in other areas of metropolitan Asante was not adversely affected by the changes in leadership in Kumase. The villages and plantations in the districts of Bekwae and Dadiase, for example, prospered. Most metropolitan region villages remained untouched by the fighting and murders in the capital. Further, commercial interchange in the Ankase market on Route VI of the Asante great-roads continued much as before; the market still attracted Asante traders from the surrounding areas and merchants from the Colony.[30] Although Asante traders were stopped and robbed on the roads leading through Adanse and Assin, the origins of this brigandage antedated 1884. In addition, trade figures recorded by clerks employed by the government of the Gold Coast Colony at Praso indicated only a negligible decline as compared with previous periods. In general economic terms, political events in the capital served to stimulate the flow of trade away from

Kumase and to the coastal ports—not directly via the Cape Coast artery —but rather over alternate routes from the interior to Saltpond, Accra, and ports other than Cape Coast.[31]

Most significant, Akyampon Panin's coup and the reduction of the Council of Kumase's power provided an impetus to certain continuing political changes on the local level, especially in the southern regions of metropolitan Asante. Coppin, who visited the southern districts of Amoafo, Bekwae, Danyase, and Dadiase between 15 April and 13 May 1885, observed that each district "maintains its own authority, and administers absolutely to its own affairs."[32] Coppin, furthermore, stressed that "formerly each of these places was tributary to Kumase,"[33] and commented:

> Affairs in Ashanti are in a transition stage. The once tributary provinces south of the capital, Amoaful, Bakwai, & c., have drunk fetish together. This ceremony of confederation, for such it is, bids fair, in time to bring about peace and order and prosperity, provided Kumasi continues to become what Kukofu is already, a desolation. Any action that in the least contributes to bring back its [Kumase's] former prestige and power will produce corresponding restlessness and variance among the various peoples in Ashanti.[34]

Politics in Asante had undergone a qualitative change. Akyampon Panin's supporters controlled and administered the urban area and worked to rebuild the diminished authority of the council in Kumase. Yet despite the attempts to increase the efficacy of his military government, the Council of Kumase under Akyampon Panin's leadership could no longer control or supervise political arrangements between the *amanhene* and other outlying district and provincial heads. In 1885 and 1886, politicians in areas outside the capital took initiatives and pursued independent courses of action both in their district's foreign affairs and in internal politics. In this period, various chiefs also increasingly began to exercise autonomous decision-making powers in order to safeguard their districts' political and economic interests. As the new political ideology of *nkabom,* or confederation for offensive and defensive purposes, became more widespread even among separatist leaders, several *ahene* organized joint programs of action against local chiefs whose politics threatened the welfare of the southern region.

The Movement to Restore the Monarchy

Despite disagreements among influential southern leaders over the nature and structure of future political relations in their region, the impetus for the movement to restore the monarchy, when it finally took hold, came

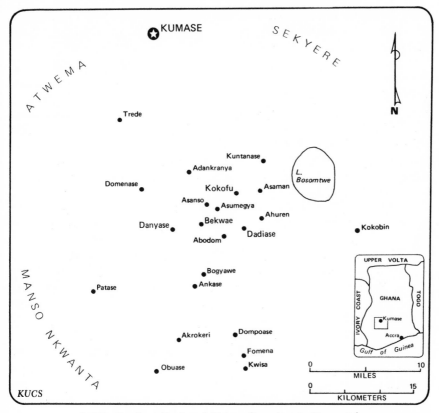

6. The Southern Region of Metropolitan Asante (Amansie)

from the Amansie district, the geopolitical area traditionally known as the cradle of the Asanteman. According to traditions, the original royal family of Asante had migrated to Kumase from this southern region, and thus it possessed special significance in the kingdom's evolution. Throughout the interregnum, Kumase officials repeatedly failed to convene a meeting to elect a new Asantehene. In July 1884 the Kokofuhene, Bekwaehene, Kuntanasehene, and Berekumhene, all from outside the Kumase district, had first requested British assistance to effect the enstoolment of an Asantehene.[35] The Akyempemhene Owusu Koko's efforts in 1884 to persuade outlying district heads to come to the capital for preliminary discussions were unsuccessful, while similar actions of the Saamanhene Akyampon Panin in 1885 also failed. Rather southern politicians, desiring a conference to nominate a new occupant for the Golden Stool, finally initiated debate over procedural matters, and in the absence of central government support, looked to other officials in the Colony to mediate the

81

arrangements. The Bekwaehene Kakari, for example, with the backing of Bekwae centralists in his district, proposed in November 1885 the nomination and election of a new monarch. The powerful Dadiasehene Amoa Fua, who as the Nifahene of Kokofu had taken over the affairs of that district, joined the movement to restore the monarchy.[36] Finally, the new Kokofuhene Osei Asibe, who was apparently appointed by Akyampon Panin in late August 1886 and who was not a member of the royal Oyoko family of the Kokofu stool, similarly lent his voice to the growing official request for monarchical restoration.[37]

Throughout June and July of 1886, reports circulated in Asante and the Colony that a political consensus had emerged over the election of a candidate to occupy the office of Asantehene. Predictably, leaders in Kumase, Kokofu, and Bekwae promoted the conference to resolve the problems surrounding the enstoolment. On 29 June 1886, the Kumase envoy Kwame Boaten, who had spoken for the Council of Kumase since October 1884, told British Governor William Brandford Griffith that officials in the capital, in Kokofu, and in other districts of metropolitan Asante wished to convene an assembly to discuss all aspects of the kingship. Further, Boaten on 3 July 1886 maintained that many Asante chiefs conducted preparations for a meeting to debate the merits of the claimants.[38] While Kwame Boaten presented the views of the Saamanhene Akyampon Panin and the Council of Kumase to officials in the Gold Coast government, the Kokofuhene Osei Asibe's envoys, the *nhenkwaa* Kwabena Agyei and Kwaku Ade, offered corroborating evidence to the British. In August 1886, the Bekwaehene Yaw Gyamfi's representative, Kwadwo Abuilmo, told the district commissioner of Cape Coast that Bekwae leaders had acted to convene an election conference.[39]

These early reports were further substantiated after the British envoy, C. W. Badger, entered Kumase on 12 September 1886. Badger consulted with a "state gathering" of Kumase authorities headed by the Saamanhene Akyampon Panin and learned that two candidates had emerged to contest the vacant throne.[40] The first was Agyeman Prempe, the third eldest son of the Asantehemaa Yaa Akyaa. Yaa Akyaa had succeeded her predecessor Afua Kobi as queen mother of Asante in late 1884. Prempe's father, the Akyebiakyerehene Kwasi Gyambibi, was a son of the Asantehene Kwaku Dua Panin by his marriage to Konadu Sompremo, a daughter of the Asantehene Osei Bonsu. Around fourteen years old in 1886, and one of thirteen children, Prempe was a brother to the Asantehene Kwaku Dua II (also known as Agyeman Kofi), and Agyeman Badu (born about 1875), another prominent member of the Kumase royal Oyoko Dako *abusua*.[41] An Asante explained that:

The name Prempe was not common in Kumase nor among Oyoko royals. Yaa Akyaa's son was either named after some person in the town of Kuma in the Kokofu *oman*, where the citizens named their male children Prempe, or the name was given by Yaa Akyaa's supporters when they pushed their candidate forward and claimed: *Wope o! Wompe o! Ye de no asi so.* "Whether you like it or not we have enstooled him."[42]

The second candidate, Yaw Atweneboanna, was born about 1860 and was the first son of Yaa Afere by her third marriage to the Sabihene of Kumase, Asabi Boakye, another son of the Asantehene Kwaku Dua Panin.[43] The contest between the two candidates that were nominated for the Golden Stool encompassed nine months of the years 1887 to 1888 and signaled the renewal, in still more violent form, of the struggle for power in Asante politics.

5

LOCALISM, CENTRALISM, AND THE SEARCH FOR A NEW POLITICS

The chiefs living outside Kumase wanted their own way. They wanted their own powers. It troubled the Kumase people.—Amakoo

LOCALIST MOVEMENTS

The emergence and proliferation of widespread localist sentiment in the aftermath of the British invasion of 1873–74 provoked heated controversy and protracted conflict in the final quarter of the nineteenth century. During late 1873 and early 1874, dissident politicians in various outlying districts and provinces made independent peace overtures to the British and commenced preliminary negotiations with leaders outside their territorial regions. The British destruction of Kumase and British military operations in Asante in early 1874 enabled several *amanhene* and local politicians to use British influence to promote their independent courses of action and to agitate for changes in the organization of the Asante political system. Their activities were encouraged by anti-Kumase officials in the Protectorate, notably Ata Fua and Kwabena Fua, rulers of Akyem Kotoku and Akyem Abuakwa, respectively, and other chiefs in Akyem Bosume, Denkyira, and Wassa.[1] These discussions between localists in Asante and leaders in the Gold Coast Colony, which continued intermittently throughout the last twenty-five years of the century, challenged the central government's power and its unceasing efforts to maintain strong ties with local officeholders who continued to favor close political union with authorities in the Asante capital.

In the broadest sense localism refers to the restructuring of the nexus of political power and authority and indicates the actions toward, and repeated demands by, outlying leaders for a redistribution of power within the Asanteman. During the reign of the Asantehene Mensa Bonsu, localists aspired to transfer power out of the central government, to modify its field of operations, and to relocate their administrative units within a new system of authority. They endeavored to construct and to institutionalize new sets of relations between their towns and the central government. All dissenting local politicians reacted against Kumase's highly centralized style of governing and its dominance in nearly all phases of political life—decision-making, appointments, prestige, control over the public sector of the national economy, and monopoly over the resources of coercion. They argued with Kumase authorities over the meaning of precedent, custom, and tradition which had sustained the structures of the nineteenth-century political kingdom.[2]

During the 1870s and early 1880s, the struggle between authorities in Kumase and localist politicians focused in the metropolitan districts of Dwaben, Adanse, Bekwae, Kokofu, and in the provinces of Kwawu and Gyaman and the northern reaches of the Bron coalition. These outlying areas also witnessed intense internal competition between centralist and localist politicians in the same era. In each of these places localism differed according to variations in local history, economics, demography, and the specific personalities of the leaders. Various forms of localism can be abstracted from the individual histories of the regions and the responses of local politicians to the specific set of conditions that prevailed during the period.

SECESSIONISM IN DWABEN

Rebellion in the populous and wealthy Oyoko *oman* of Dwaben mounted the first sustained challenge to the undisputed sovereign authority of the central government in the postwar period. In January 1874, the Dwabenhene Asafo Agyei negotiated a separate peace agreement with the British and, with his advisers, sought to assume complete responsibility for the conduct of Dwaben's internal and external affairs. The Dwabenhene demanded full authority to define his relations with Kumase and the British and was, for the most part, willing and indeed eager to be part of the Asanteman if Kumase authorities would give him or he could get that authority. Asafo Agyei's independent diplomatic and economic policies conflicted with the Asantehene Kofi Kakari's goal of national reconstruction following the British destruction of Kumase in early 1874. Kakari worked to win Asafo Agyei's allegiance and to secure the assent of the Dwaben politicians to his view of the proper structure of political relations in the metropolitan region. In spite of these attempts, Agyei's supporters in Dwaben prevailed; and, on 12 August 1874, Kakari overruled the protests of his Kumase councillors and formally recognized and pledged to uphold the Dwabenhene's right to define his own relations with the national government.[3] Dwaben could not, however, achieve full autonomy as a political reality through the grace of monarchical decree alone. The general disagreement with Kakari's unilateral decision among his councillors vitiated its effectiveness and allowed the debate to continue.

Although Asafo Agyei and his supporters did not formulate a systematic political theory, they were the first dissenters to offer a fundamentally different interpretation of the proper extent of the power of Kumase and of political relations in the metropolitan region. Localists in Dwaben apparently adhered to the view that the Asanteman, which had been established in the late seventeenth century, had been formed by contract and the voluntary act of union between Kumase and the *amanto*. Accordingly, the rulers of the *amanto*—the *amanhene*—were *de jure* of coordinate rank, while the Asantehene in Kumase was *primus inter pares*.[4] Each *amanto* in the Asanteman was sovereign in certain fields, the central government in certain others, and each was supreme in its proper sphere. Yet ultimate sovereignty resided with the *amanhene*, primarily because they were the original founding authorities. By proclaiming Dwaben's eighteenth-century historical and legal prerogatives with reference to matters of allegiance, finance, law, and warfare, Asafo Agyei disputed the legality of the restraints imposed by the central government on the autonomy of the *amanto* during the nineteenth century. As an originally sovereign community that had never yielded its sovereignty, Dwaben could assert its right to withdraw from the Asanteman in the event that the central government subverted the authority of its ruler and attempted to secure his allegiance by force.[5]

Localists argued, therefore, that the precedent of the 1830s involving the actual, though temporary, secession of the Dwabenhene Kwasi Boaten remained valid. In 1831 Boaten and a large number of his subjects had been forced to withdraw from the Asanteman to Akyem Abuakwa in the aftermath of a land, political, and financial dispute and subsequent military encounter with authorities in Kumase. Kumase's failure to replace Kwasi Boaten at that time amounted to a *de facto* recognition of his continuing authority and a tacit acknowledgment of the legality of his secession.[6] During the reign of the Asantehene Kwaku Dua Panin, in 1838 the Dwabenhene decided voluntarily to return with his supporters. He reentered the Asanteman on his own terms, which indicated that the central government reluctantly had accepted the legitimacy of Dwaben secession. Leaders in Kumase, however, looked to the more recent past and the centralizing policies of the previous two decades to find precedent for their view of the proper division of political power between the central government and the individual districts.

Localism in Dwaben, then, remained a provocative issue even after Kakari's recognition of the district's autonomy. Following the accession of the Asantehene Mensa Bonsu to the Golden Stool in late 1874, the Council of Kumase quickly repudiated Kakari's unilateral declaration and worked to restore central government control over Dwaben and to reduce the district to its pre-1874 status as one of the *Asante tete amanto num*, or five original territorial divisions of the Asanteman. Nevertheless, Asafo Agyei and his supporters during the first half of 1875 resisted the government's centralizing policies and increasingly used the threat of secession to sustain their claim to autonomy. Localists argued that the Dwabenhene repeatedly had been victimized by unlawful violations committed by authorities in Kumase. For example, Asafo Agyei had not been consulted over the installation or abdication of Kofi Kakari, nor had his advice been solicited concerning the ratification of the Treaty of Fomena and the enstoolment of Mensa Bonsu.[7] Because of these and other infractions over the previous seven years, the occupant of the Dwaben stool had been denied his proper (and customary) rights. Thus, until the Council of Kumase changed its policies, the Dwabenhene would continue to reject Mensa Bonsu's summons to come to Kumase and to participate in Asantemanhyiamu deliberations.[8] The fact that leaders in Dwaben believed that their district's exclusion from deliberations concerning Kakari's deposition and Mensa Bonsu's enstoolment abused their prerogatives indicates that the Dwabenhene resented being excluded from the larger national political processes of the Asanteman.

Asafo Agyei and his advisers enlarged their constituency and sustained their defiance of central authority on the basis of other issues which appealed to a wider cross section of the Dwaben community. Notably, Asafo Agyei's alliance with authorities in Akyem Kotoku, Akyem Abuakwa, and Kete, the important trading center on the Volta River, stimulated and safeguarded Dwaben trade in the Akyem region and consequently was backed by local merchants, while his economic policies—a continuation of the initiatives undertaken by the Dwabenhene Kwasi Boaten in the 1830s—received support from prosperous kola and other trading *asikafo* in the district.[9] Following the British invasion, the Agyei administration vigorously competed with the central government and Mampon for the Salaga trade, blocked Kumase's efforts to reassert its control over the northeastern routes, and encouraged Dwaben, Bron, Krobo, and trans-Volta traders to use alternate routes through the Volta valley to Accra, thereby circumventing the central government's monopoly over the commerce to Cape Coast. Early in 1875 agents from Dwaben conferred with dissidents in Atebubu and Kete Krakye and with leaders in the northeastern Bron coalition; and in August of that year Dwaben envoys successfully thwarted M. J. Bonnat, the Kumase envoy who, as a trader, had been recruited to negotiate the reopening of the Salaga road with the Atebubuhene.[10] Influential *asikafo* within the district who desired economic independence from Kumase and supported Asafo Agyei's endeavors to establish a new trade network in the metropolitan region steadfastly financed the local administration in Dwaben. These traders also pushed for the continued expansion of Dwaben's markets into the savanna country to the north and east of the metropolitan region.

Concomitant with its commercial policies, the Agyei administration revitalized its pact with leaders in Akyem and secured additional pledges of support from politicians in Akuapem, Accra, Cape Coast, and Fanteland and from dissenters in the Asante districts of Effiduase, Asokore, Nsuta, Edweso, and Kuntanase.[11] Emissaries from Dwaben also consulted with administrators of the Gold Coast Colony, and in February 1875 negotiated for concrete British assurances of military aid in the event of hostilities with central government forces. The Dwabenhene in turn used his rapport with Gold Coast officials, who were anxious to offer assistance to any project which restricted Kumase's influence in the Protectorate and the metropolitan region, for propaganda purposes. Asafo Agyei maintained publicly that his platform had the "assent and support" of the British.[12]

Authorities in Kumase responded cautiously to Asafo Agyei's challenge. The Dwabenhene's independent foreign policy was obviously unacceptable. Envoys from Kumase had been detained, plundered, and murdered while seeking to negotiate a peace settlement, and the Dwabenhene's aspirations and policies damaged the reconstruction aims of the central administration. Yet, despite its notable demographic and military superiority, the central government temporarily refrained from coercion. Instead, authorities in Kumase maintained that no Asante leader could claim equal status to the Asantehene. If the Dwabenhene remained on the Asantehene's lands in the metropolitan region, he would abide by the Asantehene's dictates. Further, the Dwabenhene's argument for the repossession of sovereignty was invalid because the district had formally surrendered its sovereignty when the Asantehene Kwaku Dua Panin virtually appointed Asafo Agyei in 1858 or 1859.[13] At that time, officials in Kumase reminded the Dwaben localists, there had been no disagreement with central governmental policies.

During the first half of 1875, the Asantehene and his councillors fashioned a coherent and pragmatic plan to undermine further the credibility of the localists' argument, to mobilize support for the central government, and to reassert the predominance of Kumase in the politics of the metropolitan region. Officials in Kumase indicated that the support of the founding authorities—the *amanhene*—was essential for the re-integration of Dwaben within the Asanteman. During the first half of 1874, several outlying district heads, such as the Bekwaehene, Kokofu-hene, and Kumawuhene, indignant over the Asantehene Kofi Kakari's methods of rule, had openly championed Asafo Agyei's independent course of action.[14] To persuade the dissenting *amanhene* to back the central government and to forestall further defections, Mensa Bonsu and his councillors launched a public relations campaign designed to discredit Asafo Agyei's image and his right to hold office. By focusing public attention on Asafo Agyei's questionable genealogical claim to the Dwaben stool, officials in the Council of Kumase implicitly admonished other outlying district heads that the manner by which they had attained their offices might subsequently be scrutinized if they continued to favor the Dwabenhene's platform.[15] Significantly, protest was a two-edged issue; if the *amanhene* insisted on adopting an orthodox and unbending interpretation of the original relationships between Kumase and the outlying territories, then they stood in danger, by the consistent application of this principle, of losing their offices, because the Asantehene might declare that most were not genealogically qualified to hold office.

The Asantehene, and particularly his more conservative councillors, along with their attempts to stifle the *amanhene's* dissent, depicted Asafo Agyei as a "disturber of general tranquility in the interior" and charged that he had condoned anarchy.[16] Incidents of robbery, kidnap, homicide, and rape abounded in the metropolitan region. Citizens feared to leave their towns, villages had been destroyed, local trade was at a standstill; and, noted Mensa Bonsu, an excitable and potentially violent Kumase populace agitated for decisive central government action against the rebels in Dwaben. Diplomats from Kumase, expounding this theme in their talks with officials of the Gold Coast Colony and with representatives from the European mercantile community during the first half of 1875, emphasized that Asafo Agyei's actions hindered the preservation of order in the Protectorate and the postwar revival of trade between Asante and the Colony. Cape Coast merchants in turn upheld the Asantehene's economic assessment and lobbied to keep the government of the Gold Coast neutral or pro-Kumase in the dispute. Despite the Bonsu administration's assertion that Asante coastal trade had diminished as a result of the Dwaben rebellion, reports indicate that trade from the metropolitan region to the Colony did not significantly decline until the middle of September 1875 when the government closed the southern roads in preparation for war.[17] The Asantehene and his councillors, by repeatedly emphasizing (and exaggerating) the unstable economic situation in the metropolitan region, mobilized popular support and convinced outlying district heads that Asafo Agyei's policies and the platform of the localists hurt the postwar economy of the Asanteman. In addition, the Bonsu administration's campaign in part was designed to assure administrators in the Gold Coast Colony that the rebellion—an internal political matter—could be resolved by military means without entailing a general government commitment to war.

During the second half of 1875, the central government's campaign to mobilize *amanhene* and popular support against Asafo Agyei (and in effect to call his bluff over the matter of secession) succeeded. One account of late May indicated that the Bekwaehene Yaw Opoku "has joined Ashantee, that is to say, Coomassie, and that this last town is making preparation to settle matters with the Djuabins even by force of arms."[18] Preparations were made to convene the Asantemanhyiamu, and *nhenkwaa* were dispatched to inform the outlying district heads. Representatives from Mampon, Bekwae, Kokofu, Agona, Asumegya, and Nkoransa and leading members of the Council of Kumase assembled in late August to debate the Dwaben issue. The outcome was a clear victory for the Bonsu administration: the participants agreed that Asafo Agyei "should be deposed, or war declared against him."[19] Two columns from Kumase invaded Dwaben on 21 October, and after a number of fierce engagements routed the Dwabenhene and his allies from Effiduase, Asokore, and Nsuta on Wednesday, the third of November 1875.

Asafo Agyei and his retainers escaped to Nyabo, from there to Wankyi in Asante Akyem, and thence to Kyebi in Akyem Abuakwa. During the ensuing four years, the vanquished Dwabenhene intrigued with politicians in the Colony against the central government and planned several invasions of the metropolitan region. In 1880 the government of the Gold Coast Colony, relying on spurious charges made by Edmund Bannerman of Accra, deported Asafo Agyei to Lagos where he died on 20 April 1886.[20]

Following the Bantamahene Awua's destruction of villages between Dwaben and Kumase, Dwaben citizens sought refuge in Bompata and other towns in Asante Akyem and Kwawu, while the loyalists settled in such pro-Kumase towns as Konongo and Odumaase in Asante Akyem. The bulk of the Dwaben refugees emigrated under the leadership of Asafo Boaten to Koforidua in Akyem; along with fugitives from Asokore, Effiduase, and Asaman, they founded the *oman* of New Dwaben.[21] The large-scale migration of Dwaben and other Asante citizens to Koforidua and the Akyem country created the first in a series of refugee problems which confronted authorities in Kumase during the last ten years of the nineteenth century.[22] Henceforth, Koforidua and its adjacent towns maintained an independent political and diplomatic status outside the confines of the metropolitan region; and, accordingly, their citizenry became industrious members of Gold Coast Colony political and socioeconomic life. One of the major tasks of the newly formed Prempe regime was the reintegration of New Dwaben into the Asante Nation in keeping with its policy of domestic reconciliation and national reunification.

ADANSE: CENTRALISM ON THE LOCAL LEVEL

The postwar platform of localists in Adanse, the southernmost district of metropolitan Asante, differed greatly from that of their counterparts in Dwaben. Dissident politicians in this region aspired to unite several hitherto separate units of jurisdiction into a larger, integrated local polity, better able to deal with Kumase authority, and capable of interacting with Kumase on a more equal basis. Leaders in Adanse applied to a local context the model of centralized government that was familiar on a national level. As the unification and strengthening of Adanse threatened to diminish the power of the central government, the attempt to unite the district gave rise to a clash of opinions with authorities in Kumase. Yet dissenters in Adanse in the years after 1875 did not resort to the threat of secession, primarily because the logic of their position dictated that limited autonomy was attainable without making a case for withdrawal from the Asanteman, and because their program and leadership did not possess the degree of local support necessary to achieve full realization of their political goals.

The district known as Adanse proper had constituted a largely autonomous local jurisdiction under the Adansehene, the occupant of the Fomena stool, throughout the eighteenth and early nineteenth centuries. The locus of Adanse power in the nineteenth century resided in the towns and villages adjacent to the road connecting Kumase with Cape Coast. The changing fortunes of these market towns created a situation of political instability which augured badly for Asante-coastal commercial relations. In the 1820s, for example, the town of Dompoase was the district's economic and population center. A decade later it had declined, and the town of Kwisa, four miles south, was the commercial focus of the area. By 1839 Fomena, the seat of local administration, one mile north of Kwisa, had eclipsed both towns.[23] During the reign of the Asantehene Osei Yaw Akoto (1824–33), Adanse was politically reorganized. The principal *ahene* of Fomena, Edubiase, Akrofuom, Akrokerri, Ayase, and Bodwesango became independent authorities under the responsibility of officials in Kumase and thereafter took the oath of allegiance to the Asantehene directly.[24]

The British invasion of 1873–74 precipitated the first Adanse demands for a new political status within the Asanteman. The earliest manifestation of conflict between the Fomenahene and authorities in Kumase grew out of national and local wartime politics. As a leading peace advocate in the Asantehene Kofi Kakari's war government, Kwabena Oben, the Fomenahene, believed that he had been excluded from national decision-making. To offset his political impotence, he negotiated for an alliance with anti-Kumase leaders in Wassa and Denkyira. These talks were under way at the time the British expeditionary force invaded the metropolitan region. Thus Kwabena Oben, maintaining his commitment to peace policy and responding to pressure from his new allies, declined to oppose the British and refused to mobilize his men in late 1873.[25]

Kwabena Oben's decision to remain neutral and his separate talks with the British and their allies made him *persona non grata* in Kumase, and the Asantehene apparently considered his deposition on grounds of treason. The Fomenahene, on the other hand, sensed that the British presence in southern Asante in early 1874 and his proven neutrality offered a unique opportunity for his office to increase its power and to regain its earlier authority. He assumed the role (continued by his successors) of self-appointed mediator between other dissenting Asante politicians and administrators in the Gold Coast Colony. Fomena was chosen to be the site of peace talks between envoys from Kumase and the Colony which commenced on 13 February 1874. The outcome of these talks—the Fomena Treaty—determined future relations between Adanse and the central government. The British emissaries upheld the inclusion of the name of Adanse on "the list of those to whom the King of Ashanti was to renounce all right and title."[26] The British mistakenly assumed that a literal interpretation of this clause was recognized in Kumase; but, in fact, the relationship of Adanse to Kumase remained controversial among Asante leaders despite the provision in the Fomena Treaty.

Throughout the following decade the British practiced a form of political warfare against authorities in Kumase. Administrators in the Gold Coast Colony equated—out of ignorance—localist sentiment in Adanse with the demand for separation and independence and continued to uphold the early nineteenth-century authority of the Adansehene. By maintaining that the central government in Kumase had accepted and legally recognized Adanse's sovereignty, the British legitimized their own intervention in support of Adanse localists who continually requested political assistance in the postwar era. Governor George Strahan remarked in early 1876:

> I considered that although Adansi lies outside the limits of the Protectorate, yet on account of its proximity, being immediately adjacent to the Prah, but still more by its independence having been guaranteed by the Treaty of 1874, it occupied a different

situation relatively to this Government from other countries of the interior, and that it was incumbent on me to take such measures as were in my power to obviate the tribe [district] coming at this juncture under Ashanti domination.[27]

Lonsdale, writing in 1882, noted:

Adansi is and will remain a vexed question, both for ourselves and for the Ashantis, unless some definite course be adopted. First, we claim the independence of Adansi from Ashanti, but do not recognize that Adansi is within the Protectorate, especially so far as the jurisdiction of our courts is concerned, and, therefore, do not interfere with the internal government of this portion of West Africa, beyond the advice of a political nature, given from time to time, by the Governor of the Gold Coast Colony to the King.

Secondly, the Adansis generally consider themselves within the jurisdiction of our courts, and to all intents and purposes within the Protectorate, certainly, in so far as recognising our suzerainty in contradistinction to that of Ashanti, and their right to look for us for protection against Ashanti. This is a result of the non-fulfillment of the treaty of 1874, since they still retain their land.

Thirdly, the Ashantis recognise, though unwillingly, the independence of the Adansis since the treaty of 1874, but claim that the Adansis should quit the land they occupy at present, as it belongs to the King of Ashanti. The question is whether jurisdiction shall be extended to Adansi or not. Such a course if adopted would benefit the people and be a check on Ashanti.[28]

The realities of Adanse political life in 1874 did not conform to the British interpretation. In June 1874, Kwabena Oben decided to reassume his former rank and position in the councils of government.

The situation again changed following the death of Kwabena Oben in the middle of December 1874. Two local parties openly contested the vacant Fomena stool and its subsidiary offices. In late 1875, British agents reported that both sides desired "to rejoin Coomassie," which suggests that fundamental disagreement centered on the structure of future relations between Adanse and Kumase, not on the issue of withdrawal from the Asanteman. The centralists, who aspired "to return to Ashanti allegiance," favored the late Fomenahene's intention to reestablish close ties with Kumase.[29] Such "pro-Kumase" politicians believed that Adanse under direct central government rule received greater benefits (e.g., the services of protection, road maintenance, and police patrol) than those emanating from self-government, and adhered to the view that agents from Kumase residing in the main Adanse towns effectively supervised the economy and eliminated political conflict in the district. The opposition party or "anti-Kumase" faction asserted that autonomy within the Asanteman was inseparable from local centralization and that a distinct historical precedent existed for the unification of the district under the Adansehene's authority. This group—led by Kwaku Nkansa, a member of the royal family of the Fomena stool, and Kotirko, the former Kumase diplomat and adviser to the Asantehene Kofi Kakari—evidently believed that independent negotiations with the British and officeholders in the Protectorate enabled Adanse leaders to gain a greater voice in national decision-making. They also wished to obtain exclusive control over Adanse markets (e.g., Edubiase and Kwisa) and thereby eliminate Kumase's exploitation of the district economy.[30]

The struggle for the Fomena stool dominated local politics throughout 1875, as Adanse lurched towards civil war. Commerce declined, sections of Route VI were intermittently closed to traders from the metropolitan region, and local merchants complained of robbery and violence in the markets and along the roads. Accordingly, the localists stressed that officials in the central government could not solve local law and order problems so they enlisted the British agent, Alfred C. Moloney, to mediate the election. By manipulating British prestige and receiving assurances of Protectorate support, the localists brought Kwaku Nkansa to office as the Fomena or Adansehene in February 1876. Kotirko, the new Adansehene's experienced and influential adviser, was installed as Adanse Akyeamehene, or main spokesman, for the district.[31]

During the next three years the Nkansa-Kotirko regime endeavored to broaden its political base and bolster its credibility, to minimize the influence of the central government, and to establish firm diplomatic ties with officials in the Colony and with dissidents in Sehwi and other areas of southern Asante. The administration encouraged the Wesleyan missionaries to open schools in Adanse and strove to control local markets and gain a monopoly over the trade passing through the district. By February 1879, the regime felt sufficiently confident to implement its centralization plan. The Adansehene brought deposition charges against leading pro-Kumase centralists on grounds that they had received money from Kumase and were disloyal to the district. Kwaku Nkansa appointed their successors and purged several pro-Kumase officeholders in the area.[32]

The Asantehene Mensa Bonsu and his advisers, increasingly alarmed over the regime's policies, actively contested the Adansehene's appointments. The Nkansa-Kotirko regime, in response, enlisted Acting Colonial Secretary J. S. Hay's support to rid the district of Kumase envoys who had applied financial pressure to regain local offices for the centralists. Hay's intervention was decisive. Declaring that the Kumase agents had

95

violated the Fomena agreement of 1874, Hay demanded that all central government functionaries immediately return to the capital or risk military retaliation. In April 1879, the Bonsu administration ordered its envoys to dismantle their headquarters in Fomena.[33]

Despite the accomplishments of the Nkansa-Kotirko regime and the support provided by the government of the Gold Coast Colony in the 1880s, the Adansehene and his supporters experienced severe difficulty sustaining their defiance of central authority. The central government's decision to relocate the main southern market from Edubiase to Ankase and the sanctions applied against Adanse traders in that mart more than offset the regime's struggle to achieve economic self-sufficiency and in turn alienated various Adanse asikafo who previously had backed the localists' commercial policies. Adanse chiefs became embroiled in heated disputes over land ownership with authorities in neighboring Kokofu and Bekwae. Adanse citizens made charges of maladministration, illegal seizure of property, and stringent social controls to administrators on the coast. The Council of Kumase's continual efforts to "sap the allegiance of some of the principal chiefs" and the weak personal position of the Fomenahene further eroded the consensus of opinion on which his regime depended.[34]

By 1882, then, the Nkansa-Kotirko administration was on the verge of losing its mandate to govern the district. Widespread popular and official dissatisfaction with the Adansehene's conduct in office and Kumase's persistent influence stimulated a brief revival of centralist sentiment. Late in September 1882, the ahene of Dompoase, Edubiase, and Ayase, three of the Adansehene's appointees, threatened rebellion and forcibly attempted to oust Kwaku Nkansa. The regime again solicited British assistance in the person of C. W. Badger, the British agent. Badger reasserted the standard British position: Adanse must remain united, peaceful, and strong in order to maintain its independence. He left little doubt that administrators in the Colony would only recognize an anti-Kumase leadership in the district and implied that the British would use force to sustain their goal.[35] Thus, localists remained in power for three more years and faced relatively limited opposition. Kotirko's skillful handling of Adanse external policy in the years 1883–85 was one factor in the regime's success, while the political disorder in Kumase during that period seriously undermined the prestige of the central government in Adanse. More significantly, the proliferation of dissident movements throughout the southern region of metropolitan Asante in the early 1880s made any centralist local challenge increasingly untenable. Finally, the growing confrontation with Bekwae—already evident in April 1882—masked internal conflict and fostered the first genuine signs of unification in Adanse.

BEKWAE AND CONFEDERACY

Reports of impending hostilities between authorities in Bekwae and the Nkansa-Kotirko regime in Adanse first circulated in January 1886. Throughout the ensuing six months, leaders in both districts became involved in an extensive controversy over issues that related to each district's political, economic, and territorial concerns. As the confrontation intensified, both sides enlisted allies with similar inclinations in metropolitan Asante and the northern regions of the Protectorate; concurrently, each sought to win British assistance. The controversy between Bekwae and Adanse dramatized several of the major issues in Asante politics in 1885–86. As the central authority progressively disintegrated in the mid-1880s, authorities in Kumase were unable to control political arrangements between local units and no longer arbitrated matters of war and peace between districts in the metropolitan region. The dispute highlighted differing local viewpoints regarding the election of a new Asantehene and the nature of local ties with Kumase. Furthermore, it illustrated varying local opinions over the efficacy of British influence in southern Asante affairs and focused on whether local issues (e.g., banditry on the trade routes, land ownership, and the rights of citizenry) would be resolved by local officials or the central government. The outcome of the dispute was the military defeat of the Nkansa-Kotirko faction and its allies, and the subsequent migration of several separatist leaders with their supporters into lands south of the Pra River in June and July of 1886.

In the years prior to the Bekwae-Adanse conflict, the Bekwae *oman* had shifted between centralist and localist political adherence. Bekwaehene Yaw Opoku, a leading figure in the Asante war government, argued in council for a military solution to the problems arising in the British Protected Territory in 1872–73.[36] Following the abdication of the Asantehene Kofi Kakari in October 1874, Opoku, who had been instrumental in gathering opposition to Kakari's terroristic policies, maintained close relations with officials in the Mensa Bonsu administration and upheld the central government's efforts to halt the deteriorating political and economic situation in Adanse. Yaw Opoku was outspoken on the Adanse issue, for Bekwae claimed the town of Odumaase which the Asantehene Kwaku Dua Panin had transferred to Adanse in 1831. To resolve this exclusively local issue, the Bekwaehene firmly believed in the use of military force to solve the problems of foreign affairs. In 1880, for example, Bekwaehene Opoku publicly swore to restore Adanse to Kumase's rule.[37]

Throughout his tenure in office, Bekwaehene Yaw Opoku supported the concentration of administrative power in the central government. Yet it appears that in the 1880s the Bekwaehene came under pressure from local politicians to moderate his militant stance and his centralism. Yaw Opoku died in December 1882. Although the cause of his death is unknown, reports indicated that his brother, Kwasi Adiya, killed him for backing central government policies. Kwasi Adiya undoubtedly was the spokesman for (or was put forward by) proponents of decentralism—those politicians in Bekwae who favored loose political ties with Kumase and more power in the southern region. Although in a minority, they attempted to enlarge their constituency in the district. Kwasi Adiya in turn was murdered by the supporters of Osei Yaw, who took office in early 1883.[38] Osei Yaw's accession to the Bekwae stool corresponded with the aspirations of authorities in Kumase; he was a leading partisan of the central government and probably came to office with Kumase's assistance.

Following Osei Yaw's enstoolment the Bekwae *nkwankwaa* and *asikafo* revolted against the central government, primarily because of the Mensa Bonsu administration's new tax policies in the postwar period. Representatives of the Bekwae *nkwankwaa* conferred with officials of the government of the Gold Coast Colony on 4 March 1884 and proclaimed their desire for separation from the Asanteman. Then, on 31 March and again on 3 April 1883, envoys from several Bekwae chiefs told Governor Samuel Rowe that they wished to adopt the commoners' political platform: the *ahene* announced that they would no longer serve the Asantehene and, if necessary, would resort to military measures to sustain their separatism in the face of Kumase or local opposition. Bekwaehene Osei Yaw and his remaining supporters moved to head off the rebellion and safeguard their offices. At a meeting with Knapp Barrow in Amoafo on 12 April 1883, the Bekwaehene officially renounced his centralist stance and justified his new position on political and economic grounds.[39] Bekwaehene Osei Yaw's "conversion" produced economic dividends. Six weeks later, Barrow reported "brisk trade" in Bekwae.[40]

Bekwaehene Osei Yaw's switch in political orientation for reasons of expediency and the pressure exerted by separatist politicians only temporarily safeguarded his office. The British envoy, Brandon Kirby, in February 1884 learned that Osei Yaw had been deposed and exiled to Adanse. His ouster was probably attributable to lingering resentment over his support of Kakari's restoration in 1883 and the excessive fines he levied to raise funds for Kakari. Further, Osei Yaw had "a reputation for cruelty."[41] There seems little doubt, also, that the Bekwae centralists, although temporarily out of power, challenged Osei Yaw's rapprochement with Adanse leaders throughout 1883 and probably also resented the frequent consultations of Bekwae envoys with officials of the Gold Coast Colony in that year. The Bekwae centralists joined with the *nkwankwaa* and *asikafo* in the district who also wished to rejoin Kumase once again.[42] Consequently, Bekwae's autonomy was short-lived.

Bekwaehene Kakari assumed office following the deposition of his predecessor in early 1884. Kakari's candidacy received support from politicians who favored a close political relationship with Kumase and from *nkwankwaa* who were disillusioned with the Osei Yaw administration's tax policies. By April 1884, Bekwaehene Kakari had returned his district to "Kumase authority and rule."[43] Although Kakari's administration advocated close political ties with Kumase, it differed considerably from previous Bekwae governments. This resulted from the Council of Kumase's decline in power and influence, especially in the aftermath of Akyampon Panin's military coup.

During this period the Bekwaehene joined with leaders in Amoafo, Ahuren, Dadiase, Asumegya, Kokofu, and Esiase to form a loosely structured confederation to promote mutually advantageous local goals. The Bekwae confederation was organized by leaders in Bekwae and other southern districts to promote "peace and order and prosperity" throughout the southern region of metropolitan Asante, a function previously assumed by the central government.[44] The confederation was, furthermore, a joint program of action for offensive and defensive military purposes designed to curb the actions of district chiefs whose policies threatened the welfare of the southern region. While participating in this confederation, Bekwaehene Kakari enjoyed the support of Bekwae centralists who wished to nominate and elect a new Asantehene and the support of the *nkwankwaa* and *asikafo* within his district. In April 1886, the British agent, R. E. Firminger, reported:

> This party [the centralists] became much stronger on the election to the stool of their nominee Karikari (consequent upon the death of Osai Yow) who quickly commenced negotiations with the Ashanti tribes to join the Coomassies, and together to elect a king (Quacoe Duah was dead and the stool vacant). At first the various tribes refused, relying on the advent of the white officer who, it was promised should be sent to advise them. The greatest antagonist to the new Becquai policy was Adansi, who has always feared a powerful Ashanti on her frontier, and the King of Adansi [Kwaku Nkansa] sent a sharp message to Karikari, threatening him with punishment by the Governor if he interfered in Ashanti affairs.[45]

Throughout 1885 and into early 1886, relations between authorities in Bekwae and the Nkansa-Kotirko regime in Adanse steadily worsened. Commercial traffic along Route VI repeatedly was stopped. Asante traders, mostly from Bekwae, were robbed, beaten, and murdered.[46] The

Kakari administration continually believed that Adanse citizens were the bandits and that the regime in Adanse condoned their actions. In late 1885, therefore, Bekwaehene Kakari sent special emissaries to Fomena to demand that Kwaku Nkansa pay £240 in gold dust as reparation for the losses suffered by Bekwae traders during the past year. Kwaku Nkansa, fearing the outbreak of hostilities, appealed to the British administration and maintained that the Bekwaehene lacked the authority to make such monetary demands, especially since Adanse was within the British sphere of influence. The Adansehene's refusal in 1885 to extradite the political fugitive, Dabea, to Bekwae for trial inflamed the contention between Bekwae and Adanse.[47] And Kumase's political impotence during this period can be measured by its inability to settle relations between these outlying districts or to end the rampant banditry.

Towards the end of January 1886, the Adansehene, alarmed that Bekwae would retaliate for the banditry along Route VI and the Dabea incident, increased his efforts to secure political assistance from other separatist leaders in the southern region. Further, Kwaku Nkansa requested military aid from separatist leaders in the Manso district. While Adanse and Manso forces were encamped at several locations on the Bekwae frontier, the Bekwaehene Kakari died of a "serious illness" on 1 February 1886.[48] Kakari's successor, Yaw Gyamfi, took office on the same day. The rapid transition clearly indicates that Yaw Gyamfi's constituency was similar to that which had brought Kakari to power in 1884. Yaw Gyamfi rapidly received support from the Bekwae "war party" that pressed for a military solution to the Adanse problem. The new Bekwaehene pursued a more militant policy than his predecessor; in February 1886 he sent envoys to Fomena who announced that Bekwae forces would mobilize if the town of Odumaase and the villages of Kyeaboso and Akotakye were not immediately ceded. Yaw Gyamfi also negotiated with the Saamanhene Akyampon Panin and with leaders in the towns of Asanso, Adankranya, and Abodom for a military alliance. In the first week of March, troops from these districts joined Bekwae forces encamped at Kankuase, making a total force of more than ten thousand.[49] The Bekwaehene next made political overtures to separatist leaders in Dadiase, Danyase, and Amoafo. Again, it is significant that the central government in Kumase could not control these arrangements of southern district heads and did not take the initiative to convene a peace conference or a meeting to elect a new Asantehene. In the first quarter of 1886, then, the roads through Adanse remained closed. Commerce in Cape Coast had virtually ceased, and traders from Bekwae, Kumase, Nsuta, and Adanse were again robbed, detained, and imprisoned. Bekwae and

Adanse authorities refused to surrender kidnapped traders, to underwrite economic losses, or to repatriate citizens from the border towns.[50]

Leaders in Adanse and Bekwae used British officials as mediators in the dispute to avoid a full-scale military confrontation. The reasons that prompted both sides to solicit British assistance differed considerably. The Nkansa-Kotirko regime maintained that Adanse's autonomy had been guaranteed by the government of the Gold Coast Colony according to the terms of the Fomena agreement of 1874 and believed that the British were obligated to provide military assistance to insure that status.[51] Adanse leaders hoped further that British arbitration would strengthen their credibility with hitherto uncommitted separatist leaders such as the Dadiasehene Amoa Fua. Primarily for this reason, the Adansehene publicized reports that Hausa soldiers from the Gold Coast Constabulary would join with Adanse against Bekwae and its allies. This was particularly significant because the Adanse had mobilized only some twenty-five hundred men in contrast to the much larger Bekwae force.

Bekwaehene Yaw Gyamfi's government wanted British arbitration in order to secure a pledge of British neutrality in the event of full-scale hostilities.[52] The Bekwae leaders believed that British mediators would support their efforts to reunify the Asante Nation and to convene a conference to elect a new Asantehene. An important factor in Bekwae's attempt to solicit British arbiters was the threat posed by the six-gun battery constructed by Colonel Firminger in March to command the ford and ferry at Praso. Yaw Gyamfi's government, although dominated by the war interest, acted as if this fortification was an integral part of a larger British scheme to assist the Adanse militarily. On this point, however, the Bekwae incorrectly assessed official opinion in the government of the Gold Coast Colony. In early April 1886, Firminger clearly supported the Bekwae position:

> His message [Yaw Gyamfi's], etc. gave me to understand that if fighting in earnest once begins he will not allow any interference. I must say from all I gather my sympathies are entirely with him, and I think the Adansis have behaved like murderers and robbers, and deserve a severe punishment, which, if we do not interfere, they will assuredly get.[53]

The British administration, intent on keeping the trade arteries open to the coast, would not support individual separatist leaders in metropolitan Asante.

On 8 April 1886, the Adanse council convened to discuss the situation. The deliberations indicated that, for the first time since 1875, the Adanse leaders reached substantial consensus on external affairs. At their meeting Firminger observed that "the war party was predominant" and that the Adansehene Kwaku Nkansa "commenced to find excuses and to shuffle with the object of preventing any communication between me and Yow Janfi [Yaw Gyamfi], and at last declared in a very excited manner that he did not want peace, but would follow the Becquais and fight with them wherever he found them."[54] During the deliberations Firminger, acting on instructions from his superiors in Accra, dispelled any notion that the government of the Gold Coast Colony would assist the Adanse militarily. Having failed to get British assistance, the Adanse hoped for the intervention of separatist leaders such as the powerful Dadiasehene Amoa Fua and his ally, Kofi Ahinkora of Akyem Bosume. Amoa Fua, however, did not commit himself at this stage; instead he urged the Bekwaehene Yaw Gyamfi and his allies to negotiate a peace settlement. Although the Bekwaehene personally was inclined to accept a peaceful solution to the controversy, Yaw Gyamfi acquiesced to the dominant war interest in his own district and to the militant view put forth by the envoys from Kumase and other Asante *aman*.[55] Thus, after realizing that the military installation at Praso was not directed against Bekwae and its allies and that a settlement with the Adanse was impossible, the Bekwae confederacy council decided to solve the controversy militarily.

In late April 1886, the Adanse forces launched an attack on the Bekwae headquarters at Begroase. The Nkansa-Kotirko regime apparently had secured at least a promise of military assistance from Dadiase on the seventeenth or eighteenth of April. On 10 June the Dadiase position surfaced when it was reported that:

> . . . King Amuofa of Dadiasse sends messengers to tell King Inkansah [Kwaku Nkansa] that all the Ashantis have joined the Becquais, and had made one mind to go to Coomassie and set a King on the stool there, which he Amuofa himself had joined them, and wishes Inkansah also to go and swear an oath that he will make peace with the Becquais and cease fighting.[56]

The Dadiasehene Amoa Fua's support for the confederation undercut the Nkansa-Kotirko regime's efforts to maintain Adanse's autonomy in the 1880s. The Adansehene Kwaku Nkansa—who had expressed his intention not to join the Bekwae confederation, would not work to elect a new Asantehene, and feared reprisals from Bekwae and its allies—decided to resettle in the Gold Coast Colony. Contemporary reports noted that 12,411 Adanse crossed the Pra River between 13 and 15 June 1886.[57] The loss of the Adanse communities weakened the national political fabric and generated additional problems for the central government, which continued to founder until Prempe's accession to the Golden Stool in 1888.

DISTRICT AMBITION IN KWAWU

In the province of Kwawu, located on the eastern border of metropolitan Asante and linked to Kumase by a branch of Route V of the great-roads, localists presented another kind of challenge to the authority of the central government. The populous central area of Kwawu consisted of five *nkuro*, or towns: Obo, the business center; Abene, the seat of local authority; Abetifi, the residence of the most influential local ruler; Oboman; and Apraeso. Six large and twelve small *nkuraa*, or villages, surrounded the main towns. This plateau area known as Kwawu Kodiabe was under the direct supervision of two Kumase chiefs, the Dadiesoabahene and Fantehene, who as *nhwesofo* were entrusted with administrative responsibility for the province during the greater part of the nineteenth century.[58] Concurrently, since the reign of the Asantehene Opoku Ware I (about 1720–50) who appointed Esen Kagya, ambassadors from Kumase resided in the main towns and supervised politics in the province and the Afram Plains to the north and west of the Kwawu scarp.[59]

Dissenters in Kwawu first agitated publicly for changes in the relationship with the central government in the aftermath of the British invasion, which temporarily diminished the ability of Kumase to supervise its territories directly. Following the murder of Antwi Akomea, one of the last Kumase residents in Kwawu, and the imprisonment of ambassadors from the central government in December 1875, the Abenehene Kwadwo Akuamoa II and the Abetifihene Kofi Denkyi headed the localists in the province. This group aspired to elevate the political status of their province within the Asanteman and thereby secure greater authority in local affairs and the right to pursue independent negotiations with external authorities during the postwar period. They wanted increased control over local economic decision-making and especially the construction of a new, direct route from Akyem Abuakwa via Kwawu and Krakye to the markets at Atebubu and Salaga. The artery maximized Kwawu control over its kola production and distribution. It enabled local traders to gain a monopoly over the coastal traffic to the mart at Obo via the route from Kurantumi and Kyebi.[60] Along with their attempt to control the kola trade from Akyem, Kwawu leaders encouraged entrepreneurs from the Colony to work gold mines in the region.[61]

Localists in Kwawu achieved the ability (and the *de facto* right) to control their own internal affairs in the era before 1880. Kwawu dissenters negotiated with Asafo Agyei and the Dwaben refugees and with leaders in Akuapem, Akyem, and the Asante Akyem towns. They talked with administrators in the Gold Coast Colony and the Basel missionaries at Kyebi and Begoro. These policies thus sustained Kwawu's new district status and countered the repeated political and financial efforts of the central government to bolster the influence of local centralists—notably, the *ahene* of Obo, Oboman, and Twendurase.[62] Thus, localism in Kwawu, in contrast to that of Dwaben, Adanse, and Bekwae during the same period, signified not the weakening of ties with Kumase but rather the strengthening of the power of local authorities to manage Kwawu affairs, which enabled the territory to interact on the basis of greater equality with other polities in the metropolitan region.

The situation, however, significantly changed as Basel missionary influence noticeably increased following the establishment of a permanent station in Abetifi in 1880. Kwawu commoners, responding to the pressure of the missionaries Fritz Ramseyer and Muller and of British agents, demanded the severance of all connections with the central government. Local *asikafo* actively championed the autonomous economic policies and efforts to expand the market at Obo. In addition, Dwaben fugitives in towns such as Ahiresu in Kwawu resisted any form of central government control, while outside agitators from the Colony further undermined Kumase's authority in its former dependency. Although the Abenehene Akuamoa—even in 1876 described as old and delicate—and the Abetifihene Denkyi frequently vacillated and cautiously avoided provoking reprisals from Kumase,[63] the localists after 1880 rejected compromise with the central government and considered British protection. A report of 1880, for example, indicated that participants in the Kwawu council had decided "to remain independent of Ashanti."[64] Accordingly, local authorities conducted more intensive negotiations for a pact with officials in Akuapem and Akyem and formed an alliance with leaders in the rebel northeastern Bron coalition in May 1881.[65] Localists subsequently dominated Kwawu politics with the collapse of central authority during the years 1884–88 and signed a treaty of protection with the British in June 1888. The signatories included several leading anti-Kumase figures: the Abenehene Kofi Boaten who assumed office in 1884; the Abetifihene Adu Kwame who succeeded Kofi Denkyi following his death on 15 January 1883; the Nkwatiahene Kofi Anyiripe whose supporters had executed the Kumase functionary Antwi Akomea in 1875; and the Apraesohene Kwadwo Kese who apparently was related to the mother of the Dwabenhene Asafo Agyei. Two prominent centralists, the Obohene Kwasi Asama and the Obomanhene Kofi Amankwa, also signed the treaty and had switched sides after 1880 because of Kumase's increasing unpopularity in Kwawu political circles.[66]

GYAMAN: CHALLENGE TO ASANTE IMPERIALISM

Still another manifestation of localism occurred in the northwestern province of Gyaman, a region whose military and economic contact with the central government dated to the mid eighteenth century. Since about 1740, when Asante armies had invaded the region, resident commissioners from Kumase supervised trading relations in the main towns. In the late 1870s, following the British invasion, dissenters in Gyaman also initiated a diplomatic campaign to enlist official British support in order to sustain their bid for autonomy. Discord between local authorities and officials in Kumase, as in the case of Kwawu, derived from economic considerations as well as from earlier hostilities with the central government. In the dry season of 1817–18, for example, the Asantehene Osei Bonsu personally had crushed a bloody rebellion over faltering tribute payments.[67] Led by the Gyamanhene Agyeman and the Takyimanhene Kwabena Fofie, the localists, under pressure from influential and wealthy Muslim traders in the district, sought to enlarge the market at Bonduku and to use alternate trade routes which circumvented Kumase's monopoly over commerce to and from the northwestern region. Yet Gyaman politicians differed from their counterparts in Kwawu in that they not only strove to reorient their district's lucrative gold trade to the ports of the Gold Coast Colony (as Kwawu *asikafo* desired) but also attempted to secure new outlets in the Dyula towns to the northwest and concurrently in the French ports at Kinjabo and Assini.[68] Thus, local politicians in Gyaman, although possessing similar motives and goals to those in Kwawu, had a different and broader method to achieve their aspirations: continual economic independence not only from Kumase but also from the government of the Gold Coast Colony and authorities in the adjoining provinces of Sehwi to the southeast.

THE BRON COALITION AND NKORANSA: ECONOMIC STRATEGIES IN THE NORTHEAST

The Asante economy was gravely threatened in the postwar period by other secessionist movements in the northeastern provinces. For the first three-quarters of the nineteenth century, the major northern provinces of Greater Asante—Banda, Bron, Dagomba, Gonja, Gyaman, Nkoransa, Nsoko, and Takyiman—were tributaries of the central government in Kumase. Wilks has delineated in detail the structure, development, and regularization of the relationships between local leaders and agents of the central government for the greater part of the century and has analyzed the progressive construction of an apparatus of political control in the "grasslands" (e.g., the system of resident commissioners in the northeast, Salaga, and Yendi) by which nineteenth-century Asante governments maintained stability and eliminated most interpolity conflicts. Asante control over the north was more successful than had been possible in the turbulent southern provinces.[69] After 1874, however, Asante hegemony over the northern provinces of Greater Asante was challenged by dissident political movements which directly threatened the economy of the Asanteman, the commercial relations of Kumase with its hinterlands, and the security of the southern branches of the trade arteries to Hausaland (in Northern Nigeria). In 1875 the eastern Bron, who as conscripts for the Asante armies of reoccupation had suffered severe casualties and were therefore reluctant to provide additional manpower for the Asante government, rebelled against Kumase. The revolt signaled the collapse of the government's civilian administration in the northeast.[70]

The Bron rebellion proliferated rapidly after 1875 as leaders in Krakye, Nchumuru, Buem, and Atebubu joined in the drive for autonomy and negotiated an alliance with the insurgents led by the Dwabenhene Asafo Agyei. The British administration attempted to manipulate the revolt in order to extend its own influence into the northern hinterland of Asante. Gold Coast officials strove to establish communication with the *maidugai*, or caravan-leaders, from Hausaland and Bornu who traded in the market at Salaga and with other entrepreneurs farther west in Bonduku, the capital of Gyaman, and to divert the trade of Salaga away from Kumase (and Asante *asikafo*) by encouraging traders to use a direct route down the Volta to the coast at Ada and Accra. Thus V. Skipton Gouldsbury's treaty of 8 March 1876 with the priest of Dente and the chief of Krakye was explicitly designed to underwrite this new policy of limited intervention in the northeast which, according to Carnarvon in the Colonial Office, was still in an experimental stage but was increasingly implemented throughout the 1880s and early 1890s.[71]

In May 1881, the secessionist provinces entered into a defensive alliance to consolidate their autonomy under the spiritual and political leadership of Krakye. The pact consisted of Krakye's neighbors, the Buem, of the eastern Gonja whose ruler in Kpembe controlled the market in Salaga after the revolt against Kumase in 1875, and of dissident Nsuta from metropolitan Asante who had taken refuge in Krakye in 1872 to avoid conscription. Localists in Kwawu also supported the movement.[72] The members of this alliance, in the absence of Asante political pressure, were thus able to control economic affairs on the eastern and northeastern border of metropolitan Asante throughout the 1880s. Lonsdale, who visited Atebubu on 15 December 1881, learned from the Atebubuhene Jan Kwaku that the central government administration had collapsed in the northeast. This had stimulated the creation of new local markets, especially along the Volta route to Accra. Large numbers of Hausa traders had relocated to the commercial center of Panto on the lower part of the Volta River. In the northeast, roads were closed to Asante merchants, and a new exchange center had been established in Atebubu. The eastern Bron now traded with Salaga and the coast but not with Asante.[73]

Kumase's response to widespread rebellion in the northeast was remarkably reserved considering the strategic economic importance of that area (lying between the Hausa caravans coming overland and the Asante kola-producing areas to the southwest) and Asante's loss of the Salaga market in 1875. Although two parties of Kumase envoys were massacred in Krakye while attempting to negotiate a settlement to the crisis in 1876 or 1877, the Mensa Bonsu administration chose not to make war on the northeastern secessionists, with their strong local constituencies. Instead Kumase authorities worked to establish a new trade structure and another outlet for Asante kola resources at Kintampo in the inner province of Nkoransa.[74]

The importance of the Kintampo market significantly increased after 1877. In that year David Asante and Theophil Opoku still observed a large volume of commercial transactions conducted in Salaga. Salaga had twenty thousand inhabitants. Merchants from Asante, Mossiland, Gyaman, and Hausaland regularly visited the town.[75] Lonsdale, in late 1881, maintaining that the central government in Kumase had established the entrepôt at Kintampo for the exchange of its kola, noted that Kintampo had prospered at Salaga's expense. Although traders from Kwawu still brought kola to Salaga, the town had become primarily a center for the exchange of local goods, cattle, ivory, slaves, and manufactured articles which were conveyed by Fante, Accra, and other coastal merchants along the Volta valley from Accra.[76] In early 1884, Brandon Kirby noted that Kintampo was "the largest market in this part of Africa." Some three to four thousand Asantes (along with officials of the central government) resided in the town in addition to the Hausa and other itinerant traders numbering between thirty and forty thousand during the dry season.[77] According to David Asante, Salaga, by contrast in 1884,

> is no longer what it was seven years ago. The trade has diminished and gone to Krakye, Kpando, Kpon, and Akra. The sale of human beings has also decreased. For this reason the once beautiful houses are so ruined with earth hard trampled underfoot and rubbed smooth that they can never be set to rights. The remaining trade is mainly in clothing materials, for the most part brought from Europe, meat and other food. The cattle here are said to come from the interior. There are many asses, few horses, also sheep.[78]

The Asante government's economic sanctions against Salaga and the northeast were largely successful. Kumase's decision to create the alternative market specifically at Kintampo within the territory of the Nkoransahene was based on the excellent relations between the rulers of Nkoransa and Kumase throughout the nineteenth century. Nkoransa alone among the principal polities in the northeast did not join the alliance against Kumase. Because of diplomatic pressures exerted by secessionist leaders in Atebubu and Krakye, it temporarily assumed a semi-autonomous stance ("an indifferent sort of subjugation to Ashanti") vis-à-vis the central government in the late 1870s.[79] Although the Nkoransahene Atta Fa never personally came to Kumase while the Asantehene Mensa Bonsu held office, he communicated with authorities in the capital and sent representatives to the Asantemanhyiamu deliberations during this period. But in 1881 or earlier, the Nkoransahene closed the great-road to Kumase at Kofiase in protest against the heavy tolls levied on his traders at Kintampo and against the persistent extradition demands made upon him by officials in Kumase. The central government always had insisted that Nkoransa authorities quickly return fugitive Asantes to the metropolitan region.[80]

Yet the local government in Nkoransa remained a centralist one and wished to continue its middleman role in the Kintampo kola trade and to receive the substantial revenues accruing to that position. In February 1884, Atta Fa strongly opposed the candidacy of the former Asantehene Kofi Kakari and expressed his desire to serve Kumase. The Nkoransahene would reopen his district roads to Asante traders if the new Asantehene Kwaku Dua II reformed the tax policies of his predecessor and, thereby, reduced the tolls and fines levied on Nkoransa traders and on articles passing through Kumase to the north. Following Kumase's compliance with his conditions, Atta Fa in early 1884 again joined "with the Coomassies." The district's rubber and gold enterprises greatly prospered from the Nkoransahene's move to restore ties with the central government.[81] Atta Fa's successor, Kofi Baffo (Kofi Abam) was brought to office by the centralists in the district and, consequently, remained loyal to Kumase during the forty days that he held office.[82] The next Nkoransahene, Kwasi Opoku, stayed neutral in the electoral contest of 1887–88. He refused to support any Kumase candidate for Asantehene and steadily worked to build his constituency among localists in Nkoransa who favored joining the northeastern Bron coalition.[83] The growing mood in Nkoransa for secession foreshadowed an impending confrontation with authorities in the central government who refused to recognize the localists' demands for autonomy within the Asanteman.

In response to the bewildering number of movements for autonomy throughout the Asanteman and the proliferation of localist rhetoric with all its distinctive varieties, authorities in Kumase felt a need to reinforce their own interpretation of the basis of nineteenth-century Asante political life. Officials in Kumase first stressed the hitherto unquestioned "centralist" nature of Asante politics during the reign of the Asantehene Mensa Bonsu (1874-83). Asante informants born during this administration indicated the emergence of such ideas with statements like: *Onyame boo tumi maa Kumase,* or "God created the authority for Kumase," and *Na tumi wo Kumase,* or "there was (powerful) authority in Kumase."[84] The new challenge facing leaders in the central government—justifying their right to rule which had previously been a given in Asante life—was dramatically explained by the nonagenarian Omantihene of Kumase:

> In the olden days no person defied Nana Asantehene and his chiefs in Kumase. The Asantehene had power over life and death. He and his chiefs decided who was to be killed, who was to pay taxes, who was to trade to the north and coast, and who was to swear the oath of allegiance at the Odwira. All people in Asante obeyed Nana Asantehene. Chiefs who rebelled were crushed. Even the *amanhene* were defeated. The views of all Asantes had to be like those of Nana Asantehene. The *amanhene* obeyed. The Fante obeyed as did the Akyems and Assins. After the Sagrenti [Wolseley campaign of 1873–74] War the power of Kumase was greatly challenged. It was the first time so great a challenge was made to Nana Asantehene's authority. The Asantehene and his chiefs decided that the time had again come to make Kumase all powerful. This brought much discussion and debate among the Asantehene's elders. It was a new thing for the Asantehene to have to prove he was lord of life and death.[85]

When Agyeman Prempe assumed this authority in 1888, he and his advisers were faced with the boundless challenge of successfully resolving the complex embroilments between the imperial center and local interests, local power, and local pride. Relations between the national core and the periphery had been woefully strained, neglected, and abused during the ill-managed administrations of self-styled governors who presided over Asante politics during the interregnum. Indeed, this legacy of the 1880s threatened to smash the vitality and predictability of the nineteenth-century Asante political process. Prempe's mission was one of reconciliation and national unification, and his policies were remarkable for their leniency and forbearance.

6

YAW ATWENEBOANNA, AGYEMAN PREMPE, AND THE CAMPAIGN OF 1887-1888

The elders put their faith in this young leader. It was not an easy time. Prempe and his people had to prove themselves.—Domfe Kyere

CONSTITUENCIES

The nomination of two candidates for the Golden Stool in 1886 signified a return to the traditional monarchical form of rule and an attempt to restore order in the Asante Nation. Prempe's candidacy, sponsored by the Asantehemaa Yaa Akyaa, received the endorsement of the majority of the members of the Council of Kumase. A few dissenters in the council, such as the Kyidomhene Kwame Boaten and the Anamenakohene Kwabena Dwoben I, initially favored Atweneboanna's cause and covertly backed him throughout 1887.[1] Eager to reach a consensus on the decision, the council empowered the Bekwaehene Yaw Gyamfi, who had been a leading voice in calling for the restoration of the monarchy, to conduct the preliminary arrangements for a conference to deliberate over the choices. Throughout October and November 1886, the Bekwaehene fulfilled his designated function. He polled opinion throughout the nation; the British envoy, Badger, noted that Yaw Gyamfi "has sent round to ascertain from the different Kings to know whom they have" to occupy the Golden Stool.[2] He also consulted prominent *asikafo* and leaders of the *nkwankwaa* in the metropolitan region to solicit their views on the terms or proposals that they considered essential for an elective assembly.

Contemporary and oral accounts, however, offer conflicting testimony concerning the Bekwaehene's actions during this period. Yaw Gyamfi's own statements indicate that he elicited the opinion of the Saamanhene Akyampon Panin on the nomination of a new Asantehene through the Saamanhene's son, Owusu Koko Kumaa, but that the response had been

111

evasive.[3] Akyampon Panin apparently stalled by indicating that he had to consult with the Atwema *ahene*, who had backed his coup of December 1884, before committing himself. In fact, he was well aware of Atwema opinion before November 1886; the Atwemahene Kwame Antwi Agyei and the Nkawiekumaahene Antwi Agyei leaned towards Prempe's cause. Akyampon Panin's dilatory tactics, however, gave the Atwema *ahene* time to consider the views of the Dwabenhene Yaw Sapon, the Nsutahene Adu Tire, the Agonahene Kwasi Akyampon, the Offinsohene Apea Sea, the Kumawuhene Kwasi Krapa, and the Nkoransahene Kwasi Opoku.[4] Yaw Gyamfi's report of these proceedings in late 1886 is contradicted by statements made to the British by the Kokofu envoys, Kwame Owusu and Kwabena Asafo. On 29 July 1887, they maintained that the Bekwaehene had originally opposed the proposal to elect a new Asantehene and had made arrangements for the execution of Akyampon Panin in November 1886. The Kokofu *nhenkwaa* claimed that the proposal for a conference to discuss the rules for the election of the Asantehene had originated with Akyampon Panin himself.[5] Their report, made in July 1887 concerning events that took place in November 1886, was no doubt colored by the fact that in the intervening months the Bekwaehene had ordered Akyampon Panin's murder. His motivation for the assassination was, however, not so much Akyampon Panin's support for the reinstatement of the monarchy as his backing of Atweneboanna's candidacy over that of Prempe.

Akyampon Panin, in fact, had serious reservations about the restoration of the monarchy during the preliminary stages of discussion in 1886. He had urged the Council of Kumase to proceed cautiously with the election arrangements and undoubtedly feared that the new civilian administration would conduct reprisals against his supporters for their involvement in the military actions of December 1884. Punishment might be meted out to participants in the coup by a newly empowered regime that would view the events of December 1884 as acts "committed unlawfully against the Crown."[6] The Bekwaehene tried to provide assurances against this possibility and agreed to swear an oath forbidding reprisals.[7] Yaa Akyaa's supporters in the Council of Kumase supposedly knew of Gyamfi's promise to take this oath and sanctioned it. Nevertheless, the Saamanhene had good reason to fear that treason trials would follow the enstoolment ceremonies. The excesses committed by the Akyempemhene Owusu Koko's regime in 1883–84 provided ample evidence that several members of the Council of Kumase would not hesitate to retaliate for the Saamanhene's plot. Consequently, Akyampon Panin had realistic misgivings about any election proceedings and tried to insure his own preservation. Furthermore, as Akyampon Panin represented the centralist position in the councils of government, he was naturally at loggerheads with the Bekwaehene Yaw Gyamfi who stood for the confederate position.[8] Although both leaders worked in the general direction of restoration of the monarchy in late 1886, they sharply disagreed about the structure of the new civilian government.

By the middle of January 1887, the competing factions had visibly crystallized. The principal advocates of Prempe's candidacy included the Bekwaehene Yaw Gyamfi, the Dwabenhene Yaw Sapon, and most of the members of the Council of Kumase who, according to observers, had "a large and most powerful following."[9] Yaw Gyamfi's support for Prempe largely derived from his enmity toward Akyampon Panin, who had become identified with Atweneboanna's cause. The animosity between Yaw Gyamfi and Akyampon Panin had been exacerbated by a dispute over financial matters during the controversy between Bekwae and Adanse in the first half of 1886. The Bekwaehene upheld the Council of Kumase's position in support of Prempe out of loyalty to those Kumase officials who had supplied him with men and war materials for the Adanse conflict. The Bekwaehene's support for Prempe, whose candidacy was identified with centralism, apparently contradicted Bekwae's commitment to the concept of confederacy. However, the platform of those leaders who pushed to install Prempe as the new monarch was, in fact, one of reconciliation of opposed viewpoints. Most leaders wished to create in the Asanteman a governmental structure in which the whole spectrum of political options could coexist in an environment of tolerance and mutual cooperation.[10] The Bekwaehene hoped that Prempe's domestic policies would allow the outlying districts a large measure of autonomy, especially in the field of foreign affairs. Yaw Gyamfi threw his support behind Prempe for still another, very practical reason: he thought Prempe would win, especially after the Edwesohene Kwasi Afrane Panin and the Offinsohene Apea Sea, two leaders of newly important outlying districts, had declared in his favor.[11] The Dwabenhene Yaw Sapon, who had been a Mensa Bonsu appointee in late 1876, backed Prempe because of his centralist appeal and because of Yaw Sapon's close affiliation with political sympathies in Kumase since his enstoolment.[12]

Although these Asante politicians felt that the youthful Agyeman Prempe lacked experience, they, nevertheless, believed that he was an attractive candidate for the nation's highest office. Prempe, it was argued, possessed impeccable lineage qualifications on both his paternal and maternal sides. As he was relatively unknown in Asante public life, he had not accumulated outstanding political enemies. In Kumase political circles, it was commonly known that his ambitious mother, the Asantehemaa Yaa Akyaa, had closely supervised his early education in the palace. The short, white-haired Yaa Akyaa, described as unduly proud, tenacious in pursuit of her views, and full of energy, cunning, and intelligence, prevailed over the Council of Kumase. At the age of fifty she complemented admirably her husband, Kwasi Gyambibi, an officeholder dedicated to the acquisition of financial gain who rarely took positions not in accord with the majority opinion in the councils of government but was always suspicious of the impact of European values on Asante society. Yaa Akyaa had taken great pains to encourage courageous behavior and independent thinking in her son. At an early age her gregarious child had displayed unusual confidence in his own decisions, and his self-confident, assertive mother had fully supported his intellectual inquiries. And Asantes attested to the Asantehemaa's faith in Prempe's potential and her guidance without domination.[13]

> The elders met and decided that Prempe was fit to be Asante-hene. He had the right qualities. Among Asantes there are certain things to consider before a man is made chief. The candidate has to be humble. He has to respect the elders and chiefs. He must lead a life setting a good example for others. The elders looked for these things. They found Prempe to be strong. He was never afraid to be alone in the palace. He was brave when he hunted with the Gyaasehene in Ahafo. When leopards attacked, he saved the life of one of the Gyaasehene's *nhenkwaa*. The older men were surprised. Even in the face of fear Prempe thought quickly. He decided not to run. This made all Asantes know he was not a coward. . . . Prempe was chosen because he had the right qualities to be Asantehene.[14]

Prempe's rival, the older Yaw Atweneboanna, had a lively and inquiring mind and a reputation for his distinguished oratory abilities which had been displayed before the Asantehene Mensa Bonsu's court. Atweneboanna had demonstrated strong political ambitions in the early 1880s, and several Asante politicians had noticed his leadership qualities in village gatherings. Although he was tough-minded in approach, he had treated his servants with kindness and indulgence. Yet Atweneboanna's carelessness in financial matters was a definite cause for concern. In 1883–84 he had squandered a great deal of family and private investors' money in wild-eyed rubber trade and gold-lending schemes. Many Kumase citizens believed him to be a decisive, somewhat abrasive leader whose relentless search for fortune (and other men's wives) easily had alienated many of his contemporaries. Despite his membership in the royal Oyoko group of Kumase, his family kept in the background throughout the election. They seem from the start to have had considerable misgivings about his candidacy.[15]

Most significant, however, Yaa Akyaa's supporters widely publicized Atweneboanna's physical defect which, according to custom, was in itself sufficient to disqualify him. Informants in Kokofu, Bekwae, Mampon, and Kumase repeatedly mentioned that Atweneboanna suffered from a "neck disease" since childhood.[16] The affliction had been treated in its early stages but left severe scar tissue on his neck and throat. The disease was either *scrofulosis* (swollen lymph glands) or *lymph adenitis* (an infection causing accumulation of fatty deposits in the lymph glands). The criteria for eligibility to the Golden Stool included:

> An Oyoko ɔ*dehye*, or royal, from Kumase must be known for his *ahoɔfɛ*, or handsomeness, his *anumuonyam*, or personality, and his ɔ*brapa*, or good character. ɛ*sese obi a* ɔ*bedi Asantehene yɛ obi aɔ wɔ aho fɛ anumuonyam ne* ɔ*brapa.* An Asantehene must be handsome, must have personality and must have a good character. No Asantehene may ever be touched by the knife.[17]

After the Kumase electors publicized Atweneboanna's deformity, many hitherto undecided politicians, especially those conservatives of the older generation, openly declared for Prempe's election. Captain E. A. Barnett, for example, observed that most Asante politicians "privately admitted" that Prempe was the "legitimate" candidate, a statement fully verified by Asante oral accounts.[18]

Yaw Atweneboanna's candidacy was sponsored by Akyampon Panin, who was pressured by the Asantehemaa Yaa Akyaa to return the 3,200 ounces of gold which the deposed Asantehene Mensa Bonsu had deposited in Saawua. The Saamanhene received assurances from Atweneboanna's mother that he would be allowed to keep the money in the event that Atweneboanna came to office. One informant, the Asramponhene of Kumase, a son of Mensa Bonsu, who has worked in the palace since 1885, gave the following account of this mysterious episode:

> Mensa Bonsu increased the amount [the national treasury] during his reign. The people asked him for the money. Mensa Bonsu said he would not repeat what his elder brother [Asantehene Kofi Kakari] did. Mensa Bonsu killed many people he thought were against him. He made money for the stool. Many people said he was selfish. Mensa Bonsu told the Asantes that Kakari was deposed for giving money freely to people. He asked why should I misuse stool funds and be destooled also. The Asantes insisted that he was selfish. Mensa Bonsu was destooled. He left for Saawua. He stayed in Kwabena Nkatia's uncle's house. Before he left Kumase, Mensa Bonsu filled a mattress with gold. He always slept on the mattress at Kwabena Nkatia's uncle's house. Mensa Bonsu heard the Asantes wanted him to

return the gold. He put the mattress over a pit. He cut it with a knife. The gold drained into the pit. The Saawua people recovered all the gold and shared the gold. The Saawua people thus have much money even today.[19]

Atweneboanna's cause received the additional backing of a number of *amanhene* whose towns had supported Kofi Kakari's restoration in the second half of 1883, notably the Mamponhene Owusu Sekyere II, the Nsutahene Adu Tire, the Agonahene Kwasi Akyampon, and the Kokofuhene Osei Asibe. Atweneboanna's candidacy was further championed by politicians in Dadiase, Amoafo, and Danyase, districts in which widespread localist sentiment had emerged in the early 1880s, and by leaders in the secessionist Manso towns.[20] The network of Kakari partisans in the Gold Coast Colony also supported Atweneboanna's election as did leaders in Denkyira and the Akyem country. One of the more vocal Asantes to support Atweneboanna was Yaw Awua, a *sikani* from the outlying town of Edweso, who was made *osokwani*, or hornblower, in the Asokwa Fekuo by the Asantehene Kakari and subsequently made considerable sums of money in the wild rubber trade.[21] Kofi Nti, the twenty-eight-year-old, English-educated son of the former Asantehene Kofi Kakari who had returned from the West Indies and was employed in the customs service in Cape Coast, and Nathan Davies, a former interpreter for the government of the Gold Coast, also vigorously led the lobby for Atweneboanna's cause among British officials in Accra.[22]

THE CONFERENCE OF EARLY 1887

Partisans of both candidates enlarged their respective constituencies throughout January 1887. Observers noted the intense maneuvering in Kumase, the metropolitan region, and the northern parts of the Protectorate.[23] In late January or early February 1887, a conference took place in Kumase to deliberate over the nomination. It was attended by the members of the council in Kumase, Akyampon Panin, the Bekwaehene Yaw Gyamfi, and the Kokofuhene Osei Asibe. The participants reached agreement over procedures and took an oath to work towards the enstoolment of an Asantehene from one of the rival claimants. After extensive discussions the Bekwaehene Yaw Gyamfi moved to adjourn, which indicated that a consensus had not been reached over an occupant for the Golden Stool.[24] Reports again differ over the events that followed the conference in the capital.

The Bekwaehene, according to Kokofu accounts of March 1887, ordered the detention and execution of Akyampon Panin and several Kumase leaders—the Saawuahene Kwabena Anane, the Ankobeahene

Ata Gyamfi, the Butuakwa *okyeame* Kwame Dwuben, Owusu Koko Kumaa, and the Akyeamehene of Kokofu—as these leaders were en route to their towns from the capital. Clearly, the executions were designed to eliminate Atweneboanna's remaining supporters in Kumase political circles. Then, the Kokofu sources maintained that the Bekwaehene launched a surprise attack on Kokofu town, defeated nominal opposition, and subsequently burned the town.[25] In late February 1887, the Kokofuhene Osei Asibe, a haughty and self-assertive politician, mobilized his own forces and prepared for a counterexpedition against Bekwae. The Kokofuhene had become the principal spokesman for Atweneboanna's candidacy following Akyampon Panin's death.

> Kwabena Osei Asibe I wanted Atweneboanna against Prempe. Atweneboanna was the older of the two royals. The Kokofuhene felt he was the right person to occupy the Golden Stool. Also the Asantehemaa had had her own son on the stool, and wanted her second son also to occupy it. The Kokofuhene was a bold man and wanted to be fair. Thus he challenged Kumase. He always wanted to bring out fair play. He is the senior of the Oyoko royals. The other royals went to their present areas from Amansie, "the origin of the nation," which is in the Kokofu district. So, for these reasons, Osei Asibe backed Atweneboanna. Before this, Saamanhene Akyampon led the supporters of Atweneboanna. This Saamanhene was also a proud and powerful chief. He wanted fair play. He did not want Yaa Akyaa to force her choice on the Asante Nation. The Saamanhene lived for a long time in Kumase. He had many friends. He spoke with authority. He was listened to by all. Asibe knew him to be a just and good man. The Kokofuhene followed the Saamanhene's choice. Together the two chiefs would defeat Yaa Akyaa and her supporters among the Kumase *ahene*.[26]

Other accounts stress that, after the conference, Kumase forces led by the Bekwaehene and the Edwesohene attacked Saawua and routed Akyampon Panin's supporters in his rural capital. In the aftermath of the fighting, the Saamanhene and members of his family attempted suicide. Akyampon Panin survived his self-inflicted gunshot wound and was captured by the Kumase troops. Then, after a trial in Kumase, Akyampon Panin's neck was broken on orders from the Asantehemaa Yaa Akyaa.[27] Despite differences over the details, all sources agree that forces from Bekwae invaded Kokofu and forced many Kokofu citizens to emigrate into the Akyem country.

RESORT TO ARMS

Although conflicting reports exist concerning the meeting in Kumase, one significant aspect of the electoral contest had emerged clearly by early 1887: the partisans of Agyeman Prempe and Yaw Atweneboanna eagerly employed force in order to secure the Golden Stool for their respective candidates. From February until July 1887, rumors circulated throughout southern Asante and the Colony regarding the outbreak of hostilities between Kokofu troops under Osei Asibe and Bekwae forces commanded by Yaw Gyamfi.[28] Both Kokofu and Bekwae received political support from leaders in other districts who intervened in the contest. During the early stages of the military operations, however, only the Kokofu received substantial military assistance from politicians committed to Atweneboanna's candidacy. The former partisans of Kofi Kakari in the Colony provided a continuous flow of Sniders and ammunition from Cape Coast merchants to Atweneboanna's backers in Asante. By late 1887, therefore, the Kokofuhene boasted that his six to seven thousand man army was as well equipped as the Hausa soldiers in the Gold Coast Constabulary.[29]

The assistance supplied by leaders in Dadiase, Amoafo, Danyase, and in the Colony enabled the Kokofuhene Osei Asibe to make a considerable military comeback after February 1887. Kokofu columns, for example, attacked a Bekwae outpost at the town of Ahuren, near Bekwae town, on 27 April 1887. The Kokofu forces were repelled but launched a larger offensive on the Bekwae towns of Tobretto and Dettiesu on 14 May 1887. Following a "dreadful battle" at Dettiesu, Kokofu troops destroyed Bekwae town, imprisoned several Bekwae *asahene*, and occupied Bekwae territory. This decisive, bloody victory produced political dividends. The Bekwaehene Yaw Gyamfi and his retainers fled to Kumase, and a "peace party" came to power in Bekwae which pressed for and effected the election of the new Bekwaehene Osei Kwaku Abrebrease.[30]

Toward the end of July 1887, the Kokofuhene Osei Asibe opened negotiations with Kumase and sent envoys to the Asantehemaa Yaa Akyaa proposing to settle the electoral contest peacefully.[31] Several considerations which centered on changes in political alignments between February and July 1887 motivated the Kokofuhene's request for peace terms. First, in June the Bantamahene of Kumase, Kwabena Awua, described as "a very important if not now a powerful Chief," had publicly declared his support for Prempe's candidacy.[32] Kwabena Awua was joined by other district chiefs: the Tredehene Yaw Tenkoran; the *ahene* of Pekyi, Kwadwo Adei and Kofi Boaten; the Patasehene Osei Kakan; the Adankranyahene Kwasi Pipim; the Asumegyahene Kwadwo Agyeman; the Asansohene Kwame Ankra; and the Odumaasehene Kwasi Kwinto. With this support the Bantamahene, the Bekwaehene, and the Dwabenhene had recruited a large force against Kokofu. Although the army had not moved south by the end of June, the Kokofuhene correctly predicted that it would soon take the offensive. Second, in July 1887 another conference had been held at Odaso which, according to Kokofu sources, had been attended by representatives from Nsuta, Mampon, Agona, Nkoransa, and the Bantamahene Awua who acted as the spokesman for the towns of Kwaso, Kuntanase, Gyakye, Apumase, Arbanase, Orewe, and apparently Edweso.[33] The participants had sworn a declaration to cease fighting. The outcome of this meeting served notice to the Kokofuhene that most of Atweneboanna's backers wanted to reach a political settlement, and thus Osei Asibe could count on few allies in the metropolitan region. Third, Kokofu military operations over the preceding months could be seen as vindicating the Bekwae attack after the conference in Kumase. Additional fighting would have further jeopardized Osei Asibe's position and would not have achieved any substantial political objective. Furthermore, Yaa Akyaa's supporters in the capital imprisoned Yaw Atweneboanna. A new outbreak of fighting undoubtedly would have resulted in his execution.[34] Finally, the Kokofuhene had hoped for British mediation in the confrontation with the Bekwae and had sent several diplomatic missions to Accra for this purpose in June and July 1887.[35] Osei Asibe, however, was not the only prominent Asante leader to request British help in these months. The Bekwaehene and the Bantamahene Kwabena Awua, for example, had sent a joint message to the British agent Lonsdale at Praso on 10 July 1887, requesting his assistance "to settle affairs" between the two sides.[36] In 1886 and 1887, the government of the Gold Coast Colony favored the reestablishment of a strong central government in Kumase and declined to support politicians who challenged the Council of Kumase. On 21 August 1887, Governor Griffith recorded the British position:

> It appears that the Becquais had retreated on Coomassie, with which they have hitherto acted in concert, and from whence they might be reinforced, and if this should turn out to be the case, and no decisive action should follow in favour of Kokofu, I think it would be our wisest course to leave the Ashantis to themselves. If by our intervention fighting could be put a stop to, and a strong government could be formed in Ashanti, it would be humane for us to interfere. But I question whether, looking at the matter from various points of view, it would be wise for the Gold Coast Government to take any action except as regards being represented at the coronation of the King, and that is all it was asked to do until the matter of agreement respecting who should be the king had been set to rest by such a majority of Ashantis, independent of foreign assistance and influence, as would put the chance of serious opposition to him out of the question. It might lead to undesirable complication

in the future if the Gold Coast Government sided with any party to promote the selection of any particular person as King of Ashanti.[37]

The foregoing considerations prompted the Kokofuhene Osei Asibe, who recognized that he had lost much of his advantage, to negotiate towards the end of July 1887. While his initial peace feelers were being considered in Kumase, the Kokofuhene remained at his headquarters in Agyemum on Route VI with some six thousand armed followers, "consisting of Kokofus, Didiasis, Sawuahs, Amoafuls, Adansis, and Asiamans."[38] This force convinced Yaa Akyaa's backers to take action. A column commanded by Kwabena Awua, Asafo Boakye, and other Kumase *asahene*, or military leaders, joined with forces led by Yaw Gyamfi and moved southwards from the town of Pekyi to Bekwae. It was widely publicized "that they intended to advance and wipe out Kokofu."[39] On 8 August skirmishes occurred near Agyemum. Lonsdale, for example, noted the "many dead" bodies encountered at one or two points along Route VI from Praso. Although other reports predicted that a major battle would occur on the fifteenth of August, nothing happened.[40]

The offensive of August 1887 was designed to coerce the Kokofuhene into dispersing his armed followers. Then, following the disbandment of his army, Osei Asibe either could begin meaningful deliberations or Yaa Akyaa's supporters would work for his deposition. Prempe's backers also wanted to solidify and to expand the opposition to Atweneboanna's candidacy in the outlying districts. Observers, for example, noted the numerous meetings, messages, and arguments extending over several days.[41] Yet despite the extensive military and political pressure, Osei Asibe stood firm and refused to demobilize his forces. The Kokofuhene, however, was aware of the desire to depose him, and predictably did not "feel at all secure or happy."[42] On 24 August the Kumase leaders consulted with Lonsdale in Bekwae and pushed for a hard line against Kokofu. Prempe's people stressed that Osei Asibe was an "obstructionist," that he was "the stumbling block in the way of peace," and that he "was the cause of there being no King on the Kumasi stool."[43] The Bantamahene Kwabena Awua, who was by this time the principal champion of Prempe's election, roundly called for Osei Asibe's removal because, he "is said to have broken some long established Asanti laws, which is the reason his personal enemies demand his removal."[44] Finally, the Kokofuhene, observed Lonsdale, "had deeply offended Bantama Awua's personal feelings" during the election discussions.[45] The Bantamahene, according to one Asante who knew him well, was

very angry with the Kokofuhene. This Awua was a proud man.

He wanted things to go as they always had in the olden days. He felt that the Kokofuhene did not have the right to compete for Nana Asantehene's stool. The Bantamahene said this openly. He said this many times—when he had been banished by the Asantehene to Manso, when he came back to Kumase, when Yaa Akyaa asked his help, and when he later came to be Prempe's greatest champion. The Bantamahene's anger caused him to rally his people in Atwema and his many other villages to fight the Kokofuhene Asibe.[46]

The Kumase officials' strong stand in August was temporarily successful. Authorities from Bekwae and Kokofu took an oath on the twenty-sixth of September to refrain from further hostilities and to elect an Asantehene in the coming months. "Peace negotiations," commented Lonsdale in October 1887, "have been very successful."[47] The deliberations of August and September, however, did not terminate the fighting in southern Asante. In late November or early December 1887, Yaw Atweneboanna escaped from Kumase and took refuge with the Kokofuhene in Agyemum. Atweneboanna's escape, which was undoubtedly effected by his partisans in Kumase, ushered in still another stage in the electoral contest. The Kokofuhene Osei Asibe again mobilized his forces and made new diplomatic overtures to the government of the Gold Coast Colony. At the same time, he was assisted by other Atweneboanna partisans in the south and in the Protectorate. Osei Asibe's constituency also consisted of dissident and ruthless elements in Asante society who lacked a definite political ideology. The British agent, Barnett, remarked that Atweneboanna's "following is composed of every scoundrel that wrongs the other side," and that "if any person does anything wrong," in Asante "he apparently runs" to the Kokofu camp.[48]

In early 1888, therefore, the political and economic situation in the southern region of metropolitan Asante was once again critical. Contingents from Kokofu, Dadiase, and Saawua engineered another invasion of Bekwae. Skirmishes occurred between Kokofu forces and citizens of towns in Kuntanase.[49] Following the destruction of several towns and plantations in his district, in late January 1888 the Kuntanasehene Kwabena Antwi came out strongly in favor of Prempe's candidacy.[50] Strong sentiment emerged among the Asante populace demanding an end to the struggle for power and calling for the enstoolment of a new Asantehene. An informant recounted the feeling among Asantes in Kumase and the metropolitan region over the absence of an occupant for the Golden Stool:

Asantes were tired of the bitterness and grief which followed the removal of the Asantehene Mensa Bonsu. Too much blood

121

had been shed between the supporters of Atweneboanna and Prempe. The nation wanted a new Asantehene. Even the *asikafo* and *nkwankwaa* in Kumase asked for a new Asantehene. They were the young men who had challenged Mensa Bonsu but now joined the powerful call for a new Asantehene. This the kingmakers had to listen to. The Asante people had to be heard. They wanted to live their lives in peace. It was a good thing.[51]

The first significant break in the election deadlock occurred in early February 1888. The Mamponhene Owusu Sekyere II, who by this time was recognized by Yaa Akyaa's supporters as the legitimate "leading man" of the Atweneboanna cause, and the Bantamahene Kwabena Awua, the "leading chief" from Prempe's side, reached agreement on the election procedures. Both sides, Barnett reported, "have agreed to despatch their messengers in concert to the Kings and Chiefs of Ashanti, requesting them to meet at Kumasi for the purpose of electing a King."[52] But in late February officials in Kumase learned that the Mamponhene had received a gift of £100 from the Kokofuhene. The Mamponhene Owusu Sekyere II, who had supported Atweneboanna since early 1887, had indicated that he required his "expenses paid" on the condition that he sided with the Kokofuhene in the final council deliberations. Prempe's backers subsequently confronted the Mamponhene with a charge of bribery and told Owusu Sekyere II that "Yah Kiah's son Prempeh will be put on the stool, whether he likes it or not."[53]

The Asantehemaa Yaa Akyaa's supporters in Kumase strongly opposed the Mamponhene Owusu Sekyere for pragmatic reasons. By early 1888 the Mamponhene had become the spokesman for Mampon local rights and powers. Politicians in Kumase, however, recognized that several elderly and prominent Mampon *ahene* continued to adhere to their centralist position. The Mampon envoy to Kumase, Ata—"an old and much respected Prince"—maintained that certain Mampon officeholders had "no objection to Prempeh," and, according to Barnett, "expressed his unqualified regret at the behavior of his King, saying, he is young, headstrong, and is led away by the lying and bad advice sent from the Kokofu camp (which we are led to understand comes from the Coast;) the old chiefs will force him [Owusu Sekyere] to come to Kumase or give up the stool."[54] Kumase authorities were determined either to coerce the Mamponhene into accepting Prempe's election or to exert maximum political pressure towards his deposition. There were signs that the latter course of action would succeed. Several Mampon *ahene*, Ata said on 26 March, had already "taken the big oath" that they would force the Mamponhene to come to Kumase or demand his abdication. Further, when the Gold

Coast official F. W. Sullivan, acting on Yaa Akyaa's instructions, consulted with various Mampon officials in the town of Kuna, near the district capital, he observed the differences of opinion in Mampon over the electoral contest and commented on "the general wish of the Mampons to live in peace and unity with the Kumasi people."[55]

THE INSTALLATION OF PREMPE

The extortion episode involving the Mamponhene Owusu Sekyere and the emergence of "pro-Prempe" sentiment in Mampon prompted leaders in Kumase to move rapidly to confirm Prempe as Adumhene, or heir apparent. In the second week of March, therefore, the Bantamahene formally nominated Prempe to the Adum stool. Following the nomination the electors initiated proceedings to invest Prempe with the prerogatives of the kingship. On 18 March, Barnett, the representative of the government of the Gold Coast, witnessed the procession of the Golden Stool and was told that Prempe would be installed on 26 March.[56] Although *nhenkwaa* announced the date in all the districts, the outlying heads had not arrived in the capital by 24 March. The decision to install Prempe despite the opinions held by the outlying *ahene* produced repercussions in Kokofu and Mampon. Emissaries from Kokofu arrived in Kumase on the morning of the twenty-sixth and maintained that Osei Asibe was not prepared to participate in the final deliberations unless Prempe's supporters provided guarantees that they would refrain from retaliation against Kokofu, that they would pardon crimes of adultery with chiefs' wives, and that they would approve a general amnesty for rebellion and all capital offenses.[57]

Kokofuhene Osei Asibe's demands were extensively deliberated in council on the twenty-sixth of March. The outcome of these discussions was conciliatory. The Asantehemaa Yaa Akyaa, the Bantamahene Kwabena Awua, and the Asafohene Asafo Boakye offered to meet the Kokofuhene outside Kumase and to swear "to wipe out and forget the past conduct of anyone in his camp."[58] Yet this gesture failed to reassure Osei Asibe, as, later in the same day, Kokofu and Mampon envoys requested that the installation be postponed until 27 April. Yaa Akyaa and her supporters in council opposed any further postponements for a number of reasons. Most politicians in Kumase were tired of the protracted negotiations, political and financial deals, and bitterness that had surfaced in the election.[59] Authorities in the capital correctly predicted that there was strong sentiment for the installation of a new Asantehene and for a return to civilian government. Further, by March 1888, Yaw Atweneboanna had again damaged his political image. He was publicly accused of sexual impropriety in Kokofu after his escape from Kumase. He had seduced the wives of two lesser-ranked Kokofu chiefs.[60] Several of Atweneboanna's supporters had also become associated with acts (e.g., banditry and terrorism) that were detrimental to the welfare of the southern region. One of the main terrorists was Kwaku Goroso, Atweneboanna's cousin, who had used his considerable trading wealth to finance an abortive assassination attempt on the Asantehene Mensa Bonsu in November 1879. From the town of Kwata in Assin, Kwaku Goroso raised funds from Akyem and other Gold Coast politicians in order to underwrite Atweneboanna's cause.[61]

Finally, in early 1888 the councillors in Kumase had cordial diplomatic relations with the Gold Coast government. British policy complemented the electors' centralist position. Bantamahene Kwabena Awua, for example, stressed that Prempe's supporters were "pro-peace" in the field of foreign affairs and that they would attempt to secure the roads for commerce and travel.[62] The electors wanted Barnett, the representative of the British administration, to attend the enstoolment ceremonies. But Barnett had made it clear that his party would depart for the coast by the first week in April.[63] Thus, Prempe's backers specified 26 March as the date for the installation, partly to accommodate Barnett's desire to return to Accra but primarily to forestall any increase in Atweneboanna's popularity. Consequently, in order to prevent any further delays, all the Kokofu demands were tabled. On the afternoon of the twenty-sixth, Prempe was entrusted to the care of the Kumase *akyeame*, to whom he paid the customary sixty peredwans of gold dust, and just before midnight was recognized Asantehene and given charge ("caretakership") of the Golden Stool. By early April 1888, Prempe was participating in the Council of Kumase's deliberations.[64]

Another version of the events leading up to Prempe's installation was offered by an eyewitness who was Yaa Akyaa's closest *ahenkwaa* in the palace at that time:

Before Prempe was enstooled, the Asantehemaa Yaa Akyaa consulted the Asante Nkramo and the shrines in Asante. Yaa Akyaa consulted these shrines: Adwumam Dwomo; Duase Teekwabena; Mpasaaso Dinkyini; Tepa Baanie; Bekyem Teebekoe; Manfo Boosie; and Asuhyee Teekofi. The Asante Nkramo and the priests of the shrines told Yaa Akyaa to prepare a meal. Then she should invite all the royals to the meal. A talisman was put in a big ball of fufu. The Nkramo and the priests told the Asantehemaa that any royal who took a bit of fufu which contained the talisman should be made the Asantehene. Prempe was the royal who picked the talisman in the fufu. But Goroso and Atweneboanna were not invited to the meal![65]

During the weeks following the enstoolment, Prempe and his councillors strove to reestablish order in Asante politics and sought to assert the new administration's credibility and executive capability. Concurrently, officials in Kumase attempted to legitimize Prempe's claims on the Golden Stool and in late March and early April made conciliatory overtures to win the recognition of the Kokofuhene and the Mamponhene. On 29 March a general amnesty was approved; all political prisoners were released in honor of Prempe's installation. Prempe privately told Barnett that his regime would deal "as leniently as is possible" with the rebellious Manso Nkwantahene Kwasi Mensa.[66] Further, the councillors maintained that they would minimize the use of terror in Asante public life. Barnett commented that "the King of Ashanti and Awuah of Bantama have pledged me their words that for some time past no sacrifices have taken place, and for the future none shall take place."[67] In addition, the Asantehene emphasized that his administration would begin the construction of a new route from Kumase via the town of Pekyi to Denkyira for Asante traders.

Despite attempts at reconciliation graciously proffered by Kumase, the recalcitrant Kokofuhene Osei Asibe and Mamponhene Owusu Sekyere refused to recognize Prempe as Asantehene and continued to challenge the authority of the new administration. While Atweneboanna's claim to the Golden Stool was clearly no longer tenable, his militant supporters in Dadiase and Amoafo and among the Adanse refugees from the Colony pressured Osei Asibe to champion their cause. In response, Osei Asibe tried to bribe several district *ahene* to recognize him (Asibe) as the Asantehene and sanctioned raids on towns whose leaders refused to consent to his policies. The Mamponhene, who was in constant communication with the Kokofuhene, also continued his alliance with his partisans in Mamponten and other neighboring towns.[68] In the middle of April the British administration, following the suggestions made by the council in Kumase on 4 April, intervened in the dispute and subsequently enacted legislation to prohibit the importation of war materials across the Pra River. The British also arrested and imprisoned Yaw Awua who had managed Atweneboanna's candidacy in the Colony, and brought to trial various "doubtful messengers" who unmistakably were partisans of Atweneboanna in the Protectorate.[69]

THE MOVEMENT TOWARDS CIVIL WAR

By early May 1888, all negotiations between emissaries from Yaa Akyaa and the Council of Kumase and from the Kokofuhene and Mamponhene had failed to achieve a peaceful settlement. Both sides again resorted to force to resolve the dispute. In May the Edwesohene Kwasi Afrane

Panin, the Offinsohene Apea Sea, the Kumawuhene Kwasi Krapa, and the Dwabenhene Yaw Sapon joined forces and defeated contingents under the command of the Mamponhene Owusu Sekyere, the Nsutahene Adu Tire, the Agonahene Kwasi Akyampon, and the Atonsuhene Kwadwo Dwumo at the town of Bafoso in the Edweso district.[70] This engagement concluded the intermittent skirmishes that had occurred in the Sekyere region since February 1887. The situation in most of the Sekyere towns had been critical throughout 1887 because of the raids and the detention of traders by partisans of Prempe and Atweneboanna. During the operations at Bafoso, the Edwesohene claimed the Mamponhene's *ntahara* horns and also seized the *apirede* drums, two main symbols of his office. Then, following the first defeat of his allies in the three northerly districts, Kokofuhene Osei Asibe attacked and defeated the Bekwae and, subsequently, launched an offensive on Edweso. According to informants, towards the end of May, Edwesohene Kwasi Afrane's forces defeated Kokofu, Saawua, and Amoafo troops in three battles in the Edweso district: at the Biakwaso River on the road to Cape Coast, at Odumntaa near the Onwe River, and at Aseseso on the Sampa road.[71]

During the second phase, the Bantamahene Kwabena Awua and the Asafohene Asafo Boakye moved their forces southwards to assist the Bekwae and to pacify the southern region. The Kumase troops arrived too late to aid Bekwae (Bekwae town had been destroyed) and returned to the town of Kaase, some three miles from Kumase, in order to protect the capital from a Kokofu invasion and to receive reinforcements from Kumase. During the night, the men from the towns of Dedesua, Ampabame, Sokoben, and Hwidie—allies of the Kokofuhene—captured and escaped with Awua.[72] Osei Asibe subsequently ordered his execution in Kokofu town. The treachery and capture of the Bantamahene at Kaase was described in detail by one eyewitness who graphically delineated the impressive victory of the Kumase forces under the command of the Edwesohene Afrane on 26 and 27 June:

> After Prempe was chosen Asantehene, the Kokofu people were not satisfied. They went to places and looted freely. They looted Boko-Atwema about three times. They caught sheep, goats, and took farm products. The Asantes realized that the Kokofuhene and his subjects must be punished. The Bantamahene and the Asafohene were made the joint *asahene*, or military leaders, of the Kumase forces. The Kumase troops gathered at Kaase. . . . When the Kumase troops gathered at Kaase, an *anomaa kokone-kone*, or traitor, went to the Kokofuhene secretly. The traitor told the Kokofuhene that the Kumase chiefs and troops were at Kaase and were coming to fight you. The Kokofuhene decided

to attack first to take them by surprise. This traitor was serving
in Nana Asafohene's [Asafo Boakye's] house. He was solely dependent upon Nana Asafohene. The traitor came back to tell
the Asofohene that he had been to Kokofu. He told him that the
Kokofuhene and his people were preparing to come to Kaase to
fight the Kumase people. The traitor warned the Asafohene not
to sleep with his people in Kaase that night. If they did, the
Kokofuhene and his men would take them by surprise. The
traitor did not tell this to the Bantamahene. He only told the
Asafohene because the Asafohene had shown him mercy in the
past. . . . The Asafohene did not tell the Bantamahene about
the news he received. The Asafohene came back to Kumase. He
left the Bantamahene with his troops alone in Kaase. In the night
the Bantamahene felt the Asafohene was on the other side of
Kaase. The Kokofuhene and his men surrounded the Kaase village. The Bantamahene, Awua, was in the grip of his troops.
The Kokofuhene and his men beheaded Awua. After this the
people in Kumase learned that the Kokofu people had beheaded
their military leader. Yaa Akyaa sent messages to the Atwemahene Nana Antwi Agyei, the Edwesohene, and others. She told
them to come to Kumase to think about what the the Kokofuhene had done. In those days with no one on the Bantama stool,
the Atwemahene was put in charge of the troops. They all met
in Kumase. It was decided that the Edwesohene Afrane and the
Atwemahene should go and pay the Kokofuhene in "his own
coins." Yaa Akyaa said that the killing of Awua and the counter-
attack on the Kokofuhene needed these two bold men. Yaa
Akyaa knew that fighting was necessary to punish the Kokofuhene. The Kokofuhene all the time knew that the result of his
action would mean war. The troops from Kumase took the
Kokofu road and lined up on both sides of the road until they
reached the threshold of the town. They stood so as not to be
seen easily by the people. . . . "We have set a free pass for all
to pass." The Kumase troops wanted to trick the Kokofu people.
The Kumase troops were to hide until the Kokofu troops came
halfway. Then the Kumase troops would hem in the rest of the
Kokofu troops as they followed. When they got all the Kokofu
troops surrounded, the Asantes shot at them. In the end they
found the remains of the Bantamahene Awua with the head not
there. After the Kumase troops defeated the Kokofu people, the
Atwemahene, the Edwesohene, and all the Kumase chiefs met
in Kumase. . . . When Prempe was enstooled the Mamponhene
Sekyere had also said that he would no longer serve the Golden
Stool. He said he would no longer come to Kumase. Prempe
told the Atwemahene and Akwasi Afrane to punish the Mam-

ponhene. Prempe told these two chiefs to bring Sekyere back to serve the Golden Stool. The Asantehene occupied the Golden Stool. Prempe said that any chief that rebelled against the Golden Stool should be defeated. Prempe said that he had expected other chiefs to rebel against the Golden Stool but not the Mamponhene. The Mamponhene then had a very strong army. The Kumase chiefs applied the same tactic that they used in Kokofu. They lined the road to Mampon, surrounded the people, and defeated the Mamponhene. Sekyere ran away. Later he came back to swear that he would not rebel again and would serve the Golden Stool. *Se womfom wo hene na wompewo ho woko bosomkahyire.* "When you do not want trouble from your king (or chief) you go peacefully to his palace and swear that you do not intend to rebel (or harm) that king (or chief) anymore."[73]

Following the military victory of Prempe's supporters in Kokofu in late June 1888, the Kokofuhene Osei Asibe—along with the Dadiasehene Amoa Fua, the Amoafohene Osei Panin, the Asamanhene Yaw Amoa, Kwabena Kokofu, and Yaw Atweneboanna—emigrated into the Protectorate and took refuge in Akyem Kotoku. Reports indicated that between 18,000 and 22,000 Kokofu refugees—"a large number consisted of armed men"—and 4,000 Dadiase citizens crossed the Pra and settled between the towns of Praso and Insuaim, the capital of Akyem Kotoku.[74] From his residence first in Asuoso and then in Insuaim, the Kokofuhene maintained communication with Mamponhene Owusu Sekyere and never relinquished his intention to continue the struggle in Asante. Witnesses noted in July 1888 that Osei Asibe and Owusu Sekyere planned a combined attack on Kumase from the south and the northeast.[75] Prempe's government, consequently, requested that the government of the Gold Coast Colony intervene in Akyem politics and restrain the Kokofu refugees in the Protectorate. On 9 August, ambassadors from Kumase, Bekwae, and Edweso, accompanied by "a large number of traders," emphasized to British officials that the new administration in Kumase was "very anxious to have the roads opened for trade and to be friendly with the British."[76] The Asante diplomats also requested that the British administration assume its administrative responsibilities in the Protectorate and, if necessary, deport Kokofuhene Asibe.

AKERS' MISSION OF 1888

Prempe's petition in early August 1888 for British intervention in Akyem politics brought immediate and decisive results. The Gold Coast government, anxious to maintain cordial relations with authorities in Kumase and to strengthen its own position in the Protectorate, instructed Assistant Inspector Charles E. Akers to visit the main Akyem towns. During August and September 1888, Akers consulted with Akyem, refugee Kokofu, Adanse, and Assin leaders in the towns of Kotoku, Insuaim, Insaben, Akropon, Akrosse, Yankumase, and Swedru Akinase. Akers' instructions to the refugees were, for the most part, in accord with the objectives of Prempe and his councillors in Kumase. The British, however, implemented a resettlement plan which did not meet with approval from either Kumase or the refugees themselves. This and certain other of Akers' actions illustrate the pro-Prempe orientation of the British in the Colony in the late 1880s and the early 1890s. In part, however, the mission foreshadows the dramatic reversal of British recognition of Asante sovereignty and reveals the ever-increasing British involvement in the political life of the Protectorate.

During his consultations with Asante, Adanse, Assin, and Akyem politicians, Akers emphasized that British administrative jurisdiction extended over the entire Akyem region and publicized widely his instructions that the British administration support the central government in Kumase.[77] The British maintained that they would offer neither political nor military assistance to Asante refugees resident in the Akyem towns. Akers stressed that the British administration would not permit fugitive Asante leaders to make the Protectorate a base of operations against the central government and contended that the government of the Gold Coast Colony would not condone negotiations between the Kokofuhene and the Mamponhene. This strong and unmistakably clear stand dispelled the notion accepted in refugee circles in the Protectorate that the British would assist Kokofuhene Asibe in the event of further hostilities with authorities in Kumase.[78] Akers pointed out that the Gold Coast Constabulary was planning to relocate the Kokofu refugees from towns adjacent to the Pra to the southerly parts of Akyem and to areas near the town of Agona where land had been set aside for Kokofu occupation.

The primary motive for the resettlement program, according to British sources, was to assist Prempe's government with the refugee problem and, at the same time, to eliminate the raids and banditry that issued from towns under the administrative supervision of Akyem officeholders. To carry out the program, Akers instructed Assin and Akyem leaders to encourage the movement of Kokofu and Adanse refugees southward. These operations scattered the Kokofu refugees throughout the Akyem, Essekumaa, and Agona regions. By late September 1888, it was reported that the Kokofu citizens in the Protectorate were "nowhere sufficiently numerous to be formidable."[79] Akers himself commented on the "attractive" conditions offered to the Kokofu emigrants if they remained within the Protectorate. On 25 August, he told Ata Fua, *oman-hene* of Akyem Kotoku, that "the Government was glad to welcome the Kokofus, provided that they came into the Protectorate as peaceful citizens. That land in the Aguna country had been provided for the Kokofus, and that they could settle there, build houses, make farms, or take up trading or any other industry."[80]

Akers' statements and actions concerning the Kokofu resettlement program were contrary to the reconciliation policies of Prempe's government and also ran counter to the aspirations of several Kokofu politicians and the intentions of many Kokofu citizens resident in the Protectorate. The British agent J. A. Carr noted that most of the Kokofu who had crossed the Pra in July and early August had desired to settle in Assin but were told to move to southern Akyem and the Agona district.[81] Akers observed in late August that "two or three" Kokofu chiefs, apparently possessing great influence, wished to remain in Assin and thus had hindered the success of the relocation scheme.[82] In September 1888, numbers of Kokofu were already returning to Asante. Sergeant Howard Van Dyke of the Gold Coast Constabulary remarked that various Kokofu *nkwankwaa* (among whom were women and children) were resettling in Kokofu regardless of the £1 tax in gold dust imposed by the central government in Kumase on all fugitives.[83] Even the self-willed Kokofu-hene Asibe opposed the resettlement program and repeatedly informed Akers that he wished to remain in Insuaim and thereby stay informed of the political situation in Asante. Although Osei Asibe intended to monitor the course of events north of the Pra and to communicate with his northerly allies, he also wished to avoid local political complications such as the refugee Adansehene Kwaku Nkansa had experienced in Agona.

While Kokofu leaders challenged the resettlement scheme, Ata Fua and his *ahene* in Akyem Kotoku attacked the plan too. Ata Fua, who was involved in a dispute with politicians in Akyem Bosume, had supported Yaw Atweneboanna's candidacy and had wanted the Kokofu refugees to settle in Akyem Kotoku in order to increase his "thinly populated" district.[84] Ata Fua, moreover, had promised to give Osei Asibe land in Akyem Kotoku; to renounce this promise would have further antagonized the district politicians who already pressed for his deposition. Akers hardly assuaged Ata Fua's fears when he stated that the British would work to install another candidate if Ata Fua persisted in his opposition to the resettlement program:

> I think that the Government should deal severely with Atta Fua in this matter. He is a crafty, ambitious man, full of low cunning, and is continually boasting about the way the Government treated him whilst he was recently in Accra, and has told his

people that anything he tells the Governor will be done at once. I think, too, that his idea is that by going to Accra he will so manage to represent things to his Excellency that the Kokofus will be allowed to return to Insuaim. . . . I am of the opinion that the Government should deal most severely with him, and I suggest that he should be fined the sum of 1,000 £, and be detained as a political prisoner on the coast until the fine is paid. The reasons for inflicting this fine would be, firstly, his endeavoring to induce the Kokofus to settle in Kotoko in direct opposition to the instructions given him by the Government. Secondly, tampering with the Kokofus and trying to make them reject the conditions and terms offered by myself. Thirdly, conspiring and endeavoring to bring me directly and the Government indirectly, into conflict with the Akyem people.[85]

Akers' mission also aimed to halt the importation of war materials to Asante refugees in the Protectorate. British policy on this point conformed with earlier legislation in May and June 1888 designed to stop the flow of supplies to adherents of Atweneboanna in southern Asante. Thus the constabulary blockaded the roads to Insuaim and by late August had effectively limited the influx of arms to Akyem Kotoku across the Birim River from Cape Coast, Accra, Winneba, and Saltpond.[86] Authorities in Kumase approved of the blockade. Akers did not take measures to disarm the Kokofu and admitted that supplies could still reach the refugees via other routes in Akyem. Further, he instructed local authorities in Assin and Akyem Kotoku to improve their sections of the road system, which was part of a larger British plan to modernize the network in the Akyem region. This action again benefited the Prempe regime's economic policies but also enabled British agents to step up their intelligence operations throughout the Protectorate and southern Asante. Akers made several excursions into Adanse for the explicit purpose of gathering data on Prempe's government. His trips were facilitated by improvements in the local roads system.[87]

The Akers mission of August and September alleviated the danger presented by concentrations of armed Kokofu near the borders of southern Asante and impeded the Kokofuhene's intention to launch an attack on Asante from the Protectorate. British policy towards the Mamponhene further assisted the new administration in Kumase. Towards the end of August, the Mamponhene, recognizing that Kokofuhene Asibe's support would not be forthcoming, decided to negotiate a settlement with Prempe's supporters. Owusu Sekyere appealed to the Kwawuhene Kofi Boaten to arrange for a meeting between authorities in Kumase and partisans of Atweneboanna in the northeast.[88] Kofi Boaten, the localists' representative who had signed a treaty with the British in March 1888, referred the

131

matter to the British. Gold Coast officials again responded in support of the restoration of a strong central government in Kumase. Governor Griffith noted that his "Government is on friendly terms with" Prempe and stressed that:

> The selection of the King fell upon Prempeh, now called Kwaku Dua IV [III]. He was properly placed upon the stool. I regard him as the King of Ashanti, and I shall not treat with any other person or persons connected with Ashanti except through him, and therefore, I repeat, that what the King of Mampon should do is, submit himself to his lawful sovereign.[89]

MILITARY OFFENSIVES IN SEKYERE

British policy towards the Kokofuhene and Mamponhene in 1888 prompted Prempe's supporters, who mistrusted the Mamponhene's motives, to launch an offensive against Owusu Sekyere and his northerly allies in Nsuta, Agona, and the Sekyere towns. Edwesohene Kwasi Afrane Panin, who was a member of the royal family of the Asona Ntom from Boankra, seven miles from Edweso town, was appointed, along with the Offinsohene Apea Sea, to command Prempe's army.[90] The hearty, colorful Kwasi Afrane had succeeded to the Edweso stool in 1885 after his predecessor, Kwame Wuo, was removed for maladministration and cruelty. He had been instrumental in the capture of the Saamanhene Akyampon Panin in early 1887 and had distinguished himself in campaigns against Mampon, Nsuta, Kokofu, and Saawua. Following the death of the Bantamahene Awua and the victory against the Kokofu in late June, the garrulous Afrane had become the Asantehene's special *osahene*, or military commander.[91] An *ahenkwaa* to the Edwesohene Afrane described the relationship between Afrane and Prempe: "*Obi do a na wo nso wodo no bi.* If someone loves you, you also love him. Afrane helped to put Prempe on the stool. Afrane loved Prempe. Prempe loved Afrane."[92]

Kwasi Afrane's military successes for Prempe earned him the nickname of *Anommaɔ tu a obi awuo*, "a bird which when it flies someone dies."[93] After several engagements in the Edweso district and in Nsuta town, Prempe's forces defeated the Nsutahene Adu Tire, who fled to Atebubu accompanied by some five hundred refugees. Edwesohene Afrane then attacked and smashed Owusu Sekyere's contingents in the town of Beposo, burned Mampon town, and pursued the retreating Mampon troops, who had run low on powder, to the town of Edwira. Yet the Edwirahene Yaw Safo, a chief in the Mampon district who had also supported Yaw Atweneboanna in 1887–88, refused to challenge the invasion force. Several Mampon officeholders and wealthy citizens were imprisoned in Kumase, Edweso, Offinso, and Bekwae. Mamponhene

Owusu Sekyere hastily took refuge in Atebubu and planned to launch raids on Kumase.[94] In October, Owusu Sekyere's followers were again defeated near Atebubu by the Nkoransahene Kwasi Opoku's troops. A participant in the event provided this account of the engagement near Atebubu:

> Around five hundred guns went with Kwasi [Owusu] Sekyere to Atebubu after the war. Before the war there were around one thousand guns in Mampon town. But after the war Mampon town and its surrounding villages were totally deserted. Sekyere conspired to come back to fight Afrane. He wanted to go to Gyaman to ask for troops from that side [in order] to have many men to fight the Kumase people. He wanted to go via Nkoransa and sent messages to the Nkoransahene Opoku that he should be prepared to receive him. The Nkoransahene killed himself by burning himself when he heard the Mamponhene was coming. Sekyere sent messages not to bury the Nkoransahene's body so he could look at it. The Nkoransa became annoyed and did not like to take orders from the Mamponhene. They then fought the Mamponhene's troops. The Nkoransa defeated him. He returned with his troops to Atebubu. Sekyere thus changed the Gyaman trip and decided to go to Accra instead. He went to Accra through Kwawu to get the government's protection.[95]

During the closing months of 1888, many of the Mampon refugees returned to their district. C. W. Badger, who visited Atebubu on 11 January 1889, remarked that only two or three hunderd people remained with Mamponhene Owusu Sekyere.[96] In early 1889, as a result of the Edwesohene Kwasi Afrane's political pressure, officials in Kumase appointed Kwame Apea Osokye the new Mamponhene. He ruled over divisional officeholders in the nucleated settlements of Edwira, Apaa, Asokore, Beposo, Effiduase, and Gyamase, the main units of the Mampon district. The even-tempered Apea Osokye, who had held no office in the *oman* and had courageously fought for Prempe with Kwasi Afrane's troops in Kokofu, was not related to any members of the fragmented ruling dynasty of Mampon. His wife resided in the town of Hapaase near Lake Bosomtwe in the Edweso district, and Apea Osokye had formed a close personal relationship with Kwasi Afrane while serving in the Edwesohene's palace. His father, Ata Panin from the town of Kwaso, eight miles to the southeast of Kumase, was a prominent trader and *sikani* in Mampon and had served in Kumase in the Asantehene Osei Yaw Akoto's household. As the new, opulent Mamponhene, Apea Osokye was asked to encourage the remaining Mampon refugees to return from Atebubu.[97]

Thus, Agyeman Prempe came to power in a political system marked by the pervasive use of violence to achieve political goals. His own policies broke with this tradition and followed a desire for pacification and conciliation. Having subdued his powerful opponents and quelled the outbreaks of civil strife, Prempe and his aides in the new administration turned their attention to Asante's social, political, and economic problems in the last decade of the nineteenth century, a decade that witnessed the final days of Asante sovereignty in the face of mounting British imperialism.

7

THE PREMPE ADMINISTRATION AND THE RESTORATION OF POLITICAL ORDER, 1888-1894

Nana Prempe began a new time in Asante. We had faith in his wisdom and strength. He made the nation strong again.—al-Hajj Sulāyman

POLICIES OF THE NEW ADMINISTRATION

In the years from 1886 to 1888, the contest between the supporters of Agyeman Prempe and Yaw Atweneboanna was protracted and bitter. The Asante state no longer functioned to protect private and public activity and to safeguard the values and economic pursuits of the populace. The movement towards civil war gave proof that negotiation, concession, compromise, and agreement were no longer the avenues by which political differences could be resolved. Conflict centered on the disparate views held by Asante politicians on how power should be distributed in the metropolitan region. There was general agreement, however, on the desirability of restoring civilian rule and the monarchy, and general recognition of the inability of local authorities to resolve common problems of banditry, terrorism, warfare, and economic dislocation. Championed by outlying district heads and leaders in the Colony, the candidacy of Atweneboanna symbolized the fundamental opposition to the Council of Kumase's exclusive right to nominate an Asantehene, and concurrently represented the aspirations of politicians hoping to gain autonomous status and to formalize the *nkabom* principle in the metropolitan region. By contrast, Prempe's backers in the Council of Kumase and among local centralists were committed to maintain the dominant power and authority of the central government, with certain qualifications.

When the Prempean cause prevailed in 1888, the new occupant of the Golden Stool undertook to provide leadership for the reintegration of a nation that had been racked by years of factionalism. In sharp contrast to many of his predecessors, Prempe chose to assert his strength through leniency and permissiveness rather than through repression. Whereas previous Kumase administrations had reacted to the accumulation of power within the local polities as though localist gains necessarily implied their own loss, Prempe and his advisers believed that the simultaneous growth of power on both the national and local levels was compatible. Consequently, under Prempe both the central government in Kumase and the local governments in the outlying district grew more powerful, and the system as a whole benefited from a resurgence of vitality.

The leaders who ran the central government under Prempe's administration attempted to revive public trust in national leadership that had been lost as a result of abuses perpetrated by previous regimes. They hoped to do away with excessive corruption and dishonesty (bribery, extortion, stealing) within the departments of government, to reinstate customary legal procedures, and to become a bulwark of national faith and security.[1] By creating an environment in which Asante citizens could again live secure lives, they intended to restore the prestige of the institutions of the state. Asantehenes in the late nineteenth century, occupants of the sacred Golden Stool, had lost all symbolic reverence and had come to be viewed only as politicians in the eyes of the populace. This indicated the extent to which the kingship had become demythicized and politicized during the latter part of the century. Although certain *asikafo* and *nkwankwaa* forces in Asante had wished the abrogation of the monarchy altogether, Prempe and his councillors were determined to demonstrate its worth and necessity to insure the daily functioning of the nation.[2]

The new Asantehene worked to achieve rapprochement with many of the districts that had severed close ties with earlier regimes in Kumase. In order to expedite this rapprochement, Prempe and his councillors awarded a number of local offices to loyalists. Although the granting of stools to individuals who by descent had no claims to these offices violated longstanding tradition, it was a practice that had been employed by previous Asantehenes to increase central control of the nation and to insure untroubled relations with the districts. Furthermore, in keeping with the policy of national reunification, Prempe's regime encouraged the return of dissidents and refugee populations to the metropolitan region. The Nsutahene Adu Tire made overtures to officials in Kumase in January 1889 and publicly expressed his intention to leave Atebubu for Asante. Nsuta politicians were not all of the same mind on this issue; Kofi Ben and Kwadwo Frimpon and a shrine priest, Kwaku Owusu, argued in favor of emigrating to the Colony. By November 1889, however, most of the Nsuta refugees in the northeast had returned to Asante, rebuilt the district capital, and resettled in the Kwabre towns of Bimma, Mpantuase, Atonsu, Kwakye, Didi, Kyebi, Abonkosu, and Kwagyei.[3]

The gradual return of the Mampon citizens during early 1889 had induced authorities in Kumase to appoint a new Mamponhene, Kwame Apea Osokye, an important *sikani* in the district, to replace the recalcitrant Owusu Sekyere II.[4] As a result of this action, Owusu Sekyere—who remained in exile until his reinstallation on orders from the British in 1901—and an *okyeame* from Effiduase sent envoys to Accra on 20 November 1889 to enlist British assistance. The British, however, declared that Owusu Sekyere and his few adherents in the northeast must move to and settle in the Protectorate, a suggestion not suited to the political aspirations of the refugee Mamponhene. Officials in Kumase quickly responded to these overtures and enhanced their own influence in the Mampon *oman* by appointing a new Gyamasehene, the wealthy Yaw Sekyere, who had been another prominent supporter of Prempe's candidacy.[5] Yaw Sekyere's accession to the second highest office in the district came as a reward for his centralism and complemented the orientation of the Mamponhene Kwame Apea Osokye.

Even the Nkoransahene Kwasi Opoku, antagonized by the legal and political difficulties which had arisen between his subjects and the Mampon refugees resident in his district, initially favored the restoration of political ties with Kumase in late 1888.[6] The British emissary George Ekem Ferguson noted that Kwasi Opoku "represented that there was no reason to doubt his loyalty, to prove which he swore that he would recover for the King of Ashanti his authority over the Brong tribes which was lost in 1874 when those tribes asserted their independence."[7] And throughout 1889 the Dwabenhene Yaw Sapon, a leading partisan of Prempe's election, and the new Bekwaehene, Osei Kwaku Abrebrease, who had assumed office following Yaw Gyamfi's death in early June 1888, continued to back the new regime. The Council of Kumase recompensed the Bekwae for Yaw Gyamfi's efforts to restore the monarchy and for his services to install Prempe by transferring the Kokofu towns of Anwiaam, Dome, and Amoammo to Bekwae.[8] The Kumawuhene Kwasi Krapa, a Mensa Bonsu appointee to the Twenehoa Kodua stool who had backed Prempe's election, was also rewarded for his political and military *nnwuma*, or services, to the new *amannuo*, or administration. The Kumawuhene had been forced, with many of his subjects, to retreat to the town of Agogo in Asante Akyem after Mampon and Nsuta contingents had destroyed the capital of Kumawu during the first phase of the civil war. The new administration recognized the Kumawuhene's loyalty by conferring on him the towns and subjects of Pepease and Woraso in 1889.[9]

In that year the Council of Kumase promoted the stools occupied by the Edwesohene Kwasi Afrane and the Offinsohene Apea Sea—Prempe's most vocal and militant champions who had distinguished themselves in the operations against Kokofu and its northerly allies in 1888—from the status of *abirempon* to that of *amanhene* vis-à-vis Kumase. During a conference convened in the town of Ahyiaem, the quiet and reserved Abakomadwahene (heir apparent) of Kumase, Agyeman Badu, the spokesman for officials in Kumase, and Kwaku Seekye, a royal from the town of Edweso who represented authorities in his district, swore an oath "to make peace forever."[10] The Edweso stool subsequently received the Kokofu lands extending to the town of Nnuaso in the Amansie region near the capital of Kokofu, and the town and people of Anyinasu which had been formerly attached to the Kyidom stool of Kumase. Having supported Atweneboanna's candidacy in 1887–88, Kyidomhene Kwame Boaten was clearly *persona non grata* to officials in the capital.[11] Henceforth, the Edwesohene was officially designated the Asantehene's Atufoɔhene, or keeper of the guns. He was instructed to report directly to the Asantehene for his administrative assignments and to swear the oath of allegiance to the monarch on the Mponpomsuo *afena*, the state sword reserved for the highest officials in the kingdom. Offinsohene Apea Sea by contrast did not receive any towns for his services but was elevated to take the oath of allegiance on the Mponpomsuo *afena* and like the Edwesohene was permitted to celebrate a local Odwira ceremony annually.[12] Following their promotions the Edwesohene Kwasi Afrane and the Offinsohene Apea Sea led expeditions across the Tano River to eliminate remaining pockets of resistance in the pro-Atweneboanna Ahafo towns of Nobeko, Mim, and Kukuom.[13] Political order, then, was returning to Asante public life towards the end of 1889. Prempe's supporters were firmly in power. Stability throughout the metropolitan region and the restoration of strong ties between Kumase and most outlying district heads created an atmosphere of security, order, and public confidence consistent with the new administration's central aim of *oman anoboa*, or national reconciliation.

The key element in the Prempean political machine, as it evolved after March 1888, was the *odekuro* (pl. *adekurofo*), the local official whose responsibilities deeply affected life on the town and village level. Regardless of the political opinions of Council of Kumase authorities, the *adekurofo* had to become (and to remain) partisans of the Prempean cause. Unlike previous administrations, which emphasized the importance of the *nhwesofo* on the higher tiers of the administrative hierarchy, Prempe's regime cautiously developed and strengthened political relationships with the lowest officials of the kingdom. Asantes who worked in Kumase in the early 1890s alluded to the Asantehene's efforts to elevate relatively minor *adekurofo*, to interfere in their elections and bring them into the capital for the Odwira and other official occasions, and to promote inconspicuous *adekurofo* and insist they swear directly to him on the Asanteman's senior swords.[14] Recalling that Agyeman Prempe frequently by-passed his Kumase *nhwesofo*, one informant remarked:

> Nana Asantehene did something different. He called the chiefs to him. He told small chiefs that they should act like big ones. They must carry an umbrella and have many small boys to serve them. They must use their offices wisely. He told them this on the Odwira. I myself was told this many times. It was a new thing here. The Kumase chiefs felt their power was lost. But they could do nothing. Agyeman Prempe was the Asantehene.[15]

The spatial fragmentation of Kumase office-estates in combination with close control over the *adekurofo* and other such officials on the village level would insure the success of the Council of Kumase's new political and diplomatic policies. Map 7 displays graphically the spread in the metropolitan region of the largest office-estates of the ten major *fekuo*, or administrative agencies, in Prempe's central government. Map 8 isolates sixteen of the major individual office-estates whose *nhwesofo* were generally recognized as most influential in the councils of government in the early 1890s. The sixteen are grouped according to their four defining categories within their respective *fekuo*.[16] Together the maps illustrate the spatial configuration of the web or landscape in which the Prempean regime operated and as such demonstrate that the power and authority of the central government outside the immediate environs of Kumase resided on the local level, a delicate relationship which the Asantehene and his councillors took considerable pains to preserve.

Agyeman Prempe's ascension to the highest office in the Asanteman revived the stricken Asante economy. Economic progress throughout the metropolitan region indicated that the regime was moving towards the realization of its goal of national unification. Private Asante *abatafo* again exchanged kola for savanna natural and craft products in the Kintampo, Atebubu, and Wankyi markets. Functionaries in the Bata organization regained much of the state's control over the kola, gold, and palm products trade. New regional exchange centers appeared. Reminiscent of the Asantehene Mensa Bonsu's postwar program, the administration authorized a limited flow of northern and southern immigrants into central Asante, which helped to invigorate moribund, older district markets.[17] Prempe's advisers discussed tax-reform schemes including the modification of estate taxes and death duties.[18] Legal fines in the Kumase courts returned to their customary rates. By early August 1888, steady increases

139

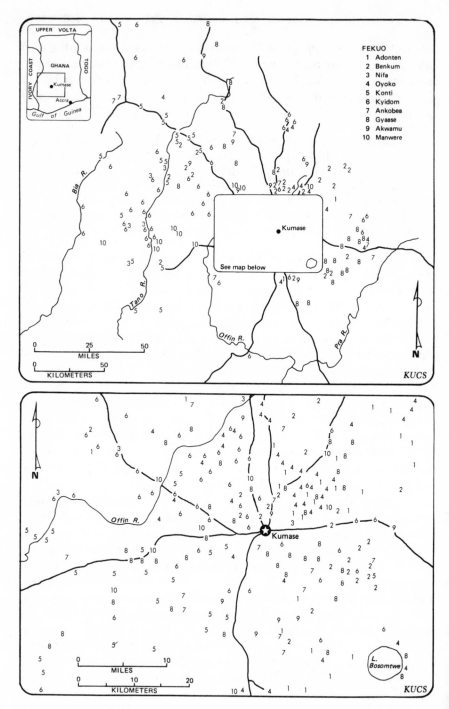

7. The Ten Main Fekuo of the Prempean Administration

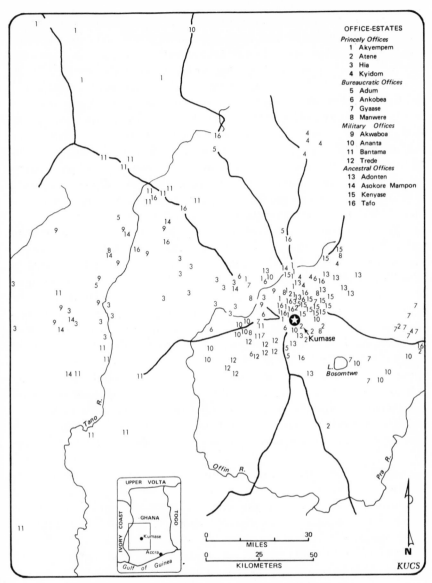

8. Principal Office-Estates of the Prempean Administration

in commercial traffic and improvements in the safety of the trade routes were noticeable. Kumase and Bekwae envoys at the start of the month, for example, told J. A. Carr, the clerk at Praso, that traders again used Route VI and its branches, which had been intermittently closed since late 1884. A delegation of Asante traders, who accompanied the diplomatic mission to the coast on 9 August, once more maintained that the British administration should assist the Asante government by patrolling and supervising the roads in the Protectorate.[19] In January 1889, still another deputation—headed by Osei Bruni, a son of the former Akyempemhene Owusu Koko—restated Kumase's desire for "peace, open roads, and trade" and exerted pressure on representatives of the European mercantile community in Cape Coast. Osei Bruni informed Macan, a partner in the firm of Messrs. Lyall and Company at Cape Coast, that "some Ashanti traders" had allegedly expressed fears over the safety of the Akyem roads. He noted that partisans of Atweneboanna, particularly refugees from Kokofu and Saawua living in the town of Essaman, north of Praso, were "obstructing the trade route into Ashanti" and planned to launch attacks on several southern Asante districts.[20]

Asante informants substantiated Osei Bruni's claims. Various influential supporters of Yaw Atweneboanna's candidacy engaged in subversive activities throughout the southern region of metropolitan Asante in 1889–90. Kwaku Goroso and Kwabena Kokofu, for instance, are particularly remembered for their actions following their emigration to the Protectorate in late 1888. Both men became wealthy *apoobofo*, or bandits (literally, "bullies"), in this period, aided several attempts to overthrow the new administration in Kumase, and instructed their local agents to plunder Asante traders en route to the coast.[21] Consequently, reacting to the pressure exerted by Kumase diplomats and Asante traders, Macan in turn expressed the concern of the Cape Coast economic establishment and convinced officials in Accra to take decisive measures to halt the banditry that originated in the northern areas of the Protectorate and, thereby, to forestall a concerted attack on Asante by dissidents in the Colony.[22]

In early 1889, the British administration, eager to improve trade relations with the central government in Kumase and to strengthen its administrative control over the Akyem towns, responded decisively. Under the command of Lieutenant-Colonel E. B. McInnis, Inspector General of the Gold Coast Constabulary, a large expeditionary force, consisting of 175 Hausa soldiers and several European officers and equipped with the latest in weaponry including a Maxim gun and rocket tubes, left Accra on 7 January 1889 for the main Akyem towns and reaffirmed the policies initiated by C. E. Akers in August and September of 1888. The official intent of the McInnis mission, according to British sources, was to assist Prempe's regime by suppressing the raids and banditry that issued from Akyem Swedru and Beronase, towns under the administrative supervision of Kofi Ahinkora, *omanhene* of Akyem Bosume. This military enterprise forcibly carried out a resettlement and internment program. The

Kokofuhene Osei Asibe and some one thousand refugees were moved from Insuaim to the town of Akrosse in Akyem Kotoku, while the Dadiasehene Amoa Fua and his *ahene* were relocated from Beronase to villages near the Ayenso River, five miles from the town of Insaban.[23]

After disarming many Asante refugees in the Protectorate, McInnis left garrisons from the Gold Coast Constabulary in the main Akyem towns. Yet, despite the officially designated purpose of this mission, the rapidity and magnitude of the British response in early 1889 suggests that officials in Accra had motives that superseded the Asante government's concern over the refugee and banditry issues and the threat to the economic welfare of southern Asante. McInnis, for example, intervened in several local elections and exerted British influence to install a number of key anti-Kumase candidates in the biggest Akyem towns. His soldiers detained various rich Akyem traders who seemed to favor the resumption of strong ties with the central government in Kumase.[24] But the McInnis expedition to the Akyem country in 1889 alleviated the banditry emanating from the northern parts of the Protectorate and thus was publicly supported by authorities in Kumase.

Throughout the remainder of 1889, the situation in the metropolitan region continued to show signs of economic revival. Observers commented on the proliferation of the new rubber industry and the large *mfaso*, or profits, realized by Asante middlemen in Ahafo, Kwabre, the Akyem towns, Sehwi, and on the coast.

> Asante middlemen sold rubber to the whites on the coast. This was the time when Nana Prempe was the Asantehene. The rubber trade had grown very big just before he became the Asantehene. Many traders became rich here in Asante. They were not chiefs. Some of these were: Kwaku Ahyia from Berekum; Yaw Sekyere from Tafo; Kwasi Bota from Offinso; Sraha from Abrepo; and one Ankra from Dwaben. They were the biggest rubber traders I remember. All rubber from Asante and Ahafo passed through their hands. They traded with people all over Asante and the Akyem country. They lent money to other traders who carried rubber to the coast. . . . Kofi Kwakye, Osei Kwabena, and Adusei from Saawua and Papa Yaw Fofuro from Boho became very rich. All were gold dust dealers before. They weighed gold dust for people to buy. They bought the gold dust from the Asantes. Then they sold it to others. They knew the whites needed their services. The whites were after the rubber to take back to their countries. They made much money from this knowledge. The rubber trade was a new thing here. Asantes with money knew they could make much more money. . . . All

the rubber traders feared that quick money would be taxed by Nana Prempe and the elders in Kumase.[25]

And Asantes described the Prempe administration's careful observance of the burgeoning industry:

> The elders watched the rubber trade grow in Asante. They felt the new money could help the nation. They told Nana Asantehene to be very wise. He must decide how much to take from the traders. He must not punish them. He must not offend them. They would run away to the coast. The rubber traders could help the nation. The chiefs told Nana Asantehene that they must be allowed to make their money here.[26]

Commercial traffic increased between the Ankase market and the coastal ports. Reports indicated that large numbers of Asante traders crossed the Pra at Praso in order to obtain manufactured articles from the exchange centers in the Colony, and that incidents of banditry along Route VI were infrequent.[27] Although Prempe's government continued to trade for most of its war materials at the French ports of Grand Bassam and Assini, the European mercantile communities in Cape Coast, Saltpond, and Accra still reported significant profits, which to a great extent reflected the restoration of political order throughout Asante. Acting Governor F. M. Hodgson in December 1889, for example, summed up the bright economic picture and observed that trade with Asante over the past year had significantly improved as measured by the number of traders who had crossed to the Colony at Praso.[28]

The improvements in trade and in the rural economy of metropolitan Asante, coupled with the renewed political order, prompted officials in Kumase to make overtures to win back Atweneboanna's adherents, many of whom still resided in the Colony. To accomplish this goal, Prempe's government strove to enlist the aid of the British administration and multiplied its diplomatic contacts with the government of the Gold Coast Colony in the period from July 1889 to August 1891. The Asantehene and his councillors sent several formal and many private missions to the coast during these two years and, with the assistance of their chief foreign policy adviser, John Owusu Ansa, they frequently corresponded with British officials in Accra and also wrote directly to functionaries in the Colonial Office in London.[29] The essence of Asante diplomacy in this era centered on issues relating to the return of Kokofu, Dadiase, Adanse, Manso, and Dwaben citizens to the metropolitan region. The full-scale discussions between Asante ambassadors and British officials in July 1890 illustrate the thrust of Kumase's diplomatic and political efforts and elucidate the difficulties faced by the new administration in its attempt to achieve national reconstruction.

In March 1890, authorities in Kumase prepared to assemble a delegation for talks with the British about the refugee problem. In a letter of 7 April 1890, Prempe informed Governor W. Brandford Griffith that the deputation would soon depart for the coast and would include some one thousand persons, representing every prominent officeholder in the metropolitan region. After several delays due to financial and accommodation difficulties and the deaths of two diplomats en route, the Asante embassy arrived in Elmina and began preliminary talks with John R. Holmes, district commissioner of Cape Coast, on 2 July 1890. On this occasion the Asante ambassadors stated the purpose of the mission: the British should instruct all Asante citizens residing in the Colony to return to Asante in order to "make Ashanti as it was in the olden days."[30] Then, on 8 July formal proceedings convened at St. George Fort in Elmina. The composition of the Asante delegation at this conference and at the subsequent meeting on 22 July reveals the degree of political consensus over policy in the field of foreign affairs. Representatives from Kumase included the Nsienehene Kofi Apea, the principal diplomat on the mission; Okyeame Yaw Boaten, whose own diplomatic career stretched back throughout the previous decade; sword-bearer Akyampon Dabban; and envoys from the Asantehemaa Yaa Akyaa, the Bantamahene Amankwatia Kwame, the Adumhene Asamoa Kwame, the Asafohene Asafo Boakye, and the Domakwaehene (or Akyeamehene of Kumase) Kwasi Akoko. The Asante embassy, in addition to these Kumase representatives, comprised emissaries from the Bekwaehene Osei Kwaku Abrebrease, the Dwabenhene Yaw Sapon, the Edwesohene Kwasi Afrane, the Offinsohene Apea Sea, the Gyamasehene Yaw Sekyere, the Abodomhene Kwaku Dua, and the Asumegyahene Kwadwo Agyeman. Envoys from Kokofu and Mampon participated too.

During the diplomatic conferences of 8 and 22 July 1890, the Asante diplomats first reaffirmed the new administration's firm commitment to "peace, trade, and open roads"—the historic "peace party" position which was consistent with Asante policy in the field of foreign affairs during the reigns of the Asantehenes Kwaku Dua Panin until 1863, Mensa Bonsu, and Kwaku Dua II. In light of the cordiality and peaceful relations between the two governments, the Asante ambassadors formally requested that the British administration assert its authority throughout the Colony and thereby assist Prempe's government to bring back the Kokofu, Adanse, Saawua, Dadiase, and Dwaben refugees. According to the diplomats, British assistance would enable the Asantehene "to rule over all and trade will improve, troubles will stop, and the roads will always be clear."[31] The Asante envoys, moreover, informed the British that initiatives designed to achieve national unity were already in progress at the

145

time the talks convened. The British, so the emissaries maintained, should thus aid the Asante government to insure the success of the program. Prempe clarified this point in a letter of 22 August 1890, which stressed that his "motto is 'Peace' ":

> I find that if it is the policy and firm determination of Her Majesty's Government not to advise any Ashanti subject that sought refuge in the Protectorate on the Gold Coast Colony to return to Ashanti, and it is not fair and reasonable for me to send for the Ashantees that sought refuge in the Protectorate without acquainting you of the fact, and if I have said that I wish my good friend the Governor will assist in restoring to me the Juabin, Adansi, Kokofu, Bekwai, and the Dadaissie peoples, or any Ashanti, I do not mean that he should force them to come, but simply to call them in the presence of my messengers, that they may deliver my message politely to them, that it is my great wish that they should return to me, and that if there is any misunderstanding still existing between us it shall be clearly settled.[32]

The Asante ambassadors subsequently asserted Kumase's stance on the particular issues under discussion in July. The public positions taken on the major issues by the Asante and British governments in 1890 and 1891 are summarized in the accompanying chart.[33]

THE IDEA OF BRITISH "PROTECTION": DWABEN AND BEKWAE

These were the major issues discussed during the talks of July 1890 and early 1891. With the exception of the Manso and the banditry issues, the British neither followed the suggestions offered by the Asante envoys nor adhered to Kumase's request for diplomatic assistance in the delicate matter involving the return of the Asante refugees from areas under British administrative jurisdiction. It was at this juncture in the history of Anglo-Asante diplomacy that Governor W. Brandford Griffith's idea of British "protection" of Asante took root. Officials in the Gold Coast Colony believed that several prominent Asante officeholders would support the extension of British political influence north of the Pra and that the Asantehene and his councillors would accept a treaty of protection. This assumption was based on two events that occurred in late 1890 and early 1891.

In November 1891, Ama Sewaa—the spokeswoman for the Dwaben community in Koforidua and a daughter of the Dwabenhemaa Afra Kuma, who died in Accra in 1886—requested an interview with Governor Griffith. Ama Sewaa and her mother had been leading supporters of the Dwabenhene Asafo Agyei's quest for his district's local rights and powers.

	Prempe Administration	Gold Coast Administration
Adanse	The 12,000 to 15,000 Adanse citizens resident in the Colony could resettle in their lands north of the Pra on the condition that their leaders agreed to return as loyal subjects. Thus Adanse politicians should: (a) acknowledge Prempe as the Asantehene; (b) abide by the laws of Asante; (c) renounce all claims to independence; (d) respect the Asantehene's oath on all local disputes and refer these to Kumase for settlement; and (e) allow the towns of Odumaase, Dumbiase, and Kyeaboso to remain in Kumase's possession. If the Adanse leaders did not agree to these terms, the Asante government would continue to implement its program of planned resettlement in Adanse: Kumase officials would settle people along Route VI to maintain the road and supervise the return of any local citizens.	The British government recognizes that Kumase desires the return of the Adanse refugees and agrees in principle but would expect that Adanse occupy the same independent position that it had prior to the conflict with Bekwae and its allies in 1886. Thus the British would advise the Adansehene Kwaku Nkansa to return on the condition that Adanse assumes its pre-1886 political status and, otherwise, would not recommend repatriation. The British adamantly oppose Kumase's plan to resettle Asantes in Adanse. As the Adanses in the Colony are not prepared to surrender the town of Dompaase, the British do not support Kumase's stance on this matter.
Atweneboanna partisans	The Kokofu, Dadiase, and Saawua leaders and some 20,000 refugees from these polities are encouraged to return to the metropolitan region. The Asantehene will refrain from any retaliations against these citizens and promises to "receive them kindly and regard them as his subjects." Kumase will continue the policies it inaugurated in March 1888 and will begin to rebuild the main towns in the Kokofu district. Thus the Asante government hopes to insure	The supporters of Atweneboanna's candidacy were driven from Asante and sought refuge in the Colony under British legal jurisdiction. They should not be troubled by Kumase's agents, and, as long as they obey British law, are entitled to remain in the Protectorate. Since the refugees entered areas south of the Pra on their own free will, they are entitled to rights of self-determination. Thus the British government would allow the refugees to return to the

	Prempe Administration	*Gold Coast Administration*
	the steady flow of refugees across the Pra to the Amansie region. If the Kokofuhene Osei Asibe resumes his activities in support of Atweneboanna, Kumase will work to enstool a successor and would again recommend that the Kokofuhene be deported to Lagos or areas outside the Colony.	metropolitan region only if they wish to do so. But, as the refugees are technically not British subjects, the government does not consider it part of its legal responsibility to suggest or to induce the refugees and their leaders to return to their respective towns in Asante nor to restore their political ties with Kumase.
Dwaben community in Koforidua	Kumase welcomes and encourages the reunification of the Dwaben district and will continue to collect for the Dwabenhene Yaw Sapon the citizens taken captive by the Asantes during the hostilities of 1875. As the reunification policy has distinct historical precedents extending into the late 1870s and early 1880s, the Asante government will continue to pursue its policies regardless of the views held by politicians in Koforidua. Further, Kumase is not concerned with the length of residence of the Dwabens in Koforidua: they are still Asante citizens. Thus the Asante government believes British assistance on this matter is essential and also desires that Accra return the stool of the *oman* to Yaw Sapon.	Accra is not prepared at this time to take any measures that would result in the reunification of the district and has no intention to return the Dwaben stool to Yaw Sapon. The Dwaben community in the Colony settled in Koforidua some fourteen years ago and has relied on British protection since that time. As they are regarded as British subjects and have peacefully pursued their economic livelihood in the Colony since late 1875, the British government will take no steps to encourage their return to the metropolitan region and would take actions to thwart the activities of Kumase's agents in Koforidua and its environs.
Manso fugitives	Kumase wants to eliminate the Manso raids from the Protectorate on Bekwae and the southern region of metropolitan Asante. As the Manso Nkwantahene	Accra will assist the Asante government on this issue. Kumase, however, should not employ its powers of coercion. The British government plans military ex-

	Prempe Administration	Gold Coast Administration
	Kwasi Mensa is an outlaw and continues to reside in Denkyira under British protection, Accra should move to restrict his activities and to deport his followers. Kumase welcomes the return of all Manso refugees following the defeat of their leaders. Even if Kwasi Mensa is not defeated by British troops, he, nevertheless, would not be allowed to return to Asante. But his subjects are encouraged to emigrate back to their towns.	peditions to suppress the rebel Kwasi Mensa's actions in the Colony. Accra will continue its policies to detain and imprison troublesome political leaders from Manso who are fomenting civil strife in Denkyira and other districts in the Colony.
Kwawu political settlement	The Asante government does not recognize the legality of the treaty of 1888 signed with the British. The citizens of Kwawu are Asante subjects and should not be encouraged to settle in the Colony. All Kwawu legal and political matters should be referred to Kumase—not Accra—for discussion. Kumase wishes to note that it resents British interference in Kwawu politics.	Accra recognizes the treaty signed with the Kwawuhene Kofi Boaten and his chiefs in March 1888. All local disputes in the district should be referred to British administrators for settlement. This would avoid bloodshed and secure a lasting settlement of all conflicts in the district. Kumase is warned not to interfere in Kwawu politics.
Banditry and Terrorism	Kumase deplores the incidents of banditry and terrorism along the southern branches of the great-road system and requests constant British assistance on this issue which is of mutual concern to both governments, especially in the ill-defined border territories. The bandits are not motivated by political or social considerations. They are unlawful killers.	Accra believes this issue is detrimental to the economic progress of the Colony and to the maintenance of cordial relations between both governments. Thus the British will continue to assist Kumase on this issue. Clearly, the bandits should be eliminated.

During her consultations with British officials in December, Ama Sewaa noted that the youthful, fiery Dwabenhene Yaw Sapon "was unwilling to trust the King of Ashanti," and thus might be induced to emigrate with his "strong and considerable following" from his headquarters at Ahyiaem, near Konongo in Asante Akyem, to lands in the Protectorate. Yet she also maintained that several Dwaben leaders in Koforidua would return to Asante if the Asantehene established a "good and safe government, and if the British permitted the Dwabens to resettle in the metropolitan region." Following the meetings with Ama Sewaa, envoys from the Dwabenhene Yaw Sapon, who arrived in Accra in early 1891, expressed the Dwabenhene's "desire to stand well" with the British and "his hope of coming under the British flag."[34] Griffith, however, maintained that the government of the Gold Coast upheld the authority of the central government in Kumase and thus would not encourage Asante citizens to leave the metropolitan region.[35] Contrary to the British response on this occasion, Griffith had urged the Mamponhene Owusu Sekyere II to emigrate into the Colony in November 1889, which indicates the pragmatism and tactical response to local conditions prevalent in British policy in these years.

While the Dwaben talks were in progress, emissaries from Bekwae met privately with officials in Accra during December 1890. According to British accounts, the Bekwae envoys hoped to learn the substance of the confidential negotiations between the Kumase diplomat Kofi Apea and Griffith in late 1890 and to express "their belief that the King of Bekwai would gladly welcome a proposition that the country [that is, Asante] be taken under British protection."[36] In their initial talks with the British, however, the Bekwae envoys apparently voiced the views of the proponents of decentralization in Bekwae and did not act on directions from the Bekwaehene Osei Kwaku Abrebrease and his adherents in council. The Bekwae *nhenkwaa*, for example, agreed "to return at once to Bekwai so as to ascertain confidentially and positively the opinion of their King upon the question."[37] Clearly, the British encouraged this initial Bekwae overture. Then, on 14 January 1891, the Bekwae *nhenkwaa* returned to Accra and allegedly proposed that a British agent proceed to Kumase in order to submit the treaty of protection. Bekwaehene Osei Kwaku Abrebrease, so the envoys claimed, would "use his influence" in favor of the British position. Strangely, the Bekwaehene had not consulted with the Asantehene or his councillors in Kumase for fear of compromising his own credibility: the council in Kumase would conclude that he was working in concert with the British administration on the question of British protection to Asante.[38] Considering their later reaction to the treaty, officials in Kumase no doubt knew of the Bekwae talks with the British but did not challenge the Bekwaehene's right to communicate with authorities in Accra. This, then, reveals one of the principal dimensions of the new regime: in 1890 and early 1891 the Council of Kumase willingly allowed outlying district heads a large degree of independence of action in the field of foreign affairs, a vestige from the mid-1880s when localism and the ideology of *nkabom* was widely accepted by leaders in metropolitan and particularly southern Asante.

Although politicians in Dwaben and Bekwae made independent overtures to the British in this period, politics in both districts were far more complicated than officials in the Colony realized. Dwabenhene Yaw Sapon's communications derived from several interrelated considerations. In the first place, politicians in Ahyiaem and Konongo made Dwaben's reunification their foremost goal. Local political opinion concurred on this issue and coincided with the diplomacy of the Asante government on the national level. Two Dwaben envoys, consequently, participated in the conferences of July 1890.[39] However, in the years that had elapsed since the turbulent Asafo Agyei rebellion of 1875, Dwaben citizens in Koforidua had become firmly entrenched politically and economically in areas lying within British jurisdiction. Despite their residence outside the metropolitan region, the Dwabens in Koforidua were considered Asante citizens by the central government in Kumase and were also British subjects. This dual citizenship presented an intricate legal as well as political problem requiring careful negotiation.

Secondly, the socioeconomic links of the Dwaben community in Koforidua—progressively constructed over a period of fourteen years and extending throughout the metropolitan region, Asante Akyem, the Akyem towns, and the Colony—impeded the community's return to Asante and complicated the entire reunification issue. When the diplomatic talks of July failed to reach a settlement, the Dwabenhene's supporters in Asante believed that they would be more successful if Dwaben negotiated independently with the British. As in the case of Bekwae, this met with the approval of the central government. But after the private meetings also failed, Yaw Sapon's adherents thought that Kumase's ratification of the treaty would facilitate the solution to the complex reunification problem. Officials in Accra and Ama Sewaa undoubtedly reinforced Yaw Sapon's intention to press for the treaty in the councils of government, while the Basel missionaries, who had worked in outstations throughout Akyem and Asante Akyem after 1874, also lobbied for the treaty among Dwaben politicians. Although the missionaries Ramseyer, Dilger, and Perregaux steadfastly disclaimed any intention of intervening in Asante politics, the missionaries repeatedly noted after 1884 that district leaders who favored loose political union with Kumase were more receptive to the introduction of schools, churches, and other ecclesiastical influences.[40] Thus the Basel agents pressed for the treaty despite (and partly because) certain influential centralists in Kumase such as Asafo Boakye and Kwasi Gyambibi strongly opposed the establishment of mission stations in Asante. It was precisely these officeholders who militantly opposed any British treaty.

The third principal factor that induced Yaw Sapon to negotiate with the British in late 1890 concerned the changed nature of political relations between Dwaben and Kumase since 1889. Yaw Sapon—a Mensa Bonsu appointee in 1875 and a grandson of Asafo Agyei and a son of Afra Kuma—was a centralist throughout the 1880s. For example, he supported the election of the Asantehenes Kwaku Dua II and Agyeman Prempe, mobilized his troops to join the Edwesohene Kwasi Afrane in the offensive against Mampon and Nsuta in 1888, and instructed his representative to attend Prempe's installation on 26 March 1888. Until 1887, Yaw Sapon resided in the town of Aboabo near Kumase under the scrutiny of officials in the capital. Kumase authorities regarded him as a headstrong, risk-taking leader with little regard for central governmental dictates.[41] Following his relocation to Ahyiaem near Konongo in late 1887, which was effected by officials in Kumase, the Dwabenhene increasingly came under the influence of localist politicians resident in the Asante Akyem towns. Yaw Sapon told Ramseyer in October 1893 that "the elders of Dwaben came to me when my grandfather and mother died [in 1886] and told me they dislike me to stay at the place [Aboabo] being too near to Kumase, so I may come to Asante Akyem."[42]

After 1887, Yaw Sapon, acting on the counsel of his advisers, maintained a measure of independence from Kumase and asserted Dwaben's autonomy in its internal affairs, while continuing cordial relations with the central government. His efforts were quite successful, primarily because Prempe's regime in the early 1890s allowed individual leaders a significant degree of independence in internal affairs (as well as in the field of foreign affairs) so long as they did not challenge the legitimacy of Prempe's office and the authority of the central government. Governor Griffith, for example, noted in March 1891 that Dwaben occupied a "strong position—apparently one of independence from Kumase influence."[43] The British envoy, Acting Travelling Commissioner H. M. Hull, observed that Dwaben sikadwumfo, or goldsmiths, had made a golden crown or cap for Yaw Sapon, which violated Asante law but symbolized the Dwabenhene's new political status. Still another indication of Dwaben's autonomy appeared in early 1891 when Yaw Sapon informed the British—not Kumase as was legally required—that he had executed one of his subjects for poisoning two persons in Konongo.[44] Dwabenhene

Yaw Sapon and his councillors in Konongo and Koforidua, therefore, supported the extension of British influence to Asante, for it would further safeguard Dwaben's new political status vis-à-vis Kumase and would enable the Dwabenhene to have a greater voice in the councils of government and in the selection of an Asantehene.

Bekwae consultations with the British in late 1890 and early 1891 also were undertaken for reasons relating to local politics. Following the conclusion of the military operations of 1888, Bekwae politicians, whether centralist or confederate, agreed on one central issue: they wished to negotiate a lasting settlement that would eliminate banditry and raiding committed against Bekwae citizens by Manso and Kokofu refugees residing in the northern reaches of the Protectorate.

> Before Nana Prempe became Asantehene the Bekwaehene Yaw Gyamfi beat the Kokofuhene in two battles. The *abirempon* of Ahuren and Esiase and their people supported Bekwae in the civil war. All the Bekwae stool subjects fought with Yaw Gyamfi against Atweneboanna's forces. . . . The Kokofuhene and his people could not withstand Prempe's power. They were beaten. They went to the lands south of the Pra River. But they continued to be a nuisance to Bekwae. They stopped Bekwae traders, killed the women, molested the children, and took money from the *abatafo*. I myself saw this when I went to the coast on the Pra Road. The Bekwaehene Yaw Boakye liked the whites. He did not intend to fight the whites when Prempe was taken away. But this Bekwaehene wanted to put a halt to the Kokofu actions against his subjects. He needed the whites to help him with this. So the Bekwaehene sent his people to tell the whites about the Kokofu. The whites received the messengers on the coast. I was sent to carry food for my people. The whites listened. They agreed to help. All Bekwae chiefs wanted these talks. Even the chiefs who liked Nana Asantehene and his elders in Kumase liked the talks with the whites on the coast. They believed it would help their *oman*.[45]

The safety of the southern roads and of Bekwae traders was intrinsically linked with this concern, which complemented Asante diplomacy on the national level. The Bekwae Akyeamehene Yaw Atabra thus participated in the conferences of July 1890, attended the discussions of January 1890 over the security of the southern routes, and joined with the Kumase diplomat Yaw Boaten in the talks with the British over the fugitive issue in January 1891.[46] Yet, despite the Bekwae support for national diplomacy throughout 1890 and 1891, political ties between the district and Kumase were severely strained. The rift initiated the Bekwaehene's stance for the extension of British influence in Asante. Bekwaehene Osei Kwaku

Abrebrease, for example, told Hull on 29 March 1891 that he would ignore the summons of officials in the central government to attend deliberations in the capital.[47]

The first points of contention related to Bekwae's role in the confederacy, the district's support for the restoration of the monarchy in 1885–86, and its backing of Prempe's election. Although Bekwae had received three towns from Kumase in 1889, local leaders in the early 1890s contended that the *oman* had been inadequately compensated for its pro-Prempe proclivities. As Bekwae's power had been seriously weakened by the frequent military engagements in the southern region since 1886 and by the virulent smallpox epidemic that ravaged Amansie in the early 1880s, Bekwae politicians hoped for financial assistance from Kumase. In March 1891, Osei Kwaku Abrebrease emphasized this point while discussing the strains in the relations between his district and Kumase. The Bekwaehene, related Hull,

> replied that he would never go to Kumasi, that a very bad state of feeling existed between himself and the Kumasis; he had fought 17 battles for Kumasi, at which 700 of his principal chiefs, captains, and headmen had fallen or been taken prisoners by the Kokofus, and notwithstanding this the Kumasis had not thought it incumbent upon them to recognize in any way his services to the common cause.[48]

This grievance was accentuated by the resentment over the drain on the district's monetary resources, which had become particularly apparent by the early 1890s. Bekwae politicians in 1891 believed that Kumase should extend compensation commensurate with the district's losses on behalf of the central government. The Bekwaehene and twenty of his *ahene*, for example, told Hull that Bekwae military operations since 1886 had cost some 3,500 peredwans of gold, or £28,000. But this economic issue, which served as another source of tension between Bekwae and Kumase, had greater implications. To compensate for their economic losses, Bekwae leaders, without the sanction of the central government, encouraged coastal entrepreneurs to begin mining operations in the *oman* in 1890. The loss of Asante gold would have been disastrous for the Asantehene because the national treasury was entitled to all gold nuggets in the kingdom. Local economic policies thus provided still another reason to explain the "ill-feeling" and "coolness" characteristic of Bekwae and Kumase relations in the early 1890s.[49]

The Bekwae also believed that the central government would be unable to maintain political order in Amansie after the Asante refugees returned from the Protectorate. Politicians, centralist and localist alike, feared the consequences of repatriating the Kokofu, Saawua, and Adanse citizens and their leaders to the metropolitan region. Bekwae uneasiness derived from their experience with the Nkansa-Kotirko regime in 1885–86, from the near collapse of the authority of the central government in the mid-1880s, and from the actions of the Kokofuhene Osei Asibe in support of Atweneboanna's candidacy in 1887–88. The Bekwaehene, noted Hull,

> is evidently master here and inclined, no doubt from a spirit of self-preservation to go to great lengths to win the support and goodwill of this Government, for he sees that if the present state of ill-feeling which exists between himself and Kumase continues, it will be an evil day for Bekwai when the Kokofus return to Ashanti, unless the support of the Government has been previously secured.[50]

The talks between envoys from Dwaben and Bekwae and the British in late 1890 and early 1891 encouraged Governor Griffith to make an official proposal to extend British protection to Asante in March 1891. The treaty did not have the prior approval of Griffith's superiors in the Colonial Office in London but was confirmed by the Executive Council of the Gold Coast Colony on 13 March 1891.[51] Kumase's acceptance, so Griffith argued, would resolve in one broad sweep the vexing, complex problems that had confronted Prempe's new administration. The pact would, he noted, settle the "uncertain political relationship" between Kumase and the districts and alleviate the "dissociated condition" characteristic of Asante public life. It would stimulate the return of the Dwaben citizens from Koforidua and the refugees from the Protectorate and allow the Adanse to resettle in southern Asante. This would keep the southern branches of the great-road system open for trade and generally "promote peace, tranquillity, and good order" in the metropolitan region as well as "assist, encourage, develop, and elevate Ashanti by the introduction of European influences calculated to secure willing obedience on the part of the people to law and order, to promote civilization, education, and industrial trading, and commercial undertakings in, and steady and progressive improvement throughout the country."[52]

In March 1891, Governor Griffith refused to acknowledge that authorities in Kumase had made significant strides toward accomplishing most of these aims. During the three years since Prempe's installation in March 1888, the Asante government had progressed towards its goal of national reconciliation and the restoration of political order in the metropolitan region. The Council of Kumase had operated with only nominal British assistance in Akyem Kotoku and Denkyira and had frequently run afoul of British interference. It is by no means clear that the British measures regarding the resettlement program and the deportation and confinement of politicians in areas such as Sehwi and Denkyira prevented opposition to the policies of the central government in Kumase or indeed benefited the Asanteman.[53] Rather, the evidence suggests that the British political and military missions in 1890 and 1891 were designed to forestall the expansion of Kumase's authority outside central Asante, to tighten British control over towns in the Protectorate (e.g., in Akyem Kotoku and Akyem Bosume) which favored the reestablishment of loose political connections with the Asante government, and to make Kumase administrators dependent on British initiatives in areas that the British maintained fell within their jurisdiction. In this period British political activities were changing from a day-to-day policy to a definite plan to gain control of Asante.

The provisions of the treaty of protection have been considered by Claridge and more recently by Tordoff.[54] The nine articles of the proposed treaty represented direct interference in Asante internal affairs. Great Britain would take Asante under its protection, would appoint a resident in Kumase, and the governor would arbitrate and have the final decision over all Asante political contests and treaties. The treaty guaranteed to British subjects unrestricted access to travel, trade, and property ownership in the metropolitan region, while only the governor of the Gold Coast could extend and consent to these privileges. Officials in Accra considered the time propitious for the proposal and believed that Prempe's regime would seriously evaluate its terms, especially Article VIII incorporating the residency clause. Although Griffith apparently was quite certain that eight of the nine articles were unacceptable to Prempe's councillors, he gambled that the Asante government's acceptance of the resident would mean its ratification of the entire treaty.

According to Griffith's own account in 1891, the treaty was not a new proposition. Apparently the British envoy, Inspector H. B. Lethbridge, had suggested to the Asantehene and his councillors in late 1888 that they should consider signing a similar agreement.[55] Interestingly, R. Austin Freeman—who accompanied Lethbridge to Asante and Gyaman and attended the public meeting with officials in Kumase on 26 December 1888 and who was meticulous about his other observations—made no allusion to Lethbridge's remarks on this point.[56] If Griffith's statement was accurate, Asante leaders would have been aware for some time that a treaty was in the offing and, consequently, would have had ample opportunity to debate the merits of the proposal before formal deliberations commenced. But, if the governor fabricated his report for reasons of political expediency, which evidence collected by this writer clearly suggests, authorities in the capital confronted the treaty question for the first time quite unexpectedly in March 1891.

The whites came to Kumase many times when Nana Prempe was the Asantehene. They came to talk about trade. They came to bring news from the coast. They came with pieces of paper and many soldiers. The Asantes always greeted the whites in the customary way. Food was given out, drinks were poured, and the chiefs assembled in the marketplace. At one meeting with the whites I came from my village in Atwema. I was a small boy and carried foodstuffs. I saw the whites come with their tents. I saw the paper handed to the Akyeamehene of Nana Asantehene. There was surprise on the faces of the Asante chiefs. There was much noise. Many people started to shout. Others ran around. Others started to return to their villages. Nana Asantehene looked sad, sad and surprised. The Akyeamehene pushed the people back. Many years later when I worked in the palace [in Kumase] I heard about this day. The paper was from the whites on the coast. It had the name of the white governor on it. It was not good for Asante. The Asantehene could not believe it. He told the governor's people to go back to the coast with this paper. It was all a great surprise to him. This all happened in the years before the white soldiers came to take Prempe away.[57]

Prempe and his councillors received the proposed treaty on 4 April 1891. During the presentation of the agreement, the council in Kumase demonstrated a "strong inclination" for discussion and clarification of its provisions and thereafter met daily. Officials in the capital, who had formulated and striven to implement their own program of national reconciliation from 1889 to early 1891, were acutely cognizant of the fact that the Gold Coast administration had officially moved diplomatic relations to a qualitatively different level of discussion.

The Asantehene's leading Kumase advisers participated in the preliminary deliberations. Agyeman Prempe leaned heavily on their strength and counsel. Several prominent officeholders of the older generation (although most were in their late forties or early fifties) had careers spanning the equivocally centralist era characteristic of the greater part of the nineteenth century.[58] The experienced, soft-spoken Asafohene Asafo Boakye, the military commander who headed the Akwamu Fekuo, was described by British sources as the "most influential factor" in the councils of government.[59] For the past ten years he had been distrustful of British aspirations on the Gold Coast but since the early 1880s had lacked overt involvement in the ideological issues of national politics. The nationalistic Nsumankwaahene Kwasi Domfe, spokesman for the

Asante shrine priests and a personal friend of the Edwesohene Kwasi Afrane, on more than one occasion had vehemently opposed the spread of literacy and European values into Asante society. Widely regarded as a man of action, Kwasi Domfe commanded forces against Dwaben in 1875 and led columns against Manso Nkwanta in 1883 and Kokofu in 1888.[60] The Adumhene Asamoa Kwame, who came to office following the death of his predecessor Agyei Kese in the operations against the rebel Dwabenhene Asafo Agyei in November 1875, was remembered as a particularly wealthy man (*sikani*) who had served in the personal bodyguard of the Asantehene Kwaku Dua Panin in the late 1860s. Asamoa Kwame's views were apparently closely followed by the new Bantamahene, Amankwatia Kwame, who had succeeded Kwabena Awua after his execution in Kokofu in June 1888. The Akyempemhene Kofi Subiri, a son of the Asantehene Kwaku Dua Panin who assumed office in 1890, still undoubtedly tested the political waters and rarely took a vocal stand on the major issues. And the Asantehene relied on his mother, the Asantehemaa Yaa Akyaa, described by most contemporary reports and informants as a "virtual ruler" in Kumase, who exerted a decisive influence on the Asantehene's reactions to the affairs of state.[61]

A less distinguished group of Kumase officeholders had staunchly backed Prempe's candidacy in the election of 1887–88. Unlike a great many of their colleagues, their careers were unblemished by charges of dishonesty or embezzlement. This group included the Hiahene Boakye Adare, the Gyakyehene Yaw Pense, the Akyeamehene (of Kumase) Kwasi Akoko, the Anantahene Adu Kofi, the Ankobeahene Yaw Kyem, the Atipinhene Kwame Boakye, and the Oyokohene Kwabena Agyekum.[62]

Several senior diplomats who had achieved rapid promotion to the higher echelons of the diplomatic service joined these centralists in the Council of Kumase's debate over the proposed treaty. Kwaku Fokuo, the occupant of the Boakye Yam Panin *okyeame* stool, had succeeded to the office held by the late Boakye Tenten in 1886 or 1887. Although he was born in the town of Oda in the Akyem region, Kwaku Fokuo's intelligence and forensic abilities had endeared him to the Kumase political establishment. The sword-bearer Akyampon Dabban and the Nketyetiahene Kwabena Bona had served the government at the diplomatic conferences of 1890 and 1891.[63] Along with the Nsienehene Kofi Apea, they advised John Owusu Ansa—son of the renowned Owusu Ansa who was born in Kumase in 1851 and educated in Cape Coast—and was generally regarded by his contemporaries as the Asantehene's principal foreign policy adviser in the 1890s.[64]

The relationship of these Kumase officeholders to Agyeman Prempe was both professional and personal. In their many deliberations and conversations, the youthful Asantehene had often showed his deep concern for good relations with his people and his love for his kingdom.

The elders were pleased. The chiefs had chosen well. All agreed. Agyeman Prempe was a man. He learned the traditions quickly. He listened carefully in council. He always considered what was said. He knew in the end he must decide things alone. The Asantehemaa had told him this in private. She helped him to rule wisely. Asantes knew he was confident. They talked about his respect for the ancestors and his nation. Prempe was a popular Asantehene. He would do anything to serve his people.[65]

CONVOCATION OF THE ASANTEMANHYIAMU

While members of the Council of Kumase deliberated, preparations were made to convene the Asantemanhyiamu, which had not met since early 1883, in order to solicit the views of a wider political audience. *Nhenkwaa* were dispatched to the outlying district heads who, by contrast with earlier summons of this type in the 1880s, arrived in Kumase during the first week of April. The Mamponhene Kwame Apea Osokye, for example, entered the capital on 6 April. Edwesohene Kwasi Afrane was already present, while the Offinsohene Apea Sea was en route to the capital. Even the Bekwaehene Osei Kwaku Abrebrease reversed his earlier stance and came to Kumase on 20 April 1891. Yet the Dwabenhene Yaw Sapon, who was repeatedly called, resisted all urgings and did not attend. Thus the Asantemanhyiamu began formal discussions over the treaty without the Dwabenhene on 28 April. Attendance for the opening session—including officeholders and *nkwankwaa*—indicated that some one thousand persons were present.[66]

During the first meeting the basic polarity emerged clearly: the Bekwaehene "asked that the earnest consideration of the Council might be given to what the white man [H. M. Hull] had said, and finally, stated for himself and his people that he agreed to sign the treaty."[67] Several influential politicians immediately supported the Bekwaehene, partly because they advocated autonomy for their districts and believed that the British presence in Asante would curtail the dominance of Kumase in internal politics, partly because some leaders championed Atweneboanna's candidacy and still hoped he might be appointed by the British, and partly because a few chiefs militantly opposed Kumase's efforts to repatriate the Kokofuhene Osei Asibe and the refugee leaders in the Protectorate. Still other "pro-British" advocates believed that the enstoolment of Atweneboanna and the creation of a residency in the capital would facilitate the regime's diplomatic relations with the British administration and would stimulate administrative and military reforms similar to those implemented in the 1870s. Therefore, various participants of the Asantemanhyiamu, according to information Hull obtained from Bekwae and Kumase Gyaase sources, decidedly "desired British protection" and maintained that Prempe would be deposed in three months if he did not sign the treaty.[68] The majority of the Kumase *asikafo* and *nkwankwaa* lobbied for ratification of the agreement due primarily to the regime's new 50 percent tax on rubber collection and production,[69] to the expectation that this would be followed by even more stringent tax measures, and to the anticonscription feelings which surfaced as a result of the war rumors that had circulated in early 1891.[70] Most Kumase rubber traders agitated for the treaty during the initial Asantemanhyiamu deliberations and following the adjournment of the first meeting.

> Many of the rubber traders in Asante always liked the whites. This was because these traders made a great deal of money from the rubber trade. Europeans with money bought the rubber. This richness made the rubber traders favor the whites. They wanted Nana Asantehene to allow the whites to trade freely here in Asante. This the Asantehene could not do. It was against the traditions of the nation. The chiefs talked much on this question. They decided and advised Nana Asantehene not to allow the Europeans to come to settle and trade in Kumase.[71]

Another eyewitness recalled:

> Before Nana Prempe I was taken away by the British, there were a few foreign cotton and kola traders in Kumase. The policy of private Asante trade in rubber, cotton, gold, and kola began probably when Mensa Bonsu was the Asantehene. During the reign of Mensa Bonsu, private traders were active in contrast with earlier periods in Asante history. These private traders, especially the rubber ones, became much wealthier when Agyeman Prempe was on the Golden Stool. Many of them supported the whites and favored the whites' cause. This was true when the whites came with their treaties to Kumase. Most rubber traders led the cause for the establishment of white firms in Kumase. Then they could make even more money. There was discussion over this question when Prempe was the Asantehene. The Asantehene himself was advised to keep the whites on the coast. They still could make money there. It was only when Prempe was taken away that all this changed. Then the Asante people had no choice left.[72]

A consensus was not reached during the meeting of 28 April 1891. The "antitreaty" faction led by the centralists within the Council of Kumase enjoyed a majority in the central government and pressed for rejection of the proposal. While debate continued in official and private circles in the capital, the Asantemanhyiamu convened almost daily until the fourth of May. After that session, the Bekwaehene privately informed the British envoys of the projected outcome: the Asantehene would *not* sign the treaty. Although the discussion at this stage ran in favor of the anti-treaty faction, their antagonists nevertheless pressed for its acceptance, which forced Prempe to ask the British envoys to remain in Kumase until the ninth of April to await further developments.[73] Hull and his party, however, left Kumase for Accra on 7 April 1891 without learning the formal announcement.

Discussion continued for a full four weeks following Hull's departure from the capital. The intervening time reflects the intensity of the debate and the strength of the arguments presented by both sides. The treaty issue had substantially polarized opinion within the Asante government. Prempe's official reply to the government of the Gold Coast Colony was a classic statement of political sovereignty and a reassertion of the platform of reconciliation for the Asanteman at a point when the nation's independence was challenged for the first time in Asante history. On 7 May 1891, the Asantehene wrote:

> The suggestion that Ashanti in its present state should come and enjoy the protection of Her Majesty the Queen and Empress of India, I may say this is a matter of a very serious consideration and which I am happy to say we have arrived at this conclusion, that my kingdom of Ashanti will never commit itself to any such policy; Ashanti must remain independent as of old, at the same time to be friendly with all white men. I do not write this with a boastful spirit, but in the clear sense of its meaning. Ashanti is an independent kingdom and is always friendly with the white men; for the sake of trade we are to bind to each other, so it is our Ashanti proverb, that the old men eat and left, it is what the children enjoyed. I thank Her Majesty's Government for the good wishes entertained for Ashanti; I appreciate to the fullest extent its kindness, and I wish that my power of language could suitably tell you how much and how deeply I appreciate those kindness of Her Majesty's Government towards me and my kingdom. Believe me, Governor, that I am happy to inform you, that the cause of Ashanti is progressing and that there is no reason for any Ashantiman to feel alarm at the prospects, or to believe for a single instant that our cause has been driving back by the events of the past hostilities.
>
> The course I should adopt for the future prosperity of the Ashanti kingdom, I may and I am most sanguine of success, and where energy is wedded to enthusiasm in any work failure is not to be thought of; it is certainly true that Ashanti to-day is very

much changed from what it was before, say 20 years past, and it is through the uncertain political relationship to the Royal Stool, I believe it will be wisest in the general interest of my kingdom of Ashanti to adopt a course calculated to bring back Ashanti to its former position, to promote peace and tranquility and good order in my Ashanti kingdom. Many thanks for the advice, and after a good consideration, a thing that is most horrible to white men, as human sacrifices, whatever precious it may cost us, I am happy to inform you I have abolished such acts totally from my Ashanti kingdom.[74]

The new polarity in Asante political opinion and the treaty's implications for Asante's independence were further dramatized during the first talks between diplomats of both administrations following the rejection of the treaty proposal. On 25 September and 2 October 1891, Yaw Boaten and Kwaku Fokuo, who headed a delegation of 240 from Kumase, Mampon, Edweso, and Offinso, once again demanded the return of the Asante refugees from the Colony. Interestingly, envoys from Bekwae, Dwaben, and Nkoransa did not attend either conference. During the meeting of 2 October, Kwaku Fokuo, responding to British inquiries, explained the absence of emissaries from these districts by maintaining that it was not the custom to include Nkoransa envoys—an assertion that concurred with the historical record—and that Bekwae and Dwaben leaders in principle approved of the talks but thought it unnecessary to send emissaries, a statement that contradicted the foreign policy discussions held in 1881, in July 1890, and throughout the year 1891. Yaw Boaten allegedly admitted that the Dwabenhene Yaw Sapon had dismissed all requests from officials in Kumase to send envoys to the coast.[75]

Boaten's statement prompted Acting Governor F. M. Hodgson and his advisers to misconstrue the nature of the debate in Asante, to foster a policy that deviated from the public positions taken by the Gold Coast government throughout 1890 and early 1891, and to lay the groundwork for future British involvement in and expeditions to Asante in the era from 1892 to 1896. Hodgson subsequently remarked:

I think the trumpery character of the message (mission?) sent down by King Prempeh, and the absence from it of representatives of the Kings of Bekwai, Juabin, and Koranza, show that the King is at his wits' end for a policy, and that he has alienated from himself the support of his most influential and powerful friends; that he is, in fact, without a united party. . . . The outlook for Ashanti is not hopeful, as matters stand at present. The people know quite well that the return of the fugitive tribes without the controlling hand of a white officer means a futher period of bloodshed and unrest, and while they all desire peace, they know that without a firm power in Ashanti, which King Prempeh certainly has not proved, further wars will be unavoidable.[76]

Although his remarks embodied the crux of British official opinion in the Colony in late 1891, Hodgson's statement neither reflected the state of Asante public life nor accurately portrayed Kumase's position on the major issues. Developments in Asante politics following the rejection of the treaty indicated that the Prempean program for national reconciliation was progressing. For example, events in Kokofu, Adanse, and Bekwae in 1892 and 1893 revealed signs of positive accomplishment. In Kwawu, moreover, leaders strove to renew close ties with the central government in Kumase, but British interference frustrated their attempt.

RAPPROCHEMENT WITH DISSIDENT DISTRICTS

In early 1889 Yaw Donko and the centralists in Kwawu—that is, those politicians who favored the restoration of close political ties with Kumase —challenged the localist (and pro-British faction) which controlled the principal offices in the province. Yaw Donko and his adherents renounced the treaty signed with the British in March 1888 by the localists in the political hierarchy. As the competition for the district's offices intensified, Yaw Donko in a symbolic act of defiance planned to send the Kwawu stool to Kumase for safekeeping.[77] In 1890 British agents acting in concert with Kwawu localists uncovered and thwarted this scheme. The British subsequently took possession of the stool (as informants claim that they had also done in Dwaben in 1875), arrested Yaw Donko because he had done "his utmost to disturb the peace in Quahoo," and imprisoned him in Accra.[78] Consequently, Kwadwo Buama, a localist leader, was brought to office with British assistance. Buama's accession, so the British argued in 1891, restored peace and order to the district, maintained the burgeoning commercial links between Kwawu and Atebubu, and stimulated the construction of a new trade artery between Kwawu towns and Atebubu. The route was to be constructed in the next dry season.[79] But it was not mentioned at the time that the plan to build this new road had been considered by localists since early 1881 and had not been accomplished by authorities in Kwawu. It required the assistance and approval of the central government in Kumase.

British actions to crush the centralist ("pro-Kumase") faction in Kwawu during 1890–91 is one instance of active involvement in Asante local politics. The Kokofu example is even more revealing. Officials in Kumase had striven continually to negotiate a settlement with the Kokofuhene Osei Asibe and his supporters in the Protectorate after the second

163

phase of the civil war in June 1888. The Prempean regime's policies towards the Kokofuhene, similar to those of the Mensa Bonsu administration, were exceedingly pragmatic. Kumase envoys offered Asibe a considerable sum of money if he would return to Asante and promised an amnesty for the partisans of Atweneboanna. They publicly reaffirmed the longstanding traditional status of the Kokofu stool and maintained that the occupant of this office must be present in Kumase for Prempe's installation to be legal and proper. By contrast Barnett observed in December 1888: "It may be information for your Excellency to know that the King of Kokofu is not a big person at all in Ashanti; he has no voice in the election of a King to the Golden Stool, and when a King is on that stool he carries a gun when he comes to Kumase, which shows that he is a Chief of lesser degree."[80] Authorities in Kumase did not initiate proceedings to install a new Kokofuhene but rather appointed a Kumase *osahene*, the Nsansahene Akyampon, to settle local disputes between the Kokofu citizens who had drifted back to the district. This Kumase official also attracted to the *oman* Kokofu refugees residing in Akyem.

> The Kokofu people in the south were very scattered. They needed much time before returning to Asante. When Prempe was enstooled, he wanted the Kokofu people to resettle. But Asibe felt there would be a new rebellion and looked to the governor for protection. So most of the Kokofu refugees stayed where they were although Prempe had invited them back to Asante. The Kokofuhene told Prempe's messengers that his people needed time to return and that they feared Prempe's followers would attack and kill them. After Asibe's death in Accra, the Kokofu people returned under Asibe's nephew, Yaw Konkroma, who became Asibe II. . . . Most of the Kokofu stayed in Akyem. Asibe himself was actually a white hostage at the coast. In the olden days the absence of the Kokofuhene was something the Asantehene could not stand. The Asantehene wanted the Kokofuhene always to be here.[81]

By 1891 Kumase's conciliatory policy, which had actually begun in March 1888, was largely successful. In that year the Kokofuhene Asibe and several of his chiefs indicated their willingness to return to Asante and declared their intention to collect the Kokofu citizens in the Colony for the migration back to their district. In preparation for their resettlement, functionaries in the Kumase Public Works Department had restored most of the edifices in the town of Kokofu and had cleared the local roads. Although a few Kokofu leaders desired to remain in Akyem Kotoku under British protection, Asibe himself renounced his support for

Atweneboanna's cause and announced that he would proceed to Kumase if the Asantehene wanted him present. After several delays the Kokofu-hene informed Hull in September 1893 during a meeting held in the town of Akyikyesu that he and his people "were now of the opinion" that the time had arrived for them to return to Asante. He wanted to depart for Kokofu in approximately sixty days.[82] On this occasion Osei Asibe, cognizant of British legal jurisdiction in the Protectorate, also requested that the British instruct the remainder of the Kokofu citizens in Denkyira to return to Asante and stated that he was most anxious to leave on "good terms with Ata Fua," the *omanhene* of Akyem Kotoku. And, finally, the Kokofuhene expressed his desire to have schools opened by the Basel Mission in his district.[83]

Despite Osei Asibe's intention to move back to Asante, Hull informed the Kokofuhene and Yaw Atweneboanna that British soldiers would not permit the Kokofu refugees to leave the Protectorate without formal approval from the governor in Accra. Then, in the event that all matters were on "proper footing" and his request was granted, the Kokofuhene should proceed directly to Asante. He should not confer with politicians in the Akyem towns of Insuaim and Asuboa. Hull believed, quite correctly, that Osei Asibe's relocation would be publicized by Prempe's agents and thus jeopardize British influence in the Akyem country. The British did have ample evidence that envoys from Kumase actively intervened in Akyem politics. In 1893 leaders in Akyem Bosume, for example, frequently communicated with officials in Kumase. Acting Governor Hodgson and his advisers consequently reinforced Hull's stance, and in September 1893 instructed Osei Asibe and Yaw Atweneboanna to visit Accra to discuss "one or two matters."[84] Accordingly, Ata Fua was warned not to permit the Kokofu to depart without first receiving written instructions from Accra and to continue gathering information on the activities of Kumase agents in Akyem Kotoku and Asante Akyem.[85] The British intelligence network was hardly a new operation. But the subsequent arrest and detention of such a prominent officeholder as the Kokofuhene was a novel undertaking. In 1894 John Kofi Kakari—Osei Asibe's son who held a minor post in the colonial civil service—petitioned the governor for his father's release. Gold Coast officials responded that Osei Asibe could return to Asante if he obeyed "all that the British government intends him to do." The Kokofuhene refused and died as a prisoner in Accra on 8 February 1895, despite Kumase's efforts in July and September 1894 to raise money to free him.[86]

While the Kokofuhene prepared to move during September and October 1893, Yaw Atweneboanna—who had remained with Osei Asibe in Akyem since late 1888—hesitantly agreed to accompany his patron to

Asante. But he too was arrested and detained in Accra so that he could reveal the location of the mysterious treasure allegedly hidden by the deposed Asantehene Mensa Bonsu. Prempe had not resorted to the instruments of political violence and terror against Atweneboanna or his supporters in Asante. The Asantehene instead had legislated to inhibit the proliferation of Atweneboanna's family and thereby remove his relatives from further competition for the Golden Stool. It was made a capital offense to have sexual intercourse with Atweneboanna's sisters. Oheneba Kwadwo Afodo, a son of the Asantehene Mensa Bonsu, participated in a trial towards the end of 1894 in which the Asoamfohene Akwasi Agyei, the leader of the Kumase hammock-bearers, was executed for having sexual relations with Atweneboanna's sister, Akosua Brenya. Afodo offered the following vivid account of the proceedings:

> After Atweneboanna went to the coast, the Asantehene made it known in Asante that no man should go to any women in Atweneboanna's family. Also no woman in Asante should go to any man in Atweneboanna's line. This law was enforced against Atweneboanna's people. Atweneboanna's sister, named Akosua Brenya, had sexual intercourse with the Asoamfohene Akwasi Agyei. They violated the Asantehene's law. Yaw Dane reported the case to the Asantehene. Yaw Dane's wife, Akosua Nsia, was the Asantehene's sister. The Asantehene heard the report from Yaw Dane. He sent me and Kwaku Dwomo from Adwumam to call the Asoamfohene to the palace. The Asantehene wanted the Asoamfohene to answer the charge. The Asoamfohene had killed two ducks to purify his soul. The Asoamfohene invited the two messengers to eat at his table. After the meal he asked them why they had come. The two messengers told him why. The Asoamfohene's house was at Ntwom Brono. The Asoamfohene got dressed. He went with the two messengers to the palace. They found the Asantehene sitting when they entered the palace. I knew that the Asantehene wanted to kill someone. The Asantehene held the tail of a mule. He had on his head the black headgear with one talisman at the forehead. The Asantehene wore the *afretakera* cloth. This attire was for important occasions. The Asantehene either would kill someone or destool an important chief. Agyei was given a seat. The Asantehene told Yaw Dane to repeat the same words he had told the Asantehene. Yaw Dane spoke through the Akyeamehene. Dane told Nana his elder brother had done something sacred. Agyei violated the Asantehene's law. Dane told the court that at dawn he came out to urinate. He saw Akosua Brenya with her cloth over her head coming from Agyei's house. The Asantehene asked Dane to repeat. Dane said the same thing. The Asante-

hene asked Agyei to defend himself. Agyei did not accept what Dane had said. He said Dane's story was untrue. Dane challenged Agyei. He said he would swear the Great Oath. Dane said he would tell the kind of cloth Akosua Brenya was wearing that morning. Dane said he would call people who saw the cloth that morning. Dane then swore the Great Oath. Agyei accepted his guilt. He pleaded to the Asantehene through the Bantamahene and the Asafohene. The Asantehene did not accept the plea. Agyei pleaded again through the Nsutahene Adubiawuo. The Asantehene again did not accept the plea. The Asantehene asked for Agyei's execution. Agyei pleaded. The executioners beat him each time he pleaded. The executioners took Agyei to the house of Kwaku Fe. Kwaku Fe was the guardian of the Asantehene's children. The Asantehene was very angry. He left the court. On that day he did not work in court. The elders of the court went home. The Asantehene undressed and came to take his meal. Many elders were at the table with the Asantehene. The Asantehene dipped his hand twice into the bowl of fufu. He stopped eating. He called Kofi Dakwa from Akyease. Kofi Dakwa was the Asantehene's elder cousin. Their mothers were sisters. The Asantehene told Dakwa to bring Baafo Ahen to Dietwaso. Dietwaso was the place [*brono*] for executions. The executioners stopped eating with the Asantehene. They brought Ahen to Dietwaso. The executioners were in a hurry. They put the rod [*sepɔ*] through Agyei's mouth. They undressed him. They bound Agyei's hands behind his back. The executioners came out with Agyei in the middle. The Asantehene gave orders. When he finished his meal, Agyei was to be killed. All the people in the palace rushed to Dietwaso. On such occasions every *ahene* brought drums to the scene. After the execution the *ahene* rubbed the blood into the drums. After the execution news was taken to Accra that Agyei was executed because he had sexual intercourse with Atweneboanna's own sister. Atweneboanna and Yaw Awua started to make a campaign against the Asantes. They told the whites the Asantes would never stop killing. The whites decided to come to Asante.[87]

Although the British frustrated the Prempean regime's attempt to secure the repatriation of the Kokofuhene Osei Asibe and Yaw Atweneboanna, the Asante government had greater success with most of the dissident Kokofu, Manso, and Saawua leaders resident in the Colony. In the case of Adanse, Kumase's policies were tangibly rewarded. The Agonahene (of the Colony) in September 1893, for example, informed Hull that the Adansehene Kwaku Nkansa and the majority of the Adanse refugees had returned to the metropolitan region. By the end of 1893, members of the British Western Boundary Commission verified the Adanse move and observed that Adanse towns north of the Pra were repopulated. The inveterate Kotirko, however, remained in Insuaim under British protection and urged the Gold Coast administration to thwart the Adanse movement back to Asante because "Ashanti will again become a powerful nation and a source of trouble."[88]

Signs of improvement in the relationship between Bekwae and the central government in Kumase further underscored the trend toward national unity and the emerging consensus over the reconstruction program. In early May 1893, the Bekwaehene Osei Kwaku Abrebrease was deposed amidst rumors (which were later discredited) that he had been murdered. The official charges made against the Bekwaehene centered on his orders to execute his Nseniehene and another local *ohene* without the consent of the Bekwae council and on his administration's stringent tax policies, a recurrent source of friction in district politics since the early 1880s. Despite these charges, the Bekwaehene undoubtedly was removed for his pro-British stance on the treaty issue in March 1891 and for his negotiations with the Gold Coast administration in 1890. Osei Kwaku Abrebrease's successor, the new Bekwaehene Yaw Boakye, came to office in late May 1893 and represented the centralists in Bekwae. The Asantehene either appointed Yaw Boakye or he attained office through the pressure exerted by envoys from the central government. Thus the Bekwae *okyeame*, Kofi Yam, attended the council deliberations in Kumase on 19 October 1893 and, by contrast with earlier Bekwae relations, was favorably received by officials in the capital.[89] The central government's role in Yaw Boakye's installation is further substantiated by the events surrounding the attempted coup in Bekwae in October 1893. During this incident Okyeame Yaw Atabra, a leading advocate of localism in Bekwae throughout the early 1890s, and his associate, Yamua, committed suicide or were executed after attempting to depose Yaw Boakye. Their activities no doubt were thwarted by Prempe's agents working in concert with centralist politicians in the district.[90]

Warfare in Nkoransa

Despite increasing British involvement in Asante politics in the early 1890s, Prempe's government had made a significant beginning in its efforts to achieve national reconciliation and restoration of confidence in *abankesemu*, or central authority, in the aftermath of the election of 1887–88. The politics of the conflict in Nkoransa in 1892–93 serves as still another illustration of the growth of national unity in Asante, especially over issues pertaining to economic welfare and internal security.

In early 1888, when Agyeman Prempe assumed caretakership of the Golden Stool, Kwasi Opoku was the Nkoransahene. Despite Opoku's professions of loyalty to the new administration in Kumase, he refused to concede formally his allegiance to Prempe and continued to balance the debate in his district between the centralists who argued on historical and traditional grounds for reaffirming political ties with Kumase and those politicians who favored joining the rebel eastern Bron coalition for its local political and economic advantages. A major aspect of the localists' platform was Kumase's decision to encourage the growth of the market at Wankyi at the expense of Kintampo which directly threatened the economy of Nkoransa.[91] In early 1889, following the death of Kwasi Opoku and the failure of the central government to respond in time to the request for an alliance made by leaders in the district, the Nkoransa decisively defeated the refugee Mamponhene Owusu Sekyere II who had been unable to solicit military assistance from the Atebubuhene Kwabena Asante. The policy to develop the Wankyi market and the absence of support from Prempe's regime in 1889 virtually insured the election of a secessionist candidate. The new Nkoransahene Kofi Fa promptly refused to take the oath of allegiance to Prempe, to send back the remaining refugees from Mampon and Nsuta who had fled to his district during the second phase of the civil war, or to pay annual tribute to Kumase.[92]

The rebellion in Nkoransa in 1889–90 presented a grave threat to Asante's economic interests in Kintampo and Wankyi and also to Kumase's relations with its northern hinterlands. The Nkoransahene Kofi Fa subsequently negotiated with Atebubu and Krakye to join the northeastern alliance and made overtures to leaders in Mo, the country west of Kintampo, and to the British administration.[93] A diplomatic mission from Kumase offered considerable sums of money to the Nkoransahene and several district *asikafo* but failed to convince Kofi Fa to end his talks with leaders in the northeastern Bron coalition.[94] The danger was further augmented by two diplomatic incidents beyond the Asante government's control which underscored the extension of British authority into the northern provinces and justified the Gold Coast administration's active intervention in polities whose rulers had signed treaties with its agents. First, in mid March 1888 the British and German governments had entered into an agreement to partition the area specified as the "neutral zone." Salaga, Yendi, Yegyi, and the neighboring districts thus came to be regarded as neutral territory outside the British sphere of influence.[95] This European pact and the subsequent German diplomatic activities in the Krepi country and throughout the northeast meant that the government of the Gold Coast had inadvertently lost the bulk of the Salaga and trans-Volta trade through Krakye to the Germans. Consequently, Accra was forced to expand its own interest in the northwest in Kintampo to provide alternate outlets for British trade. Governor Griffith, who since 1887 had warned his superiors against German expansion, stressed the importance of extending and preserving British trading relations and British jurisdiction in areas outside the Colony's administrative influence.[96] In mid December 1892, the governor brought Kintampo to the Colonial Office's attention:

> The large and important market town of Kontempo [Kintampo] is a town in the country of Nkoranza. To it, equally as to Bontuku on the west and Salagha on the east, come the Mahommedan caravans from the interior and a very large trade is transacted there. Now, therefore, that Salagha and Bontuku are no longer within the sphere of English influence, Kontempo assumes an importance which cannot be undervalued as an outlet for the trade of this Colony, and it is on that account that I have thought it desirable to show your Lordship [Ripon] the position which Nkoranza holds towards Ashanti and the condition of that country at the present time.[97]

To strengthen its commercial ties with Nkoransa and the northwestern markets, the Gold Coast administration concluded a Treaty of Protection with the Gyamanhene Agyeman on 24 January 1889.[98] The treaty was also designed to counter French encroachments in the northern Ivory Coast. In May 1888, Captain Louis-Gustave Binger and the French trader Treich-Lapléne had signed treaties with prominent anti-Kumase authorities in Kong, Bonduku, and the surrounding Dyula-dominated entrepôts. Binger's mission to Kong and Bonduku and his travels through Salaga, Kintampo, and Mamprussi contributed to major changes in France's West African policy. The venture revitalized French colonial ambitions in the interior of the Ivory Coast and had stimulated French imperial plans to develop the Ivory Coast as another base for the penetration of the Niger bend and the opening of that region to French trade.[99] Although the British treaty was challenged by centralist politicians in Gyaman,[100] it nevertheless legitimized future British claims in the northwest and subsequently enabled the Gold Coast administration to increase its own efforts—which actually started in the late 1870s—to channel the flow of trade from the northwest to the western ports of the Colony via routes beyond the control of the Asante government.

When the Atebubuhene Kwabena Asante entered into a similar compact with the British administration on 25 November 1890, the era of limited British intervention in the northeast ended. The Gold Coast administration formally supported the eastern Bron alliance. As a result of these treaties and of the rebellion in Nkoransa, the Asante government faced the possibility of an extensive northern coalition of dissident provinces aided by the British and stretching from Krakye on the northeast to Bonduku on the northwest.[101] Prempe's regime was forced to safeguard its own interests in the northern hinterlands and to thwart a dire threat to the nation's independence.

Asante troops therefore invaded and pillaged the main towns of Nkoransa in the middle of 1892. Despite significant casualties during the engagement at the town of Kumfa in August, government forces were victorious and returned with civilian prisoners to the metropolitan region towards the end of that year. Rather than negotiate with Prempe's envoys—one of whom was the refugee Mamponhene Owusu Sekyere II who seemingly hoped to win Kumase's favor—the Nkoransahene instead requested British protection in October and launched retaliatory strikes against the Banda allies of the central government. Furthermore, Nkoransahene Kofi Fa sought military assistance from Atebubu, Krakye, and other polities in the rebel northeastern alliance. Consequently, in 1893 Prempe's army, under the command of the Bantamahene Amankwatia Kwame and the Edwesohene Kwasi Afrane, launched a major offensive and strove to occupy the province.[102] According to the British agent, G. E. Ferguson, the expeditionary force, equipped with some three to seven hundred Snider weapons, numbered between ten and seventeen thousand. The Asante army which secured and encamped at Kintampo was estimated at fifteen thousand.[103] The extent of district participation indicates still further the degree to which national unity existed on issues pertaining to Asante's economic welfare and its political sovereignty. Contingents from Kumase, Mampon, Nsuta, Offinso, Edweso, Kumawu, Kwaman, Bekwae, and Asokore were mobilized to join the enterprise. Even the Agogohene in Asante Akyem and the Dwabenhene Yaw Sapon, the leaders of "pro-British" districts in the metropolitan region, furnished their respective quotas, the latter supplying men from Konongo and the towns of Asante Akyem under the leadership of the Dwaben *osahene* Ampetsi, a son of the rebel Dwabenhene Asafo Agyei. Then, following an initial setback in the first full-scale engagement—a result of the assistance the Nkoransahene received from Gyaman and from several polities in the eastern Bron coalition—the government forces defeated all opposition and forced Kofi Fa (along with the rulers of Yegyi, Gwan, Basa, and Wiase) to cross the Pru River and seek refuge first at Wiase in the eastern Bron country and then at Atebubu. Thereupon, government troops seized the Nkoransa stool with its regalia, occupied the province and the Kintampo mart, and apparently took measures to install a new Nkoransahene.[104] An eyewitness, offering this account of the conflict in Nkoransa, explained the significance of Kumase's victory for the birth of a future Asantehene, Kwame Kyeretwie or the Asantehene Osei Agyeman Prempe II, who took office in April 1933 and died in June 1970.

The Nkoransahene Bafo Twum [Kofi Fa] said he would not serve Kumase. He spoke these very words: *Borɔ deɛ a ahana a ani hwɛ Kumase no ɔrenni bi da.* "I will never take the fruit of the flowering plaintain that points toward Kumase." The Nkoransa *ohemaa* at this time was named Yaa Okanka or Boahemaa. In those days the main Kumase chiefs were the Offinsohene Kwadwo Kwawu, the Edwesohene Kwasi Afrane, the Bantamahene Amankwatia Kwame, and the Atwemahene Antwi Agyei. These four chiefs were sent along with many other chiefs to Nkoransa. The first attempt to crush the Nkoransahene was not favorable. The Nkoransahene proved to be stronger than the chiefs who were sent against him. The Kumase people only said *akwaaba,* or welcome, when the chiefs returned to Kumase. The Kumase chiefs had not been victorious. The chiefs again decided to go back to Nkoransa. They did not see why the Nkoransahene should drive them away. The Nkoransahene's shrines were called Susa Ntoa and Kukuma Ntoa. Each of the shrines had Ntoa attached to its name. Ntoa means disturbance. The shrines were believed to be the powers that assisted the Nkoransa to drive the Asante away. In the second encounter the Kumase chiefs met the Nkoransa at Brofo Koko. This time the Asante troops with their Kumase chiefs defeated the Nkoransa troops. The Nkoransa ran away. The Kumase chiefs returned to Kumase. This time the people in Kumase said, *mo no ko,* or well fought, to the troops. In the course of this war, the Nkoransahene changed himself into a leopard. It was juju. The leopard visited the house of Nana Prempe's wives called Hiaa. News was brought to Prempe that a leopard was with his wives. Prempe instructed his *asoamfo,* or carriers, to kill the leopard. The *asoamfo* made torches from the dried palm leaves. They went up and down with the torches. The leopard backed away from the torches and attempted to jump on one *soamfoni.* The rest of the *asoamfo* caught the leopard in the air and cut off his head. They brought the head and placed it at the junction of Hiaa and Boagyawe wards in Kumase. They informed Prempe that the leopard had been killed. Prempe asked the young *nhenkwaa,* or servants, in the palace to follow him to the scene. I was one of these servants. Prempe put one foot on the leopard and sprinkled white clay on the leopard three times. Prempe then said, "if the leopard had brought bad luck to the Asantes, it must be cursed." But, "if otherwise it would be good luck for the Asante warriors fighting in Nkoransa." The Asantehemaa then sent people to Prempe. She said she had given birth to a new child. Prempe rushed to where the Asantehemaa was and put his hand on the head of the newborn baby. Prempe said, "the baby should be called Kwame Kyeretwie." This new-born baby was the late Asantehene Prempe II. He was named Kwame because he was born on Saturday. Kyeretwie meaning "leopard caught," on that same day. If the *asoamfo* had not succeeded in killing the leopard, the Asantes felt that the Nkoransahene would have defeated them a second time. Since this war with the Nkoransa, the Asantes did not fight until Nana Prempe was taken overseas.[105]

In the aftermath of the impressive military victory against Nkoransa, Prempe and his councillors revived their program of conciliation and once more strove to negotiate a political settlement with the northeastern secessionists during the second half of 1893. Kumase's overtures to the leaders of the eastern Bron coalition in this period (which had started in 1892 and was particularly evident in July 1893) were primarily designed to reintegrate the Bron polities into the Asanteman and to thwart increasing British intervention in the affairs of the northeast. Thus in late September 1893 officials from Kumase—the herald Kofi Akwa and the sword-bearer Opoku—working in concert with Kwame Agyei, a subject of the refugee Mamponhene Owusu Sekyere II, told authorities in Atebubu:

The King of Ashanti presents his compliments to you all. He has heard that the people of Atabubu and the Brong people are deserting their country. They should stay in their country. If they like peace Prempe is for peace. If they like war they will have it. Prempe desires that the King of Atabubu and the King of Mampon should return to serve him; that they should eat fetish with him, after which they are to make peace between him and the King of Nkoranza. That the King of Atabubu, the King of Nkoranza, and the Brong people should take their oath of allegiance to Prempe. Should they not do so they are not for peace with Ashanti. If they are for peace the King of Ashanti is for peace. If the messengers return with an unfavorable reply to their King and the army then at Abease would proceed against Atabubu and the Brong people. Should the invasion of Atabubu and the Brong people as well as the capture of the Nkoranza King not be feasible now, the army would retire to Kuntampo and wait there till it can fight them. Five days were given to consider the demands of the King of Ashanti.[106]

The government's message was carefully considered and debated in Atebubu by the centralists (i.e., in this context, those politicians who wished to remain neutral in the struggle between Nkoransa and Kumase) led by the Atebubuhene Kwabena Asante and his adviser, the *okyeame*

Yaw Yami, and by the secessionists represented by the Prasihene Kwaku Mensa and the Nkoransahene Kofi Fa. The proposal was conveyed concurrently to other eastern Bron leaders in Gwan, Basa, and Krakye, but the localists and secessionists, who held a majority in the Atebubu council, rejected Kumase's overture. Consequently, the Atebubuhene requested British protection on 29 September 1893 and thereby legitimized the presence of a British force consisting of three hundred Hausa soldiers, equipped with one Maxim gun, stationed in the town in early October.[107] The Prempe administration still maintained that it would not authorize an attack on Atebubu and continued to press for negotiations with dissident eastern Bron leaders. The Asantehene, in turn, promised the Hemanhene of Kumase that he would place the town of Atebubu under Heman's administrative supervision if the Atebubuhene and his councillors accepted Kumase's overture.[108] Kumase envoys towards the end of October again inquired "whether the King of Nkoranza is now willing to give his allegiance to Prempe" and reemphasized "that Prempe has the most friendly intentions towards the Brong people." Indeed the response was predictable: ". . . the Chief Priest of Kraki swore to the Nkoranzas that he will restore them to their country and would make Atabubu his base of operations against the Ashantis."[109] Regardless of the prevailing anti-Asante climate in the northeast, Kumase emissaries pressed for a settlement and, according to Ferguson, maintained on 18 November in Atebubu:

> I [the Asantehene] have no palaver with them [the Atebubuhene and the eastern Bron leaders], so why should they leave their homes. I have no enemy among them. My operations will be conducted against Nkoranza only. It is not during my reign that the Brong people have severed their connection with Ashanti. They did so in the time of my predecessors. I am a young king. I do not know them, and they do not know me, no messenger of mine has been to see them, nor has theirs come here. Go and tell them that I am on the best terms with them, and that after my forces, now at Kuntampo have returned I shall send to give them my compliments and exchange peace relations with them.[110]

ALLIANCES IN THE NORTH

The efforts of the central government in Kumase to reassert its political control in the northeast and to counteract British intervention in that region were complemented by other Asante initiatives in the northern hinterlands. In the northwest, Kumase officials in late December 1893 negotiated for an alliance between the Bole of Gonja—who had signed a Treaty of Friendship and Trade with the British in June 1892—and the Banda, to whom Kumase promised jurisdiction over a large portion of Nkoransa territory. The Asante government also supplied war materials and money to compensate for Banda losses in the military operations against the rebel Nkoransahene's Mo allies. Further, Prempe's regime sought to reopen communications with the Kpembewura Yusuf, who desired Asante support for his contemplated attack on Yegyi whose authorities had intervened in the Salaga civil war.[111] The Yegyihene before 1880 was under the administrative supervision of the Anamenako-hene of Kumase whose office-estate included the towns of Abase, Dwa-man (between Atebubu and Krakye), Potrikrom, and a portion of the Volta River at Yegyi.[112] Kumase apparently utilized the services of Mus-lims from Bole—described by British sources as "possessing the same sympathies as Salaga"—in an attempt to rebuild direct trade relations with Salaga in the aftermath of the destruction of Kintampo in the second half of 1893.[113]

The members of the Asante Nkramo community in Kumase and their other principal location, the town of Nkankansu, situated sixty miles north of the capital, vigorously urged the Asantehene to reestablish commercial ties with Salaga and used their group influence to support Prempe in this endeavor.[114] The prospect that the Prempe administration would reconstruct commercial links between metropolitan Asante and Salaga posed a significant threat to the Gold Coast administration's own plan to divert the trade of Salaga and Kintampo to the growing market towns of Krakye, Panto, and Accra. The British Acting Governor, F. M. Hodgson, thus believed that this "was another very strong argument for dealing with Ashanti at the present time so as to endeavor to prevent an alliance of Ashantis and Salagas." According to Hodgson, this imminent danger to the economy of the Gold Coast Colony was a crucial factor "in favour of a forward policy with regard to Ashanti and its absorption within the protectorate."[115] Aware of the increasing international rivalry for West African markets and the resurgence of Asante governmental power and authority, the acting governor pushed Colonial Office officials for territorial expansion and the annexation of the Asanteman.

Despite the antagonism from British officials in Accra and London, from Liverpool, Glasgow, and coastal mercantile lobbies, and from out-lying dissident leaders in metropolitan Asante and within the confines of the imperial ambit who had allied themselves with these foreign interests, Agyeman Prempe, born and bred in a world of competing political ideas and heir to an immeasurably complicated political legacy, had succeeded with the counsel of his experienced Kumase advisers in restoring a large measure of political order to the Asante kingdom. Unlike previous administrations with powerful and far-reaching centralizing policies, Agyeman Prempe and his councillors had achieved their goals of the reassertion of royal power, the concentration of administrative authority in the central government, the modification of political relations between Kumase and the *amanto*, and the restoration of public confidence in the integrity of Kumase's leadership and its institutions, without resort to the principles and instrumentality of authoritarian violence. Under this new regime, a diversity of political affiliations and ideas was permitted. The new monarch, strikingly puissant for all his youth, never took on those attributes of arrogance, isolation, and political fantasy commonly associated with most nineteenth-century Asantehenes who habitually exercised authoritarian power. Tragically, the Prempean years—years of hope, rejuvenation, and revitalization in Asante political culture—were all too short. Before the policies of the young Asantehene could reach fruition, British imperial designs augured the end of two hunderd and fifty years of Asante sovereignty.

8

YEARS OF MISCALCULATION, 1894-1900

We were honest with the whites. They lied. Nana Prempe sacrificed himself for the nation.—Kwabena Baako

FORWARD POLICY

The Gold Coast administration's "forward policy," implemented in the years 1893 and 1894, signaled its official abandonment of support for the restoration of effective central government in Kumase. British officials in the Colony were convinced that Asante must be annexed in order to open and preserve the northern hinterlands to British trade and advocated a firm policy of territorial expansion which would extend British control, by force if necessary, to the Asanteman. This new policy consisted of interrelated military, diplomatic, and propaganda initiatives which reflected a remarkable switch in British attitudes and presaged the end of Asante's political sovereignty. Ultimately, the "forward policy" received full Colonial Office support in mid-1895 and led to direct British military intervention in metropolitan Asante and the arrest and deportation of Agyeman Prempe and the main members of the political elite of the capital. Contrary to British expectations, however, the Prempean administration continued to carry on the affairs of government in the Asantehene's absence in defiance of British attempts to establish their own authority in Kumase and the outlying districts.

On the military level, the Gold Coast administration took measures to encircle Kumase, blockade the roads leading to the capital, and station detachments of British and Hausa soldiers in and around the metropolitan region. Thus, during the first half of 1894, the British increased the expeditionary force in Atebubu and the garrison at Praso, and sent troops to Bompata (forty miles east of Kumase), Patriansa, Abetifi (the main Kwawu town), Amantin (thirty miles from Atebubu on the road to

Kumase), and other towns in Asante Akyem and Sehwi situated in close proximity to the Asante capital.[1] That same year several influential military commanders such as Colonel Francis Scott and Captain J. I. Lang joined the missionaries Ramseyer and Perregaux and other Basel personnel working in Kwawu and Akyem in calling for the annexation of Asante. Lang, for example, argued on economic grounds for the military occupation of the metropolitan region:

> The early acquisition of Ashanti is of paramount importance to this Colony; the central position occupied by her enables the King to exercise much control over the trade to the coast. The country would settle down, traders would enter it in confidence, and the opening of a direct road through Kumasi to Kuntampo would afford an easy means of reaching the coast from the interior.[2]

The Gold Coast administration increasingly monitored the supply of war materials entering Asante from the Colony at Praso, and in mid-1893, prohibited the sale of arms, ammunition, and lead to Prempe's envoys in the Colony districts of Cape Coast, Elmina, Chama, Saltpond, and Anomabo. Although the Asante government continued to obtain limited supplies from Winneba, Accra, and the French port at Assini, it was clear that the British were prepared to work in concert with the French and Germans to embargo all war materials to Asante. The British agent, G. E. Ferguson, in late 1893 reported that the Asante army in Nkoransa suffered from acute ammunition shortages, while Acting Governor Hodgson in February 1894 observed that the Asantehene "is without the means of providing himself with sufficient munitions of war."[3] The armaments blockade, coupled with the expansion and improvement of the telegraph system and the modernization of the road network in the Colony (which besides aiding the growth of local trade also accelerated British intelligence operations), helped to establish a suitable military position if an invasion of the metropolitan region was warranted.[4]

On the diplomatic front, Ferguson, Lang, and other agents from Accra entered into a series of additional treaties of friendship and trade with secessionist leaders in the northeastern provinces as well as with pro-British (or "anti-Kumase") politicians in towns such as Agogo (twenty-three miles north of Bompata in Asante Akyem) and in Sehwi and Ahafo. Agreements were signed with Nkoransa, Abease, Mo, Amantin, Boase, Buem, Ofumai, Nkra, Wankyi, and Nsoko in February 1894.[5] The British thereafter claimed that these districts were independent of Asante control and were considered to be legally within the Protectorate (although in previous years Accra had specified that residence south of the Pra River was an essential criterion for Protectorate status). A crucial aspect of this treaty-making diplomacy, frequently noted by present-day informants and contemporary reports alike, was the monetary gifts to pro-British politicians, a practice not dissimilar from the Asante government's own actions in the post-1874 era.

> I remember as a small boy that the whites gave money out freely to people. The chiefs, of course, got most of this money. One day some whites arrived in my town. I was in Ahafo. My uncle was hunting and tapping rubber there. I saw great excitement. The small boys were running in the streets. The women stopped pounding the fufu for the evening meal. The whites and the chief of this town sat down together. One Kwame was the interpreter. The whites opened a chest with a big golden lock. They took out many, many silver coins. The whites told the chief he could buy things on the coast with this money. The chief at first did not understand. He was used to gold dust for buying things here in Asante. I saw the whites take out a piece of paper. This Kwame told the chief the message on the paper. The chief did not know how to answer. He waited. The silver coins made noise. The chief slowly told Kwame he would look at the paper. This chief was angry with Nana Asantehene. He knew the whites would help him to rebel. He liked the silver coins. I saw this happen many times in the towns of Ahafo. I was a small boy. I did not know what it all meant.[6]

Throughout late 1893 and 1894, officials from Kumase challenged the validity of most of these compacts and attempted to persuade (mostly with economic arguments) anti-Kumase politicians in the northeast and in Agogo, Ahafo, and Sehwi to rejoin the national polity. During Prempe's reign Sehwi Wiawso, Sehwi Bekwae, and Bunusa fell under the administrative responsibility of the Bantamahene of Kumase who shared a common boundary with the French colony in the Ivory Coast at the Bia River.[7] Accra repeatedly warned that further interference from Kumase would justify armed action against its officials. By contrast, Prempe's regime never threatened military action when Ferguson intervened in the internal politics of Salaga, Bole, Banda, and Krakye, prevented the formation of the northwestern alliance, and inhibited the activities of Kumase envoys in the northern hinterlands.[8] Prempe's government had little objection to local leaders in Sehwi, Asante Akyem, and Ahafo signing treaties of trade and friendship with the British. But authorities in Kumase were never certain whether such treaties specified protection or whether they were confined to commercial relations. Asante informants who witnessed treaty discussions in Sefwhi and Ahafo maintained that many of the so-called treaties of protection which Ferguson and other

179

British agents brought back to the coast had never been approved or signed by the local officials whose signatures appeared on the document.[9] Kumase agents claimed that some pacts were invalid because oath-swearing ceremonies had not taken place. And the Asante government always believed that a treaty made by local politicians was a temporary, reversible measure.[10]

The administration in Accra in the years 1893–95 also launched an intensive propaganda campaign in the Colony designed to discredit Prempe's legitimacy and to undermine the reconstituted power and authority of the central government. Unlike official statements emanating from the Colony in the late 1880s, this invective had the sanction of a section of Colonial Office personnel primarily because of increasing pressure from London, Manchester, Glasgow, and Liverpool mercantile groups who had close business connections with the Cape Coast Chamber of Commerce and other coastal trading interests.[11] Yet several of the issues raised by officials in Accra were clearly contrived. The British, for instance, argued that the nkwankwaa-led anticonscription movement in Asante during the second half of 1893 reflected the weakness of Prempe's regime and stressed that the Asantehene and his councillors desired peace only because they were unable to resolve the political and diplomatic problems that had emerged in the aftermath of the turbulent election of 1887–88. They also maintained that Prempe had publicly promised to rule in accordance with "the advice and wishes of the Gold Coast Government," and that Kumase still owed a balance of 49,000 ounces of gold which the Asante government had agreed to pay by the treaty of 1874, a sum that the Mensa Bonsu administration in the late 1870s had long renegotiated and paid.[12]

A major feature of the propaganda promulgated by the British at this time was the issue of "human sacrifice." Both the British and the missionaries had traditionally invoked this concept to denote all forms of political executions and killings, whether legitimate or illegitimate. The periodic mass public executions that the British had observed in Asante in the 1870s and 1880s no longer took place under Agyeman Prempe. The Asantehene personally disdained instruments of political repression. Asante citizens, for example, were not killed for looking at the Asantehene. Politicians and leaders were not eliminated for holding differing political views, as had been the case in the 1880s. Prempe's administration had virtually dismantled the apparatus of state terror in response to the pressure of reforming councillors in his government and to the widespread horror that these killings had evoked among Asante citizens in the 1880s.[13] Thus, the instrument of terror had already been voluntarily reduced at the time when the British were slandering the Prempean administration with accusations of the practice of rampant and uncontrolled human sacrifice. Prempe's government, however, had not abolished capital punishment as a sanctioned legal measure for major offenses against the state, for murder, or for violations of the nation's religious codes. But the number of people executed for committing these offenses had been greatly reduced.[14] Prempe, who seems personally to have been opposed to all capital punishment, received considerable respect from Asante citizens for his actions. "King Kwaku Dua III," it was reported, "abhors human sacrifice as much as any one in his position can do."[15] An adviser to the higher echelons of government offered this account of the offenses which resulted in the death penalty under the Asantehene Prempe:

> Capital punishment in Asante meant beheading. The victims were convicted criminals. If a man interfered with a chief's wives and was found guilty of the offense, he would surely be beheaded. Those people who spied on the Asantes or interfered with custom, when found guilty at a trial, were executed also. No execution took place without a trial in which a person was found guilty. Even disloyal Asantes were tried at the Asantehene's court. The lucky ones were fined. But if the fine was not paid, execution would result. As a general rule, no executions took place without a trial to determine guilt. Murderers were prosecuted. Violations of a taboo or things forbidden meant death for those who were captured. Public executions were sanctioned by the state and did take place. But public executions were very scarce when Nana Agyeman Prempe was on the Golden Stool.[16]

An *ahenkwaa* who witnessed several legal executions in the early 1890s noted:

> There were many *asomfo* [servants] in the palace. The Asantehene had about thirty wives. The Asantehene could not sleep often with all his wives. If any woman induced an *asomfo* to sleep with her and she became pregnant, the Asantehene questioned his wife. . . . The man was caught and killed. The Asantehene's wife was not punished immediately. She first gave birth to the child. Then the Asantes killed her. The newborn baby was given to the shrine called *asenampɔn* in Kumase. This, like Tano, is one of the many Asante shrines. An *owundini* [murderer] was also executed in the open here in Kumase for all people to see. The place for executions was near the present Central Post Office. The *owundini* first had a trial at the Asantehene's palace. Before Prempe was taken away, the Asantehene's palace was located at the present Glamour area. Also if anybody insulted the Asantehene, he was killed after a trial. These

181

were Asante laws. Asantes killed. But not without a cause. Asantes made sure the offender deserved the death penalty.[17]

The British either misunderstood or purposely disregarded the legitimate nature of the executions carried out at Prempe's court, and continued to manipulate the issue of "human sacrifice" to justify their forward policy in Asante.

Other issues publicized at this time, while not explicitly contradicting the record nor directly challenging the statements of Asante diplomats nor the actions of officials in Kumase, were either oversimplifications of exceedingly complex events or were designed to legitimize the extension of British imperial power into the metropolitan region. To convince the Colonial Office to intervene in Asante, the British governor, for example, maintained that the Bekwaehene was "found anxious to have British protection," the Dwabenhene Yaw Sapon desired to enter into the Protectorate, and all the outlying (or subordinate) towns had deserted the Asantehene.[18] Furthermore, the British envoy, Hendrick Vroom, argued that "the Kings of Ashanti have always been false, as well as treacherous, in all their dealings with this Government," and Hodgson wrote that the Mamponhene and Kokofuhene continued to regard Yaw Atweneboanna as the rightful heir to the Golden Stool.[19] Thus Governor Griffith in October 1894 summed up Accra's position vis-à-vis the Asante government:

> I think due notice of the change of attitude of the Government ought without delay to be given to the King of Ashanti. For 20 years we have striven loyally and earnestly to prop up Ashanti, but all to no purpose. Ashanti is now practically in a state of disintegration, and to any tribe who seeks it we should grant our protection as a preliminary course of procedure; but I am most strongly of the opinion that the wisest, safest, most prudent and inexpensive course of action will be to pursue a resolute policy, and if the sections of Ashanti which are still independent of the Gold Coast decline to accept its rule they should be compelled to do so.[20]

By contrast, Ramseyer pressed for annexation for precisely the opposite reason, that is, the new cohesion of central authority and the resiliency of Asante power in the early 1890s:

> . . . it has come to what we were afraid of. The power of the King, instead of having been abated, has, on the contrary, in the last months, so increased, that those provinces which were imploring the English Government to be taken in the Protectorate, receiving no answer and seeing that their hope has been frustrated, are returning to serve Coomase. More than that, for even those provinces which are already under English jurisdic-

182

tion are now so wavering, for fear of increasing Ashantee power, that if occasion would allow it, they would not wait long before submitting to the King of Coomassee, and accept his offers by which he is constantly trying to decoy them.[21]

It is ironic that diametrically opposed views of the state of the Asante polity should have led Griffith and Ramseyer to the same conclusion.

THE ASANTEMANHYIAMU OF JUNE 1894

As Ramseyer had indicated, the Prempean administration had succeeded by 1894 in achieving a substantial degree of national reconciliation and in winning considerable support for its policies to reintegrate the Asanteman despite the significant escalation of anti-Asante invective from the British. After a decade of intense political conflict, coups, bloodshed, and brief civil war, Asante for the first time since 1883 possessed a strong central authority with the aura of legitimacy and with a consensus to govern. In early May, therefore, preparations were conducted for the formal installation of Prempe upon the Golden Stool the following month. The Asantemanhyiamu, attended by "district Kings, Chiefs, and principal men of Ashanti" with the exception of the Kokofuhene, was convened and met in session on 4 June. Prempe, or Kwaku Dua III, at the age of twenty was enstooled on Adae Monday, 11 June; thus his regime became the fully legitimate government of Asante.[22]

Following the ceremonies the Asantemanhyiamu remained in session for a full two weeks, until 24 June, to consider a second proposal, which had been conveyed to the council in Kumase by Hendrick Vroom in mid March, for a treaty of protection and the establishment of a resident in Kumase. Discussion of the participants in the Asantemanhyiamu focused on the future course of Asante diplomacy vis-à-vis the Gold Coast administration.

During the opening sessions, the Nsumankwaahene Kwasi Domfe and the Atwemahene Antwi Agyei strongly argued for military preparedness and even mobilization to force the British to withdraw their constabulary from Atebubu, Praso, and the towns of Asante Akyem and Kwawu.[23] The British military presence on the borders of the metropolitan region was totally unacceptable. Although a few Kumase officeholders supported a show of force, most Kumase and outlying district heads opposed the idea. Since its inception in 1888, the Prempean administration had been steadfastly committed to maintain peace principles in the field of foreign affairs, and the government's pacific intentions were repeatedly manifested in the series of diplomatic talks with Gold Coast administrators in the late 1880s and early 1890s. The majority of politicians in

Kumase and the districts—aware of Britain's relatively enormous military means for conquest and the forward policy implemented by functionaries in Accra after 1893—believed that mobilization would not achieve national diplomatic goals nor advance the reconstitution of central authority and the return to political order. More probably, it would result in years of warfare and the subsequent annexation and incorporation of the Asanteman within the Colony. Furthermore, armed confrontation or even potential conflict with the British was entirely contrary to the government's need for cooperation in resolving the complicated refugee, land, and economic difficulties arising in areas within the administrative jurisdiction of the Colony. Until late in 1895, when several Kumase officeholders first agitated for mobilization and unsuccessfully attempted to oust the peace advocates and depose (and perhaps murder) the Asantehene,[24] this ideological position was widely accepted and upheld by councillors with divergent political orientations, notably such politicians as the Bantamahene Amankwatia Kwame, the Asafohene Asafo Boakye, the Asantehemaa Yaa Akyaa, and the Akyebiakyerehene Kwasi Gyambibi, who were distrustful of British intentions and motives, and the more pro-British politicians such as John Owusu Ansa, the Kyidomhene Kwame Boaten, and the Bekwaehene Yaw Boakye. Thus the Prempean administration's foreign policy stance and the apparent cordiality between Kumase and Accra (only one brief war scare occurred in 1891) militated against the extremists' concern for preparedness against the British.

Certainly, Kumase's misapprehension of the scope of British imperial ambition in Asante and its reliance on peace initiatives and the sanctity of the pledged word contributed to the decision not to mobilize. Other political and practical military considerations reinforced reluctance in Kumase to take up arms against the British. The bitter Nkoransa campaigns of 1893 revived the popular anticonscription and antiwar movements of the early 1870s. It joined with protest against the government's tax measures of April and May 1894, to cause alarm among authorities in the capital. The Basel missionary Haasis reported from Abetifi in September 1893 that many *nkwankwaa*, seeking to avoid involvement in the Nkoransa war, fled from the metropolitan region into the Colony.[25] Colonel Scott's similar account of late 1893 elated British intelligence agents in Kwawu and Asante Akyem:

> My latest information from Kumasi, procured on excellent authority, is to the effect that the dissatisfaction in the town is considerable. The young-men state openly that, were the forces of the Government to advance tomorrow on Kumasi, they would refuse to fire a shot, indeed would gladly welcome us, and refer us to their Chiefs who have caused them so much trouble lately

by continual fighting, of which they themselves are heartily tired. There is undoubtedly much truth in the above report.[26]

In October 1895 Ramseyer informed the governor that his sources over the past year were confident that the "young men of the Ashanti tribes do not want to fight," while in early 1896 the British governor noted that "it is probable that there is widespread dissatisfaction with the present regime, and that there is little disposition among the people to take up arms for the favourites and adherents who have surrounded and influenced Prempeh."[27]

The depth of antiwar feeling among Asante commoners and *asikafo*, the split between the old and young over the inherent purpose and value of military exercises, and the distinct possibility that the government would be unable to raise sufficient manpower to wage war made even the most militant of the Asantehene's councillors hesitate to commit the nation to a trial of arms. Despite rising public confidence for the Prempean administration's policies, officials in Kumase were keenly aware that there were limits to the Asantehene's domestic success. Thus, the Asafohene Asafo Boakye, the Adumhene Asamoa Kwame, and other influential politicians with long careers of public service were wary of any signs of widespread social unrest. They undoubtedly feared popular uprisings of the sort experienced during the reigns of the Asantehenes Kofi Kakari and Mensa Bonsu. Accordingly, authorities of all political persuasions in the capital approached the entire military question gingerly.

Vivid memories of the last war against the British were still present in the councillors' minds. In 1873–74 several of the Asantehene's advisers had fought against Sir Garnet Wolseley's regiments, and others had worked in the Asante commissariat in the metropolitan region and the Colony.[28] The painful truth of British superiority in weapons was again brought home with demonstrations of the awesome efficiency of the Maxim gun and British artillery during expeditions of the late 1880s and early 1890s in the Colony and the northeast. Furthermore, the counsel and expert opinion of Abu Bakr, Kramo Serekye, and other Asante Nkramo leaders in Kumase whose subjects had witnessed or received information via their network of Dyula contacts attested to the dreaded formidability of European weapons. The Asante Nkramo—set aside to say prayers for the Asantehene—urged Prempe not to prepare for war.[29]

Shortages of war materials, a consequence of the British embargo enacted with French cooperation in early 1894,[30] and the obsolescence of Asante weaponry, particularly the Ananta, Akuapem, and Dane guns, also undercut the possibility of success for any major or long-term war effort. Kwadwo Donko, who served as an *ahenkwaa* to the Gyaasewahene of

185

Kumase in 1894, maintained that the metropolitan Asante villages and towns had

> little gunpowder or guns. The Asantes made their own gunpowder with "brimstone and bullets." The bullets were made from the bark of trees. The bark was beaten to make it soft and then mixed with brimstone. Then the bullets were laid to dry in the sun after they had been shaped. The metal was brought from the coast lands. It was the size of a small stone. The bullet with the powder was put in the barrel of the Atwereebotuo gun. The click was pulled back, and the gun put to the chest. The Asantes tied the bullets around their waist and reloaded after every shot. . . . Otherwise, the Asantes had no supplies to fight. The Asantes also used the Ananta gun. The barrel of the Ananta gun is tall. It was used to hunt elephants. The Atwereebotuo [flint] gun was used for hunting deers, antelopes, grasscutters, and many other animals. It has a very small barrel. The Akuapem gun [or *etuopa*] varies. There are small and big ones. All were used for fighting. The barrel of the small Akuapem gun was around two inches. The length of the barrel of the large Akuapem gun was about six feet. When there was no war, the Asantes sent the Akuapem guns to the north for hunting.[31]

A number of wealthy rubber and gold *asikafo* lobbied, as they had in 1891, for British protection and objected to all military preparations.[32] Because of their vested interest in the maintenance of cordial relations with the British and the preservation of an uninterrupted flow of trade to the coastal ports, these Asante entrepreneurs believed that hostilities would undermine their gains made over the past decade by depriving them of their income and of their newly achieved middle-class status. Governor William Maxwell observed in June 1895 that it could "be safely assumed that there will be at Kumasi a fairly strong party who will be unwilling (when it is realized that we are in earnest) to enter upon a struggle in which all that they have of value is risked, and which can only end disastrously for the Ashanti cause."[33]

Many of these *nouveaux riches* had acculturated to Western clothing, tastes, and styles. Thus the entrepreneur-diplomats John and Albert Owusu Ansa and other members of the new Asante commercial elite, such as the most prominent rubber *asikafo* in Bekwae, Yaa Kode, Adu Gyamfi, and Kofi Fofie, and in Kokofu, Kwaku Ateme, Kwame Aboaa, and Kwabena Boahene, had a cultural and emotional stake in British protection and admired Western political and constitutional models.[34] This vocal, vital interest group profoundly influenced the Prempean administration's decision to refrain from any displays of force or hostilities with the British.

The Asantemanhyiamu's deliberations over military preparations concluded with new proposals for peace, good trade, and open roads from Asante to the Colony. During the ensuing days the Asantehene, his councillors, and the outlying district *ahene* considered the state of the country and how it could "regain its past glory and renown."[35] Two noteworthy decisions came out of the meetings. First, the government levied a special tax of .4 peredwans per head of household to pay the expenses of repatriating the Kokofuhene Osei Asibe, the Adansehene Kwaku Nkansa, and their subjects, and, subsequently, required each district in the metropolitan region to contribute an additional 40 peredwans (or £320) to underwrite their return to Asante. Of this money, 1,000 peredwans were offered to the Gold Coast administration for its assistance in the repatriation proceedings. The Asantehene insisted that the *amanhene* also contribute to this expense from their district's treasuries. The Sanaa, or Treasury, would not be responsible for the entire payment.[36]

Discussion in the Asantemanhyiamu over the proposed British treaty of protection and its residency clause emerged as the main subject of debate. The notion of a British resident (or consul) stationed in Kumase had been considered by Asante governments throughout the nineteenth century and had continually met with disfavor in Kumase political circles. In 1891, Governor Griffith's proposal had been handily turned down. But the political climate in Kumase had substantially changed when Hendrick Vroom presented the newest British offer. Although a number of the Asantehene's more traditional councillors continued to oppose the establishment of a permanent British agency in the capital, most politicians by 1894 were inclined to support the residency clause for its obvious diplomatic and political advantages.

A resident would serve the Asante government as a legal, political, and diplomatic intermediary to facilitate communication between Kumase and the Gold Coast administration. He might assist in future relations with all European powers, which would preclude misunderstandings of the type so often experienced in the past, and he could also advise authorities in the capital in their dealings with localist leaders in the outlying regions. Most prosperous rubber and gold *asikafo* backed the proposal for the British resident because he might restrict the Prempe regime's ability to supervise and control the steady infusion of European capital and entrepreneurs into the gold-mining areas of Bekwae, Danyase, and Adanse and because he might exert British influence to limit the state's control over the economy of the Asanteman.[37] Nevertheless, despite the prevailing trend to accept the residency clause, politicians of differing political views were convinced that a delegation to London could negotiate a compromise treaty which would guarantee the integrity of the central government and safeguard the operations and supremacy of Asante courts and social institutions.[38] Thus, most Asante politicians by 1894 no longer objected to the appointment of a British resident in Kumase provided the Asante government received concrete assurances that the consul would have restricted and clearly defined advisory functions.

Authorities in Kumase believed that the terms of the resident's appointment would be clarified in face-to-face negotiations with functionaries in the Colonial Office. The diplomatic talks in London would also consider British proposals for the manumission of slaves in the metropolitan region. Besides rejecting the British offer of protectorate status, the Asantemanhyiamu's members overwhelmingly opposed the abolition of slavery. Led by the Asantehemaa Yaa Akyaa and the Asafohene Asafo Boakye, the Asantehene's more traditional councillors insisted that the imperial government agree to uphold the system of domestic slavery and consequently refrain from interfering with this integral aspect of Asante social structure and the national plantation economy. Even reform-minded councillors such as the Bekwaehene Yaw Boakye and John Owusu Ansa stressed the profound importance attached to the slavery issue.[39] Along with money, wives, and houses, slaves constituted primary indices of wealth and mobility, and the owners achieved status in the late nineteenth-century Asante political establishment according to their possessions. The Prempean administration, seemingly assured by Governor Griffith that the consul would not intervene in judicial matters nor tamper with domestic slavery, was prepared to concede the residency issue and to negotiate an alternate treaty to guarantee Asante's political sovereignty and the integrity of the kingdom's boundaries. And British officials in London were inclined to provide assurances of this sort, particularly on the slavery question. The Colonial Office functionary A. W. L. Hemming, a leading proponent of Accra's forward policy, in his minutes of 22 October 1895 remarked:

> It would be a mistake to frighten the King of Kumasi and the Ashantis generally on the question of slavery. We cannot sweep away their customs and institutions all at once. Domestic slavery should not be troubled at present. We can talk of these things when definite treaty or negotiations take place. This is assuming we have peace. If we have war, we can impose any terms we like on Kumasi. Then we might probably apply laws of protection and proclaim the pardon of all slaves.[40]

Hemming demonstrated in a subsequent minute of 26 October 1895 his awareness of the Asante *asikafo's* reaction to legislation to free their slaves.

The question of slavery concerns not only Kumasi. Our quarrel is with Kumasi only, but slavery concerns all the Ashanti kings and provinces. If we make it known that we have entered a crusade against slavery, we will not have any allies and they might all combine against us. So we should move very warily and carefully in this matter. To abolish domestic slavery would mean a social revolution of the greatest character. All in Ashanti who have anything to lose would gravely resist this act.[41]

Clearly, the decision to receive a resident was both logical and pragmatic. Participants in the Asantemanhyiamu knew that local newspapers, chambers of commerce, missionaries, and coastal lobbies were pressing for direct action against Prempe's government. Failure to accept the resident might result in annexation and the status of a colony with little or no specific provisions for the preservation of central authority and the maintenance of revered institutions. Confident that a delegation to England would insure the independence of the Asante Nation, the Asantemanhyiamu implemented still other tax measures to finance an Asante embassy to London (and possibly also to Paris and The Hague) and a delegation to the coast consisting of some three to five hundred envoys with their retainers.[42] After the deliberations concluded, the Asantehene wrote to Governor Griffith on 28 June about the aspirations of his government.

> I pray and beseech my elders, as well as my gods, and the spirits of my ancestors, to assist me, to give me true wisdom and love, to rule and govern my nation, and I beseech you, my good friend, to pray and ask blessings from your God to give me long life and prosperous and peaceful reign, and that my friendship with Her Majesty's Government may be more firm and more closer than hitherto had been done, that bye-gones will be bye-gones, that the Ashanti nation will awake herself as out of sleep, that the hostilities will go away from her, that the evils which the constant wars brought upon her, like destroying our jewels, may die everlastingly from her, and that I shall endeavor to promote peace and tranquility and good order in my Kingdom, and to restore its trade, and the happiness and safety of my people generally, by making it to the advantage of the refugees to return, inhabit, and cultivate their respective countries, and thus raise my Kingdom of Ashanti to a prosperous, substantial, and steady position as a great farming and trading community such as it has never occupied hitherto, and that the trade between your Protectorate and my Kingdom of Ashanti may increase daily to the benefit of all interested in it.[43]

The contents of the Asantehene's letter was also conveyed in early

189

May 1895 to the Colonial Office by the Asante embassy to the Court of St. James. The delegation was headed by the well-educated, articulate forty-three-year-old John Owusu Ansa, described by British sources as a "most skillful, diplomatic, and capable agent," who had been instrumental in securing the interest of European firms in the development of Asante industry. Like his father, Owusu Ansa, who had been a senior political and economic adviser to the Mensa Bonsu government in the 1870s, John Owusu Ansa was the catalyst behind the Asante government's efforts to solicit the participation of European enterprises in the development of Asante. The embassy also included Albert Owusu Ansa, another son of the older Owusu Ansa, who was a partner in the prosperous export firm of Johnson and Ansa in Axim. The experienced Kumase diplomats Kwaku Fokuo, Yaw Boaten, Kwaku Nkruma, Kwadwo Tufuo, the sword-bearer Akyampon Dabban, and the herald Bandar rounded out the delegation.[44]

The Asante emissaries intended to express their government's willingness to receive a British resident in Kumase and hoped to circumvent officials in Accra, whom Kumase increasingly regarded with distrust and suspicion, in beginning negotiations for a treaty which would recognize Asante's political sovereignty. In the event an agreement could not be consummated in London, the ambassadors were instructed to seek diplomatic recognition from Paris and The Hague.[45] Although the ambassadors received journalistic and legal assistance and enlisted the help of sympathetic members of Parliament, Owusu Ansa's repeated efforts over six months to meet with British officials were completely rejected. Rumors even circulated that he was threatened with deportation for "interfering in Ashantian politics." The brusque repudiation of the Asante embassy was a result of mounting British opposition to Asante's continuing independence.[46] There could be no agreement over the terms of Asante's political sovereignty. In this age of high imperialism, the Colonial Office, under the new leadership of the expansionistic ex-businessman, the new Colonial Secretary, Joseph Chamberlain, had finally adopted a consistent policy, lacking for twenty years, towards Asante. The British intended to open the Asanteman to their commerce and administration and would reduce the Asantehene's power and circumscribe his territory. To this John Owusu Ansa and the Asante envoys could never agree. In September 1895 the ambassadors sorrowfully learned that the British government was planning the military take-over of the Asante kingdom.[47]

The failure of John Owusu Ansa's mission to the Colonial Office also stifled the Prempean administration's innovative economic program for enlisting European capital and skills to promote more rapid economic development in the metropolitan region. Following the precedent established by Mensa Bonsu's government in the late 1870s, Prempe and his councillors since 1892 had made a major effort to solicit British financial and managerial assistance in Asante railroad and industrial expansion. In April 1892, for example, the Asantehene had agreed to grant a charter for gold mining and timber concessions to the British entrepreneur Dr. J. W. Herivel. Herivel's proposed company would assume responsibility for overseas marketing arrangements and would raise the capital for the venture. Intense British opposition to the scheme forced Herivel in 1894 to abandon his plans. He did not receive Parliament's approval for the charter.[48] The proposed Reckless Concession of 1895, which John Owusu Ansa negotiated with the London businessman George Reckless, who was backed by the Liverpool firm of Radcliffe and Durant, was even more ambitious. It authorized the creation of a British chartered company to manage for the Asante government the development of public works, factories, schools, and a national printing press. Prempe's government was to have received one-quarter of the net profits of the company. Yet Owusu Ansa's talks with British businessmen largely depended upon the success of his negotiations with officials in the Colonial Office.[49] The British government, however, had no intention of permitting the Prempean administration to modernize Asante economic life and instead were committed to their own control of the Asanteman's economic development.

While Asante statesmen deliberated in Kumase and ambassadors and entrepreneurs attempted to negotiate in London, Lord Salisbury's new Unionist government had decided to take control of Asante for reasons relating to Britain's larger designs in West Africa. Joseph Chamberlain, appointed in June 1895, pressed the prime minister for a new policy of building and consolidating a colonial empire and of greater state responsibility to promote the rapid development of new markets for private enterprise and British industry.[50] A zealous advocate of the extension of imperial authority, the colonial secretary heartily agreed with officials in the Gold Coast Colony who feared that their stronghold in West Africa was jeopardized by the Asante government's increasing diplomatic, political, and economic contacts with other European and African powers. The Gold Coast administration's growing anxiety had been heightened by the revival of Asante influence in Salaga, Bole, and the northern hinterlands and by the activities of and treaties made by German political agents in the "neutral zone," Yendi, Krakye, the trans-Volta provinces, and Togoland. New French military operations in the northwest, particularly evident following the Gyamanhene Agyeman's acceptance of French protection on 12 July 1893, and the new supplies of war materials (e.g., Snider rifles and ammunition) obtained by Asante traders from French merchants in the Ivory Coast in 1894–95 increased the sense of urgency in the Colony to reduce the threat from Asante.[51] The prospect that Prempe's government might enter into an argeement with France, after the French diplomatic mission to Kumase in early 1895, lent support to the British justification for military intervention.[52]

Most significant for British policy-makers was the possibility that the Asantehene and Almami Samori would continue the negotiations started in 1895 and would develop, as British contemporary reports (and my informants) noted, a full-scale military alliance or at the very least a program of mutual cooperation.[53] In that year Samori's soldiers, having occupied Kong and Bonduku, established garrisons in the northwestern towns of Banda, Gbuipe, Bole, and Mengye and forced the Gyamanhene Agyeman into exile on the grounds that he had refused to allow Samori's troops to open a trade route through his territory.[54] From these towns Samori's armies ranged in all directions to establish the political and economic sinews of a new state. His commanders, seeking to control the urban centers and thus the trade routes of the northwest, penetrated Sikasso, Gonja, the Zabarima, the Lobi, and Bobo-Diolasso. And his lieutenants everywhere sought political alliances, resources of guns, horses, and captives for the remarkable Samorian military and state organization.

According to one eyewitness, who is the father of the present Asantehene Opoku Ware II and who as a young boy in the Asantehene's palace saw the meeting in Kumase in 1895, Samori exchanged several messages with Prempe and also dispatched a delegation consisting of three men and two women. When the envoys entered the capital the women held two guns as a symbol of peace.

> Prempe and Samono [i.e., Samori] were friends for a long time. The Asantes went to the north to buy slaves from Samono for a piece of white calico. Samono never came to Kumase. The Asantes went north. He wanted to save Prempe, but the Asantehene asked him not to come to Asante. Samono was not afraid of anything in the world. Samono wanted to help the Asantes against all white men. Prempe sent messages to Samono to tell him not to come to fight here. Prempe was taken away before the messengers returned to Kumase.[55]

Samori's emissaries remained in Kumase for nearly a week. The Asantehene, other observers reported, responded by sending an embassy of three hundred envoys and retainers with a gift of one hundred ounces of gold for Samori. Upon arriving in Bonduku in late October 1895, the Kumase emissaries expressed Prempe's desire for Samori's military assistance against Nkoransa in particular and the north in general. Yet another account, however, indicated that the council in Kumase considered Samori's request of one thousand ounces of gold to finance an attack on Nkoransa too costly. Apparently Samori was not overly eager to enter into a military alliance with Prempe's government. During the last two years he had moved four hundred miles east with his armies and a large section of the local population in response to relentless French military pressure from their Niger posts. From his new capital at Dabakala, south of Kong, the Almami needed time to replenish his stock of arms and horses. Conflict with the British, with whom he hitherto had excellent diplomatic relations, was to be avoided at all costs. Samori feared that the government of the Gold Coast would close the coastal roads to his envoys and, perhaps, might join the French in an effort to smash his forces in the northern Ivory Coast. And Samori's troubles with rebellious local authorities in Kong and the Watara and Tarawiri states were already evident by early 1895. He apparently doubted that the Asante government, which was already low on war materials, could supply him with supplies for warfare in the northwest.[56] Nevertheless, intermittent contact between the Almami and officials in Kumase continued in the ensuing two years, and the prospect of an alliance repeatedly alarmed administrators in the Gold Coast Colony.[57]

The Asante government's negotiations with Samori and the French in 1895 and the reconstituted power of the central authority in the 1890s impelled the British to expedite their measures to incorporate Asante within the imperial ambit. Acting on direct orders from Chamberlain, Governor William Maxwell, who had taken over from Griffith in May, dispatched Hendrick Vroom and Captain Donald Stewart to Kumase in September 1895 with an ultimatum constituting the third and final offer of protection and requiring compliance by the thirty-first of October. Authorities in Accra, realizing that Kumase had already accepted their maximum demands and that the embassy to London had failed to negotiate a compromise treaty, repeatedly increased their political and financial demands. Maxwell, aware that the imperial government had decided to send an expedition to Asante, informed the Asantehene that his administration had violated the Treaty of Fomena "by the encouragement and practice of human sacrifice, by placing hindrances in the way of trade and by failing to carry out the guarantee contained in Article 7 of the said treaty with regard to the construction and maintenance of a road from Kumasi to the Prah river."[58] In still a further contradiction of the evidence, the new British governor accused Prempe of aggression, of obstructing the development of commerce and communication between the Colony and the metropolitan region, and of refusal to pay the indemnity stipulated in the agreement of 1874. Vroom and Stewart were instructed to gather up-to-date intelligence on political and military affairs in the metropolitan region and to publicize the terms of the ultimatum and the impending offensive to centralist politicians in Mampon,

Nsuta, Agogo, Kumawu, Kwawu, Nkoransa, Sehwi, and even Gyaman who, it was stressed, were not "held responsible for the faults of Kumase, provided that they separate themselves from King Prempeh and place themselves under Her Majesty's protection."[59] Thus the mission's secondary design was to isolate Kumase and pressure district leaders into signing treaties with agents from the Gold Coast Colony and to make certain that the heads of the outlying districts did not begin mobilization to resist the invasion.

Maxwell and his advisers were aware that the Prempean administration's new centralizing policies, particularly evident following the Asantehene's formal installation in June 1894, and the Asantehene's growing reliance on the opinions of his centralist councillors had once again provoked resentment in several outlying areas. Strong pro-British sentiment had emerged among several hitherto committed (but vacillatory) district leaders who in 1893–94 had favored close political ties with the capital. The Bekwaehene Yaw Boakye's decision (influenced by gold and rubber *asikafo* in his *oman*) to grant a mining concession to the European entrepreneurs Smith and Cade, for example, was forcefully disputed by the central government in 1895.[60] The political and financial pressure exerted by Kumase's agents had again antagonized the Dwabenhene Yaw Sapon, the refugee Adansehene Kwaku Nkansa, and the heads of several Asante Akyem towns. Various localist leaders on the borders of the metropolitan region, openly defying the authority of the central government, indicated to the British that they would sign separate treaties of protection.[61] Thus by cooperating with the British, they again strove to augment their power at the expense of the council in Kumase and to assert their local rights and privileges in the Asanteman. These sentiments mirrored the feelings of most rubber traders in the metropolitan region.

> I myself was a rubber trader for many years. I made much money through it. We traders collected rubber from Asante and carried it to the coast and sold it to the whites. But first we had to go through the middlemen such as Adusei, Yaw Foforo, and Sraha. They were from Saawua and ran to the coast after Prempe defeated Yaw Atweneboanna. They became rich from rubber and also because they exchanged gold for silver. They took a commission from this. They traded with the Asantes, the Gas, and the Fantes. . . . Most of the traders I talked with wanted the whites to come to Asante. The whites promised them offices here. They would not have to pay the Asantehene's taxes. They could trade without any restrictions. The whites told them they would have greater influence in the councils in

Kumase. That is why the rubber traders on the coast quietly waited for the whites to make their move.[62]

Authorities in Kumase "warmly received" the British envoys on Monday, 7 October, and held the first in a series of council meetings three days later. Preparations were made to convene the Asanteman-hyiamu in order to consider the ultimatum and evaluate John Owusu Ansa's report on the results of his trip to England. Ansa's arrival in the capital was delayed by administrators in the Gold Coast Colony who harassed him and charged him with forged credentials, intrigue, and deception.[63] Vroom and Stewart did not remain in Kumase to learn the outcome of the Asantemanhyiamu sessions in spite of Asafo Boakye's private and the Council of Kumase's official requests to attend the council deliberations.[64] They departed for Bekwae and the coast on 10 October. Vroom stayed briefly in Kaase on the outskirts of the capital. Informants recount that many Asantes perceived his mission to be a symbol of the provocativeness of the missionary and terror issues, and Vroom himself represented the anti-Kumase invective expounded by British officials and missionaries to justify the forward policy and the impending military maneuvers. Adu Gyamera, one of the *nhenkwaa* assigned to supply the emissaries with provisions and gifts, offered his version of the proceedings:

The governor of the Gold Coast sent Fromu [Vroom] and Ramseyer to Prempe. The two messengers told Prempe to allow education in Asante. When the messengers came to Kumase, Prempe called the Asante chiefs and their subjects to a meeting here in Kumase. The chiefs and people met. The two messengers spoke to the Asantehene through his *okyeame*, named Kwaku Fokuo. The messengers told the Asantehene and the chiefs that the Queen in England wanted the Asantes to accept education. The Queen felt that education would put a stop to the rampant human sacrifice. There was nothing to gain in killing people. For example, if a person said an Asante oath [*ntam*] without substance in what he said, he was killed after a trial. If the person said the truth, he would go free. But the two messengers did not believe that the Asantehene only killed a person after a trial before the chiefs. At the meeting the Asantehene spoke through Kwaku Fokuo. He told the two messengers to go back to the Queen and tell her that the Asantes were not prepared to accept education. Several Asante chiefs said that the British should put the schools "on your head." *Asantefo ka kyere abrofo se wommesi asore wo won mpampam.* This was an insult. The Asante knew it was impossible for the whites to build the schools on their heads! The Asantes at this meeting hooted [*huro no*] at the messengers. The messengers said they would not sleep in Kumase. They said they were not treated well. The two messengers slept at Kaase that night. Prempe sent *nhenkwaa* with gifts to the two at Kaase. I was one of the people sent by the Asantehene. I carried three fowls to the messengers at Kaase. The two saw the Asantehene's people and concluded that the Queen and the Asantehene were one. But the two messengers refused the gifts. They said that if the Queen and the Asantehene were one, then the Asantes should not have hooted when they came to Kumase. Later the two messengers decided to take certain things from the gifts. They said that they would take something back to show that they had been to see the Asantehene. The two messengers left. About forty days after the messengers left, the Asantes heard that the British troops were coming to fight the Asantes. The Asante traders who often visited the coast brought news that the British troops really meant to fight the Asantes. These traders added that the people on the Gold Coast who favored the British molested them when they traded in the coast lands. They did this because they knew the British were coming to Kumase.[65]

Another eyewitness, Oheneba Kwadwo Afodo—who was in his twenties at the time the ultimatum was delivered—further discussed the significance of Vroom's mission but, contrary to most oral and written accounts, maintained that the Asantehene did not agree to minimize the application of terror:

Prempe went overseas because of the human sacrifice in Asante. Fromu [Vroom] came from Edena [Elmina]. Oben, an *okyeame*, was the nephew of Fromu. Fromu sent Oben to Prempe. Oben told Prempe to stop the killings. Oben told Prempe to stop cutting off noses, ears, and lips. Fromu and Oben came again to see Prempe on this issue. They told Prempe that they had warned Kakari about this. Kakari did not agree. This caused the war between the Asantes and the whites. The Asantehene again did not agree. Fromu came to Kumase a third time. Fromu said to the Asantehene, "Nana, I am from Edena. I am your subject. I brought the message from the whites. If you do not agree, the whites will come to fight you." The Asantehene told Fromu that he would not mind if the whites came on that very same day. Prempe said that killing was done for the power of the Golden Stool. He would not stop the sacrifice. Prempe said that sacrifice made a difference between royals and subjects. If a person insulted a royal, he should be killed. Prempe told Fromu that a non-royal who slept with a royal must be killed. All the killing was to frighten people not to have sexual intercourse with royals and not to insult royals. . . . Fromu suggested to Prempe that he should get a curved, iron rod with a sharp end. He should put the sharp end of the iron rod on the wrist and drive it into the ground. This would no longer be sacrifice. Fromu told the Asantehene first to ask the offender for money. If the offender did not have money, he should get the iron rod. The Asantehene said that he had enough money in the palace. He wanted people to fear him. Prempe did not take any of Fromu's suggestions.[66]

Kwaku Fokuo and Yaw Boaten clarified the Asante government's position with respect to the third and last offer of protection during their consultations with the British governor at Cape Coast on 18 December 1895. They reaffirmed "consent on behalf of the King of Kumase to a British Resident at Kumase"[67] and said that their British counsel, Thomas Sutherst, had been instructed to inform the Colonial Office that Kumase was ready to discuss the terms on which a resident could be stationed in the capital. The Asante envoys accused Maxwell of suppressing information he had received some four weeks earlier which specified that the Prempean administration had accepted the residency clause and noted that the governor had prematurely (and falsely) telegraphed his superiors that the Asantehene did not reply to the ultimatum. Unaware that the British were no longer adhering to usual diplomatic procedures, the envoys vainly endeavored to inaugurate a new era of peaceful relations and to "bring down our big Chiefs to negotiate with the Governor."[68] They assured Maxwell that the Asantehene would pay all verifiable debts. Maxwell's reaction was predictable: "I am the servant of Her Majesty the Queen, and I cannot accept mere words; this is not child's play; when thousands of men are brought across the sea, they are not to be sent back again because you bring me words."[69]

The British Expedition of January 1896
and the Arrest of Prempe

In early January 1896 a large expeditionary force under the command of Colonel Francis Scott moved along Route VI into the metropolitan region. It was equipped with artillery and aided by the field telegraph. As Kwaku Fokuo had maintained, the Prempe administration was prepared to accept the governor's terms, and an executive proclamation of late 1895 ordered local forces to refrain from hostilities.[70] Accordingly, British columns encountered no opposition en route to the capital and entered Kumase without firing a shot on 17 January. The Asantehene and his councillors, believing that the British had arrived to negotiate a treaty, sheltered and provisioned the regiments which, according to one Kumase observer, "came like black ants with many tents and guns" and whose "number was uncountable."[71] Governor Maxwell entered Kumase on the eighteenth and promptly demanded that prior to treaty discussions the Asantehene agree to underwrite the cost of the expedition—estimated at £230,000 to £250,000—and the balance of the indemnity of 1874 (which had earlier been recomputed and paid), and insisted that Prempe make a public statement of submission in the main marketplace at Dwaberem Brono on Monday, the twentieth of January.[72]

Several Asante eyewitnesses offered accounts of these momentous days. Kwadwo Afodo commented on Asafo Boakye's attempts to begin negotiations at the Pra and related the preliminary operations conducted by British contingents in the capital.

> When the whites came to Kumase, the Asantehene sent Asafo Boakye, the Asafohene, to meet the whites halfway at the Pra River. Asafo Boakye had gifts and gold for the whites. Asafo Boakye told the whites the Asantes would kill no more. The whites should return to Accra. The whites did not accept this. They still came to Kumase. The whites arrived in Kumase on a Friday. They rested on Saturday. On Sunday the Asantehene went to take gifts to welcome the whites to Asante. The Asantehene invited the whites to his palace on that Monday. He wanted the whites to tell him why they had come to Kumase. Before the whites came to Kumase, Yaw Atweneboanna, Yaw Awua, the Saawua people, and others told the whites the Asantes had gunpowder and bullets stocked in a building at Asem [a Kumase ward]. The Asantes were surprised to see the whites collect the powder and bullets on Friday. The Asantes wondered how the whites knew where the powder and bullets were kept. Later the Asantes found out who told the whites. On Friday, the whites started to dig trenches for the fort. The Asantes did not take this seriously. They felt the whites were digging trenches to sleep in. But the whites had brought nothing to sleep on.[73]

Domfe Kyere, who was an *ahenkwaa* and *sikadwumni*, or goldsmith, in Manhyia during the 1890s, observed the hurried and strenuous endeavors to comply with Maxwell's inflated and audacious monetary demands:

> Prempe did not have much money in the Sanaa when the whites came to Kumase. He had spent a good deal of money to pay for the enstoolment and the civil wars. Prempe asked the chiefs to pay additional taxes. Few responded. Only for the mission of Kwaku Fokuo [to London] did the chiefs tax the people to pay for the mission. But the *amanhene* grumbled over this burden. It was these *amanhene* who advised the Asantehene to melt the palace property to pay the whites. Nana Osokye, the Mampon-

hene, directly told Prempe that he had no money, and the
Asantehene should order the gold to be melted down. . . . The
Asantehene's goldsmiths started to melt down the gold stocks on
swords, guns, and drums. Everything with gold was melted to
get the bulk to pay the Asantehene's debt. I myself saw this
happen. I was working in the palace at that time. The whites
then told the Asantehene that they would like to meet Prempe
and his chiefs at 7 A.M. on Monday. The Asantehene went to
the meeting. The Asantehene told the whites he was preparing
the gold for them. Before the Asantehene came out of the
palace, some of the whites already surrounded the place. They
rushed into Manhyia and took away much of the palace property. Some *nhenkwaa* who tried to hide the royal property had
it taken from them by the whites. Then the whites asked about
Prempe's mines. They looked for these mines but only found
them in Manso some years later.[74]

During the early morning hours of the twentieth, the Asantehene and his
Asantehemaa Yaa Akyaa, and the Mamponhene, Nsutahene, Offinsohene,
and Edwesohene, in the presence of their Kumase councillors, formally
submitted to the governor and, cognizant of the cannons pointing directly
at their *ahene*, acquiesced to the demand that Asante come under British
protection. Kwadwo Afodo vividly related the proceedings:

On Monday the Asantehene, his chiefs and subjects met at
Dwaberem. They saw some whites coming to them. The whites
held the bones of some people who had been executed. The
white leader, named Afontokuro [dimples], asked the Asantehene to come to where he was sitting. The Asantehene moved
toward the white leader. Drums were beating. The drummers
followed the Asantehene. The Asantehene came near the whites.
The Asantehene asked the drummers to stop. The drummers
beat harder. People danced. The white soldiers started to beat
people with the stocks of their guns. The Asantehene told the
drummers to calm down. He wanted to listen to what the whites
had to say. At this point the Asante chiefs first realized the
whites came for war. Most Asantes wanted to go back to get
their guns. The Asantehene told his subjects to stay. He said
he did not want his nation to be destroyed. The white leader
stretched his arm to the Asantehene. They shook hands. The
white leader spoke to Nana. He told Nana the Queen had sent
him to bring the Asantehene to her. The Asantehene wanted to
know if the white leader meant Prempe. The white leader said,
"yes." The Asantehene told his subjects, chiefs, and elders nobody should fire a gun. He said he would sacrifice himself for
the nation. Asantes started to weep when they heard this. The

whites then started to loot Kumase after the meeting. Many Asantes insisted they wanted Prempe back. The whites caught the Asantehene on Monday. The Asantehene remained in a tent at Dwaberem. The whites and their soldiers had over one thousand tents all over Kumase. On Wednesday the whites took the Asantehene away from Kumase. The whites felt if they kept the Asantehene in Kumase for long the Asantes would fight.[75]

Thus, Maxwell, taking advantage of his immediate and obvious military strength and flouting the Asantehene's hospitality and his government's expectation that a treaty would be consummated on Monday, took the extreme and unsanctioned step—violating all conventional diplomatic procedures—of arresting and detaining the Asantehene, the Asantehemaa, and several prominent Kumase councillors and family members.[76] Among them were the Asafohene Asafo Boakye, Bantamahene Amankwatia Kwame, Akyempemhene Kofi Subiri, Oyokohene Kwabena Agyekum, Akyeamehene Kwasi Akoko, Akomofodehene Boakye Ansa, Akyebiakyerehene Kwasi Gyambibi, and Abakomadwahene Agyeman Badu. Three of the most outspoken centralist district leaders were also imprisoned: the Mamponhene Kwame Apea Osokye, the Edwesohene Kwasi Afrane Kumaa (Kofi Tene), who as the grandson of the Edwesohemaa Yaa Asantewaa had succeeded his uncle, Kwasi Afrane Panin, in 1894, and the Offinsohene Kwadwo Kwawu, who came to office following Apea Sea's death in early 1893.[77]

Various firsthand Asante accounts focusing on the arrest and detention of the Asantehene and his councillors concurred on the deception inherent within British diplomacy in late 1895 and further dramatized the governor's treacherous performance at Dwaberem. Significantly, the Omantihene of Kumase, who was present at the meeting, noted that the governor arrived with a list of *ahene* who were to be arrested.

> The whites knew the important chiefs who had to go. They came to Kumase with a number of names supplied by Yaw Atweneboanna's people on the coast. The whites had heard of all the important chiefs in Kumase. They read the list. The chiefs were called and asked to stand. The whites' soldiers brought to Kumase those who were not present.[78]

Kwabena Baako—generally considered the "senior historian" in Edweso and in his late twenties at the time of Prempe's seizure—attended the meeting as an *afenakurani*, or sword-bearer, to the Edwesohene.

> Prempe asked the Asantes to come to the meeting. They came. I was his subject. He was my lord. I came. The Offinsohene came. So did the Mamponhene, the Kokofuhene Asibe, the

Atwemahene Adu Kofi, the Nkoransahene Bafo, the Dwabenhene Yaw Sapon, the Edwesohene Afrane Kumaa, the Wamfie-
hene Boaten, the Dormaahene Adu Antwi, the Asokorehene
Gyima, the Kumawuhene Tweneboa Kodua [his stool's name],
and the Nsutahene. The *amanhene* came with their people to
the meeting. An *omanhene* does not come without his people.
Prempe called the meeting. He wanted the chiefs and people
to meet the whites who came from the coast. But the Bekwaehene [Yaw Boakye] did not attend. He rebelled. He supported the whites. . . . I never came to a meeting so large. The
Asantehene called the meeting to welcome the whites to Kumase. I took the Edweso–Krapa–Kwamo–Fumesua–Kenten-
krono–Oduom–Kumase road to the meeting. . . . The Asantes
got settled. Then the whites told them they had come to build a
fort in Kumase. The whites said they must take the Asantehene
away. He was killing people. Prempe did not kill anyone.
Rather Mensa Bonsu Kumaa was fond of killing people. When
the whites came, Prempe was on the stool. Bonsu Kumaa was
destooled. The whites took Bonsu's actions to be those of
Prempe. The whites said they must advise Prempe to stop the
killing. The wives and children of the Asantehene began to
weep. Prempe was not afraid. Prempe told his family not to
weep. He said he would return after the whites advised him.
He said he wanted Yaa Akyaa, his mother, to go with him. Yaa
Akyaa told the whites she would go with her son. . . . There
was no need to fight. Prempe told the Asantes not to fight the
whites. Prempe said he would come back. He said he did not
want the nation to be destroyed. . . . At Dwaberem it was not
possible to fight the whites. The Asantes could have fought
earlier. They could have stopped the whites from coming to
Kumase. The Asantes were surprised. They knew the whites
were coming. They did not know the whites came to take Nana
away. The Asantes prepared to meet the whites. They thought
the whites would bring good news to Asante. At Dwaberem
Prempe said: *Mede me ho medi.* "I will sacrifice myself." *Moma
aboro fo mfa me nko.* "Let the whites take me away." *Na yekoa
afotuo na wose worekatu me. Mesan saba!* "When we go they
are going to advise me. I shall return!" The Asantes thought the
whites came to advise the Asantehene how to administer the
nation. The Asantes never expected the whites to come to take
Nana away.[79]

Adu Gyamera, who came from the Atwema town of Boko, was also
present for the assembly and maintained:

The British came in great numbers with long swords hanging
on their sides and drums beating. The Asantes found it to be

tough. The whites were carried in palanquins. They came on many roads—the Kaase road, Denkyira road, Wassa road—followed by their African soldiers. When the British troops arrived in Kumase, the Asantehene and his subjects were at a meeting called to welcome the whites. The British arrived on Sunday. They told the Asantes that they would meet the Asantehene on the following Monday to tell him what they had in mind. On Monday the British told the Asantehene that the Queen says she is sorry that the Asantes did not treat her two messengers well. The British said that they had come to take Prempe away. Prempe refused the piece of advice given by the Queen. If the Asantes wanted the Asantehene to stay with them, they should pay gold to the value of £1000. Prempe agreed to pay £1000. The next morning a number of troops marched in the streets and beat drums. The British troops surrounded the Asantehene's palace. The British leader stood up and called Prempe. Prempe was a bold ruler. He got up and went to the British military leader. He stood in front of the white man and the troops. The British military leader called Prempe's mother, Yaa Akyaa, Prempe's father, Kwasi Gyambibi, Prempe's brother, Agyeman Badu, the Bantamahene, the military leaders of the Asantes. . . . The British took them away. Soon after this there was a very severe famine. The Asantes said Prempe should not walk barefoot. Thus the famine came to Asante. I myself am very sad when I recall these events. I was present when this took place. It was a very sad time for Asante.[80]

Another informant, Yaw Safo—who traveled to the capital with his uncle (one of the Asantehene's *akyeame*) from the town of Hyeman on the Mampon road and was in his early teens when Prempe was arrested—stressed that:

> the Asantes heard the whites were coming to Kumase. The Asantes did not know the whites came to take Nana away. Asantes felt the whites came to talk with Nana about "special topics." The whites and the soldiers surrounded Kumase town. They blocked all the roads. The Asantehene knew this. He told the Asantes not to fight. . . . The Asantes did not know the whites surrounded the town. They became aware when the whites were already around the town. The Asantes were deceived by the whites.[81]

Kwadwo Mosi, who at the age of ten had just returned to Kumase from the coast with his father (a salt trader), recalled that as British regiments entered the capital:

> all the Asantes were sad and remained calm. Prempe declared

that no one should fight because this would destroy Kumase and its people. Prempe wanted to save the Asanteman. Before Prempe was arrested, all the paramount chiefs of Kumase and the nation came to a meeting in Kumase. Almost all of the Asantes [i.e., chiefs] attended the meeting. The Edwesohene was there. The meeting was held where the fort now stands. It was held for the arrival of the new British Gold Coast Governor. The Asantes met to receive him. At this meeting the whites said that Prempe should be arrested. The Asantes had guns but did not use them.[82]

Kofi Afrane was a fifteen-year-old *ahenkwaa* to the Edwesohene and traveled to attend the *nhyiam*, or meeting, from his home in the Edweso district.

The Asantes were taken by surprise. . . . The whites told the Asantes they were taking Nana away. The Asantes thought the whites were coming to visit Kumase. When the Asantes heard that the whites were coming to Kumase, the whites had already surrounded Kumase. The whites blocked all the roads leading to Kumase. The whites shook hands with the Asante chiefs. Just after this the whites arrested the Edwesohene Kofi Tene, the Asantehene, and many other chiefs. The whites told the Asantes they were taking Prempe overseas to advise him. Prempe called the meeting. Prempe did not know the whites would take him away. Prempe would have fought if he knew. The Edweso people were very surprised.[83]

Although Adu Buobi resided in Kokofu and was not present when the Asantehene was arrested, he offered an account of the reaction he observed in his district:

The Kokofu citizens heard that Prempe was taken away. This was a surprise. The Kokofus did not know the whites were coming to do this. The whites took precaution and brought many soldiers with them. They thought the Asantes would not take this quietly. The whites passed near Asumegya, not Kokofu, and were happy that so few Kokofu lived in Amansie because they would have fought to save Prempe. Then the Asantehene gave instructions not to fight. If not for this, people would have challenged the whites and sent them back to the coast. But the Kokofus in Asante were small in number and had few guns and ammunition.[84]

Kwako Anno, who lived in the Boagywe Brono of Kumase and whose father was an *okyeame* to the Asantehemaa Yaa Akyaa, provided his interpretation of the reasons for Prempe's arrest:

The whites came because Prempe did not put a stop to the killings. I have heard this from the elders and the British. If Prempe stopped the killings, the whites said they would not have taken him away. The whites told the Asantes they would bring Prempe back. The Asantes wanted to fight when the whites came to Kumase. The Asantehene did not let the Asantes fight. Prempe told the Asantes that there was a civil war when he came to occupy the stool. Prempe said he did not want the nation of his ancestors to be destroyed during his reign. The whites did not want to kill him. The Asantehene said anyone who wanted could follow him overseas. The whites told the Asantes they would bring the Asantehene back after he was educated to administer the nation. He would return after all killing was gone from Asante.[85]

According to another eyewitness, al-Hajj Sulāyman, a member of the Asante Nkramo community in Kumase, the Asantehene was taken to the Asante Kotoko Brono—"the whites would not let him sleep in the palace that night"[86]—and remained there for thirty-six hours under heavy guard. The prisoners and a number of their attendants subsequently were escorted by the British column to Elmina. Kwadwo Afodo related his final act of service for the Asantehene in Kumase:

On Wednesday the whites took the Asantehene away from Kumase. They did this because they felt the Asantes were very angry. The whites felt if they kept the Asantehene in Kumase for long the Asantes would fight. On Monday, the day of the arrest, I and my people went to Odumanafo in the Kwabre area. I went with my elder "brother" and his two "sisters." The two "sisters" were Prempe's wives—Afua Mfum and Adwoa Baayie. The two wives prepared thirty balls of kenkey and a pot full of palm wine. I took this to Kumase. I carried the kenkey. One Akua Odum carried the palm wine. We arrived in Kumase. The whites were at Asafo with the Asantehene. The whites kept the Asantehene at Dwaberem for two days. I presented the kenkey and the palm wine to the Asantehene. I told Prempe his wives had sent me to bring the kenkey and the palm wine. The Asantehene told the whites to bring his palanquin. Asantes brought the palanquin to Nana. The Asantehene asked for his own stool, the *kukurubo*. He wanted to take it with him. Asantes brought the *kukurubo*. The Asantehene sat in his palanquin. His subject, named Yaw Dabre, carried the stool. Yaw Dabre died recently. The Asantehene gave me £4 to take back to his two wives. Asafo Boakye gave me £1.6s. I took this money to the Asafohene's sister, named Akosua Krapayenam. She was my mother.[87]

The youthful Agyeman Prempe I and his principal councillors thus submitted to the *coup de grace* of the British forward policy. Up to this point the Asantehene had not relied on personal charisma, as had heads of earlier nineteenth-century administrations. He had dedicated himself to the maintenance and legitimization of royal power rather than the increase of that power and had not pursued programs to create new offices and *fekuo* in order to augment his position. Prempe had allowed outlying district heads a greater voice in national decision-making and a large measure of independence, particularly in the field of foreign affairs, and had diminished the instrumentality of the state use of terror as a means to substantiate the aura of fear surrounding his office.[88] This administration, dominated by experienced but not overly ambitious officeholders, embraced mild, lenient, and permissive policies coupled with economically modernizing reforms which were formulated to instaurate the Asanteman through an abiding belief in and actualization of the supremacy of *esom*. Prempe's last service and self-sacrifice for what he believed to be the good of the Asante Nation demonstrates the majesty, maturity, and patience that he brought to the Golden Stool at an exceedingly difficult time. Ironically, Agyeman Prempe's submission failed to save the sovereignty of the Asante kingdom.

The prisoners and a number of their attendants subsequently were escorted by the British column to Elmina. Late in 1896 Agyeman Prempe and his detained councillors were deported to Sierra Leone and on 19 August 1900 were exiled along with other Asante political prisoners to the remote Seychelles Islands. The Asantehene did not return to his homeland until 1924 in the status of a "private citizen." One of the last Asantes to talk with Prempe before he left the nation of his ancestors recalled that

> when the British came, the Asantes did not fight because Nana Prempe told them not to. . . . Okomfo Anokye, the shrine priest who lived at the time of Osei Tutu, made a prediction that the whites would come to Kumase, would arrest Prempe, and would eventually rule all of Asante. He made this prediction through the tail of a cow. This shrine priest was believed by the Asantes because he enabled the Asantes to conquer the Akyems, Denkyiras, Gyamans, Fantes, and Assins. Okomfo Anokye's prophecies all came true. The Asantes were very successful. Prempe believed that the whites would come to arrest him. Prempe believed the predictions. He told Yaa Akyaa, his mother, that he would go quietly. He was proud of his country. He was proud of his people. Prempe asked the Asantes not to react when he was taken away. Asantes were very sad. We all cried. Women

threw themselves to the ground screaming. Kumase was a sea of tears.[89]

Another informant who brought the Asantehene his last meal in Kumase remembered that Agyeman Prempe

> was proud but so sad. The whites brought so many people into Kumase. They came well-armed. There was no need to sacrifice the Asanteman for one man. So Prempe ordered the Asante people not to fight and went with the governor's troops. But he refused to say one word to the white soldiers. They respected and feared him. Prempe told them with a wave of his hand what he wanted. They knew. The Asantehene only wanted peace in the Asanteman. He went with his head held high. Prempe loved his nation more than himself. He knew he would always serve his people. Asantes knew he would return. We went to our villages quietly and waited.[90]

BRITISH RESIDENT AND THE TRIUMVIRATE

Following the invasion of Asante, Governor Maxwell and his advisers misconstrued the nature of the Asante political process and erroneously believed that the arrest and detention of the Asantehene and his most outspoken centralist councillors would precipitate the collapse of the Asante government, thereby enabling British officials to appoint various advocates of localism and other dissatisfied politicians from among the former partisans of the candidacy of Yaw Atweneboanna to influential positions in a newly created administration. For example, Yaw Awua, Kofi Nti, Kwaku Goroso, and Kwabena Kokofu were quickly considered prime candidates for the new posts.[91]

British authorities immediately after the Asantehene's capture invoked the now-standard rhetoric that Asante in the 1890s "was no longer a compact state but had been split into sections" and that Prempe's installation in June 1894 "was illegal and had no binding force."[92] Arguing that the Asantehene had "only ruled Kumase," they took measures to promote the principle of *nkabom* as a means to augment the resident's restricted administrative powers. Although the British militarily occupied Asante, they lacked adequate legal standing and title to the Asanteman since their claims to legitimacy were neither based on treaty with the lawful government nor on rights of conquest. Asante in 1896 could not be treated as a conquered country because there had been no resistance to British forces. And administrators in the Gold Coast Colony continually feared that their precarious legal position would be undercut if the exiled Asantehene entered into treaty relations with France or Germany.

The intervention of Gold Coast authorities in the electoral process on the local level, and their assurances that the resident, Captain Donald Stewart, could be consulted on all occasions and would work to restrict the influence of the Council of Kumase, persuaded various outlying district heads—always fully aware of the political and economic advantages of cooperating with the British—to follow the example of the Bekwaehene Yaw Boakye and other southern leaders and sign separate treaties of protection. Accordingly, the Nsutahene Adu Agyei, a former supporter of the candidacy of Yaw Atweneboanna who desired British assistance to procure the release of his subjects in Dwaben, Offinso, Edweso, and Kumawu, entered into a similar agreement on 30 January 1896. The Mamponhene Owusu Sekyere II, another prominent Atweneboanna partisan who was reinstated by the British and received the support of most politicians in his district after Maxwell rejected the applications of the pro-Kumase Gyamasehene Yaw Sekyere and the Effiduasehene for separate recognition, quickly followed suit. Owusu Sekyere, the new Kokofuhene Asibe II (Yaw Konkroma), a nephew of the late Osei Asibe whom the British brought to office, the Dwabenhene Yaw Sapon, the Agonahene Kwabena Akyampon, the Kumawuhene Kwame Afram, and representatives from Edweso and Offinso signed treaties in Kumase on 10 February.[93]

The treaties of early 1896 recognized each of the *amanto* and the main districts of the metropolitan region as independent administrative units constituting a largely autonomous local jurisdiction. They were legal instruments formulated to fragment the Asante political structure and, thus, to restore the eighteenth- and earlier nineteenth-century political model in order to facilitate British control over the Asanteman. These treaties with the *amanhene* were of dubious legal validity but strengthened British claims to authority. The pacts, consistent with the aims of the forward policy, were designed to arrest the progressive accumulation of power and authority in the central government.[94] They aimed to restrict the decision-making prerogatives of the Council of Kumase and to formalize the principal goals sought by localists and proponents of decentralization over the past two decades. Yet despite these agreements with the *amanhene*, the presence of the resident in the capital, and the imprisonment of the highest executive officer (and top bureaucrat), together with several members of the Asante political elite, the extension of British protection neither seriously undermined Kumase's influence in the metropolitan region nor markedly affected the operations of most sections of the well-organized bureaucracy. One informant, Domfe Kyere, for instance, delineated the functions of the Public Works Department in the period immediately following the detention of the Asantehene:

The people who weeded the bushy parts were called the *akwan-mofo*. They were an *ekuo* [group] in the Gyaase Fekuo. The group had its own stool and chief called the Akwanmofohene. The stool is still here, but its services are no longer needed. The people weeded paths from Kumase to the villages. They kept the roads clean throughout Asante. The Asantehene's Akwan-mofohene supervised, went round, and asked people to weed their grounds. His people went to areas around the Asantehene's capital such as Sepe and Pankrono. The *amanhene* had their own *akwanmofo* who supervised the clearing of weeds in their own districts. The people in this *ekuo* were responsible for felling trees across rivers for bridges. They had to cut the trees into pieces and move them across the road. The services of the nearest village were also needed. The villagers were responsible with the Asantehene's people for clearing trees within their bounds. The Asantehene's people remained permanently in Kumase. Every morning they grouped themselves and went up and down to find the work to be done. At times they stayed for three or four nights outside Kumase. They were given money and food by the people of the villages where they stayed. The *odekuro* or *ohene* of the village became the host to them wherever they went. They had no special uniform. They carried canes for their positions. The Akwanmofohene all the time stayed in Kumase. He went around the Kumase wards and gave instructions to people who had weeds to clear. . . . The overall number of the group was around one hundred. The number depended on the number of places they went at a time. If they had to go to four places, they grouped themselves into four groups and went. The chief of the group decided where they should go. They were not paid for this. They got hospitality from the people in the villages as a form of payment. . . . This was a full-time occupation. Sons inherit this stool. The next in command was the Mmammahene—the chief of the sons of the men in this group. He also had a stool. . . . The only other duty of the group was to insure good sanitation in Kumase and other towns of the Kumase district. . . . The Akwanmofohene swore the oath of allegiance to the Asantehene. The people in this group came from the villages around Kumase. Sons followed their fathers in this role. If a son chose not to follow his father, the father would let him alone. Many sons said they would trade instead. When they came back from trading, they assisted their fathers in their jobs. It had great prestige to say you were the Asantehene's *akwanmoni*. The people in this *ekuo* continued to work after Prempe was taken away but were seen no more after the Yaa Asantewaako.[95]

Despite modifications in the *akwansifo* organization—essential to the protection and regulation of state trade and control of immigration and the passage of traders—the fundamental workings of this section remained unchanged.

> The Asantehene had people stationed on the different roads who asked people why they were coming. If a person said he was coming in the name of the Asantehene, the guards called *akwansifo* or *abansifo* would first find out from Kumase if this was so. The Asantehene had to approve. This was so when Kakari, Bonsu, and Prempe were the Asantehenes. The guards stayed for a short time after Prempe was taken away. They checked those coming out who committed crimes and those coming in. They stopped traders to make sure they were trading. They stopped the foreigners and Asante kola traders going to the northern markets.[96]

The Omantihene of Kumase, whose uncle served as an *okwansini*, or highway policeman, stationed at Edwira on the Mampon road in the late 1890s, commented further on this section of the bureaucracy:

> On the road from Bekwae to Cape Coast, there was a point—Osa Nkwanta—where many *abansifo* stayed. They stopped all traders from Asante. They would only allow the traders to go after Kumase verified that they were traders and not criminals. . . . All roads that led out of Kumase had *abansifo* on them: the Wankyi, Atebubu (or Mampon), Cape Coast, and Elmina roads. The roads had junctions. The *abansifo* had to be on these junctions to watch the traders. The *abansifo* could ask the traders not to cross by saying the Great Oath. . . . The Asantehene directly appointed the *abansifo* from two groups: the Esen and the Afenasoafo. They went with their people to the roads. They watched in turns. Each time of day and night they watched. They brought news to the Asantehene. The Asantehene sent messages from Kumase to them. The Asantehene had his own traders called *adwadifo* or *asokwafo*. These traders would blow their horns to tell that they were the Asantehene's traders. People used the *asokwafo* as an advantage. If a person wanted to go quickly to the north, he would ask one of the *asokwafo* to take him so their group did not lose time waiting for permission from Kumase. . . . The Asantehene appointed elderly ones whom he had gotten to know well because they stayed with him for a long time. If one was appointed, he becomes an *ohene* because the *abansifo* settled Great Oath cases at their points. They gave the Asantehene some of the money and kept their own share. They had no stool. They had the power to act like

an *ohene* at these points. My uncle was an elderly person when he did this. He had guns given to him by the Asantehene. . . . Traders going to and fro had to give the *abansifo* dashes [*akyedee*]. If a person sold kola nuts, he had to parcel their dash separately and put it down in a different cloth when passing the check-point. . . . The whites after Prempe's arrest wanted to destroy the *abansifo* and allow free trade and people into Kumase.[97]

The concept of *esom*, political behavior, and the science of government were institutionalized to the degree that Asante officialdom and public alike were prepared to accept and support an administration no longer headed by a member of the royal Ankanese of the Oyoko matriclan. Despite the extraordinary catalogue of political disruption, social and economic transformation, foreign and civil war, and conflict over the very nature of the Asante state, administrators in the lower echelons of the bureaucratic apparatus continued to carry out their mundane and routinized tasks such as road maintenance, police control, housing construction and sanitation, tax collecting, and immigration regulation. The administrative infrastructure and the concept of *esom* were so deeply ingrained as to be beyond the reach of political upheavals. Although the political system was much transformed and indeed almost threatened with destruction, the viability of the civil administration was not seriously disrupted. Thus in early 1896 the bureaucracy continued to function relatively unimpaired even following the Asantehene's arrest.[98] Furthermore, the threat of disruption of personal lives was minimized by Asante functionaries' performance of their duties as long as conditions permitted.

The statement often made by Kumase informants, that most citizens believed that the Asantehene would return in some three or four years, reflected hopeful expectation after the governor's unprecedented and shocking action.[99] Yet more significantly, sentiments of this sort also underscored Asante confidence that the government in Kumase would continue to function smoothly in 1896 without the Asantehene. Asante citizens did *not* need the Asantehene for the government to carry out its operations. In fact, the issue of whether the Asante polity could exist without the monarchy had been a subject of considerable debate since the popular rebellion of early 1883 which ousted the Asantehene Mensa Bonsu and first forced politicians to consider alternative modes of rule. Clearly, the years from 1896 to 1900 demonstrated the viability of the Asante political structure without an occupant of the Golden Stool.

In late January 1896 the Gyaasewahene Opoku Mensa, who was the occupant of the Pinanko stool, the Okyeame Nantwi Kaakyire, and the Atwemahene Kwame Antwi Agyei—three members of the Prempean administration and of the Council of Kumase—were empowered by the council to administer the central government, oversee the operations of the bureaucracy, and hold regular court sessions in consultation with the resident for minor criminal, civil, and land cases.[100] Governor Maxwell reported that he appointed this so-called Committee of Administration after rejecting the proposal made by authorities in Kumase, led by the Mamponhene and the Kokofuhene, for "a provisional Ashanti Government with full control in the name of the Golden Stool, over all subordinate Kings, Chiefs, and tribes."[101] But Asante accounts indicated that the triumvirate was independently selected by the Council of Kumase and that the senior Kumase diplomat, Kwaku Fokuo, was dispatched to the Gyaasewahene's town of Atimatum to escort the elderly, semiretired Opoku Mensa to the capital. Asante leaders considered Opoku Mensa to be the "successor to the Asantehene."[102] The Atwemahene Kwame Antwi Agyei—a leading supporter of the Saamanhene Akyampon Panin's coup in late 1884 who had backed Prempe's election and had already assumed many of the legal responsibilities of the detained Bantamahene Amankwatia Kwame—and the Okyeame Nantwi Kaakyire were likewise appointed by the council to take charge of political and legal affairs in urban Kumase.[103] Kwame Antwi Agyei died in late 1896. His official duties were divided between his successor, Osei Kwame, and the Toasehene Kwame Afrifa, who assumed office in the early 1890s following the death of his predecessor, the Toasehene Ampofo.[104]

The Council of Kumase with British approval authorized the trio to encourage Kumase citizens to resettle in the capital as many had migrated to their villages and to Ahafo following the Asantehene's arrest. They worked to sustain public confidence in commercial activities, rubber transactions, and European capital investments in the form of mining concessions and mercantile firms. These leaders also allowed the establishment of Basel and Wesleyan mission stations in Kumase and the outlying district capitals. The triumvirate received assistance from influential members of the council, several of whom had careers extending over the previous two decades: the Adumhene Asamoa Kwame, Anantahene Adu Kofi, Nsumankwaahene Kwasi Domfe, Hiahene Boakye Adare, Atipinhene Kwame Boakye, Ankobeahene Yaw Kyem, Gyaasewahene Manwere Poku, and Gyakyehene Yaw Pense. Other less senior Kumase centralists had supported Prempe's candidacy in 1887–88 and had participated in his administration during the previous eight years.[105] The experience and support provided by these leaders guaranteed a smooth and rapid transition to the government by triumvirs and enabled the Council of Kumase, utilizing the resident's political and legal advice, to continue its management of the affairs of government.

During the ensuing three years Opoku Mensa and his councillors took steps to reaffirm the authority of the central government in the metropolitan region. They also reopened negotiations for an alliance with the Almami Samori and levied taxes to raise funds for legal fees to effect the release of the Asantehene. In June 1897, the Dwabenhene Yaw Sapon complained "of the Chiefs of Kumasi interfering with the affairs of his country, requiring him to obey their orders, and accounting to them all fines for swearing the great oath," while the Kokofuhene Asibe II reported that authorities in the capital were "meddling with his affairs."[106] "Prempe's supporters," observed Vroom, "are frequently guying the Bekwais," and the Council of Kumase concurrently encouraged centralists in Ahuren, Esiase, Asanso, Asumegya, and other southern towns to organize against the leadership of the pro-British Bekwaehene Yaw Boakye.[107] Further, officials in Kumase assisted the centralist Gyamasehene Yaw Sekyere in his efforts to oust the Mamponhene Owusu Sekyere on charges of malfeasance over legal and financial matters, and disputed the installation of the pro-British Agonahene Kwame Boakye, who succeeded Kwabena Akyampon—appointed by the Asantehene Kwaku Dua II—in late May 1897.[108] In Edweso, agents from Kumase cooperated with the main centralists—the Edwesohemaa Yaa Asantewaa, the Gyaasehene Kwasi Boadu, and the Abontendomhene Saakode—who ran the local administration following the arrest of the Edwesohene Kwasi Afrane Kumaa. Edweso, noted Vroom, "appears flourishing" under its new leaders, and "the Ejesus are seemingly on the most friendly terms with (the) Kumasis."[109]

The Council of Kumase similarly backed centralist politicians in Offinso and appointed an Offinso royal, Afranewa, to supervise the district in the absence of the Offinsohene Kwadwo Kwawu.[110] The Offinso stool, like that of Edweso, remained vacant. Prominent officeholders in Ahafo also responded to Kumase's new, vigorous centralizing policies. During the greater part of the nineteenth century, Ahafo was under the direct supervision of a number of Kumase *nhwesofo*, notably the Bantamahene, Akwaboahene, Akyempemhene, Atipinhene, Hiahene, Akuroponhene, Asokore Mamponhene, Banmuhene, and Akrafohene.[111] Localist sentiment had emerged in this region after 1874, and several leaders had signed separate treaties of protection with the British in the early 1890s. In 1897, however, it was reported that "Ahafu, Tekiman, Wam, and Brekum [Berekum] already recognise the Kumase Chiefs as their head-Chiefs, and prefer perhaps to refer their differences to the Native Committee rather than the Resident."[112] Accordingly, Vroom summarized the dismal failure of British policy to contain the Opoku Mensa administration's politics in the metropolitan region:

The arrangement would have worked well if the Committee had confined its actions to Kumasi and its villages. As far as I can see the Committee aims to reclaim prestige long lost to the King of Kumasi in those districts which revolted against Kumasi; and they may succeed if not checked in time, for an idea is generally entertained that all their actions have received the sanction of the Government. I am afraid the Chiefs are slowly returning to their old ways, so distasteful to us. . . . There is no doubt that much of their doings are unknown to the Resident.[113]

THE GENESIS OF THE YAA ASANTEWAA WAR

The measures taken by the central government to reassert its predominance in the metropolitan region and to restore towns and villages to their former Kumase *nhwesofo* augmented the extension of judicial authority outside the capital. Opoku Mensa and his councillors in May 1897 sought permission from the resident to adjudicate Ntam Kese, or Great Oath, cases involving both Kumase and *amanto* citizens, to retain fines accruing from such trials, and thus to reverse the current practice whereby district leaders presided over and withheld financial penalties from these trials.[114] Despite British efforts to confine the scope of Kumase courts to "petty cases in which no political question with independent Kings and Chiefs arises,"[115] Opoku Mensa—without the resident's knowledge—conducted political and criminal trials involving the swearing of the Great Oath and imposed heavy fines on guilty citizens from Kumase as well as the *amanto*. The Omantihene of Kumase, for example, recounted:

> The whites had their soldiers. Opoku Mensa had his own *nhenkwaa* who saw to it that anybody who spoke the Great Oath would be brought to him and tried. He and his elders in Kumase decided certain cases. Murder and other serious cases were decided by the whites. In the absence of the Asantehene, there was no one to try cases. Opoku Mensa played the role of Asantehene and did this willingly.[116]

The centralizing policies implemented by the Prempean administration in the years 1894–95 and continued by Opoku Mensa and his councillors after 1896, together with the Council of Kumase's support for local centralists in the outlying districts, precipitated a new wave of resentment among most pro-British leaders, particularly the Bekwaehene, Dwabenhene, Mamponhene, and Agonahene. Kumase's regained powers, concurrently, antagonized administrators in the Gold Coast Colony who naïvely believed that the establishment of the residency in the capital and the arrest of the Asantehene and his most vocal anti-British advisers would curtail the powers of the central government. District heads and others favoring the extension of British protection for its formal sanction of the confederacy principle and its support for localist rights once again manipulated British influence in order to safeguard their new autonomy. They relied exclusively on Gold Coast officials to achieve local political and economic goals, many of which violated the aims of authorities in Kumase. Their cooperation with the British (e.g., providing carriers and laborers, and supplying food) and their independent dealings with European entrepreneurs (e.g., Bekwae's local monopoly over mining concessions in the south),[117] in turn, provoked hostility from a majority of the politicians in the capital who increasingly agitated for direct action to quell the localists' activities.

Disagreement over British measures to create a confederate political structure constituted one major source of tension between the Council of Kumase and administrators in the Gold Coast Colony. The politics of former partisans of the candidacies of Kofi Kakari and Yaw Atweneboanna and other Kumase dissenters were intrinsically related to the *nkabom* issue. Following the Asantehene's arrest, Yaw Awua, Kofi Nti, Kwasi Adabo, Kwaku Goroso, Kwabena Kokofu, Kwakye Nkatia, and their supporters openly defied the Prempean administration's ban on their activities in the metropolitan region, reentered Kumase politics, and competed again for positions in the government. Agitating for *nkwan-kwaa* and *asikafo* support and relying on British assistance, these long-standing dissidents touted their superior administrative capabilities and demonstrated their willingness to spend considerable financial resources to take over the government.[118]

A number of resourceful and wealthy rubber middlemen—who had lobbied for British protection prior to 1896—backed these dissatisfied politicians and strove to form an opposition party, staunchly pro-British, by advocating a platform of free trade, the confederacy, and unrestricted European capital investment in the metropolitan region. Aside from personal grievances and the desire to enhance their wealth through free trade, the Kumase dissidents raised several provocative issues previously championed by the Asantehene's more liberal councillors in the 1880s and earlier 1890s. Advocating further changes in the Asante judicial process and reduced taxes, they favored the introduction of missionary education and Western cultural styles and objected to the Council of Kumase's efforts to control the proliferation of foreign business enterprises and the pace of development in the southern mining industry. By cooperating with the resident and other British officials, they ignored the government's secrecy laws and revealed the location of the Golden Stool in the town of Wawase to the northwest of Kumase. They supplied information pertaining to the storage and importation of war materials and exposed clandestine military preparations occurring first in the Edweso and Offinso districts and after 1898 in the towns of Atwema.[119]

Although it is difficult to identify all these individuals, since many wished to remain anonymous and most Kumase informants refer to them as "traitors," "bullies," and "extortionists"[120] because of their material and political support for the British in the post-1896 era and especially in the hostilities of 1900, some of these wealthy politicians occupied the Asante-man's most prominent stools after 1901. Kwame Tua—an *osokwani* and *ntahara* blower in the Prempean administration who was born in the town of Amorman—was appointed Gyaasewahene (i.e., the occupant of the Pinanko stool) by the British after 1900. His brother, Kwasi Nuama from Amorman, succeeded Akyeamehene Akoko who in 1896 was arrested with Prempe. Yaw Berko, a royal to the Mampon stool, followed the imprisoned Offinsohene Kwadwo Kwawu, while Kofi Nsenkyire, also a royal to the Mampon stool and a rubber and cloth *sikani*, was appointed Ankasehene or Kyidomhene of Kumase. Osei Mampon and Kwaku Dua Mampon, both rubber *asikafo* from Mampon, were installed respectively as Bantamahene and Atipinhene of Kumase. Kwabena Tooto, a son of the Adumhene Agyei Kese who likewise did not hold office in the Prempean administration, became the Adumhene of Kumase. Bosompra, a former slave to Kofi Ansa, an influential Kumase *sikani*, was installed Atutuehene of Kumase. Kofi Domfe, Kwame Kusi, and Yaw Kusi from the town of Gyimakye were appointed respectively Oyokohene, Anko-beahene, and Nsumankwaahene of Kumase. Akwasi Traa and Kofi Fofie from the town of Tweneduruase on the Bekwae road were enstooled respectively as the Hyeawuhene and Nkonsonhene of Kumase. Kwame Frimpon from the town of Baaman near Bonwire, who resided for the most part in the Colony during the 1890s, became the Adontenhene of Kumase. Kwame Ntahara, a *sikani* and a *ntahara* blower in Prempe's government, was appointed the Abontendomhene of Edweso in 1901 by the newly installed Edwesohene Yaw Awua. Thus these *asikafo*, joining with the former supporters of Kofi Kakari and Yaw Atweneboanna, strove to take over the government in the post-1896 era.[121]

The presence and interference of European missionaries and the Fante, Assin, and Akuapem agents who staffed their outstations also contributed to mounting tensions between the Asante government and the British authorities. Responding to the pressure of reformist Kumase councillors, the Opoku Mensa administration cautiously allowed Ramseyer and Perregaux to establish the first Basel Mission in the capital in late February 1896, and two months later permitted the Wesleyans to return to Kumase to open their own school. Both societies subsequently enlarged their field of activities to a number of outlying districts includ-

215

ing Edweso, Offinso, Agona, Mampon, and Ahafo. By June 1897 thirteen Basel and six Wesleyan schools, with 182 and 209 pupils respectively, were operating in the metropolitan region.[122] Yet, after a brief experimental period, the policies and attitudes of the missionaries rapidly reinforced recurrent conservative opposition and antagonized even the more liberal elements in the Asante government. The efforts by missionary agents to influence local politicians into repudiating the Council of Kumase's authority and their attempts to undermine the legal process (e.g., the Basel missionaries' agitation against customary Great Oath litigations) stimulated anti-British sentiment in Kumase political circles and in several outlying districts.[123] Regretfully, Vroom observed, "some of the agents would not keep away from interfering with the Native Chiefs and their palavers."[124] In promoting the abolition of domestic slavery—an institution supported by most Kumase politicians and citizens as well as by local officeholders and earlier guaranteed by British policymakers—and by employing, training, and allotting land to communities of freed slaves, the missionaries further provoked widespread official and popular resentment. Vroom noted the increasing Asante opposition to European interference with domestic slavery:

> It may be remarked generally that the Ashanti-land is at present unsettled. There are feelings of dissatisfaction in many parts of Ashanti arising from our interference with the question of slavery; so great a social change could not be effected without engendering feelings of irritation, or even incurring some risks. . . . To a casual observer, the country may appear peaceably settled by the seeming rebuilding and repopulation of a few towns and villages; but the careful observer will not fail to see that much remains to be done by judicious administration before the country could be considered as settled. Those districts who opposed Prempe or revolted from his rule entertain grave doubts as to our future domestic policy, or intentions of the Government, particularly with Prempe.[125]

These tensions and cleavages were exacerbated by a host of additional factors operative in the post-1896 era. Asante, Asante Nkramo, Dagomba, Gonja, Silsila, Fante, and Ewe informants who lived and worked in that period provided insights into the multilayered nature of this Asante discontent. A major source of resentment centered on the competition arising from the influx of northern and Colony *ahoho* who contended with Asante entrepreneurs in the rubber, gold, and kola industries and persistently challenged the Council of Kumase's efforts to preserve the economic benefits of these industries for the Asanteman. The Prempean administration in the early 1890s had permitted a limited flow of foreign traders into the metropolitan region, but governmental restrictions curtailed their trading opportunities. A few Hausa, Gonja, and Wangara traders from Kintampo, Salaga, Yegyi, and Atebubu, for example, were allowed to reside permanently in Mbrom on the outskirts of Kumase. Their number never exceeded twenty at any one time, and their spokesman, Muhammad Tune, a wealthy, articulate kola trader from Kano, reported directly to the Asafohene Asafo Boakye whose own *nhenkwaa* carefully supervised foreign kola, cattle, and cloth enterprises. Kumase officials specified the metropolitan regional markets open to these merchants, monitored their journeys to the northern and southern marts, and prohibited all northern or *ntafo* traders from engaging in money-lending operations with Asante citizens. Although authorities in Kumase did not levy special taxes on Tune's companions, they were required to give nearly one-fifth of their merchandise to central governmental functionaries in the Wankyi and Ankase markets. Despite these restrictions, the Hausas in particular reaped sizeable profits from their lucrative trading relationships in the environs of Kumase.[126]

Opoku Mensa and his advisers had difficulties supervising foreign traders and maintaining restrictive immigration policies. Encouraged by officials in the Gold Coast Colony, northern and southern merchants flocked to the Asante capital. British soldiers pressured the Asante *nkwansrafo*, or road guards, to open the arteries to all strangers. After 1896, Asante toll collectors were frequently bribed and were careless in discharging their duties, and British interference with the Bata organization allowed increasing numbers of immigrants to reside in the towns and villages of the metropolitan region.[127] Muslim entrepreneurs gained a large share of the kola trade which gradually was reoriented from the northern to the southern coastal outlets. Akyem, Akuapem, Ewe, and Fante middlemen, attracted by bountiful profits from the Asante rubber trade, engaged in speculative credit and gold-mining schemes and charged exorbitant interest rates on loans to Asante farmers, chiefs, and private Asante *asikafo*. Backed by capital from European and African coastal firms, some Colony entrepreneurs acquired plantations around Kumase and thereby undercut the prices Asantes obtained for their foodstuffs in the Kumase markets and the regional exchange centers of Atwema, Kwabre, Edweso, and Offinso. Several prominent Asante families in these areas went into debt over loan repayments, lower food prices, and the loss of their plantations and laborers.[128] The newly arrived strangers from the Colony and the north, consequently, were bitterly resented by various public and private Asante *asikafo* and *nkwankwaa* in Kumase and the outlying districts.

These economic concerns were compounded by labor complications attending the proliferation of large European mining concessions in Bekwae, Adanse, and along the Pra River after 1898 and the establishment of mercantile firms in several of the urban centers of the metropolitan region.[129] Asantes complained of the European's forced recruitment of carriers for transporting merchandise and machinery to the coast, low pay and discriminatory wage scales, unemployment fines, and a flooded labor market because of freed slaves and migrants from the north and the Colony. British direct taxes and fines to raise revenue to recoup the cost of the expedition of 1896 and to meet the administrative expenses of the resident's office and the newly constructed fort in Kumase (with a garrison of 130 troops) were an affront to segments of the asikafo who had originally lobbied for British protection in hopes of favorable fiscal policies. And the European take-over of the state-owned Manso and Sankore gold fields and the Asantehene's "secret" mines in Asante Akyem, on which Agyeman Prempe had drawn heavily in his last years of office, reduced the flow of capital necessary to support functionaries in the kingdom's bureaucratic apparatus.[130] Competition with foreign traders and the loss of income from the royal gold mines aggravated soaring food costs and insidious inflation in the metropolitan region.

Rising unemployment and higher costs of living thus affected many Asantes' daily existence. Molestations, rape, and banditry committed by Sierra Leone ("Konsoko"), Hausa, and northern troops and carriers of the occupation Gold Coast Constabulary and the inability of Asante citizens to receive due process of law over such incidents intensified the growing Asante dissatisfaction.[131] British punitive expeditions launched in Atwema and Ahafo in 1898–99 against suspected rebel villages further inflamed Asante discontent.[132] Indeed, the issue of discrimination against Asante nationals in British courts and the resident's tendency to uphold the legal claims of and grant preferential treatment to northerners and immigrants from the Colony heightened the xenophobia which had surfaced throughout metropolitan Asante following the establishment of the residency and the Basel and Wesleyan outstations.[133] All of these irritants contributed greatly to the strains between the Opoku Mensa administration and British officials. The belief that the Gold Coast administration might install the rejected candidate, Yaw Atweneboanna, whose partisans had never ceased working towards this end since 1888 and who himself spread false rumors about limitless treasure buried in the environs of Kumase,[134] merely added to the wave of anger and resentment sweeping Kumase and its surrounding villages. Domfe Kyere, voicing the views of many Asantes who hoped that Prempe's return might alleviate most of these mounting tensions, recalled the increasing Asante agitation over the intolerable situation.

The soldiers of the whites bullied Asante traders. They asked the Asante traders to carry their loads on roads up and down the coast. The soldiers did not pay the Asantes for carrying their loads here in Kumase or to the coast. When the Asantes brought drinks from the coast, the soldiers opened the cases and drank without giving the Asantes anything from them. . . . The resident heard of what the soldiers were doing on the coastal road. But the Asantes did not make complaints because the *abatafo* did not like to spend so much money on litigation. In Kumase the whites took the Asantes to court and fined them even for urinating in the streets. Also the whites were carried in *ahomankaa*, or small palanquins. If an Asante man returned from farming, he would be asked to carry the white man. The whites' carriers were paid. But the Asantes who did this were not paid by the whites. Asantes were asked by the whites to carry things, travel distances, and the like. Some were paid. Others were not. We all in Kumase wished Nana Prempe would return. He would know what to do and how to handle the whites' soldiers and people. For some time before the whites came to ask for the Golden Stool, the Asantes had their grievances against the whites. People who were involved in this treatment told others. The word went around.[135]

All these provocations, then, created enormous unrest and anticipation that culminated with Governor Hodgson's unwarranted request for payment of the interest on the war indemnity of 1874 and the expedition of 1896 and his statement of 28 March 1900 that Prempe and Atweneboanna, despite their Colony supporters' petitions, would not be allowed to return to Asante. On that fateful day the governor, seeking to strengthen British claims to authority in Asante, made his shocking, inflammatory demand for Kumase officials to surrender the Golden Stool.[136] Following Opoku Mensa and his councillors' refusal to reveal the location of the symbol of Asante political sovereignty, the governor ordered his military attache, Captain C. H. Armitage, to force the people to tell him. One eyewitness, al-Hajj Sulāyman, recounted the subsequent events of early April.

Four years after Prempe was taken away, Armitage came to Kumase. He went from village to village looking for the Golden Stool. Where he met opposition from the Asantes, Armitage beat the people. He went to Edweso, and the Edwesohemaa told him she did not have the Golden Stool. . . . The Golden Stool was all the time hidden at Wawase. When Armitage went to Wawase, the people of Wawase did not know where the Stool was. Armitage went to Nkwantakese from Wawase. He found nothing there. Armitage continued on to Bare but still did not find the Golden Stool. Armitage beat people at Bare. Kwame Tua and his friends used sticks to whip people with their hands bound. The people at Bare found it too much. They took arms against Armitage and killed one Hausa soldier. Armitage shot back. He and his people ran away. The Bare people were stronger. Armitage and his people were met by the Toasehene Afrifa at the village of Ntemede. Armitage came back to Kumase from Ntemede. This was the beginning of the Yaa Asantewaa War of Independence.[137]

Another informant, Kwadwo Afodo, gave the following account of the situation in the town of Bare to the north of Kumase.

When Prempe was taken away, the Asantes took the Golden Stool from Kumase. They hid it outside Kumase. Kwame Tua blew the *ntahara* in the palace. The *ntahara* is a special horn. It has a special name. It warns people when the Asantehene is about to speak. Kwame Tua told the white men he would help them to get the Golden Stool. The Asantes heard of this. The Asantes said they must shoot if the whites came for the Golden Stool. All the Kumase chiefs swore an oath calling the shrine. They kept calm. One white man, named Armitage, did not want the Asantes to see Kwame Tua. The white soldiers carried Tua on their heads. They covered him with clothes. The Kumase people saw Kwame Tua. They knew he was with Armitage and his men. Kwame Tua learned that the Kumase people knew he was with Armitage. Tua told Armitage his nephew would take his place. Kwame Tua's nephew, named Adu Boahene, was unknown to the stool carriers. The whites carried Adu Boahene in the same way. He was covered. They went to Bare. The Bare people heard Armitage was coming to their village. They left the village. They left their children in the streets. The children cooked kenkey and yams and sold them. The whites asked the children why the elderly people were not in town. The children told the whites their fathers had gone hunting in the bush. The white man asked the children to call their fathers. The children said they did not know where their fathers were hunting in the bush. The white man asked the children where the Golden Stool was kept in Bare. The white man said he would beat the children if they did not bring their fathers from the bush. The children told the white man not to call their fathers. If he wanted to beat them, he should do it. The children knew the whites were coming for the Golden Stool. The children did not fear beating. The white soldiers began to bully and beat the children. The elderly people were around the village. They would not allow the whites to bully their children. Then the white men searched for the Golden Stool themselves.

The Bare people did not allow the white men to come back to Kumase. They knew if Armitage went back to Kumase he would trouble the elderly people in Kumase for the Golden Stool. So the Bare people gave the first shot.[138]

Following the Bare incident of 2 April 1900, a full-scale military confrontation was inevitable. Governor Hodgson ordered the destruction of a number of centralist strongholds to the south and east of the Asante capital and reinforced British garrisons stationed in Kumase, the local centers of administration, and Atebubu, Bompata, Nkoransa, and Gyaman. British agents pledged modern war materials, financial resources, and rewards of high political office and career advancement to their most vociferous official, rubber *asikafo*, and commoner backers in the outlying localist districts of Agona, Bekwae, Dwaben, Mampon, Manso, and Nsuta. Various former partisans of the candidacies of Kofi Kakari and Yaw Atweneboanna also received guarantees of rapid promotion in the Asante political establishment. Agyeman Prempe's councillors in the Opoku Mensa administration, concurrently, mobilized their own supporters in the towns and villages of Atwema, Ahafo, Amansie, and Kwabre. Contingents from Edweso and Offinso quickly joined their cause. Then, on the twenty-third of April, two thousand troops under the joint command of the Nsumankwaahene Kwasi Domfe, the Nkonsonhene Kofi Fofie, the Suamehene Yaw Dane, the Antoahene Antoa Mensa, the Gyakyehene Yaw Pense, and the Edweso Gyaasehene, Kwasi Boadu, launched reprisals against British troops at the town of Fomesua, seven miles from Kumase. For the first time in twenty-six years, the Asante and British governments were at war.

During the ensuing four months, Asante combatants barricaded the capital and besieged 750 British soldiers, the governor and his staff, and several European entrepreneurs and missionaries in the fort, the intensely unpopular symbol of British power and influence in the metropolitan region. Despite heavy losses from British artillery, starvation, water shortages, and smallpox, the morale of the poorly equipped Asante forces remained high. The surge for independence was embodied in the feisty, gallant Yaa Asantewaa, the fifty-year-old *ohemaa* of Edweso, who relentlessly inspired the Asante drive for freedom. Yet Yaa Asantewaa and the remaining Prempean officials in Kumase could not overcome Great Britain's unwavering commitment to rule Asante. In September 1900, additional detachments of the West African Frontier Force from Accra, Lagos, and the northern hinterlands crushed the bloody, short-lived War of Independence.[139] Edweso, Offinso, Kokofu, and the villages on the outskirts of Kumase were razed. Thirty-one principal Asante *asahene* were either arrested, executed, or detained at Elmina Castle. Their families were plundered, their farms and plantations ravaged, and their property confiscated. Yaa Asantewaa and her closest companions were deported as political prisoners along with the exiled Asantehene Agyeman Prempe and his advisers to the distant Seychelles.

The agony of the Opoku Mensa administration had ended. A new era of postwar reorganization opened. In the aftermath of the hostilities, Britain finally gained its right to rule Asante by conquest. The royal prerogatives of nineteenth-century occupants of the Golden Stool had been destroyed, and the structure of the Asante government and its terri-torial jurisdiction forever altered. On 26 September 1900, Asante was annexed by an Order in Council as a separate Crown Colony. British colonial rule with its new judicial, administrative, and financial institu-tions was formalized and consolidated. But, as British administrators, European concessionnaires and missionaries, and foreign soldiers traveled throughout the districts and towns of the metropolitan region in the early twentieth century, they never crushed the recurrent, spirited, and pro-foundly optimistic chant of Asante men, women, and children in every *abusua*, village, and community of the Asanteman.

ɔmane yi nnye mo deɛ,	This nation is not yours,
Nana Yaa deɛ,	It belongs to Nana Yaa,
ɔmane yi nnye mo deɛ oo!	This nation is not yours!
Yaa Akyaa deɛ,	It belongs to Yaa Akyaa,
ɔmane yi nnye mo mane, a oo!	This nation is not your nation!
Nana Prempe deɛ.	It belongs to Nana Prempe.
Nana Prempe nni hɔ na moredi	Nana Prempe is away, and you
n'adeɛ.	are occupying his office.[140]

APPENDIXES

The major historical figures mentioned in the text are listed here with short biographical comments.

Osei Kwaku Abrebrease—Bekwaehene; chief of the outlying district of Bekwae; came to office in 1887; supported candidacy of Agyeman Prempe.

Kwame Adwetewa—Mamponhene; ruler of the outlying *oman*, or district, of Mampon; slain in the Kenyase hostilities of 1883–1884.

Kwasi Afrane Kumaa—Edwesohene; head of the outlying district of Edweso, thirteen miles from Kumase; imprisoned by the British and deported with the Asantehene Agyeman Prempe in 1896.

Kwasi Afrane Panin—Edwesohene; one of the leading military supporters of Prempe in the electoral contest of 1887–1888; his district was elevated to *oman* status as a reward for his services.

Kwame Afrifa—Toasehene; chief of Toase; served in the triumvirate administration post-1896.

Asafo Agyei—Dwabenhene; ruler of Dwaben and leader of rebellion and secessionist cause in 1874–1875; defeated by the Mensa Bonsu administration and exiled in Colony.

Agyeman—Gyamanhene; ruler of Gyaman polity; leading localist and supporter of Gyaman independence in late 1880s.

Yaw Akroma—Nsutahene; chief of Nsuta; vocal supporter of the unsuccessful candidacy of Kofi Kakari in the contest of 1883.

Kwadwo Akuamoa II—Abenehene; a political authority in province of Kwawu; leader of localists in mid 1880s.

Yaa Akyaa—Asantehemaa; queen mother of Asante; mother of Prempe; brought to office in 1884; imprisoned by British in 1896.

Kwasi Akyampon—Agonahene; chief of Agona town; supporter of Kakarian candidacy in 1883 and Atweneboanna's candidacy in 1887–1888.

Akyampon Panin—Saamanhene; chief of Saawua, eight miles from Kumase; leader of military coup against Akyempemhene Owusu Koko in December 1884; supported Atweneboanna and executed in 1887.

Yaw Amponsa—Manso Nkwantahene; chief of Manso district; led local rebellion against Kumase's authority in early 1880s; backed Akyampon Panin's coup in late 1884.

John Owusu Ansa—son of Owusu Ansa; chief diplomat, foreign policy adviser, and economic innovator in Prempe regime in 1890s.

Kwabena Antwi—Kuntanasehene; Oyoko ruler of Kuntanase town; late supporter of Prempe's candidacy.

Kwame Antwi Agyei—Atwemahene; ruler of district of Atwema; key supporter of Prempe in 1887.

Kofi Apea—Nsutahene; military supporter of Atweneboanna in 1887–1888; took refuge in Atebubu and supported British policy in the northeast; localist leader.

Yaa Asantewaa—Edwesohemaa; queen mother of Edweso; symbolic leader of War of Independence of 1900–1901; mother of Afrane Kumaa.

Osei Asibe—Kokofuhene; ruler of Kokofu; came to office in early 1887; outstanding Atweneboanna backer; took refuge in Colony after 1888.

Asibe II (Yaw Konkroma)—Kokofuhene; nephew of Osei Asibe; came to office in early 1890s; supporter of extension of British authority to Asante.

Yaw Atweneboanna—Kumase royal; unsuccessful candidate against Prempe in electoral contest of 1887–1888; banished to Colony in late 1880s; outspoken against Kumase in 1890s.

Kwabena Awua—Bantamahene; one of the two senior military commanders of Kumase; leading conservative force in late 1870s; banished by Mensa Bonsu to Manso in early 1880s; killed in 1886.

Yaw Awua—Edweso royal; wealthy rubber trader; supported Kakari and Atweneboanna; appointed Edwesohene by British after 1900; became blind in office and deposed.

Agyeman Badu—Abakomadwahene; younger brother of Prempe; occupant of heir apparent stool in 1890s; imprisoned and exiled by British in 1896.

Yaw Berko—wealthy rubber trader; supported Kakari and Atweneboanna; appointed Offinsohene by British after 1900; favored British presence in Asante.

Asafo Boakye—Asafohene; one of two major military commanders of Kumase; extensive military and political career throughout 1870s, 1880s, and 1890s; imprisoned and exiled with Prempe in 1896.

Kofi Boaten—Abenehene; called Kwawuhene by British; brought to office in 1884; signed treaty with British in June 1888; localist leader.

Adu Bofo—Gyaasewahene; occupant of Gyaasewa stool; titular treasurer and military commander under the Asantehene Kofi Kakari; principal Kumase traditionalist in Bonsu administration; died in 1883.

Mensa Bonsu—Asantehene; occupant of the Golden Stool from 1874 to 1883; deposed by popular coup in March 1883; headed modernizing but economically repressive administration; died by poisoning in 1896.

Osei Bruni—son of Akyempemhene Owusu Koko; diplomat in Prempe regime and leading advocate of commercial reform.

Kofi Denkyi—Abetifihene; ruler of the most influential Kwawu town; came to office in early 1870s; died January 1883.

Kwaku Dua Kumaa—Asantehene; occupant of the Golden Stool for forty days in 1884; elder brother of Prempe; competed against Kofi Kakari and symbol of Kumase centralists in 1884; probably murdered.

Atta Fa—Nkoransahene; chief of northeastern district of Nkoransa in early 1880s; led localists' rebellion against Kumase from 1881 to 1883; promoted renewed ties with Kumase in 1884; out of office in 1885.

Kofi Fa—Nkoransahene; came to office late 1888; led rebellion against Prempe regime in early 1890s; partisan of secessionism.

Kwaku Fokuo—Prempean diplomat; attended embassy to London in 1896.

Amoa Fua—Dadiasehene; Nifahene of Kokofu district; led rebellion in southern districts from 1883 to 1885; advocate of confederacy ideal and restoration of monarchy in 1886; very influential southern leader.

Ata Fua—chief of Akyem—Kotoko in Protectorate; supported Kakari and Atweneboanna; opposed Kokofu resettlement scheme in 1888.

Kwabena Fua—chief of Akyem—Abuakwa; localist; opposed Kumase in the 1880s; British supporter.

Kwaku Goroso—elderly Kumase royal; implicated in assassination attempt against Mensa Bonsu in 1879; wealthy trader and supporter of Atweneboanna post-1888 from Colony.

Kwasi Gyambibi—Akyebiakyerehene; father of Prempe and husband of Yaa Akyaa; chief of Antoa; imprisoned and exiled with Prempe in 1896.

Ata Gyamfi—Ankobeahene; head of the Asantehene's household and personal bodyguards; a main Kumase supporter of Kwaku Dua Kumaa and Akyempemhene Owusu Koko; captured and killed in Atwema in late 1884.

Yaw Gyamfi—Bekwaehene; brought to office in early 1886; led war effort against Adanse; opposed Saamanhene Akyampon Panin; confederate spokesman.

Nantwi Kaakyire—Kumase *okyeame*; member of the triumvirate administration post-1896; was appointed by Kumase chiefs.

Kofi Kakari—Asantehene; occupant of the Golden Stool, 1867–1874; headed war interest and presided over Kumase during British invasion of 1873–1874; forced to abdicate for illegal policies and resurfaced to contest with Kwaku Dua in 1883; was executed by Owusu Koko in June 1884.

Kwasi Kasa—a Manso chief; militant rebel against Kumase's authority in early 1880s; fled to Akyem in 1886; instrumental in forcing Kumase attack in 1884.

Afua Kobi—Asantehemaa; queen mother of Asante; mother of Mensa Bonsu and Kofi Kakari; predecessor of Yaa Akyaa; advocate of peace policies; deposed 1884.

Owusu Koko—Akyempemhene; chief of the Kumase princes (sons and grandsons of the Asantehene); foremost peace advocate under Kwaku Dua Panin; banished in 1867; reemerged as a leading centralist and backer of Kwaku Dua Kumaa; ruthlessly dominated Kumase politics in 1883–1884.

Owusu Koko Kumaa—son of Saamanhene Akyampon Panin; a main Kumase diplomat in the 1880s.

Kwabena Kokofu—wealthy rubber trader; ally of Goroso; Atweneboanna partisan; pro-British; became Saawuahene post-1900.

Kotirko—adviser to Asantehene Kofi Kakari, 1869–1872; *okyeame* and main adviser to Adansehene Kwaku Nkansa.

Kwasi Krapa—Kumawuhene; ruler of outlying district of Kumawu; appointed by Mensa Bonsu; a key supporter of Prempe in 1888; elevated in political status by Prempe.

Amankwatia Kwame—Bantamahene; successor to Awua; important councillor to Prempe; imprisoned by British in 1896.

Asamoa Kwame—Adumhene; head of the Kumase police force; brought to office in late 1870s; served under Prempe.

Kwadwo Kwawu—Offinsohene; came to office in early 1893; followed Apea Sea; imprisoned with Prempe; died in exile.

Kwaku Dua Mampon—Atipinhene; Mampon royal; opposed Prempe; appointed to office by British after 1900; wealthy gold, kola, and cloth trader.

Osei Mampon—Bantamahene; rubber trader and Mampon royal; pro-British; appointed to office by British after 1900.

Opoku Mensa—Gyaasewahene; Kumase chief; headed triumvirate administration; staunch Prempe supporter; died in 1900.

Kwaku Nkansa—Adansehene; ruler of Adanse; localist who lacked widespread district support; fought with Bekwae authorities in 1886; fled to Colony.

Kofi Nti—son of Kofi Kakari; educated in West Indies; Kakari and Atweneboanna supporter; appointed Dadiesoabahene by British after 1900.

Kwabena Oben—Fomenahene; most important local ruler in Adanse; peace advocate; negotiated with Wolseley in late 1873; early localist; defeated by Bekwae.

Yaw Opoku—Bekwaehene; war advocate in 1870s; opposed Adanse territorial claims; leader of opposition against Asantehene Kakari in 1874.

Kwame Apea Osokye—Mamponhene; appointed by Kumase in late 1888; wealthy trader; strong Prempe supporter; allied with Edwesohene Afrane Panin.

Agyeman Prempe—Asantehene; occupant of the Golden Stool in 1888; also known as Kwaku Dua III; son of Yaa Akyaa and Kwasi Gyambibi; captured by British in 1896; exiled from Sierra Leone to Seychelles Islands in 1900.

Almami Samori—Muslim reform leader; attempted first unification of Dyula towns in northern Ivory Coast; negotiated with Kumase in 1895; executed by French in 1899.

Yaw Sapon—Dwabenhene; appointed by Asantehene Mensa Bonsu; early supporter of Prempe; pro-British in 1890s; advocate of Dwaben unification.

Apea Sea—Offinsohene; leader of Offinso district in 1880s; supported Prempe and Kumase centralists; out of office in early 1890s.

Ama Sewaa—Dwabenhemaa; spokeswoman for Koforidua Dwaben community in Colony; pro-British; supported Dwaben unification.

Owusu Sekyere II—Mamponhene; a principal supporter of Atweneboanna's candidacy in 1887; defeated by Prempe's supporters; fled to Atebubu; refused to return to Asante; negotiated with British in 1890s.

Yaw Sekyere—Gyamasehene; leader of most populous town in Mampon district; supported Prempe; came to office in early 1889; centralist in 1890s.

Boakye Tenten—occupant of the Boakye Yam Panin *okyeame* stool; second husband of Afua Kobi; chief Kumase diplomat in 1870s and 1880s; foremost civil administrator; killed in late 1884.

Kwame Tua—hornblower in the Asantehene's palace; wealthy rubber trader; pro-British in 1890s; appointed occupant of Pinanko stool post-1900.

Osei Yaw—Bekwaehene; installed with Kumase's assistance in early 1883; localist; rebelled against Kumase; pro-British; deposed early 1884; probably executed by Kumase agents for his localist and British leanings.

B. PRINCIPAL PARTICIPANTS IN THE COUNCIL OF KUMASE IN THE LATE NINETEENTH CENTURY

Konti Fekuo:	Kontihene (Bantamahene)	Toasehene
	Bamuhene	Atwema Agogohene
	Afarihene	Abontemhene
	Barehene	Tredehene
	Assuowinhene	Atwemahene
	Akwaboahene	Nkawiekumaahene
Akwamu Fekuo:	Akwamuhene (Asafohene)	Akrafohene
	Adumhene	Twafohene
	Suaduhene	Nkwantakesehene

	Ohwimhene	Baworohene
Adonten Fekuo:	Adontenhene	Sekyehene
	Amakomhene	Abenkyimhene
	Antoahene	Yasehene
	Kwamohene	Adankranyahene
	Akyawkromhene	Asansohene
Nifa Fekuo:	Asokore Mamponhene	Beposohene
Benkum Fekuo:	Tafohene	Fomesuahene
	Abodomhene	Hemanhene
	Apiaduhene	Tikromhene
	Bomanhene	
Oyoko Fekuo:	Oyokohene	Anyinasehene
	Atutuehene	Pampasohene
	Mampontenhene	Oyoko Bremanhene
	Kenyasehene	Aburasohene
	Wadie Adwumakasehene	
Kyidom Fekuo:	Akyempemhene	Akumantihene
	Kyidomhene	Akuroponhene
	Hiahene	Ofoasehene
	Domakwaehene (Akyeamehene)	
	Adumasehene	Krapahene
	Saawuahene	Adensehene
	Asemhene	Amormanhene
	Konahene	Ampabamehene
	Amoakohene	
Gyaase Fekuo:	Saamanhene (Gyaasehene)	Buokromhene
	Dadiesoabahene	Donyinahene
	Kronkohene	Akyeasehene
	Anantahene	Beposohene
	Esasehene	Pamenasehene
	Hiawuhene	Ofoasehene
	Adwumakasehene	Tepahene
	Nsumankwaahene	Kaasehene
	Nkonsonhene	Asromasohene
	Fantehene	Wirempehene
Ankobea Fekuo:	Ankobeahene	Atenehene
	Atipinhene	Apesemakahene
	Anamenakohene	Atene Akotenhene
	Apagyahene	Mamensenhene
Manwere Fekuo:	Manwerehene	Onokyehene
	Asabihene	Nkabomhene
	Asramponhene	Nyinahinihene

Akyeame of the Asantehene

C. Seventy-Seven Wards of Kumase in the
Late Nineteenth Century

These wards comprised the urban capital of Asante, and informants commonly referred to them in their accounts of the past. Each ward had political, ritual, and

historical significance for nineteenth-century Asante political life. As the residences of senior Kumase officeholders, they were also points of identification for Asante citizens.

Abromam	Asokwa	Kotoko
Adenkyemenaso	Asratoase	Manhyia
Adonnwe	Asramponso	Nitibanso
Adontene	Asumenam	Nkramom
Adum	Atani	Nkramu
Adwaa	Atuatu	Nkukua
Akanase	Atweneboanna	Nnono-kro
Akuomem	Bantama	Nsene
Akyeremade	Boagyawe	Nsuase
Anamenako	Bodomase	Ntanosu
Ankobea	Bohenmoho	Ntommemu
Ankra-Asuman	Bonsamoho	Ntuom
Anokye-ko-manmu	Daboase	Nwerem
Anonomsa	Dadiesoaba	Oanoasi
Anowu	Dampankeseho	Odumase
Anyinase	Deduakrase	Senteao
Apagya	Denteso	Sentewosoro
Apeboso	Dominase	Serebosakyi
Apempoa	Domponinase	Sodo
Apoboe	Dontoaso	Sraman Nnyeduase
Apremoso	Dwaberem	Tonsuoanim
Asabi	Hemaneho	Topreduase
Asafo	Hiawu	Topreman Nkwanta
Asafo-Aboraso	Kagyatia	Wawase
Asaman-Akodane	Kete	Worakese
Asikasu	Kose	

NOTES

Abbreviations used in the notes.

Acc. No.	Accession Number, Accra Archives
ADM	Administrative Files, Accra Archives
BMA	Basel Mission Archives, Basel
C.	Papers Presented to the United Kingdom
CCA	Chief Commissioner, Asante
C.O.	Colonial Office, London
Conf. M.P.	Confidential Minute Papers
dd.	dated
GNQ	Ghana Notes and Queries
IAS	Institute of African Studies, University of Ghana
JAH	The Journal of African History
MMA	Methodist Mission Archives, London
NAG	National Archives of Ghana, Accra
PRO	Public Record Office, London
SNA	Secretary for Native Affairs, Gold Coast
THSG	Transactions of the Historical Society of Ghana

CHAPTER 1

1. See W. Walton Claridge, A History of the Gold Coast and Ashanti (two vols., London, 1915), II, chs. VIII–XXII; W. E. F. Ward, A History of Ghana (London, 1967), fourth edition, passim; Sir Francis Fuller, A Vanished Dynasty: Ashanti (London, 1921), pp. 132–184; David Kimble, A Political History of Ghana: The Rise of Gold Coast Nationalism, 1850–1928 (Oxford, 1963), pp. 264–300; William Tordoff, Ashanti under the Prempehs, 1888–1935 (London, 1965), pp. 1–109.
2. Ivor Wilks, Asante in the Nineteenth Century: The Structure and Evolution of a Political Order (Cambridge, 1975).
3. Complete texts of the interviews cited are found in Lewin, "The Structure of Political Conflict in Asante, 1875–1900" (two vols., Ph.D. thesis, Northwestern University, 1974), The English Involvement in Ashanti around 1900 (Legon, 1968), and the writer's field-notes. All interviews listed in the sources section are on public deposit in the libraries of Northwestern University and the University of Kansas. Field interviews were conducted in the environs of Kumase and the districts of Asumegya, Bekwae, Dwaben, Effiduase, Edweso, Kenyase, Kokofu, Kumawu, Mampon, Mamponten, Manso Nkwanta, Nsuta, Offinso, and the Sekyere towns and villages of the Asante metropolitan region. In addition, both open-ended and structured, direct question interviews were conducted with

116 senior officials in the Kumase political establishment. This represents nearly all of the principal Kumase administrators whose ancestors controlled lands and subjects in the metropolitan region. Ten of the Asantehene's *akyeame* or spokesmen were interviewed and all the leaders of the outlying districts and their advisers. Interviews were also held with descendants of influential Asante merchant families. Finally, interviews were conducted with descendants of Muslim and other stranger communities in an effort to amass and recheck oral data received from Asante citizens. Probing of informant memories of events, situations, and relationships and of details these informants had heard from their older relatives regarding the nature and involvement of their villages and towns within the late nineteenth-century political process was also crucial. Constant efforts were made to coordinate specific with general data. All inconsistencies and anomalies were investigated. All answers were fully recorded, and keenly interested, knowledgeable interpreters from urban and rural environments were carefully screened and employed extensively in this phase of the research. Fortunately, influential Asante and non-Asante citizens—some of whom claimed to be well over one hundred years old—were still able to recount their own *first-hand*, broad range of experiences with the precolonial situation.

4. I intend to discuss fully the subject of interpretation and my own research experience and field interviewing procedures in a future paper. The value of survey interviews in relation to specialized interviews with key Asante and non-Asante informants will be assessed. Surveys underscored the significance of lists of officeholders and genealogies, and other formal (or fixed) texts of oral tradition which are occasionally maintained locally throughout the Asante region. And the survey method was especially useful in isolating facts stored away in individuals' memories which are best elicited by subsequent question-and-answer interviews. This paper, then, will constitute the first full-scale treatment of the remarkably rich and diverse Asante oral heritage.

CHAPTER 2

1. For the politics of population and general demographic features of central or metropolitan Asante in the eighteenth and early nineteenth century, see Wilks, *Asante in Nineteenth Century*, pp. 80–102, and pp. 106–11 for an overview of the origins of the kingdom's political order. The creation of the Asante agrarian order and the formation of matriclans in the forest heartlands in the seventeenth century is considered in Wilks, "Land, Labour, and Capital and the Forest Kingdom of Asante: A Model of Early Change," in J. Friedman and M. Rowlands (eds.), *Evolution of Social Systems* (London, 1978), pp. 487–534, passim. See also Kwamina B. Dickson, "Trade Patterns in Ghana at the Beginning of the Eighteenth Century," *The Geographical Review* 56 (1966), 417–25, for general ecological patterns of the Asante forest zone and southern Akan society.

2. A discussion of the importance of this trade route and its distributive network in the Western Sudan can be found in Wilks, *The Northern Factor in Ashanti History* (Legon, 1961), pp. 1–13, and Wilks, "A Medieval Trade-Route from the Niger to the Gulf of Guinea," *JAH* 3 (1962), 337–41. Kwamina B. Dickson, *A Historical Geography of Ghana* (Cambridge, 1971), pp. 269–322, discusses hunting, mining, and agricultural activities in the modern period. For a summary of the career and reign of the Asantehene Osei Tutu (died 1712 or 1717), see J. K. Fynn, *Asante and Its Neighbours, 1700–1807* (London, 1971),

pp. 27–56, and Wilks, *Asante in Nineteenth Century*, pp. 110–12, for his illustrious military campaigns.

3. On the social structure and geography of this area, see M. Fortes, "Ashanti Survey, 1945–46: An Experiment in Social Research," *Geographical Journal* 110 (1947), 149–51, 160–70; R. W. Steel, "The Population of Ashanti: A Geographical Analysis," *Geographical Journal* 112 (1948), 64–76; Kwasi Boaten, "An Historical Geography of Northern Asante, 1702–1945" (M.A. thesis, University of Ghana, 1969), pp. 1–83.

4. For a discussion of Asante regalia and its significance for the kingdom's traditions and political life, see A. A. Y. Kyerematen, *Panoply of Ghana* (London, 1964), pp. 11–115, passim. See also Wilks, "Ashanti Government," in D. Forde and P. M. Kaberry (eds.), *West African Kingdoms in the Nineteenth Century* (London, 1967), p. 208.

5. Ibid., pp. 211–12, and for a further discussion of the extent of the Asante empire, see Wilks, *Asante in Nineteenth Century*, pp. 1–79, passim, which considers the process of conquest, incorporation, and communication in the creation of the empire. The relationship of interior trade and Asante and European commercial involvement is discussed in M. A. Kwamena-Poh, *Government and Politics in the Akuapem State, 1730–1850* (London, 1973), pp. 72–110.

6. For a discussion of commercial flows in the eighteenth and early nineteenth century, see Wilks, *Asante in Nineteenth Century*, pp. 126–41, 193–98, 261–66; Wilks, "Asante Policy towards the Hausa Trade in the Nineteenth Century," in Claude Meillassoux (ed.), *The Development of Indigenous Trade and Markets in West Africa* (London, 1971), pp. 124–32; Kwame Arhin, "The Financing of the Ashanti Expansion (1700–1820)," *Africa* 37 (1967), 283–91.

7. For analyses of these developments, see Tordoff, "The Ashanti Confederacy," *JAH* 3 (1962), 399–417; Kwame Arhin, "The Structure of Greater Ashanti (1700–1824)," *JAH* 8 (1967), 65–85; Wilks, "Ashanti Government," pp. 206–38; G. P. Hagan, "Ashanti Bureaucracy: A Study of the Growth of Centralized Administration in Ashanti from the Time of Osei Tutu to the Time of Osei Tutu Kwamina Esibe Bonsu," *THSG* 12 (1971), 43–62.

8. A point noted by nearly all aged Asante informants in their accounts of the past. Most nineteenth-century European visitors to the capital did not disagree. See further, Wilks, *Asante in Nineteenth Century*, pp. 374–476, passim, and Lewin, "Structure of Political Conflict," II, passim.

9. The vitality, excitement, pathos, and fluidity in Asante political culture form a backdrop to all discussions of late nineteenth-century political life.

10. Lewin, field-notes: interview with Omantihene Owusu Nkwantabisa, 4 Feb. 1971.

11. See, e.g., T. Edward Bowdich, *Mission from Cape Coast Castle to Ashantee* (London, 1819), pp. 323–24. And see also pp. 332–37 for artisans and immigrants in Kumase.

12. For descriptions of the city of Kumase in the early and middle nineteenth century, see Wilks, *Asante in Nineteenth Century*, pp. 374–87, and Thomas C. McCaskie, "The Paramountcy of the Asantehene Kwaku Dua (1834–1867): A Study in Asante Political Culture" (Ph.D. thesis, University of Cambridge, 1974), pp. 152–84, which also discuss the relationship between the city's spatial structure and the Asantehene's immense political control in the urban area.

13. See, e.g., Wilks, *Asante in Nineteenth Century*, pp. 381–83, 386, 451, for the types of official business conducted in these bureaus or offices in Kumase.

14. Lewin, field-notes: interviews with Omantihene Owusu Nkwantabisa, 4 Feb. 1971, and Domfe Kyere, 9 Feb. 1971; and for the early nineteenth century, see Bowdich, *Mission from Cape Coast*, p. 388.
15. Lewin, "Structure of Political Conflict," II, p. 434: interview with Domfe Kyere, 7 Apr. 1971. Domfe Kyere, born around 1872, is an *osomfo-panin* (elder or adviser) in the Nsumankwaa Fekuo. As an *ahenkwaa* in the Asantehene's palace in Kumase, he witnessed the deposition of the Asantehene Mensa Bonsu in 1883, carried yams to Kumase troops in the military encounters of 1887–88, participated in the ceremonies surrounding the installation of Agyeman Prempe in 1894 and the reception for the British in 1896, and fought in the Yaa Asantewaa War of 1900. Living in Kumase his entire life, Domfe Kyere never held office but worked as a *batani* (trader), goldsmith, and plantation overseer. Since 1880 he has had close ties with other elderly *nhenkwaa* in the Asantehene's palace and after converting to Islam in 1967 broadened his connections in the Asante Nkramo community of Asante and among other metropolitan region *asikafo*.
16. Ibid., p. 434: interview with Domfe Kyere, 7 Apr. 1971. See also the seventy-seven wards of nineteenth-century Kumase in Appendix C.
17. Ibid., pp. 433–34: interview with Domfe Kyere, 7 Apr. 1971.
18. Bowdich, *Mission from Cape Coast*, pp. 324–25, and Lewin, field-notes: interview with Domfe Kyere, 10 May 1971.
19. Lewin, "Structure of Political Conflict," II, p. 364: interview with Omantihene Owusu Nkwantabisa, 29 Dec. 1970.
20. See Arhin, "Aspects of the Ashanti Northern Trade in the Nineteenth Century," *Africa*, 40 (1970), 370, and Wilks, "The Golden Stool and the Elephant's Tail: The Rise of the Asante Middle Class," in George Dalton (ed.), *Studies in Economic Anthropology* (1979), forthcoming, for discussions of symbols of wealth displayed by officeholding groups in the metropolitan region.
21. S. S. Djang, *The Sunlight Reference Almanac* (Aburi, 1936), p. 114. Most present-day Asante informants agree with this description and stress that the term *asikafo* should be used for public and private individuals possessing wealth in the form of slaves, liquid assets, houses and farms, and wives. See, e.g., Lewin, "Structure of Political Conflict," II, pp. 448–49: interview with Domfe Kyere, 13 Apr. 1971.
22. Arhin, "Aspects of the Ashanti Northern Trade," 365–68; Lewin, "Structure of Political Conflict," II, pp. 440–43: interview with Domfe Kyere, 10 Apr. 1971.
23. Ibid., p. 441: interview with Domfe Kyere, 10 Apr. 1971.
24. Ibid., p. 185: interview with Kwadwo Bo, 3 Sept. 1970.
25. Ibid., p. 449: interview with Domfe Kyere, 13 Apr. 1971.
26. Ibid., pp. 448–49: interview with Domfe Kyere, 13 Apr. 1971; and see also Wilks, *Asante in Nineteenth Century*, pp. 178–79, 264, 310–12.
27. Lewin, "Structure of Political Conflict," II, pp. 443–44: interview with Domfe Kyere, 10 Apr. 1971.
28. Ibid., pp. 61, 134, 138–39, 242–43: interviews with I. K. Agyeman, 8 July 1970; Adu Gyamera, 17, 27 Aug. 1970; Akyempemhene Boakye Dankwa II, 2 Oct. 1970; see also Wilks, *Asante in Nineteenth Century*, pp. 80–96, passim, and 102–6. I. K. Agyeman, eighty-seven years old in 1971, has played a leading role in Asante politics over the past fifty years. His grandfather was the Kyidomhene of

Kumase, and his great-grandfather was the Asantehene Osei Bonsu I. I. K. Agyeman was one of the founders of the Asante-Kotoku-Union Society in 1916, which was the earliest nationalist organization in Asante, was senior secretary of the Kumase State Council as well as secretary and president of that body. In July 1945, Agyeman represented Asante in the embassy that met with the British secretary of state over new legislation for Asante and the Colony. During the installation ceremonies of June 1970, this informant closely supervised the installation proceedings of J. Mathew Poku, the current Asantehene Opoku Ware II.

29. Ibid., pp. 106–10; Lewin, "Structure of Political Conflict," II, pp. 257–58, 261, 265: interviews with Kyidomhene Osei Yaw, 16 Oct. 1970; Manwerehene Kwabena Boaten, 16 Oct. 1970; Saamanhene Osei Kwaku II, 23 Oct. 1970.

30. For an expanded discussion of the late nineteenth-century spread of Kumase office-estates and their spatial configuration, see Thomas J. Lewin and Dennis Fitzsimmons, "The Political Organization of Space in Asante: Part I," *Asante Seminar '76* 4 (1976), 25–33, and "The Political Organization of Space in Asante: Part II," *Asante Seminar '76* 5 (1976), 15–21.

31. A comprehensive description of the *odekuro*, his council of elders, and the basic patterns of Asante social organization in the villages is found in R. S. Rattray, *Ashanti* (Oxford, 1923); *Religion and Art in Ashanti* (Oxford, 1927).

32. See Rattray, *Ashanti*, passim; Lewin, "Structure of Political Conflict," II, pp. 313, 329: interviews with Atutuehene Opon Wadie, 27 Nov. 1970; Atwemahene Antwi Agyei IV, 11 Dec. 1970.

33. See, e.g., ibid., p. 320: interview with Atwema Agogohene Owusu Afriyie I, 4 Dec. 1970.

34. Lewin, field-notes: interviews with Adu Gyamera, 16 Feb. 1971; Domfe Kyere, 18 Feb. 1971. Adu Gyamera stated his age at 115 years. He was born in the town of Boko-Atwema in the Atwema region shortly before Kofi Kakari became Asantehene in 1867. Adu Gyamera's grandfather was Atwemahene, and his father was an *ahenkwaa* in the Asantehene's palace in Kumase. As a young man Adu Gyamera followed in his father's footsteps and worked in the group whose responsibility it was to fill the Asantehene's smoking pipes. He performed this service (i.e., *taahyɛ*) until 1896 and subsequently made a great deal of money in the rubber and cocoa trade. He represents the viewpoint of Atwema "nationalists" and had many associates in the *asikafo* and *nkwankwaa* segments of nineteenth-century Asante society.

35. Ibid., interview with I. K. Agyeman, 17 June 1970.

36. See, e.g., ibid., interview with I. K. Agyeman, 6 Feb. 1971.

37. Lewin, "Structure of Political Conflict," II, pp. 319–20, 329–30: interviews with Atwema Agogohene Owusu Afriyie I, 4 Dec. 1970; Atwemahene Antwi Agyei IV, 11 Dec. 1970.

38. See, e.g., ibid., pp. 391–93: interview with Kokofuhene Osei Asibe III and Adu Buobi, 19 Mar. 1971.

39. See, e.g., Lewin, field-notes: interview with Domfe Kyere, 8 Apr. 1971. For a treatment of the relationship between Bron Ahafo and the Asante kingdom, with particular reference to the late nineteenth and early twentieth centuries, see John Dunn and A. F. Robertson, *Dependence and Opportunity: Political Change in Ahafo* (Cambridge, 1973), pp. 10–41, and 224–38.

40. An extensive account of the nature of bureaucratic and socioeconomic change in Asante during the early and middle years of the nineteenth century is in Wilks,

"Aspects of Bureaucratization in Ashanti in the Nineteenth Century," *JAH* 7 (1966), 215–32, and *Asante in Nineteenth Century*, pp. 445–76; Hagan, "Ashanti Bureaucracy," 43–62; McCaskie, "Paramountcy of Kwaku Dua," pp. 16–76, 113–52, 192–240.

41. For the restricted traditional role of the Asantehene and the nature of Asante "parties" (or aggregated interest groups) in the first three-quarters of the nineteenth century, see Wilks, *Political Bi-Polarity in Nineteenth Century Asante* (Edinburgh, 1970), pp. 2–12, and especially p. 14, and *Asante in Nineteenth Century*, pp. 477–90, for an expanded discussion of this argument. The historical significance of the Golden Stool is considered by Rattray, *Ashanti*, pp. 287–293; Kyerematen, "The Royal Stools of Ashanti," *Africa* 39 (1969), 1–10; Hagan, "The Golden Stool and the Oaths to the King of Ashanti," in *University of Ghana Institute of African Studies Research Review* 4 (1968), pp. 1–33; IASAS/33: Ceremony of Enstoolment of Otumfuo Asantehene, recorded by J. Aygeman-Duah, 1962; Lewin, field-notes: interview with Bantamahene Owusu Amankwatia IV, 14 Oct. 1970.

42. For the crucial role of the Asantehene's personality in Asante politics, see Lewin, "Structure of Political Conflict," I, pp. 47–50, 90–97, 146–62. I am preparing a more detailed discussion of the impact of monarchical personality on the late nineteenth-century Asante political process based upon eyewitness reports of Asantes who lived in the 1870s and 1880s.

43. Wilks, *Asante in Nineteenth Century*, pp. 387–92, delineates the origins, recruitment, and principal issues of deliberation in the early nineteenth-century Asantemanhyiamu, also commonly referred to as the Kotoko Council. See A. Triulzi, "The Asantehene-in-Council: Ashanti Politics under Colonial Rule, 1935–50," *Africa* 42 (1972), 98–111, for the activities of the Asantemanhyiamu in a different era.

44. See Wilks, *Asante in Nineteenth Century*, pp. 392–93.

45. Ibid., pp. 393–98, discusses the development, membership, and significance of this council in the first decades of the nineteenth century.

46. Ibid., pp. 396–98; Lewin, "Structure of Political Conflict," II, pp. 173, 241, 244, 246–47, 249, 251, 255, 257, 261, 278: interviews with Amakomhene Mensa Yiadom II, 2 Sept. 1970; Akyempemhene Boakye Dankwa II, Hiahene Mensa Bonsu, 2 Oct. 1970; Adumhene Asamoa Totoe II, Gyaasehene Opoku Mensa II, and Atipinhene Osei Kwame, 9 Oct. 1970; Bantamahene Owusu Amankwatia IV, 13 Oct. 1970; Oyokohene Kofi Poku, Kyidomhene Osei Yaw, and Manwerehene Kwabena Boaten, 16 Oct. 1970; Adontenhene Agyeman Nkwantabisa, 30 Oct. 1970.

47. See, e.g., ibid, pp. 246–47, 255–56, 267–68, 278–80: interviews with Adumhene Asamoa Totoe II, 9 Oct. 1970; Oyokohene Kofi Poku, 16 Oct. 1970; Buokromhene Owusu Bempah, 23 Oct. 1970; Adontenhene Agyeman Nkwantabisa, 30 Oct. 1970.

48. Wilks, *Asante in Nineteenth Century*, pp. 394–95; Lewin, "Structure of Political Conflict," II, pp. 66–72, 79–81, 87–88: interviews with al-Hajj Sulāyman, 10, 21 July 1970; Mamunatu, 3 Aug. 1970, confirm the Muslim role in this council. Now totally blind and in his late nineties, al-Hajj Sulāyman is the oldest member of the Asante Nkramo community in Kumase and the metropolitan region. He served as a young man in Prempe's palace and left Kumase in the 1890s only for infrequent trading trips to Salaga and Kintampo. He witnessed

the capture of Prempe in 1896, fought against the British in 1900 and 1901, and subsequently entered the cocoa business. His physical handicap disqualified him from becoming the official leader of the Muslim community in Kumase, but he is widely recognized as the foremost adviser to the Asantehene on spiritual matters and the leading legal authority in the Muslim community.

49. For the bureaucratic process, see Wilks, "Aspects of Bureaucratization," 215–32, and *Asante in Nineteenth Century*, pp. 465–76. Following more-or-less a Weberian model, Wilks cites several factors to indicate the presence of a bureaucracy including a system of recruitment through achievement, the specialization of administrative role, the existence of promotional hierarchies, and the continuous remuneration of service through fixed commissions.

50. Ibid., pp. 472–76, discusses the patterns of recruitment and promotion in the bureaucratic process in Kumase. See also Lewin, "Structure of Political Conflict," II, pp. 241, 244, 249, 268, 281: interviews with Akyempemhene Boakye Dankwa II, Hiahene Mensa Bonsu, 2 Oct. 1970; Atipinhene Osei Kwame, 9 Oct. 1970; Anantahene Apia Dankwa II, 23 Oct. 1970; Ankobeahene Poku-Dum, 4 Nov. 1970, for confirmation.

51. For an overview of the major and radical structural changes in early nineteenth-century Asante and the Ankobea's role, see Wilks, "Ashanti Government," pp. 213–14; Lewin, "Structure of Political Conflict," II, p. 281: interview with Ankobeahene Poku-Dum, 4 Nov. 1970; McCaskie, "Paramountcy of Kwaku Dua," pp. 56–60, 62–63.

52. The significance of the *nkwansifo* (or *nkwansrafo*) is discussed by Wilks, "Ashanti Government," pp. 217–18, and Lewin, "Structure of Political Conflict," II, pp. 317–18, 364–66: interviews with Omantihene Owusu Nkwantabisa, 4, 29 Dec. 1970.

53. Wilks, "Ashanti Government," p. 218, and *Asante in Nineteenth Century*, pp. 126–93, passim, treats this section of the bureaucratic structure with reference to the southern provinces of the empire.

54. For an elaboration of this relationship, see Wilks, "Ashanti Government," pp. 221–22, and *Asante in Nineteenth Century*, pp. 43–60, passim; Lewin, "Structure of Political Conflict," II, passim. The interaction between late nineteenth-century Asante office and administrative patterns and the spatial distribution of political power is currently being explored by the author based primarily on the reconstruction of Kumase officials' lands at the turn of the century and into the colonial era.

55. Wilks, "Ashanti Government," pp. 221–23; McCaskie, "Paramountcy of Kwaku Dua," pp. 56–75, passim; Lewin, "Structure of Political Conflict," II, passim.

56. For a discussion of the ascriptive nature of governmental positions, see Wilks, *Asante in Nineteenth Century*, pp. 445–55.

57. Wilks, "Ashanti Government," pp. 210–13. On the customary (constitutional) obligations of district (or divisional) rulers, see R. S. Rattray, *Ashanti Law and Constitution* (Oxford, 1929), pp. 72–126.

58. Wilks, "Ashanti Government," pp. 210–13. The significance of district and local history (that is, "the politics of the periphery") for a greater understanding of the Asante political system is a theme requiring immediate, extensive investigation.

59. The rulers of the outlying districts of Adanse, Kokofu, Dwaben, and perhaps Mampon were appointed by the central government in Kumase in the 1840s

and 1850s. This trend became more noticeable towards the end of the century. For the middle of the nineteenth century, see McCaskie, "Paramountcy of Kwaku Dua," pp. 131–33, 135–36, 140–41, 145–46, 149–51. Compare this view with that of Rattray, *Ashanti Law*, pp. 398–407, who misappropriately applied an anthropological, synchronic analysis to explain temporal change. Rattray's interviews were conducted in the 1920s. The "model" he created refers to the early twentieth century, especially with reference to the power of Kumase; and by delineating the confederal idea as the original norm of the Asante political structure, Rattray mistakenly projected a relatively late (or restored) development into the Asante past.

60. For a discussion of the commoners' influence in twentieth-century Asante politics, see Kofi A. Busia, *The Position of the Chief in the Modern Political System of Ashanti* (London, 1951), pp. 10, 11, 21.

61. Lewin, "Structure of Political Conflict," II, pp. 116, 133: interviews with Adu Gyamera, 10, 17 Aug. 1970; Malam Haruna, 5 Aug. 1970. See also Wilks, "The Position of Muslims in Metropolitan Ashanti in the Early Nineteenth Century," in I. M. Lewis (ed.), *Islam in Tropical Africa* (London, 1966), pp. 318–41.

62. See Rattray, *Ashanti*, pp. 86, 90–91, 145–58, and *Religion and Art*, pp. 1–47; A. B. Ellis, *The Tshi-Speaking Peoples of the Gold Coast of West Africa* (London, 1887), pp. 9–33; Lewin, "Structure of Political Conflict," II, pp. 85, 90, 129, 133, 140–42, 170–71, 207, 361–63: interviews with Mamunatu, 3 Aug. 1970; Malam Haruna, 4 Aug. 1970; Akyereapem, 11 Aug. 1970; Adu Gyamera, 17, 27 Aug. 1970; Kwadwo Bo, 1 Sept. 1970; Amakoo, 11 Sept. 1970; Nana Opoku, 28 Dec. 1970.

63. Ibid., interviews of 11 Sept., 28 Dec. 1970 cited above.

64. For the colonial period in Asante, see Tordoff, *Ashanti under Prempehs*, pp. 111–352; Kimble, *Political History*, pp. 479–506; Claridge, *Gold Coast*, II, pp. 567–75.

CHAPTER 3

1. For a discussion of British trading activities in the eighteenth and early nineteenth centuries, see E. Collins, "The Panic Element in Nineteenth Century British Relations with Ashanti," *THSG* 5 (1962), 79–144; Kimble, *Political History*, pp. 1–4; Adu Boahen, "Politics in Ghana, 1800–1874," in J. F. A. Ajayi and Michael Crowder (eds.), *History of West Africa* (London, 1974), II, pp. 167–89.

2. R. A. Kea, "Firearms and Warfare on the Gold and Slave Coasts from the Sixteenth to the Nineteenth Centuries," *JAH* 12 (1971), 188–89, and also see 190–210, passim.

3. See, e.g., Kimble, *Political History*, pp. 3–10.

4. Ibid., p. 65, and also see pp. 65–70 for a discussion of the changes this decision in 1843 produced on the Gold Coast.

5. For the principal lines of diplomacy between Asante and the British in the years 1831–74, see Wilks, *Asante in Nineteenth Century*, pp. 126–242; Kimble, *Political History*, pp. 168–261; Claridge, *Gold Coast*, II, pp. 3–144; G. E. Metcalfe, *Maclean of the Gold Coast* (London, 1962), pp. 150–250; Francis Agbodeka, *African Politics and British Policy on the Gold Coast, 1868–1900* (London, 1971), pp. 1–76.

6. Wilks, *Asante in Nineteenth Century*, pp. 126–66, and McCaskie, "Paramountcy

of Kwaku Dua," pp. 1–16, 76–90, treat several dimensions characteristic of this uncertain situation in the south.

7. See Wilks, *Asante in Nineteenth Century*, pp. 166–206, for a discussion of a number of these points of contention.

8. This policy remained in effect until the early 1890s. For a discussion of the "fresh" policies of Sir Benjamin Pine, who came to the Gold Coast in 1857 and quickly found British authority severely limited in the Colony, see Kimble, *Political History*, pp. 182–91. There seems little doubt that Pine at times exaggerated the Asante "threat" in order to receive additional funding from his superiors in London and to bolster his own position on the coast. During the early 1860s the Colonial Office usually followed his advice.

9. For an extended discussion of this debate, see Wilks, *Political Bi-Polarity*, pp. 2–12, and *Asante in Nineteenth Century*, pp. 477–97.

10. On the nature of Asante military expansion from 1700 to 1750, see Arhin, "Financing of the Ashanti Expansion (1700–1820)," 283–91; Wilks, "Ashanti Government," pp. 206–25.

11. F. A. Ramseyer and J. Kühne, *Four Years in Ashantee* (New York, 1875), p. 243; Wilks, *Political Bi-Polarity*, pp. 8–9.

12. Ramseyer and Kühne, *Four Years*, p. 201.

13. Ibid., p. 202.

14. J. Miles, "The Ashanti War of 1873–4: A Study in Ashanti Military Organization and Techniques" (M.A. thesis, University of London, 1968), treats the composition, mobilization, and commissariat of the Asante armies in 1873 and estimates that some eighty thousand troops were mobilized from the metropolitan region alone. A systematic investigation of Asante military theory and practice in these years needs to be undertaken. Numerous accounts of the military operations exist, but most are written from a British point of view and fail to delineate Asante strategy, the structure of the army, and the conflicts of interest prevalent among Asante field commanders. See, e.g., J. F. Maurice, *The Ashantee War, a Popular Narrative* (London, 1874), pp. 30–70; E. Wood, *The Ashanti Expedition of 1873–4* (London, 1874), pp. 4–22; G. A. Henty, *The March to Coomassie* (London, 1874), pp. 56–57, 125, 203, 222–23, 374–92; Frederick Boyle, *Through Fanteeland to Coomassie* (London, 1874), pp. 270–310.

15. Ramseyer and Kühne, *Four Years*, pp. 136, 181, 206, 220, 229–30, 250–51, 260, 268; Henry Brackenbury, *The Ashanti War; a Narrative* (two vols., London, 1874), II, pp. 217–19; Miles, "Ashanti War of 1873–4," pp. 18, 37.

16. Ramseyer and Kühne, *Four Years*, p. 236.

17. Brackenbury, *Ashanti War*, II, pp. 338–39.

18. Ramseyer and Kühne, *Four Years*, p. 182. See also *The African Times*, III, No. 29, p. 52: Owusu Ansa to Pine, dd. Cape Coast, 16 Sept. 1873.

19. Brackenbury, *Ashanti War*, II, pp. 160–79, 215–19; Henty, *March to Coomassie*, pp. 374–92; Boyle, *Through Fanteeland*, pp. 281–341.

20. For the events of early February, see Brackenbury, *Ashanti War*, II, p. 233; Henty, *March to Coomassie*, p. 364; A. B. Ellis, *A History of the Gold Coast of West Africa* (London, 1893), pp. 333–34; W. W. Reade, *The Story of the Ashantee Campaign* (London, 1874), pp. 346, 348–49. See Kimble, *Political History*, p. 274, for the legal debate concerning the formation of the Gold Coast Colony from the Protected Territory or Protectorate.

21. Brackenbury, *Ashanti War*, II, pp. 266–67; *Correspondence Relating to the Affairs of the Gold Coast*, C. 1140, 1875, p. 38: Carnarvon to Lees, dd. London, 3 July 1874, and p. 61: Strahan to Carnarvon, dd. Cape Coast, 7 July 1874.

22. See, e.g., Lewin, field-notes: interviews with Domfe Kyere, 25 Apr. 1971; Kwadwo Afodo, 27 Apr. 1971. Oheneba Kwadwo Afodo, who claims to be over 110 years old and is a son of the Asantehene Mensa Bonsu, by his marriage to Akosua Krapayenam, has been closely associated with the royal family of Kumase since the early 1880s. He has held minor administrative posts under the Asantehenes Kwaku Dua III and Prempe II and is now the Asramponhene of Kumase. This office is in the Manwere Fekuo, and the occupant is in charge of the area where the Asantehene sits while deciding legal cases in the Bampenase, the Asantehene's court. Afodo was the key adviser to the newly installed Asantehene Opoku Ware II in 1970, and his opinion was repeatedly solicited by Kumase authorities in regard to customary enstoolment procedures.

23. For a discussion of the reforms designed to modernize the administrative, military, and economic structures of the state, see Lewin, "Structure of Political Conflict," I, pp. 64–74, and Wilks, *Asante in Nineteenth Century*, pp. 605–21.

24. Ibid., pp. 292–94; *Affairs of the Gold Coast and Threatened Ashanti Invasion*, C. 3064, 1881, pp. 47–48: Mensa Bonsu to Griffith, dd. Kumase, n.d., in Griffith to Kimberley, dd. Cape Coast, 6 Feb. 1881, and p. 21: Griffith to Asantehene, dd. Cape Coast, 24 Jan. 1881.

25. Ibid., pp. 2–3: Griffith to Kimberley, dd. Cape Coast, 24 Jan. 1881, and p. 80: Griffith to Kimberley, dd. Elmina, 27, 28 Feb. 1881.

26. Ibid., p. 94: Dudley to Hay, dd. Cape Coast, 28 Feb. 1881, citing information from an Assin trader who was present at the Bantama meeting.

27. Ellis, *History of Gold Coast*, p. 238.

28. *Affairs*, C. 3064, 1881, p. 85: Buck and Huppenbauer to Jackson, dd. Dweraso, 18 Feb. 1881.

29. Ibid., p. 74: Brackenbury to Richards, dd. Elmina, 18 Feb. 1881.

30. Ibid., p. 69: Dudley to Colonial Secretary, dd. 17 Feb. 1881, pp. 134–35: Rowe to Kimberly, dd. Praso, 19 Apr. 1881, pp. 139–41: Notes taken at interview at Praso, 17 Apr. 1881, and pp. 151–53: "Official Record of the Message of Prince Buaki," dd. Elmina, 30 May 1881. For the distinguished nineteenth-century career of Boakye Tenten, see Asante Collective Biography Project: Boakye Tenten.

31. For a discussion of this slogan in the early nineteenth century, see Wilks, *Asante in Nineteenth Century*, pp. 479–82.

32. On this aspect of British policy, see, e.g., PRO, C.O. 96/124, No. 171: Lees to Hicks Beach, dd. Accra, 15 Aug. 1878, and *Further Correspondence Regarding Affairs of the Gold Coast*, C. 3687, 1883, pp. 111–16: Lonsdale's report on his mission of 1882. On the major Asante roads see Wilks, *Asante in Nineteenth Century*, pp. 1–17.

33. See, e.g., *Affairs*, C. 3064, 1881: p. 68–69: Dudley to Colonial Secretary, dd. 17 Feb. 1881.

34. Lewin, field-notes: interview with Malam Gariba, 28 Nov. 1970.

35. See, e.g., *Further Correspondence*, C. 3687, 1883, pp. 87–88: Moloney to Griffith, dd. Lagos, 14 Oct. 1882, and pp. 89–90: Strahan to Carnarvon, dd. Cape Coast, 19 Feb. 1876. This remained the case until 1895 when the Colonial Office finally adopted a definite policy vis-à-vis the Asante government.

36. See chapter 6. *Further Correspondence*, C. 5615, 1888, pp. 9–10: Griffith to Knutsford, dd. Accra, 13 Apr. 1888, p. 20: Barnett to Colonial Secretary, dd. Edwabin, 14, 22 Jan. 1888.

37. See, e.g., *Further Correspondence*, C. 4906, 1886, pp. 9–10: Griffith to Granville, dd. Accra, 1 Apr. 1886, and p. 36: Firminger to Governor, dd. Praso, 15 Apr. 1886.

38. Several of these provocative issues and the changes that resulted—such as the presence of European missionaries in Kumase, the termination of domestic slavery and the position of emancipated slaves in Asante society, the regulation of terror as an instrument of governmental authority, and the power and legitimacy of the Council of Kumase—are discussed in this chapter.

39. On the attributes of the Colony as a prototype for socioeconomic and political change, see Kimble, *Political History*, pp. 301–15, 330–40, 458–64, 528–37, 554–62. A great deal of research is needed on the influence the Gold Coast Colony exerted on Asante reformers and reformism in the 1880s and early 1890s. This topic is completely neglected in the literature.

40. For a general overview of state controls over the economy, see Wilks, *Asante in Nineteenth Century*, pp. 414–45; "Ashanti Government," pp. 216–20; and "Asante Policy," pp. 124–41.

41. See Wilks, *Asante in Nineteenth Century*, pp. 418–40, passim, for details on a few of the major forms of taxation and the limitations placed on the emergence of an Asante middle class in the early part of the nineteenth century.

42. Ibid., pp. 419–50, passim; Lewin, field-notes: interview with Domfe Kyere, 6 Feb. 1971.

43. See, e.g., Lewin, field-notes: interviews with Adu Gyamera, 9 Jan. 1971; Domfe Kyere, 6 Feb. 1971.

44. See, e.g., ibid.; interviews with Yaw Safo, 9 Feb. 1971; Kwadwo Bo, 14 Feb. 1971.

45. For a discussion of restricted immigration as an economic policy, see Wilks, *Asante in Nineteenth Century*, pp. 243–310, passim.

46. See chapter 5. On this general theme, see A. G. Hopkins, *An Economic History of West Africa* (London, 1973), passim.

47. *Further Correspondence*, C. 3386, 1882, pp. 71–73: Lonsdale's report on his mission of 1881–82.

48. Ibid., p. 59: Lonsdale's report on his mission of 1881–82, and see *Further Correspondence*, C. 3687, 1883, p. 84: Griffith to Kimberley, dd. Accra, 16 Nov. 1882.

49. *Further Correspondence*, C. 3386, 1882, p. 59: Lonsdale's report on his mission of 1881–82.

50. Ibid., p. 13: Rowe's instructions to Lonsdale, dd. Christiansborg, 15 Oct. 1881.

51. *Affairs*, C. 3064, 1881, p. 81: Griffith to Kimberley, dd. Elmina, 27, 28 Feb. 1881; PRO, C.O. 96/129, No. 11180: Ellis to War Office, dd. 30 June 1879, submitting report on Asante.

52. *Papers Relating to Her Majesty's Possessions in West Africa*, C. 1402, 1876, p. 84: Strahan to Carnarvon, dd. Cape Coast, 6 Sept. 1875; *Papers*, C. 1343, 1875, p. 59: Bonnat to Colonial Office, dd. Liverpool, 6 Mar. 1875. On Bonnat's economic pursuits and career in Asante and the Colony, see Johnson, "M. Bonnat on the Volta," *GNQ* 10 (1968), 4–17; R. F. Burton and V. L. Cameron, *To the Gold Coast for Gold* (London, 1883), II, pp. 271, 297–99; J. Gros,

Voyages, Aventures et Captivité de J. Bonnat Chez les Achantis (Paris, 1884), pp. 264–65, 269.

53. PRO, C.O. 879/38, African (West) No. 451, p. 37: Brun to Colonial Secretary, dd. Elmina, 18 Jan. 1881, in Griffith to Kimberley, dd. Elmina, 11 Feb. 1881; NAG, ADM 12/5/111: Ansa to French Foreign Secretary, dd. London, 13 June 1895; Gros, *Voyages*, p. 265; H. J. Bevin, "The Gold Coast Economy about 1800," *THSG* 3 (1956), 77.

54. See, e.g., *Papers*, C. 1402, 1876, p. 86: Mensa Bonsu to Governor, dd. Kumase, 26 Aug. 1875.

55. *Affairs*, C. 3064, 1881, p. 14: Griffith to Kimberley, dd. Cape Coast, 24 Jan. 1881, citing information from Owusu from Gyaman. See also Lewin, "Structure of Political Conflict," II, pp. 401–2: interview with Domfe Kyere, 24 Mar. 1971, for confirmation.

56. See, e.g., ibid., p. 134: interview with Adu Gyamera, 17 Aug. 1970, who described in detail the rubber collection and distribution process.

57. Ibid., pp. 449–50: interview with Domfe Kyere, 13 Apr. 1971. This is one of a great number of similar accounts on the early rubber industry in the metropolitan region. On the Asante rubber trade, see Arhin, "The Ashanti Rubber Trade with the Gold Coast in the Eighteen-Nineties," *Africa* 42 (1972), 32–43; and for the Colony, see R. Dumett, "The Rubber Trade of the Gold Coast and Asante in the Nineteenth Century: African Innovation and Market Responsiveness," *JAH* 12 (1971), 79–101.

58. Kimble, *Political History*, p. 63, and see also pp. 62, 64, 71–72.

59. Ibid., pp. 70–72.

60. Ibid., p. 64. The Wesleyan Methodists in 1858 had twenty-nine schools in the coastal areas with about 1100 pupils, while the Basel Mission had opened seventeen with over 250 children enrolled for primary education. The Basel missionaries' principal educational thrust had commenced in 1843 with the foundation of their school in the Akropong district of the Colony.

61. For a discussion of this theme, see McCaskie, "Innovational Eclecticism: The Asante Empire and Europe in the Nineteenth Century," *Comparative Studies in Society and History* 14 (1972), 36–39. The Asante Nkramo, who were the traditional physicians and spiritual advisers to the Asantehene, apparently opposed the practice of medicine by these aliens and further objected to the presence of missionaries because it threatened their exclusivity in literacy. See, e.g., Lewin, "Structure of Political Conflict," II, p. 104: interview with Malam Haruna, 5 Aug. 1970, who indicated that all his father's contemporaries in the Nkramo community in Kumase feared the threat posed by the introduction of Christianity into Asante.

62. Ibid., p. 273: interview with Domfe Kyere, 30 Oct. 1970. See also Kimble, *Political History*, p. 74, 153, and Wilks, *Asante in Nineteenth Century*, pp. 595–96.

63. Lewin, "Structure of Political Conflict," II, p. 58: interview with I. K. Agyeman, 30 June 1970.

64. McCaskie, "Innovational Eclecticism," 34, develops this subject; see also 30–32, 35–36, 44–45.

65. See, e.g., interview of 30 June cited in note 63. Most informants born in the 1870s and early 1880s agree with this issue.

66. Lewin, field-notes: interview with Domfe Kyere, 28 Apr. 1971. Various political leaders in the Colony likewise believed that the emancipation of slaves would

be detrimental to their rural economies and would create social dislocation in the coastal regions. Several chiefs stressed these points in their petitions to Governor G. C. Strahan after his proclamation of 17 Nov. 1874 abolished slavery on the Gold Coast. See, e.g., *Further Correspondence,* C. 1159, 1875, p. 8: Petition of Chiefs of Gold Coast to Strahan, dd. Cape Coast, 30 Dec. 1874. See also pp. 1–3: Strahan to Carnarvon, dd. Cape Coast, 3 Jan. 1875, for the social changes produced by manumission in the Colony.

67. Lewin, "Structure of Political Conflict," II, pp. 61, 67, 71–72, 183–86, 195, 276–77: interviews with I. K. Agyeman, 8 July 1970; al-Hajj Sulāyman, 10 July 1970; Kwadwo Bo, 3 Sept. 1970; Kwaku Anno, 4 Sept. 1970; Domfe Kyere, 30 Oct. 1970. For a discussion of social servitude in Asante, see A. Norman Klein, "West African Unfree Labor before and after the Rise of the Atlantic Slave Trade," in L. Foner and E. D. Genovese (eds.), *Slavery in the New World* (Englewood Cliffs, 1969), pp. 89–92; and see J. D. Fage, "Slavery and the Slave Trade in the Context of West African History," *JAH* 10 (1969), 394–95, 398–404, for an examination of the general views held about West African slavery, and Hopkins, *Economic History,* pp. 23–27, 143–44, 225–28 for an overall analysis of the colonial response to this dominant institution. For oral accounts of slavery in Asante, see Rattray, *Ashanti Law,* pp. 33–55, and pp. 285–93 for accounts of nineteenth-century legal practice.

68. Bowdich, *Mission from Cape Coast,* pp. 235, 254, 260, 282, 317. Lewin, "Structure of Political Conflict," II, pp. 183–84: interview with Kwadwo Bo, 3 Sept. 1970.

69. For a discussion of this demonstration of wealth, see Arhin, "Aspects of the Ashanti Northern Trade," 370, 372.

70. Lewin, "Structure of Political Conflict," II, p. 183: interview with Kwadwo Bo, 3 Sept. 1970.

71. Arhin, "Aspects of the Ashanti Northern Trade," 371, and Hopkins, *Economic History,* pp. 225–27, passim.

72. See, e.g., Bowdich, *Mission from Cape Coast,* pp. 310–14, for a description of their labor in the confines of Kumase.

73. Ibid., pp. 316–17. The entire problem of the role of slaves in Asante social history requires urgent investigation. No detailed study has been made for the nineteenth century, and generalizations from Dahomey and other centralized West African kingdoms are apparently not valid for Asante.

74. See, e.g., ibid., pp. 262, 277, 279, 281, 283, 289, 296, 300, for one observer's comments on these killings.

75. Lewin, "Structure of Political Conflict," II, p. 214: interview with Kwabena Baako, 14 Sept. 1970.

76. Such allusions are common in missionary field reports. See, e.g., BMA, Basel: Ramseyer to Neuchatel Friends, dd. 20 Aug. 1883, and Ramseyer to Basel, dd. 28 Aug. 1883. For other refutations of these misleading popular views, see Kimble, *Political History,* p. 131, Rattray, *Religion and Art,* pp. 117–22, and especially Collins, "Panic Element," pp. 121–22, who has shown how European observers misrepresented Asante executions.

77. Rattray, *Religion and Art,* pp. 112–13, and see also p. 109. Informants in the 1970s confirmed Rattray's findings on this point.

78. See Rattray, *Religion and Art,* p. 106.

79. Ibid., p. 92.

80. A theme noted by nearly all of my informants who were alive in the mid and late 1870s. A comprehensive study of violence in particular has yet to be undertaken in the Asante context. Such a study would have major implications for an analysis of the nature and role of violence in precolonial African political cultures. The notion of popular consensus for governmental violence is well developed in Eugene V. Walter, *Terror and Resistance, a Study of Political Violence* (New York, 1969), pp. 3–55, passim, and especially p. 29. See also McCaskie, "Paramountcy of Kwaku Dua," pp. 93–99, 110–12, for abuses of judicial violence in the 1860s.
81. Lewin, "Structure of Political Conflict," II, p. 123: interview with Adu Gyamera, 10 Aug. 1970.
82. Ibid., pp. 90–91: interview with Malam Haruna, 4 Aug. 1970.
83. See, e.g., Lewin, field-notes: interviews with Domfe Kyere, 25, 28 Apr. 1971.
84. The death of the Asantehene Kwaku Dua II, discussed in chapter 4, is an excelcent example of this type of distortion.
85. Authorities in Kumase were increasingly aware that a number of Asante commoners were beginning to take positions on ritualized killing which were not too far from those of the European missionaries. See, e.g., BMA, Basel: Haasis' report to Basel, dd. 9 July 1894, in which the Asantehene Agyeman Prempe also maintained that he would never accept a teacher in Kumase.
86. For a discussion of this issue, see Arhin, "The Missionary Role on the Gold Coast and in Ashanti: Reverend F. A. Ramseyer and the British Take-over of Ashanti, 1869–1894," *University of Ghana Institute of African Studies Research Review* 4 (1968), 4–15.
87. *Correspondence*, C. 1140, 1875, p. 57: Strahan to Carnarvon, dd. Cape Coast, 30 June 1874, citing information from Kumase envoys.
88. MMA, London: Picot to Boyce, dd. Cape Coast, 3 May 1876.
89. Lewin, "Structure of Political Conflict," II, p. 95: interview with Mamunatu, 5 Aug. 1970.
90. *Affairs*, C. 3064, 1881, p. 115: Fletcher's memorandum of an interview with Asante messengers on 18 Mar. 1881, in Rowe to Kimberley, dd. Elmina, 18 Mar. 1881.
91. Lewin, "Structure of Political Conflict," II, p. 33: interview with J. W. Opon, 8 June 1970.

CHAPTER 4

1. On the secondary issues involved in the protracted electoral contest of 1883–84, see Lewin, "Structure of Political Conflict," I, pp. 146–71.
2. Ibid., pp. 156, 159–60, 168–69. A discussion of his career is in McCaskie, "Paramountcy of Kwaku Dua," pp. 61, 246–53, 290–97, 301–7.
3. See, e.g., *Further Correspondence*, C. 4052, 1884, pp. 46–47: Asante's statement to Barrow, dd. 3 May 1883, citing Kofi Kakari; p. 54: Barrow's report, dd. 5 July 1883; and p. 83: Barrow to Colonial Office, dd. Sussex, 16 Oct. 1883.
4. Lewin, "Structure of Political Conflict," I, 175–76. For an analysis of the fundamental opposition between adherents of the "peace" and "war" interests in the government, see Wilks, *Political Bi-Polarity*, pp. 10–18, and *Asante in Nineteenth Century*, pp. 477–549. See chapter 3 for the British influence in Asante foreign policy and central government decision-making.
5. Lewin, "Structure of Political Conflict," I, pp. 155, 166–68.

6. Lewin, "Structure of Political Conflict," II, pp. 377–78: interview with Agyei Maniampon Abrebrease, 14 Mar. 1971. Agyei Maniampon Abrebrease was born in the reign of the Asantehene Mensu Bonsu, was enstooled Safohene of Mampon in 1921, and has been closely associated with Mampon palace affairs since he became an *ahenkwaa* to the Mamponhene in the mid 1880s. He was the Mamponhene's "special" envoy in the 1890s while also serving as foremost hunter and cook in that *omanhene*'s palace. He is generally regarded as the senior adviser to the present Mamponhene. He was ninety-eight years old in 1971.

7. *The Gold Coast Times*, III, No. 111, 7 Sept. 1883, pp. 3–4; III, No. 112, 14 Sept. 1883, p. 3; III, No. 114, 28 Sept. 1883, p. 2. *Further Correspondence*, C. 4052, 1884, p. 80: Rowe to Derby, dd. Accra, 7 Sept. 1883, citing information from the Kumase envoy, Kwaku Kra.

8. For the confused reports surrounding the formal installation and the murders of both rivals for the Golden Stool, see Lewin, "Structure of Political Conflict," I, pp. 173–75, 178–85.

9. *Further Correspondence*, C. 3687, 1883, p. 158: Barrow to Rowe, dd. Kumase, 27 Apr. 1883, citing information from Boakye Tenten and the Council of Kumase. See also Wilks, *Political Bi-Polarity*, pp. 2–16, and *Asante in Nineteenth Century*, pp. 477–549, for development of this diplomatic motto.

10. Lewin, "Structure of Political Conflict," II, p. 379: interview with Agyei Maniampon Abrebrease, 14 Mar. 1971. For British accounts, see Claridge, *Gold Coast*, II, p. 275; Fuller, *Vanished Dynasty*, p. 158; Ellis, *History of Gold Coast*, p. 377.

11. *Further Correspondence*, C. 4477, 1885, p. 135: Young to Derby, dd. Accra, 11 July 1884, citing information from a Kumase envoy. But also see Basel Mission Archives, Basel: Ramseyer to Basel, dd. 23 July 1884.

12. See, e.g., *The Gold Coast Times*, IV, No. 144, 23 July 1884, p. 3; *Further Correspondence*, C. 4477, 1885, p. 135: Young to Derby, dd. Accra, 11 July 1884.

13. *Further Correspondence*, C. 4906, 1886, p. 6: statement by envoys from Kumase, dd. 16 Oct. 1884. See also genealogical sketch enclosed.

14. Lewin, "Structure of Political Conflict," II, pp. 407–8, 144–45: interviews with Domfe Kyere, 28 Mar. 1971; Kwadwo Afodo, 27 Aug. 1970. Kyeretwe should not be confused with the Asantehene Prempe II's personal name.

15. For a detailed discussion of the southern rebellions of 1883, the increasingly erratic behavior of the Asantehene Mensa Bonsu following the assassination attempts on his life, and the popular coup that deposed the monarch, see Lewin, "Structure of Political Conflict," I, pp. 87–101. See also Wilks, *Asante in Nineteenth Century*, pp. 564–89, for the uprising spearheaded by the *nkwankwaa* of Kumase who were instrumental in driving Mensa Bonsu from power.

16. *Further Correspondence*, C. 4052, 1884, pp. 42–43: Barrow's report, dd. 5 July 1883; *Further Correspondence*, C. 4477, 1885, pp. 92, 95: Kirby's report, dd. Accra, 15 Apr. 1884. See Arhin, "Succession and Gold Mining at Manso-Nkwanta," *University of Ghana Institute of African Studies Research Review* 6 (1970), 101–9, for traditional gold mining in the Manso region, and Lewin, "Structure of Political Conflict," II, pp. 60–64: interview with I. K. Agyeman, 8 July 1970, for the Asantehene's "secret" Manso gold resources.

17. *Further Correspondence*, C. 4052, 1884, pp. 42–43: Barrow's report, dd. 5 July 1883; *Further Correspondence*, C. 4477, 1885, p. 79: Kirby to Colonial Secre-

tary, dd. Kumase, 5 Feb. 1884. See also *Further Correspondence*, C. 3687, 1883, p. 131: interview of Manso representatives with Governor Rowe, dd. Elmina, 4 Mar. 1883, and *Further Correspondence*, C. 4906, 1886, p. 6: statement by envoys from Kumase, dd. 16 Oct. 1884.

18. *Further Correspondence*, C. 3687, 1883, p. 104: Daniel to Private Secretary, dd. Cape Coast, 24 Feb. 1883, citing information from Manso envoys; *Further Correspondence*, C. 4477, 1885, pp. 147–48: Carr to District Commissioner, Cape Coast, dd. Praso, 12 Dec. 1884, citing information from Asante traders. "Atwema" means "to draw people" for governmental service in the capital, a term that derives from the earliest political relationship between the Asantehene and the Atwemahene who provided *nhenkwaa* for the palace in Kumase. The Atwema, Atwema Agogo, Toase, and Nkawiekumaa stools are *annouem*, or brothers, in the Konti Fekuo. Furthermore, before 1900 the stools of Manso Nkwanta, Yawkrom, Abodom, Wirempe, and Odaho swore directly to the Asantehene on the Mponpomsuo *afena*, or sword. The Manso Nkwantahene was promoted to *omanhene* status by the British after 1901 for his "pro-British services" in the War of 1900. Consequently, after 1901 most of the Manso area chiefs took the oath of allegiance directly to the Manso Nkwantahene rather than to the Asantehene. The Yawkromhene and Abudiahene, e.g., now swear to the Manso Nkwantahene. The Abodomhene and Wirempehene swear directly to a Kumase chief, the Nsumankwaahene, while the Odahohene swears now to the Danyasehene. Presently, the Yawkromhene, Keniagohene, Abiramhene, Abudiahene, Abenansehene, Asamanhene (all Manso chiefs), and the Manso Nkwantahene must pass through the Asafohene of Kumase in order to see and greet the Asantehene. The Aborehene, Teteremhene, and Ahwerewahene (the chiefs whose stools supported Bantamahene Kwabena Awua in 1882–83 during his enforced exile in Manso Nkwanta) currently must pass through the Bantamahene of Kumase to see the Asantehene. The Esase Bonmuhene and Atwedehene and several other Manso district chiefs must pass through the Anamenakohene, another Kumase chief, while the Wirempehene and Abodomhene pass through the Nsumankwaahene of Kumase. See Lewin, "Structure of Political Conflict," II, pp. 319–22, 329–30, 436–39: interviews with Atwema Agogohene Owusu Afriyie, 4 Dec. 1970; Atwemahene Antwi Agyei, 11 Dec. 1970; Yawkromhene Kwaku Ti, 8 April 1971.

19. *Further Correspondence*, C. 4477, 1885, p. 147: Yaw Awua to Colonial Secretary, dd. Cape Coast, 8 Dec. 1884, and pp. 147–48: Carr to District Commissioner, Cape Coast, dd. Praso, 12 Dec. 1884. See also Lewin, "Structure of Political Conflict," II, pp. 304–5: interview with Tredehene Nubin Asare II, 27 Nov. 1970.

20. *The Gold Coast Times*, IV, No. 154, 12 Feb. 1885, p. 3. *Further Correspondence*, C. 5357, 1888, p. 51: Lonsdale to Governor, dd. Sehwi Wiawso, 19 Feb. 1887.

21. *Further Correspondence*, C. 4906, 1886, p. 6: statement by Kumase envoys, dd. 16 Oct. 1884; *Further Correspondence*, C. 4477, 1885, p. 147: Yaw Awua to Colonial Secretary, dd. Cape Coast, 8 Dec. 1884.

22. Ibid., p. 17: Torry to Governor, dd. Accra, 28 Dec. 1883, citing information from Nantwi of Saawua. NAG, ADM 1/9/153: Torry to Governor, dd. Accra, 12 Nov. 1883.

23. Lewin, "Structure of Political Conflict," II, pp. 133–36, 236–38: interviews

with Adu Gyamera, 17 Aug. 1970, and Yaw Safo, 25 Sept. 1970; *The Gold Coast Times*, IV, No. 144, 23 July 1884, p. 3; *Further Correspondence*, C. 4906, 1886, p. 6: statement by envoys from Kumase, dd. 16 Oct. 1884. Before 1900 the Saamanhene of Kumase was also the chief of Saawua, the Saawuahene, and his stool was in the Gyaase Fekuo. Although the town of Saawua and its land now belong to the Saawuahene, most of the people of Saawua still serve the Saamanhene of Kumase, who is no longer the Saawuahene. On the traditional relationship between Kumase and Saawua, see Lewin, "Structure of Political Conflict," II, pp. 359–60, 247–48, 265–66: interviews with Saawuahene Kwabena Edusei, 22 Dec. 1970; Gyaasehene Opoku Mensa II, 9 Oct. 1970; Saamanhene Osei Kwaku II, 23 Oct. 1970.

24. *Further Correspondence*, C. 5615, 1888, p. 122: Barnett's report on Asante, received Accra, 10 May 1888; *Further Correspondence*, C. 5357, 1888, p. 35: Kwadwo Yinna et al. to Lonsdale, dd. Cape Coast, 17 Jan. 1887.

25. NAG, ADM 11/1/1482, No. 752: Stewart to Colonial Secretary, dd. Praso, 22 Jan. 1887. See also *Further Correspondence*, C. 5615, 1888, p. 122: Barnett's report on Asante, received in Accra, 10 May 1888.

26. MMA, Journal of Coppin's visit to Asante, 1885, entry dd. Kumase, 28, 29 Apr., 2 May 1885. For the career of Owusu Koko Kumaa, see Wilks, *Asante in Nineteenth Century*, passim.

27. *Further Correspondence*, C. 4906, 1886, p. 3: District Commissioner, Cape Coast, to Colonial Secretary, dd. Cape Coast, 16 May 1885, quoting information from Coppin. See also NAG, ADM 11/1/1482: Coppin to Lt. Gov. Griffith, dd. Cape Coast, 18 May 1885, and MMA, Journal of Coppin's visit to Asante, 1885, entry dd. Kumase, 29 Apr. 1885.

28. *Further Correspondence*, C. 4906, 1886, p. 4: Coppin to Lt. Gov. Griffith, dd. Cape Coast, 18 May 1885.

29. Ibid., pp. 4–5: Coppin to Lt. Gov. Griffith, dd. Cape Coast, 18 May 1885. Compare this account with *Further Correspondence*, C. 4052, 1884, pp. 92–93: Kirby's report, dd. Accra, 15 Apr. 1884.

30. MMA, Journal of Coppin's visit to Asante, 1885, entry dd. Fomena, 22 Apr. 1885. See also entry dd. Bekwae, 22, 23 Apr., dd. Dadiase, 4 May 1885.

31. *Further Correspondence*, C. 4906, 1886, pp. 3–4: District Commissioner, Cape Coast, to Colonial Secretary, dd. Cape Coast, 16 May 1885, and p. 3: Merchants of Cape Coast to District Commissioner, dd. Cape Coast, 14 May 1885.

32. Ibid., p. 4: Coppin to Lt. Gov. Griffith, dd. Cape Coast, 18 May 1885.

33. Idem.

34. Ibid., p. 5: Coppin to Lt. Gov. Griffith, dd. Cape Coast, 18 May 1885.

35. A discussion of these overtures is in Lewin, "Structure of Political Conflict," I, pp. 225–31, especially the political relations between Kokofu and Bekwae and the British in the period.

36. Ibid., pp. 231–34. *The Western Echo*, I, No. 3, 9 Dec. 1888, p. 4: I, No. 6, 8 Jan. 1886, p. 4: I, No. 7, 20 Jan. 1886, p. 4: I, No. 2, 28 Nov. 1885, pp. 4–5. *Further Correspondence*, C. 4906, 1886, p. 64: Carr to Colonial Secretary, dd. Praso, 13 June 1886, citing information from Adanse envoys.

37. *Further Correspondence*, C. 5357, 1888, p. 7: Badger to Governor, dd. Christiansborg, 20 Oct. 1886; Rattray, *Ashanti Law*, p. 203; Lewin, "Structure of Political Conflict," II, p. 192: interview with Kwaku Anno, 4 Sept. 1970.

38. *Further Correspondence*, C. 5357, 1888, p. 3: Governor to Badger, dd. Accra,

28 Aug. 1886. *Further Correspondence*, C. 4906, 1886, p. 69: interview with Boaten from Kumase and Kwabena Agyei and Kwaku Ade from Kokofu, dd. Christiansborg, 29 June 1886.

39. *Further Correspondence*, C. 5357, 1888, p. 3: Governor to Badger, dd. Accra, 28 Aug. 1886.
40. Ibid., p. 61: statement of the Kokofuhene's messenger, in District Commissioner, Cape Coast, to Colonial Secretary, dd. Cape Coast, 25 Mar. 1887; Ibid., p. 7: Badger to Governor, dd. Christiansborg, 20 Oct. 1886.
41. Lewin, field-notes: interview with Domfe Kyere, dd. Kumase, 25 Apr. 1971; McCaskie, "Paramountcy of Kwaku Dua," p. 240, and see pp. 241–42. For a detailed account of the royal dynasty, see Wilks, *Asante in Nineteenth Century*, pp. 327–74, which discusses the genealogy for the greater part of the eighteenth and nineteenth centuries. Lewin, "Structure of Political Conflict," II, pp. 106–7, 147–48, 407–8: interviews with Adu Gyamera, 6 Aug. 1970; Kwadwo Afodo, 27 Aug. 1970; Domfe Kyere, 28 Mar. 1971.
42. Ibid., p. 423: interview with Domfe Kyere, 4 Apr. 1971, and see also p. 384: interview with Bekwaehene Osei Kwadwo II, Kwadwo Donko, and Kwabena Antwi, 19 Mar. 1971.
43. Ibid., pp. 407–8, 147–48: interviews with Domfe Kyere, 6 Aug. 1970; Kwadwo Afodo, 27 Aug. 1970. The oral accounts of these elderly informants differ somewhat from the genealogical material contained in Wilks, *Asante in Nineteenth Century*, pp. 327–33, passim, which is largely based on the compilation authored by Prempe I, *The History of the Ashanti Kings and the Whole Country Itself*, a work written in the early twentieth century by the exiled Asantehene from his enforced residence in the Seychelles.

CHAPTER 5

1. See, e.g., *Correspondence*, C. 1140, 1875, p. 15: extract from *The Gold Coast Times* of 29 Apr. 1874, in Lees to Carnarvon, dd. Cape Coast, 4 May 1874, p. 21: Maxwell to Kimberley, dd. Cape Coast, 19 Mar. 1874, p. 40: Lees to Carnarvon, dd. Cape Coast, 8 June 1874, p. 57: Strahan to Carnarvon, dd. Cape Coast, 30 June 1874, and p. 61: Strahan to Carnarvon, dd. Cape Coast, 7 July 1874.
2. Localism is an appropriately descriptive term with various traits of identification and must be evaluated with reference to its diagnostic features. Its significance for understanding politics is far too often obscured by synchronic and unidimensional definitions. For this reason and also for want of a more precise term in the Asante context, I define localism only within the context and situation to which it applies. Nineteenth-century European observers (and Asante informants) were only too aware of the nature of this process: for example, "the Kings of the large divisions of the country are unwilling, and, I believe, determined not to come again under the rule of Coomassie as it existed formerly, although they do not wish to see Coomassie altogether effaced, and would probably yield something to maintain at least friendly relations with the capital." *Further Correspondence*, C. 4906, 1886, p. 33: Governor to Firminger, dd. Accra, 17 Apr. 1886.
3. *Correspondence*, C. 1140, 1875, pp. 82–83: Lees to Strahan, dd. Cape Coast, 31 Aug. 1874, and see pp. 63–64: Strahan to Carnarvon, dd. Cape Coast, 13 July 1874, citing information from Dwaben envoys on the coast.

4. For a general discussion of this early relationship, see Wilks, "Ashanti Government," pp. 209–11, and *Asante in Nineteenth Century*, pp. 374–414, passim.

5. The rebellion in Dwaben on this level can be seen as a conflict between nationalism and particularism. The platform of the Dwaben localists represented the earliest formulation of the particularistic idea, although the theory as such did not assume definite form in Asante until the 1880s.

6. C. C. Reindorf, *The History of the Gold Coast and Asante* (Basel, n.d., prob. 1895), pp. 276–96, provides a detailed account, largely based upon oral sources, of the controversy. See also McCaskie, "Paramountcy of Kwaku Dua," pp. 116–30, for a discussion of the events preceding the enstoolment of Dwabenhene Asafo Agyei. Kumase's policy in the 1830s was similar to that of the American President James Buchanan who in early 1861 maintained that secession was illegal but nevertheless declared that he would not coerce the South and would rather seek to negotiate its return to the Union. In effect Buchanan's declaration recognized the fact (not the theoretical legality) of Southern secessionist aspirations.

7. Rattray, *Ashanti Law*, p. 175; Lewin, "Structure of Political Conflict," II, pp. 371–73: interview with Boaten Sapon, 12 Mar. 1971. Despite the claim that Asafo Agyei was not consulted over the Fomena agreement, a Dwaben *okyeame*, Kwabena Ampea, signed the treaty that Kumase envoys presented to the British in March of 1874. See *Further Correspondence*, C. 1006, 1874, pp. 10–11: Treaty of Fomena, 1874, in Maxwell to Kimberley, dd. Cape Coast, 18 Mar. 1874.

8. *Papers*, C. 1343, 1875, p. 55: Strahan to Carnarvon, dd. Cape Coast, 8 Jan. 1875. Dwaben informants maintained that Asafo Agyei never entered Kumase while Mensa Bonsu held office. The Dwabenhene, however, was active in council deliberations during the reign of Asantehene Kofi Kakari and was apparently a moderate war advocate who frequently sided with peace politicians. See Ramseyer and Kühne, *Four Years*, pp. 93, 135, 157–59, 180–81, 187, 205.

9. *Correspondence*, C. 1140, 1875, pp. 63–64: Strahan to Carnarvon, dd. Cape Coast, 13 July 1874; *Papers*, C. 1402, 1876, p. 83: Asantehene Mensa Bonsu to Strahan, dd. Kumase, 16 July 1875, p. 85: Strahan to Carnarvon, dd. Cape Coast, 12 Oct. 1875, p. 107: Strahan to Gouldsbury, dd. Cape Coast, 14 Nov. 1875. On Dwaben activities in Kete Krakye, see D. Weaver, "Krachi Dente in Politics in the Late 19th Century" (draft paper, Legon, 1973), pp. 5–7. For an overview of this period, see Adu Boahen, "Juaben and Kumasi Relations in the Nineteenth Century" (seminar paper, Legon, 1965).

10. *Papers*, C. 1402, 1876, pp. 76–78: Strahan to Carnarvon, dd. Cape Coast, 14 Aug. 1875. See Johnson, "M. Bonnat on the Volta," *GNQ* 10 (1968), 5, 11, 16, and "Kumasi, Juaben, and M. Bonnat," *THSG* 12 (1971), pp. 38–40.

11. *Papers*, C. 1402, 1876, p. 83: Asantehene Osei (Mensa) Bonsu to Strahan, dd. Kumase, 16 July 1875, p. 102: Gouldsbury to Strahan, dd. Kyebi, 29 Oct. 1875, and p. 85: Strahan to Carnarvon, dd. Cape Coast, 12 Oct. 1875. Rattray, *Ashanti Law*, p. 176.

12. *Papers*, C. 1402, 1876, p. 71: Asantehene Mensa Bonsu to Lyall et al., dd. Kumase, 19 July 1875. See also *Papers*, C. 1343, 1875, p. 96: Strahan to Carnarvon, dd. Cape Coast, 5 June 1875, and p. 62: Strahan to Carnarvon, dd. Cape Coast, 14 Feb. 1875; Lewin, "Structure of Political Conflict," II, pp. 371–74: interview with Boaten Sapon, 12 Mar. 1971.

13. *Papers*, C. 1402, 1876, p. 71: Asantehene Mensa Bonsu to Lyall et al., dd. Kumase, 19 July 1875, p. 81: Mensa Bonsu to Governor, dd. Kumase, 11 June 1875, and p. 113: Gouldsbury to Strahan, dd. Kumase, 16 Nov. 1875.

14. See, e.g., ibid., p. 81: Asantehene Mensa Bonsu to Governor, dd. Kumase, 11 June 1875.

15. Lewin, "Structure of Political Conflict," II, pp. 372–74: interview with Boaten Sapon, 12 Mar. 1971; Rattray, *Ashanti Law*, p. 174. The Kokofuhene and Mamponhene, similarly brought to office by officials in the central government, were two such prominent *amanhene*. See McCaskie, "Paramountcy of Kwaku Dua," pp. 134–36, 137–39, 149–51, for a discussion of these two rulers.

16. *Papers*, C. 1343, 1875, p. 55: Strahan to Carnarvon, dd. Cape Coast, 8 Jan. 1875; *Papers*, C. 1402, 1876, pp. 71–72: Mensa Bonsu to Lyall et al., dd. Kumase, 19 July 1875, and p. 80: Bonnat to Strahan, dd. Kumase, 11 June 1875.

17. Ibid., p. 90: Strahan to Carnarvon, dd. Cape Coast, 25 Oct. 1875, p. 84: Strahan to Carnarvon, dd. Cape Coast, 17 Aug. 1875, p. 72: Lyall et al. to Mensa Bonsu, dd. Cape Coast, 4 Aug. 1875, and pp. 92–93: Bonnat to Governor, dd. Cape Coast, 30 Sept. 1875.

18. *Papers*, C. 1402, 1876, p. 80: Bonnat to Strahan, dd. Praso, 31 May 1875.

19. Ibid., p. 87: Mensa Bonsu to Governor, dd. Kumase, 2 Sept. 1875.

20. PRO, C.O. 96/173, No. 138: Griffith to Granville, dd. Accra, 28 Apr. 1886; C.O. 96/172, No. 73: Griffith to Stanley, dd. Aburi, 16 Feb. 1886, which refers to Bannerman as the Asantehene's "agent and spy." See also C.O. 96/131, No. 154: Ussher to Hicks Beach, dd. Accra, 11 May 1880, and C.O. 96/122, No. 226: Hay's report of 1877, in Freeling to Carnarvon, dd. Accra, 13 Sept. 1877; and Lewin, "Structure of Political Conflict," I, pp. 120–22, which discusses the violence attending the Dwaben migration from Asante.

21. Reports estimate some 6,500 Dwaben took refuge in Kwawu and Asante Akyem, while about 8,000 refugees migrated to Koforidua in the 1870s. Asafo Boaten, a son of Asafo Agyei, was a well-known trading *sikani* in Dwaben. PRO, C.O. 96/141, No. 293: Moloney to Kimberley, dd. Accra, 12 July 1882; C.O. 96/122, No. 226: Freeling to Carnarvon, dd. Accra, 13 Sept. 1877; and C.O. 96/203, No. 208: Hodgson to Knutsford, dd. Accra, 15 July 1889.

22. Asante Akyem, another region in which frequent migration took place in the final years of the century, was also marked by widespread localist sentiment. The towns of Agogo, Domeabra, Bompata, Konongo, Odumaase, Petrensa, Dwansa (the Asante Akyem capital in the 1860s), Obogu, Wankyi, and Amantra were under the administrative supervision of the Gyaasehene of Kumase and other senior officials in the capital. The region lost much of its population following the migration of the Akyem south of the Pra River during the reign of the Asantehene Opoku Ware I around 1800. While the Asantehene Kwaku Dua I held office, several towns were rebuilt, apparently to serve as buffers in the supervision of Akyem movements across the Pra. After the British invasion of Asante in 1873–74, leaders in Asante Akyem negotiated with other dissidents in Akyem Abuakwa, Akyem Kotoku, Dwaben, and Kwawu and the British. Some officeholders in Asante Akyem wished to continue close ties with Kumase (e.g., the Agogohene and Konongohene), while others, failing to preserve their neutrality, sought alliances with authorities in the Gold Coast Colony in the late 1870s. See Ramseyer and Kühne, *Four Years*, pp. 183, 240, 295. PRO, C.O. 96/127, No. 229: Ussher to Hicks Beach, dd. Accra, 8 Sept. 1879; NAG, ADM 11/1/3: Davidson-Houston to CCA, dd. Kumase, 1 Apr. 1903.

23. Wilks, *Asante in Nineteenth Century*, p. 100.
24. NAG, L. 448, No. 62: Report on Land Disputes in the Adansi Division, Obuasi District, dd. 24 Mar. 1947, pp. 1-3, 23; Ramseyer and Kühne, *Four Years*, pp. 297, 308; T. B. Freeman, *Journal of Various Visits to the Kingdoms of Ashanti, Aku, and Dahomi, in Western Africa* (London, 1844), pp. 18, 22, 40, 43. On the morphology of the Asante roads system, see Wilks, *Asante in Nineteenth Century*, pp. 1–50, which discusses the importance of Adanse on the trade route to the coastal ports.
25. *Correspondence*, C. 1140, 1875, p. 40: Lees to Carnarvon, dd. Cape Coast, 30 June 1874, p. 57: Strahan to Carnarvon, dd. Cape Coast, 30 June 1874, and p. 64: Strahan to Carnarvon, dd. Cape Coast, 13 July 1874. Brackenbury, *Ashanti War*, II, pp. 270–72; Ramseyer and Kühne, *Four Years*, p. 284.
26. Brackenbury, *Ashanti War*, II, p. 270, and see also pp. 271–72, and *Further Correspondence*, C. 1006, 1874, pp. 10–11: Treaty of Fomena of 1874, in Maxwell to Kimberley, dd. Cape Coast, 18 Mar. 1874.
27. *Further Correspondence*, C. 3687, 1883, p. 90: Strahan to Carnarvon, dd. Cape Coast, 19 Feb. 1876.
28. Ibid., p. 109: Lonsdale's report on his mission of 1882.
29. Ibid., p. 87: Moloney to Griffith, dd. Lagos, 14 Oct. 1882, and see pp. 89–90: Strahan to Carnarvon, dd. Cape Coast, 19 Feb. 1876.
30. Idem. See also Ramseyer and Kühne, *Four Years*, pp. 156–57, 173–74, 208, 249, 251–54, 257, and PRO, C.O. 96/145, No. 591: Griffith to Kimberley, dd. Cape Coast, 21 Dec. 1882.
31. *Further Correspondence*, C. 3687, 1883, p. 89: Strahan to Carnarvon, dd. Cape Coast, 19 Feb. 1876, and p. 87: Moloney to Griffith, dd. Lagos, 14 Oct. 1882.
32. Ibid., pp. 108–9: Lonsdale's report on his mission of 1882. PRO, C.O. 96/126, No. 83: Hay to Lees, dd. Accra, 29 Mar. 1879, dd. Fomena, 7 and 9 Mar. 1879.
33. PRO, C.O. 96/126, No. 32: Lees to Hicks Beach, dd. Cape Coast, 25 Feb. 1879, and Lees to Mensa Bonsu, dd. Cape Coast, 19 Feb. 1879.
34. *Further Correspondence*, C. 3386, 1882, p. 58: Lonsdale's report on his mission of 1881–82, and p. 103: Cade to Private Secretary, dd. Cape Coast, 28 June 1882; *Further Correspondence*, C. 3687, 1883, p. 84: Griffith to Kimberley, dd. Accra, 16 Nov. 1882.
35. Ibid., p. 95: Badger to Private Secretary, dd. Accra, 4 Dec. 1882, and see p. 87: Kwaku Nkansa to Governor, dd. Fomena, 2 Oct. 1882, and p. 91: Griffith to Adansehene, dd. Accra, 9 Nov. 1882.
36. Ramseyer and Kühne, *Four Years*, pp. 93, 135, 157–59, 180–81, 187, 189.
37. *Affairs*, C. 3064, 1881, p. 4: Griffith to Kimberley, dd. Elmina, 5 Jan. 1881, and p. 8: Griffith to Parker, dd. Elmina, 5 Jan. 1881. *Further Correspondence*, C. 4906, 1886, p. 41: Firminger to Governor, dd. Praso, 17 Apr. 1886.
38. *Further Correspondence*, C. 3687, 1883, p. 96: Badger to Private Secretary, dd. Accra, 4 Dec. 1882; Rattray, *Ashanti Law*, p. 151.
39. *Further Correspondence*, C. 3687, 1883, pp. 147–48: Barrow to Rowe, dd. Amoafo, 23 Apr. 1883, and pp. 132–34: interviews between Rowe and Bekwae *nkwankwaa* held on 4, 28 Mar. and 3 Apr. 1883. See Lewin, "Structure of Political Conflict," pp. 385–88: interview with Bekwaehene Osei Kwadwo II, Kwadwo Donko, and Kwabena Antwi, 19 Mar. 1971, for Bekwae stool lands and principal subordinate chiefs in this period.
40. *Further Correspondence*, C. 4052, 1884, p. 35: Barrow's report, dd. 5 July 1883.

41. Lewin, "Structure of Political Conflict," II, p. 385: interview of 19 Mar. 1971, cited above; Rattray, *Ashanti Law*, p. 151; *Further Correspondence*, C. 4477, 1885, p. 91: Kirby's report, dd. 15 Apr. 1884.

42. Idem. *Further Correspondence*, C. 3687, 1883, p. 149: Kirby to Barrow, dd. 23 Apr. 1883.

43. *Further Correspondence*, C. 4477, p. 91: Kirby's report, dd. 15 Apr. 1884.

44. *Further Correspondence*, C. 4906, 1886, p. 5: Coppin to Griffith, dd. Cape Coast, 18 May 1885, and see p. 47: Firminger to Governor, dd. Praso, 24 Apr. 1886.

45. Ibid., p. 41: Firminger to Governor, dd. Praso, 17 Apr. 1886.

46. See, e.g., ibid., p. 13: District Commissioner, Cape Coast, to Colonial Secretary, dd. Cape Coast, 4 Feb. 1886, and NAG, ADM 1/7/17, No. 47: Griffith to Firminger, dd. Aburi, 15 Mar. 1886.

47. *Further Correspondence*, C. 4906, 1886, pp. 11–12: Kwaku Nkansa to Governor, dd. Edubiase, 10, 18 Jan. 1886.

48. Ibid., p. 41: Firminger to Governor, dd. Praso, 17 Apr. 1886.

49. Ibid., p. 36: Firminger to Governor, dd. Praso, 15 Apr. 1886, and p. 12: Yaw Awua to Colonial Secretary, dd. Cape Coast, 25 Jan. 1886. Many Kumase troops were armed with Sniders, indicating the support of Akyampon Panin for the Bekwae position.

50. Ibid., p. 36: Firminger to Governor, dd. Praso, 15 Apr. 1886. See also PRO, C.O. 96/173, No. 107: Griffith to Granville, dd. Accra, 6 Apr. 1886, for another reason explaining the "dullness of trade" at Cape Coast—the refusal of Asante traders to accept the low prices offered by Cape Coast merchants.

51. *Further Correspondence*, C. 4906, 1886, pp. 26–27; Firminger to Kwaku Nkansa, dd. Praso, 26 Mar. 1886, and pp. 31–32: Firminger to Governor, dd. Fomena, 8 Apr. 1886, citing information from Kotirko and the Adanse council.

52. Ibid., p. 42: Firminger to Governor, dd. Praso, 17 Apr. 1886, p. 27: Firminger to Kwaku Nkansa, dd. Praso, 26 Mar. 1886, and p. 50: Firminger to Governor, dd. Praso, 30 Apr. 1886.

53. Ibid., p. 21: Firminger to Governor, dd. Praso, 17 Mar. 1886.

54. Ibid., p. 31: Firminger to Governor, dd. Fomena, 8 Apr. 1886.

55. Ibid., p. 40: Firminger to Governor, dd. Praso, 17 Apr. 1886, and pp. 36–38: Firminger to Griffith, dd. Praso, 15, 19 Apr. 1886. Kofi Ahinkora, *ohene* of Akyem Bosume, like many localist leaders in the Colony, had supported Kofi Kakari's restoration in 1883.

56. Ibid., p. 64: Carr to Colonial Secretary, dd. Praso, 13 June 1886, citing information from Adanse envoys.

57. Ibid., p. 63: Griffith to Granville, dd. Accra, 21 June 1886, and p. 65: Carr to Colonial Secretary, dd. Praso, 16 June 1886.

58. Lewin, "Structure of Political Conflict," II, pp. 285–86, 291–93: interviews with Fantehene Kwame Ti, 6 Nov. 1970; Dadiesoabahene Yaw Boaten, 13 Nov. 1970; BMA, Basel: Ramseyer's Jahresbericht for Abetifi, 1878, dd. 29 Jan. 1879, Mohr's report on his expedition to Kumase with Ramseyer in 1881, dd. Feb. 1881, and Clerk's report for 1890, dd. Buem, n.d. On Kwawu in the nineteenth century, see P. Steiner, *Ein Besuch in Akwawu* (Basel, 1882), passim; E. Perregaux, "A Few Notes on Kwaku, 'Quahoe,' a Territory on the Gold Coast Colony," *Journal of the Royal African Society* 2 (1903), 44–47; A. J.

Walker, "The Kwahus," *The Gold Coast Review* 1 (1925), 15–28; and the geographical comments by Dickson, *Historical Geography,* pp. 60, 275.

59. K. Ameyaw, "Kwahu—An Early Forest State," *GNQ* 9 (1966), 45.

60. Idem. BMA, Basel: Ramseyer to Basel, dd. Kyebi, 17 Jan., 8 Feb. 1876, and report of journey in early 1884, dd. Abetifi, 9 Mar. 1885. *Further Correspondence,* C. 3386, 1882, p. 75: Lonsdale's report on his mission of 1881–82.

61. *Evangelische Heidenbote,* Nov. 1875, No. 11, pp. 81–84, and May 1876, No. 12, pp. 5 and 33–34.

62. For the constant stream of diplomatic overtures from Kwawu localists, see *Correspondence,* C. 1140, 1875, p. 21: Maxwell to Kimberley, dd. Cape Coast, 19 Mar. 1874, and p. 66: Gouldsbury to Strahan, dd. Elmina, 12 July 1874; BMA, Basel: Ramseyer to Basel, dd. Kyebi, Abetifi, Neuenburg, 8 Feb. 1876, 12 May 1888, and 16 Oct. 1885, and Mohr to Basel, dd. Begoro, 22 Mar. 1875.

63. BMA, Basel: Ramseyer to an "unspecified lady," dd. Abetifi, 11 Sept. 1878, Ramseyer to Basel, dd. Abetifi, 12 May 1888 and 25 Nov. 1879, and Mohr to Begoro, dd. 28 Oct. 1879.

64. Ibid., Ramseyer to Basel, dd. Abetifi, 28 Aug. 1878, enclosing letter from Owusu Ansa, dd. 16 July 1878.

65. *Further Correspondence,* C. 3386, 1882, p. 78: Lonsdale's report on his mission of 1881–82.

66. PRO, C.O. 96/192, No. 213: Treaty with Kwawu, in Griffith to Colonial Office, dd. Accra, 22 June 1888.

67. PRO, C.O. 96/124, No. 171: Lees to Hicks Beach, dd. Accra, 15 Aug. 1878, citing information from Owusu Ansa, and C.O. 96/120, No. 39: Freeling to Carnarvon, dd. Cape Coast, 26 Jan. 1887, citing information from Gyaman envoys. For earlier interaction between the Bonsu administration and Gyaman dissenters, see Wilks, *Asante in Nineteenth Century,* pp. 287–95, passim, and Agbodeka, *African Politics and British Policy,* pp. 88–89.

68. PRO, C.O. 96/120, No. 39: Freeling to Colonial Office, dd. Accra, 26 Feb. 1877, citing interview with envoys from the Gyamanhene Agyeman and Kwaku Kyei, *ohene* of Sehwi Wiawso, and see C.O. 96/128, No. 251: Ussher to Hicks Beach, dd. Accra, 8 Nov. 1879, citing information in J. Smith's report of 1879; *Further Correspondence,* C. 3687, 1883, pp. 111–13, 125–26: Lonsdale's report on his mission of 1882.

69. See Wilks, *Asante in Nineteenth Century,* pp. 243–71. For general comments on Kumase's relations with the North, see J. Goody, "Ashanti and the North-West," *University of Ghana Institute of African Studies Research Review,* Supplement 1 (1965), pp. 38–61; Arhin, "Ashanti and the North-East," *University of Ghana Institute of African Studies Research Review,* Supplement 2 (1970), pp. 1–38; H. J. Hobbs, "History of Nkoranza," *The Gold Coast Review* 3 (1927), 117–21. On Asante's commercial contacts with its northern hinterlands, see Wilks, *The Northern Factor,* pp. 3–36, and "A Medieval Trade-Route," 337–41, and "Asante Policy towards the Hausa Trade," pp. 124–41; Arhin, "Aspects of the Asante Northern Trade," 363–73, and "The Development of Market Centers at Atebubu and Kintampo since 1874" (Ph.D. thesis, University of London, 1969), pp. 6–150; Goody, "Salaga in 1876," *GNQ* 8 (1966), 1–5. For the role of Salaga in Asante and European power politics, see J. A. Braimah and J. Goody, *Salaga: The Struggle for Power* (London, 1967).

70. *Further Correspondence,* C. 3386, pp. 70, 74, 78: Lonsdale's report on his

mission of 1881–82, pp. 100–1: Concise History of Abruno Rebellion against Ashanti, recorded by C. V. E. Graves, dd. Dec. 1881. According to Graves' informants, the Asantehene Kakari had sought the advice of the priest of the Dente shrine at Krakye before authorizing the reoccupation of the southern provinces in 1872–73. The priest advised against the project. Subsequently, Kakari and "the Ashantis always had the knack of placing the Brunfo [eastern Bron] to the hottest and most uncomfortable positions" during the military operations.

71. Ibid., pp. 69, 79, 82: Lonsdale's report on his mission of 1881–82, pp. 99–100: Graves' report, dd. Dec. 1881; PRO, C.O. 96/119, No. 5162: Gouldsbury's report of 1876, printed as African No. 95, for use of Colonial Office, pp. 1–7, in Gouldsbury to Strahan, dd. Accra, 27 Mar. 1876; minutes by A. W. L. Hemming, R. Meade, and Carnarvon, dd. 1, 3, 12 May 1876. Carnarvon, among others, noted that Gouldsbury's "experiment will be applied on a larger scale with advantage," and that this would be a most effective policy to pursue in the future, especially in light of the breakdown of political and commercial relations between Asante and Salaga after 1875.

72. *Further Correspondence*, C. 3386, 1882, pp. 71–75, 78–79: Lonsdale's report on his mission of 1881–82.

73. Ibid., pp. 69–70, 80–81: Lonsdale's report on his mission of 1881–82, and Lonsdale's treaty with the chief of Panto.

74. Ibid., pp. 72, 78: Lonsdale's report on his mission of 1881–82.

75. BMA, Basel: Reports on the Salaga Journeys of 1877: D. Asante to Basel, dd. 19 Sept. 1878. Manuscript on T. Opoku's Journey from Salaga down the east bank of the Volta in 1877, dd. Feb. and Mar., 1877 (cited in Paul Jenkins, *Abstracts of Basel Mission Gold Coast Correspondence*, pp. 77–91).

76. *Further Correspondence*, C. 3386, 1882, pp. 71–73: Lonsdale's report on his mission of 1881–82.

77. *Further Correspondence*, C. 4477, p. 94: Kirby's report, dd. 15 Apr. 1884.

78. David Asante, "Account of a Journey to Salaga in 1884," *Mitteilungen der Geographische Gesellschaft zu Jena* 4 (1886), 16 (translated and cited by Johnson, *Salaga Papers* (two vols., Legon 1965), I, acc. no. ASL/5/1. See also J. G. Christaller, "Eine Reise in den Hinterlandern von Togo," *Mitteilungen der Geographischen Gesellschaft für Thuringen* 8 (1889), 1–28, which includes an account of P. Hall's journey to Nkonya and Buem in early 1887.

79. *Further Correspondence*, C. 7917, 1896, p. 135: Memorandum by Ferguson, dd. 9 Nov. 1893, in Ferguson to Hodgson, dd. Atebubu, 24 Nov. 1893.

80. *Further Correspondence*, C. 3687, pp. 95–96: Badger to Private Secretary, dd. Accra, 4 Dec. 1882; *Further Correspondence*, C. 4477, 1885, p. 85: Kirby to Colonial Secretary, dd. Kyekyewere, Asante, 10 Mar. 1884, and p. 94: Kirby's report, dd. 15 Apr. 1884.

81. Ibid., pp. 93–94: Kirby's report, dd. 15 Apr. 1884.

82. J. Goody and C. Y. Boateng, "The History and Traditions of Nkoranza," *University of Ghana Institute of African Studies Research Review*, Supplement 1 (Legon, 1965), p. 179.

83. *Further Correspondence*, C. 7917, 1896, p. 136: Memorandum by Ferguson, dd. 9 Nov. 1893.

84. See, e.g., Lewin, "Structure of Political Conflict," II, pp. 368–69: interview with Domfe Kyere, 2 Jan. 1971.

85. Lewin, field-notes: interview with Omantihene Owusu Nkwantabisa, dd. Kumase, 5 Dec. 1970.

CHAPTER 6

1. Lewin, "Structure of Political Conflict," II, pp. 257, 428–29: interviews with Kyidomhene Osei Yaw, 16 Oct. 1970; Anamenakohene Kwabena Dwoben II, 4 Apr. 1971.
2. *Further Correspondence*, C. 5357, 1888, p. 7: Badger to Governor, dd. Christiansborg, 20 Oct. 1886.
3. Ibid., p. 12: memorandum by Yaw Gyamfi, dd. Bekwae, 24 Nov. 1886.
4. Idem. Lewin, "Structure of Political Conflict," II, pp. 319, 329: interviews with Atwema Agogohene Owusu Afriyie I, 4 Dec. 1970; Atwemahene Antwi Agyei IV, 11 Dec. 1970.
5. *Further Correspondence*, C. 5357, 1888, p. 73: interview with Kokofu envoys and Yaw Awua, dd. Accra, 29 July 1887.
6. Ibid., p. 13: memorandum by Yaw Gyamfi, dd. Bekwae, 24 Nov. 1886.
7. Idem. It is not known whether authorities in Kumase sanctioned the Bekwaehene's offer to swear an oath. Yet the evidence suggests that Yaa Akyaa's supporters approved of his action.
8. See chapter 4, and, e.g., *Further Correspondence*, C. 5357, 1888, p. 6: Griffith to Stanhope, dd. Accra, 30 Oct. 1886.
9. Ibid., p. 35: Kwadwo Yinna et al. to Lonsdale, dd. Cape Coast, 17 Jan. 1887. The Antoahene Antoa Mensa, Gyakyehene Yaw Pense, Akokofehene Boahene, Beposohene Esen Kwaku, Atwemahene Kwame Antwi Agyei, Nsumankwaahene Kwasi Domfe, and Pinankohene (Gyaasewahene) Opoku Dum were among the most vocal Kumase supporters of Prempe at this stage in the contest. See Lewin, "Structure of Political Conflict," II, pp. 130, 193, 455, 461: interviews with Akyereapem, 11 Aug. 1970; Kwaku Anno, 4 Sept. 1970; Domfe Kyere, 15, 17 Apr. 1971.
10. See, e.g., Lewin, field-notes: interviews with Domfe Kyere, 25 Apr. 1971; Kwadwo Afodo, 27 Apr. 1971. *Further Correspondence*, C. 5357, 1888, p. 35: Kwadwo Yinna et al. to Lonsdale, dd. Cape Coast, 17 Jan. 1887.
11. Lewin, "Structure of Political Conflict," II, pp. 204–5, 221–22, 455–56, 460: interviews with Amakoo, 11 Sept. 1970; Kofi Afrane, 15 Sept. 1970; Domfe Kyere, 15, 17 Apr. 1971.
12. Ibid., pp. 371–72: interview with Boaten Sapon, 12 Mar. 1971. This informant is a son of the Dwabenhene Yaw Sapon by his marriage to Afua Akyaa of the Agona matriclan of Dwaben. Oheneba Boaten Sapon holds the office of *ahenemma*, or chief of the children of the chief, a position which he claims enables him to speak as the "leading authority" on Dwaben affairs. See also *Further Correspondence*, C. 5357, 1888, p. 35: Kwadwo Yinna et al. to Lonsdale, dd. Cape Coast, 17 Jan. 1887.
13. See, e.g., Lewin, field-notes: interviews with Domfe Kyere, 6 Jan. 1971; Kwadwo Afodo, 8 Jan. 1971.
14. Ibid., interview with Kwadwo Afodo, 11 Jan. 1971.
15. Ibid., interviews with Domfe Kyere, 13 Jan. 1971; Adu Gyamera, 1 Feb. 1971; Kwadwo Afodo, 6 Feb. 1971.
16. Lewin, "Structure of Political Conflict," II, pp. 377, 384–85, 391–92, 462–63: interviews with Agyei Maniampon Abrebrease, 14 Mar. 1971; Bekwaehene Osei

Kwadwo II, Kwadwo Donko, and Kwabena Antwi, 19 Mar. 1971; Kokofuhene Osei Asibe III and Adu Buobi, 19 Mar. 1971; Kumawuhene Otuo Akyampon II, 18 Apr. 1971.

17. Ibid., p. 407: interview with Domfe Kyere, 28 Mar. 1971.

18. *Further Correspondence*, C. 5615, 1888, p. 34: Barnett to Governor, dd. Edwabin, 10 Mar. 1888.

19. Lewin, "Structure of Political Conflict," II, pp. 146–47: interview with Kwadwo Afodo, 27 Aug. 1970. *Further Correspondence*, C. 5615, 1888, p. 122: Barnett's report on Asante, received in Accra, 10 May 1888.

20. *Further Correspondence*, C. 5357, 1888, p. 66: Lonsdale to Administrator, dd. Akwaboso, 13 June 1887, and p. 50: Lonsdale to Governor, dd. Wiayawusu, 19 Feb. 1887; Lewin, "Structure of Political Conflict," II, pp. 377, 391–92, 454: interviews with Agyei Maniampon Abrebrease, 14 Mar. 1971; Kokofuhene Osei Asibe II and Adu Buobi, 19 Mar. 1971; Domfe Kyere, 15 Apr. 1971.

21. Ibid., pp. 57, 222: interviews with I. K. Agyeman, 16 June 1970; Kofi Afrane, 16 Sept. 1970. Yaw Awua actually was born in Deduako, near Edweso, some ten miles from Kumase. He was an *aheneba* as his father had been Edwesohene. Awua was appointed Edwesohene by the British in about 1901 and was forced to abdicate in 1910 due to blindness which, according to informants, was caused by Edweso citizens who resented his continual support for the British position in Asante. For his career, see Boyle, *Through Fanteeland*, pp. 276–77; NAG, ADM 11/1770, Palaver Book, 1877–1887, p. 110: interview of 12 Aug. 1884; Lewin, *The English Involvement in Ashanti around 1900* (Legon, 1968), interview with Owusu Ansa, dd. Kumase, 13 Aug. 1968.

22. *Further Correspondence*, C. 5357, 1888, p. 6: Griffith to Stanhope, dd. Accra, 30 Oct. 1886, and p. 7: Badger to Governor, dd. Christiansborg, 20 Oct. 1886. See Ramseyer and Kühne, *Four Years*, p. 177, for the career of Kofi Nti, a son of the Asantehene Kofi Kakari, who was appointed Dadiesoabahene (of Kumase) by the British in 1901.

23. See, e.g., *Further Correspondence*, C. 5357, 1888, p. 34: Lonsdale to Governor, dd. Mampon, 30 Jan. 1887.

24. Ibid., p. 61: statement of the Kokofuhene's envoy, in District Commissioner to Colonial Secretary, dd. Cape Coast, 25 Mar. 1887.

25. Idem.

26. Lewin, field-notes: interview with Kokofuhene Osei Asibe III and Adu Buobi, dd. Kokofu, 20 Mar. 1971. The present Kokofuhene, born in 1903, was enstooled in 1951 and is a nephew of Osei Asibe I, who was also known as Asibe Panin. Adu Buobi, who was born in Assini in the Nsuta district about the time Osei Asibe I was enstooled (i.e., 1884), is generally regarded by the Kokofu elders as the leading historian in his *oman*.

27. *The Western Echo*, II, Nos. 39/40, 14–28 Feb. 1887, p. 5, and Nos. 41/42, 16–31 Mar. 1887, p. 4; *Further Correspondence*, C. 5357, 1888, p. 32: Stewart to Governor, dd. Akrofom, 31 Jan. 1887; Fuller, *Vanished Dynasty*, p. 162.

28. See, e.g., *Further Correspondence*, C. 5357, 1888, p. 57: Lonsdale to Administrator, dd. Cape Coast, 9 June 1887.

29. *Further Correspondence*, C. 5615, 1888, pp. 121–22: Barnett's report on Asante, received Accra, 10 May 1888.

30. *Further Correspondence*, C. 4906, 1886, p. 16: Firminger to Colonial Secretary, dd. Praso, 10 Mar. 1887; *Further Correspondence*, C. 5357, 1888, p. 59: Hay-

ford to Colonial Secretary, dd. Praso, 4 May 1887, p. 57: Lonsdale to Administrator, dd. Akwaboso, 30 May 1887, p. 55: statement of Kokofuhene's envoys, in Administrator to Lonsdale, dd. Cape Coast, 1 June 1887, p. 66: Lonsdale to Administrator, dd. Boasi, 22 June 1887, and p. 73: interview with Kokofu envoys and Yaw Awua, dd. Accra, 29 July 1887.

31. Ibid., p. 62: Lonsdale to Administrator, dd. Akwaboso, 10 June 1887.
32. Idem.
33. Ibid., p. 73: interview with Kokofu envoys and Yaw Awua, dd. Accra, 29 July 1887.
34. Ibid., p. 62: Lonsdale to Administrator, dd. Akwabosu, 10 June 1887.
35. See, e.g., ibid., p. 72: White to Holland, dd. Accra, 5 Aug. 1887.
36. Ibid., p. 70: Lonsdale to Administrator, dd. Praso, 11 July 1887.
37. Ibid., p. 71: Minutes by Sir B. Griffith, dd. 21 Aug. 1887. See also *Further Correspondence*, C. 5615, 1888, p. 10: Griffith to Knutsford, dd. Accra, 13 Apr. 1888.
38. Ibid., p. 30: Barnett to Governor, dd. Edwabin, 24 Feb. 1888.
39. Ibid., p. 31: Barnett to Governor, dd. Edwabin, 24 Feb. 1888; see *Further Correspondence*, C. 5357, 1888, p. 75: Lonsdale to Administrator, dd. Edwabin, 22 Aug. 1887.
40. Idem.
41. See, e.g., *Further Correspondence*, C. 5615, 1888, p. 19: Barnett to Colonial Secretary, dd. Edwabin, 6 Jan. 1888, and p. 17: Barnett to Colonial Secretary, dd. Edwabin, 31 Dec. 1887.
42. *Further Correspondence*, C. 5357, 1888, p. 76: Lonsdale to Administrator, dd. Asante, 27 Aug. 1887.
43. Idem. See *Further Correspondence*, C. 5615, 1888, p. 23: Barnett to Governor, dd. Edwabin, 23 Jan. 1888.
44. *Further Correspondence*, C. 5357, 1888, p. 76: Lonsdale to Administrator, dd. Asante, 27 Aug. 1887.
45. Idem.
46. Lewin, field-notes: interview with Adu Gyamera, dd. Kwadaso, 15 Aug. 1970.
47. *Further Correspondence*, C. 5357, 1888, p. 79: White to Holland, dd. Accra, 3 Oct. 1887, quoting Lonsdale.
48. Ibid., p. 20: Barnett to Colonial Secretary, dd. Edwabin, 14 Jan. 1888, and p. 122: Barnett's report on Asante, received Accra, 10 May 1888.
49. Ibid., p. 17: Barnett to Colonial Secretary, dd. Edwabin, 31 Dec. 1887, and p. 20: Barnett to Colonial Secretary, dd. Edwabin, 14 Jan. 1888.
50. Idem. Lewin, "Structure of Political Conflict," II, p. 432: interview with Kuntanasehene Kofi Boaten II, 5 Apr. 1971. The Kuntanasehene and his "junior brother," the Akokofehene, do not belong to a *fekuo* in Asante, are grouped together in the Dako Nton, and swear directly to the Asantehene on the Mponpomsuo sword, the senior sword of the nation. The informant must pass through one of the Asantehene's twelve *akyeame* to see the Asantehene, and the full name of this ancestral, hereditary stool is Kyere ne Boaten. The symbol of office is represented by the Atoaa tree.
51. Lewin, field-notes: interview with Domfe Kyere, dd. Kumase, 25 Apr. 1971.
52. *Further Correspondence*, C. 5615, 1888, p. 28: Barnett to Governor, dd. Edwabin, 15 Feb. 1888.
53. Ibid., p. 29: Barnett to Governor, dd. Edwabin, 23 Feb. 1888.

54. Ibid., p. 43: Barnett to Governor, dd. Kumase, 29 Mar. 1888.
55. Ibid., p. 44: Sullivan to Barnett, dd. Kumase, 26 Mar. 1888.
56. Ibid., p. 42: Barnett to Governor, dd. Kumase, 24 Mar. 1888, and p. 38, Barnett to Governor, dd. Kumase, 20 Mar. 1888.
57. Ibid., p. 42: Barnett to Governor, dd. Kumase, 29 Mar. 1888.
58. Idem.
59. Ibid., p. 43: Barnett to Governor, dd. Kumase, 29 Mar. 1888.
60. Ibid., p. 34: Barnett to Governor, dd. Edwabin, 10 Mar. 1888.
61. Kwaku Goroso's implication in the political violence of Nov. 1879 virtually disqualified him from competition for the kingship in 1887–88. Although he appeared to have had no open support, informants noted that the Kokofuhene Osei Asibe at one stage in the election did suggest his candidacy as an alternative to that of Atweneboanna. Goroso's close connection with the partisans of Atweneboanna in Asante meant that Kumase politicians would have retaliated for the support Goroso lent to the Atweneboanna cause. While residing in the Colony, Goroso engaged in trading, especially rubber. By 1896 he was a wealthy entrepreneur with renewed ambitions north of the Pra River. See Lewin, "Structure of Political Conflict," II, pp. 111–12, 118–19, 273–74: interviews with Akyereapem, 7 Aug. 1970; Adu Gyamera, 10 Aug. 1970; Domfe Kyere, 30 Oct. 1970.
62. *Further Correspondence*, C. 5615, 1888, p. 111: Barnett's report on Asante, received Accra, 10 May 1888.
63. Ibid., p. 112: Barnett's report on Asante, received Accra, 10 May 1888.
64. Ibid., pp. 121–22: Barnett's report on Asante, received Accra, 10 May 1888. See also Fuller, *Vanished Dynasty*, p. 164.
65. Lewin, "Structure of Political Conflict," II, p. 193: interview with Kwaku Anno, 4 Sept. 1970.
66. *Further Correspondence*, C. 5615, 1888, p. 122: Barnett's report on Asante, received Accra, 10 May 1888. See p. 125: Halm to Barnett, dd. Kumase, 3 Apr. 1888, and p. 127: Badger to Barnett, dd. Kumase, 2 Apr. 1888. One of the released prisoners was the Ankobeahene Ata Gyamfi who had been allegedly executed following the conference in Kumase in early 1887.
67. Ibid., p. 122: Barnett's report on Asante, received Accra, 10 May 1888.
68. Idem. See also p. 126: Halm to Barnett, dd. Kumase, 3 Apr. 1888, and p. 159: District Commissioner, Cape Coast, to Colonial Secretary, dd. Cape Coast, 9 Aug. 1888; Lewin, "Structure of Political Conflict," II, pp. 391–93: interview with Kokofuhene Osei Asibe III and Abu Buobi, 19 Mar. 1971.
69. *Further Correspondence*, C. 5615, 1888, p. 144: Griffith to Knutsford, dd. Accra, 12 July 1888.
70. Ibid., p. 159: District Commissioner, Cape Coast, to Colonial Secretary, dd. Cape Coast, 9 Aug. 1888, citing information from Prempe's envoys; Lewin, "Structure of Political Conflict," II, pp. 207–9, 222–23, 454–57: interviews with Amakoo, 11 Sept. 1970; Kofi Afrane, 15 Sept. 1970; Domfe Kyere, 15 Apr. 1971.
71. Ibid., pp. 207–8, 205–7, 223–25; interviews with Amakoo, 11 Sept. 1970; Kwabena Baako, 14 Sept. 1970; Kofi Afrane, 15 Sept. 1970. The *ntahara* horn is only sounded immediately before the Asantehene or an important district head is about to speak in court.
72. *Further Correspondence*, C. 5615, 1888, pp. 147–48: Carr to Colonial Secretary,

dd. Praso, 3 July 1888, and p. 159: District Commissioner, Cape Coast, to Colonial Secretary, dd. Cape Coast, 9 Aug. 1888, citing information from Prempe's envoys; Lewin, "Structure of Political Conflict," II, pp. 342, 385: interviews with Ampabamehene Kwabena Kwaku II, 17 Dec. 1970; Bekwaehene Osei Kwadwo II, Kwadwo Donko, and Kwabena Antwi, 19 Mar. 1971.

73. Ibid., pp. 119–21: interview with Adu Gyamera, 10 Aug. 1970. Fuller, *Vanished Dynasty*, p. 156, maintains wrongly that a Bekwae man betrayed Bantamahene Awua.

74. Lewin, "Structure of Political Conflict," II, pp. 391–93: interview with Kokofuhene Osei Asibe III and Adu Buobi, 19 Mar. 1971; *Further Correspondence*, C. 5615, 1888, pp. 170–71: Griffith to Knutsford, dd. Accra, 18 Sept. 1888, p. 147: Carr to District Commissioner, Cape Coast, dd. Praso, 1 July 1888, p. 164: Akers to Colonial Secretary, dd. Insuaim, 25 Aug. 1888, and p. 158: Griffith to Knutsford, dd. Accra, 20 Aug. 1888.

75. Ibid., pp. 162–63: Griffith to Knutsford, dd. Accra, 4 Sept. 1888, and p. 163: Akers to Colonial Secretary, dd. Insuaim, 25 Aug. 1888.

76. Ibid., p. 157: District Commissioner, Cape Coast, to Governor, dd. Cape Coast, 9 Aug. 1888.

77. Ibid., p. 158: Griffith to Knutsford, dd. Accra, 20 Aug. 1888; NAG, ADM 1/7/19, No. 483: Griffith to Colonial Secretary, dd. Accra, 15 Aug. 1888; PRO, C.O. 96/199, No. 25353: Akers to Colonial Office, dd. 22 Dec. 1888.

78. See, e.g., *Further Correspondence*, C. 5615, 1888, pp. 173–74: Akers to Colonial Secretary, dd. Insuaim, 7 Sept. 1888.

79. Ibid., p. 175: Akers to Colonial Secretary, dd. Insuaim, 7 Sept. 1888.

80. Ibid., p. 166: Akers to Colonial Secretary, dd. Insuaim, 27 Aug. 1888.

81. Ibid., p. 172: Akers to Colonial Secretary, dd. Insuaim, 7 Sept. 1888.

82. Ibid., p. 173: Akers to Colonial Secretary, dd. Insuaim, 7 Sept. 1888.

83. Ibid., pp. 180–81: Van Dyke to Akers, dd. Akukuaso, 11 Sept. 1888.

84. Ibid., pp. 175–76: Akers to Colonial Secretary, dd. Agona Swedru, 13 Sept. 1888.

85. Ibid., p. 178: Akers to Colonial Secretary, dd. Agona Swedru, 13 Sept. 1888, and see pp. 47–50: Turton to Colonial Secretary, dd. Moseaso Akyem, 5 May 1888.

86. Ibid., pp. 164, 167: Akers to Colonial Secretary, dd. Insuaim, 27 Aug. 1888, and p. 144: Griffith to Colonial Secretary, dd. Agona Swedru, 15 Sept. 1888.

87. Ibid., p. 167: Akers to Colonial Secretary, dd. Insuaim, 27 Aug. 1888; PRO, C.O. 96/156, Nos. 161, 449, 25353: Rowe to Derby, dd. Accra, 18 Mar. 1884, Turton to Griffith, dd. Accra, 18 Dec. 1888, Akers to Colonial Office, dd. 22 Dec. 1888.

88. *Further Correspondence*, C. 5615, 1888, p. 167: Boaten to Governor, dd. Abetifi, 24 Aug. 1888.

89. Ibid., p. 168: Griffith to Boaten, dd. Accra, 3 Sept. 1888.

90. Lewin, "Structure of Political Conflict," II, pp. 205–7, 215–16, 222–24: interviews with Amakoo, 11 Sept. 1970; Kwabena Baako, 14 Sept. 1970; Kofi Afrane, 15 Sept. 1970. Fuller, *Vanished Dynasty*, pp. 162, 165. *Western Echo*, I, No. 9, 22 Oct. 1888, p. 3.

91. Lewin, "Structure of Political Conflict," II, pp. 221–24: interview with Kofi Afrane, 15 Sept. 1970. In the Edweso district there are three *adehyea abusua*, or royal families. One resides in the town of Boankra, the second in Besease,

and the third in Edweso proper. The Edwesohene always comes from one of these towns. Kwasi Afrane, e.g., was born in Boankra, while his predecessor, Kwame Wuo, deposed for maladministration, issued from Edweso town.

92. Ibid., p. 209: interview with Amakoo, 11 Sept. 1970.

93. Ibid., p. 207: interview with Amakoo, 11 Sept. 1970.

94. Ibid., pp. 378–80: interview with Agyei Maniampon Abrebrease, 14 Mar. 1971; Fuller, *Vanished Dynasty*, p. 165; *Further Correspondence*, C. 5615, 1888, p. 9: Hodgson to Knutsford, dd. Accra, 9 Dec. 1889, and p. 159: District Commissioner, Cape Coast, to Colonial Secretary, dd. Cape Coast, 9 Aug. 1888, citing information from Kumase ambassadors.

95. Lewin, "Structure of Political Conflict," II, pp. 379–80: interview with Agyei Maniampon Abrebrease, 14 Mar. 1971.

96. *Further Correspondence*, C. 7917, 1896, p. 9: Hodgson to Knutsford, dd. Accra, 9 Dec. 1889, citing information from Badger.

97. Lewin, "Structure of Political Conflict," II, pp. 380–81: interview with Agyei Maniampon Abrebrease, 14 Mar. 1971. Rattray, *Ashanti Law*, p. 241, notes that his name was Kwame Osokye.

CHAPTER 7

1. A point repeatedly emphasized by my Asante and non-Asante informants. See, e.g., Lewin, field-notes: interviews with Domfe Kyere, 25 Apr. 1971; Kwadwo Afodo, 27 Apr. 1971.

2. Lewin, field-notes: interview with Domfe Kyere, 25 Apr. 1971.

3. *Further Correspondence*, C. 7917, 1896, p. 9: Hodgson to Knutsford, dd. Accra, 9 Dec. 1889, and p. 136: Memorandum by Ferguson, dd. 9 Nov. 1893. Lewin, "Structure of Political Conflict," II, p. 454: interview with Domfe Kyere, 15 Apr. 1971. The *ahene* of the Nsuta towns of Ntonso, Asaman, and Dako-Gyakye, who as *abirempon* to the Nsutahene had supported Atweneboanna's candidacy, also returned to the metropolitan region in late 1889.

4. See chapter 6.

5. *Further Correspondence*, C. 7917, 1896, p. 12: Hodgson to Mamponhene, dd. Accra, 23 Nov. 1889. Lewin, "Structure of Political Conflict," II, p. 381: interview with Agyei Maniampon Abrebrease, 14 Mar. 1971.

6. *Further Correspondence*, C. 7917, 1896, p. 9: Hodgson to Knutsford, dd. Accra, 9 Dec. 1889.

7. *Further Correspondence*, C. 7917, 1896, p. 136: Memorandum by Ferguson, dd. 9 Nov. 1893.

8. *Further Correspondence*, C. 5357, 1888, p. 73: Statement of Kokofu messengers, dd. Accra, 29 July 1887. Lewin, "Structure of Political Conflict," II, p. 384: interview with Bekwaehene Osei Kwadwo II, Kwadwo Donko, and Kwabena Antwi, 19 Mar. 1971.

9. Ibid., pp. 457, 462: interviews with Domfe Kyere, 15 Apr. 1971; Kumawuhene Otuo Akyampon II, 18 Apr. 1971. BMA, Basel: Dilger to Basel, dd. 9 Aug. 1883.

10. Lewin, "Structure of Political Conflict," II, pp. 208, 210–11, 263–64: interviews with Amakoo and J. M. Tando, 11 Sept. 1970; Nsumankwaahene Domfe Gyeabo III, 23 Oct. 1970. Edweso district lands and *nkoa* from the 1889 meeting include the towns of: Anyinasu (the richest in rubber and now cocoa resources), Bepo Ayase, Tanodumaase, Abrakaso, Beposo, Boankra, Hwesreso, Ampabame,

Adadentem, Manhyia, Besease, Edweso, Donoaso, Abenase, Dumakwae, Dwenase, Asotwe, Bonwire, Apenkra, Nuaso, Nyinataase, Bosore, and Onwe.

11. Ibid., pp. 257–58: interview with Kyidomhene Osei Yaw, 16 Oct. 1970.

12. Ibid., pp. 263–64, 455–56: interviews with Nsumankwaahene Domfe Gyeabo III, 23 Oct. 1970; Domfe Kyere, 15 Apr. 1971.

13. See, e.g., Lewin, "Structure of Political Conflict," II, p. 253: interview with Bantamahene Owusu Amankwatia IV, 13 Oct. 1970.

14. Most Asantes agree completely on this aspect of the Asantehene Prempe's policies. See, e.g., ibid., pp. 329–30: interview with Atwemahene Antwi Agyei IV, 11 Dec. 1970.

15. Lewin, field-notes: interview with Domfe Kyere, 8 Apr. 1971.

16. Ancestral, bureaucratic, military, and princely offices are the four major categories within the sixteen *fekuo* of central government. Nineteenth-century Asantehenes created most of the offices in the last three categories. For a discussion of the geopolitical spread of these officeholders, see Lewin and Fitzsimmons, "Political Organization of Space in Asante: Part II," 15–17, and "Part III," 22–30.

17. See, e.g., Lewin, "Structure of Political Conflict," II, pp. 51–52, 62–63: interviews with I. K. Agyeman, 16 June and 8 July 1970.

18. Lewin, field-notes: interview with Omantihene Owusu Nkwantabisa, 1 May 1971.

19. *Further Correspondence*, C. 5615, 1888, p. 157: Colonial Secretary to Governor, dd. Victoriaborg, 7 Aug. 1888, and Griffith to Knutsford, dd. Accra, 13 July 1888.

20. *Further Correspondence*, C. 7917, 1896, p. 1: Griffith to Knutsford, dd. Accra, 8 Jan. 1889, and pp. 2–3: Colonial Secretary to Inspector-General, dd. Accra, 6 Jan. 1889.

21. Ibid., p. 37: Griffith to Knutsford, dd. Accra, 19 May 1891; Lewin, "Structure of Political Conflict," II, pp. 118–19, 396: interviews with Adu Gyamera, 10 Aug. 1970; Domfe Kyere, 21 Mar. 1971. Kwabena Kokofu did not hold office in the early 1890s but had served as an *ahenkwaa* in the Asantehene's court in the 1880s and had solidly supported the candidacy of Atweneboanna. He fled to the Colony in 1888 and came to be regarded as the Saawuahene-elect by the Saawua exiles south of the Pra. Kokofu, who was born in Saawua, amassed much wealth and political favors while in the Colony. This insured his installation, with British approval, as Saawuahene in the aftermath of the 1900 conflict.

22. *Further Correspondence*, C. 7917, 1896, p. 1: Griffith to Knutsford, dd. Accra, 8 Jan. 1889.

23. Ibid., pp. 4–5: Griffith to Knutsford, dd. Accra, 13 May 1889, and pp. 5–8: Inspector-General to Colonial Secretary, dd. Accra, 20 Mar. 1889.

24. Ibid., p. 4: Griffith to Knutsford, dd. Accra, 13 May 1889.

25. Lewin, "Structure of Political Conflict," II, p. 185: interview with Kwadwo Bo, 3 Sept. 1970. Ibid., pp. 236–37: interview with Yaw Safo, 25 Sept. 1970. See also NAG, ADM 11/1/1482, No. 48: District Commissioner, Cape Coast, to SNA, dd. Cape Coast, 16 Oct. 1889; Turton to Acting Colonial Secretary, dd. 24 Oct. 1890; interview held in Accra on 29 Jan. 1890, citing information from Sehwi envoys.

26. Lewin, "Structure of Political Conflict," II, p. 184: interview with Kwadwo Bo, 3 Sept. 1970.
27. *Further Correspondence*, C. 7917, 1896, p. 1: Griffith to Knutsford, dd. Accra, 8 Jan. 1889, and p. 45: return of persons crossing the Pra during 1890, dd. Accra, 29 Apr. 1891.
28. Ibid., p. 10: Hodgson to Knutsford, dd. Accra, 9 Dec. 1889. See also PRO, C.O. 96/194, No. 326: Griffith to Knutsford, dd. Accra, 8 Sept. 1888, transmitting estimates for 1889; C.O. 96/204, No. 247: Hodgson to Knutsford, dd. Accra, 3 Aug. 1889, transmitting estimates for 1890; C.O. 96/215, No. 61: Griffith to Knutsford, dd. Accra, 19 Feb. 1891.
29. See, e.g., *Further Correspondence*, C. 7917, 1896, pp. 12-13: Hodgson to Asantehene, dd. Accra, 26 Nov. 1889, p. 16: Kwaku Dua III (Prempe) to Acting Governor, dd. Kumase, 27 Dec. 1889, and p. 19: Griffith to Knutsford, dd. Accra, 8 Sept. 1890.
30. Ibid., p. 21: District Commissioner to Governor, dd. 8 July 1890, citing information from Asante chiefs. See also p. 20: Asantehene to Governor, dd. Kumase, 7 Apr. 1890, pp. 25-26: Governor to Asantehene, dd. Accra, 16 July 1890, and p. 23: Report of proceedings of a deputation from Asante Chiefs, dd. Elmina, 8 July 1890.
31. Ibid., p. 24: Governor to Asantehene, dd. Accra, 16 July 1890, transmitting statement of Asante diplomats during Elmina talks.
32. Ibid., pp. 34–35: Kwaku Dua III to Governor, dd. Kumase, 22 Aug. 1890.
33. This chart is abstracted from data contained in: PRO, C.O. 96/204, No. 276: Griffith to Knutsford, dd. Accra, 11 Sept. 1889; C.O. 96/213, No. 287: Griffith to Knutsford, dd. Accra, 3 Dec. 1890; C.O. 96/188, No. 19610: Griffith to Knutsford, dd. Accra, 28 Sept. 1887; C.O. 96/247, No. 241: Griffith to Ripon, dd. Accra, 18 Aug. 1894; C.O. 96/189, No. 4: Griffith to Holland, dd. Accra, 12 Jan. 1894. *Further Correspondence*, C. 7917, 1896, pp. 14–15: Hodgson to Knutsford, dd. Accra, 11 Jan. 1890, pp. 46–49: Governor to Asantehene, dd. Accra, 11 Mar. 1891, pp. 34–35: Kwaku Dua III to Governor, dd. Kumase, 22 Aug. 1890, pp. 43–44: Kwaku Dua III to Governor, dd. Kumase, 20 Jan. 1891, and pp. 25–28: Griffith to Asantehene, dd. Accra, 16 July 1890. NAG ADM 11/1/1482, No. 2444: Memorandum by Hodgson, dd. Accra, 21 May, 1889, Acc. No. 1563/56: Kwaku Dua III to Governor, dd. Kumase, 7 May 1891, ADM 1/7/26, No. 731: Governor to Osei Mampon et al., dd. Kumase, 15 Dec. 1905, and ADM 11/1/1482, No. 2444: Minute by Hodgson, dd. Accra, 21 May 1889.
34. *Further Correspondence*, C. 7917, 1896, p. 38: Griffith to Knutsford, dd. Accra, 19 May 1891. See p. 46: Griffith to Kwaku Dua III, dd. Accra, 11 Mar. 1891, citing information from Dwaben envoys.
35. Ibid., p. 38: Griffith to Knutsford, dd. Accra, 19 May 1891.
36. Idem.
37. Idem.
38. Idem. NAG, ADM 11/1/1482, No. 40: Minute by Turton, dd. Accra, 27 Jan. 1890, and Notes of interview on 23 Feb. 1891.
39. *Further Correspondence*, C. 7917, 1896, p. 23: Report of proceedings at a meeting of deputation from Asante Chiefs, dd. Elmina, 8 July 1890, and p. 35: Kwaku Dua III to Governor, dd. Kumase, 22 Aug. 1890.
40. See, e.g., BMA, Basel: Ramseyer to Basel, Neuchatel Friends, dd. Abetifi, 9,

20 Aug. 1883 and 6 Nov. 1888; Perregaux to Basel, dd. 10 May 1894; *Further Correspondence*, C. 7917, 1896, pp. 113, 128–29: Ramseyer to Acting Governor, dd. Abetifi, 31 Oct. and 11 Nov. 1893, and p. 115: Ramseyer to Scott, dd. Abetifi, 2 Nov. 1893.

41. Lewin, field-notes: interview with Domfe Kyere, 25 Apr. 1971.
42. *Further Correspondence*, C. 7917, 1896, p. 111: Message from Yaw Sapon to Ramseyer, dd. Abetifi, 30 Oct. 1893.
43. Ibid., p. 48: Griffith to Asantehene, dd. Accra, 11 Mar. 1891. See also Lewin, "Structure of Political Conflict," II, pp. 371–72: interview with Boaten Sapon, 12 Mar. 1971, for a similar account.
44. *Further Correspondence*, C. 7917, 1896, p. 48: Griffith to Asantehene, dd. Accra, 11 Mar. 1891, and p. 64: Hull to Governor, dd. Kumase, 6 Apr. 1891.
45. Lewin, field-notes: interview with Kwabena Antwi, dd. Bekwae, 20 Mar. 1971.
46. *Further Correspondence*, C. 7917, 1896, p. 24: Governor to Asantehene, dd. Accra, 16 July 1890, transmitting statement of Asante diplomats during Elmina talks, p. 23: Report of proceedings at a meeting of deputation from Asante Chiefs, dd. Elmina, 8 July 1890, and p. 38: Griffith to Knutsford, dd. Accra, 19 May 1891.
47. Ibid., p. 62: Hull to Governor, dd. Kumase, 6 Apr. 1891, citing information from Bekwaehene and his *akyeame*.
48. Idem.
49. Ibid., pp. 63–64: Hull to Governor, dd. Kumase, 6 Apr. 1891. See Lewin, "Structure of Political Conflict," II, p. 63: interview with I. K. Agyeman, 8 July 1970, for a discussion of mining in Bekwae in the early twentieth century.
50. *Further Correspondence*, C. 7917, 1896, p. 67: Hull to Governor, dd. Kumase, 6 Apr. 1891.
51. Ibid., p. 45: Extract from Executive Council minutes, Gold Coast Colony, held on 13 Mar. 1891, in Griffith to Knutsford, dd. Accra, 19 May 1891.
52. Ibid., p. 39: Griffith to Knutsford, dd. Accra, 19 May 1891, and see p. 48: Griffith to Asantehene, dd. Accra, 11 Mar. 1891.
53. Ibid., pp. 35, 43–44: Kwaku Dua III to Governor, dd. Kumase, 22 Aug. 1890, 20 Jan. 1891; PRO, C.O. 96/189, No. 4: Griffith to Holland, dd. Accra, 12 Jan. 1888, and C.O. 96/247, No. 241: Griffith to Ripon, dd. Accra, 18 Aug. 1894.
54. Claridge, *Gold Coast*, II, pp. 352–56; Tordoff, "Brandford Griffith's Offer of British Protection to Ashanti (1891)," *THSG* 7 (1962), 31–49.
55. *Further Correspondence*, C. 7917, 1896, p. 50: Griffith to Asantehene, dd. Accra, 11 Mar. 1891. See pp. 52–54, for full text of the treaty, in Griffith to Knutsford, dd. Accra, 19 May 1891, and PRO, C.O. 96/217, No. 179: Minute by A. W. L. Hemming, dd. 9 July 1891, which indicates that Griffith made the offer of protection without prior Colonial Office approval, although the residency issue had been seriously under consideration in London since early 1887.
56. R. A. Freeman, *Travels and Life in Ashanti and Jaman* (London, 1898), pp. 110, 124–25, 129. Compare with Tordoff, "Griffith's Offer," 33–34, and Claridge, *Gold Coast*, II, p. 333, who accept the validity of Griffith's remarks.
57. Lewin, field-notes: interview with Kwadwo Afodo, dd. Kumase, 28 Apr. 1971.
58. *Further Correspondence*, C. 7917, 1896, pp. 59–60, 65, 67: Hull to Governor, dd. Kumase, 3, 6, 22 Apr. 1891. Compare with *Further Correspondence*, C. 4052, 1884, pp. 41–42: Nominal roll of chiefs present for Barrow's reception in Kumase on 26 Apr. 1883, with *Further Correspondence*, C. 4477, p. 80: Chiefs

present in Kumase to meet Kirby on 4 Feb. 1884, and with *Further Correspondence*, C. 5615, 1888, pp. 39–40: Nominal roll of chiefs present in Kumase to meet Barnett on 15 Mar. 1888.

59. *Further Correspondence*, C. 7917, 1896, p. 15: Hodgson to Knutsford, dd. Accra, 11 Jan. 1890; Lewin, "Structure of Political Conflict," II, p. 263: interview with Nsumankwaahene Domfe Gyeabo III, 23 Oct. 1970; Brackenbury, *Ashanti War*, II, p. 274; Ramseyer and Kühne, *Four Years*, p. 309.

60. Lewin, field-notes: interview with Nsumankwaahene Domfe Gyeabo III, 29 Apr. 1971.

61. Lewin, "Structure of Political Conflict," II, pp. 426–27: interview with Domfe Kyere, 4 Apr. 1971. *Further Correspondence*, C. 7917, 1896, p. 55: Griffith to Hull, dd. Accra, 11 Mar. 1891, p. 73: Hull to Governor, dd. Accra, 27 May 1891, and p. 87: Hull to Acting Governor, dd. Manso, 14 Sept. 1893.

62. Ibid., p. 60: Hull to Governor, dd. Kumase, 3 Apr. 1891, and pp. 75–76: Hodgson to Knutsford, dd. Accra, 5 Oct. 1891. Lewin, "Structure of Political Conflict," II, pp. 366–67: interviews with Omantihene Owusu Nkwantabisa, 29 Dec. 1970, Domfe Kyere, 2 Jan. 1971.

63. Ibid., interviews of 29 Dec. 1970 and 2 Jan. 1971, cited above. The *nketia* are short hats worn by certain *nhenkwaa* in the Asantehene's palace, especially by members of the Esen Fekuo, which is one of the two groups from which the *abansifo* and *asokwafo* were recruited. *Further Correspondence*, C. 7917, 1896, pp. 25, 28: Governor to Asantehene, dd. Accra, 16 July 1890.

64. Ibid., p. 84: Hodgson to Ripon, dd. Accra, 23 Sept. 1893. Lewin, "Structure of Political Conflict," II, pp. 426–27: interview with Domfe Kyere, 4 Apr. 1971. Manwere Poku, arrested by the British in early 1892, was tried for robbery and violence for his political activities in Asante Akyem and sentenced to seven years of penal servitude. Kokofuhene Osei Asibe formally protested the charges from his enforced residence in the Colony. On the career of J. Owusu Ansa—from teacher and businessman to diplomat—see Wilks, *Asante in Nineteenth Century*, pp. 589–666, passim, *Further Correspondence*, C. 7917, p. 67: Hull to Governor, dd. Kumase, 22 Apr. 1891, pp. 187–88: Ansa to Governor, dd. Kumase, 5 Apr. 1894, and NAG, ADM 11/1/1482, No. 436: Stewart to Governor, dd. Accra, 3 Mar. 1895, which discusses Ansa's commercial pursuits in the Colony.

65. Lewin, field-notes: interview with Adu Gyamera, 28 Apr. 1971.

66. *Further Correspondence*, C. 7917, 1896, pp. 63–68: Hull to Governor, dd. Kumase, 6, 22 Apr. 1891.

67. Ibid., p. 72: Hull to Governor, dd. Accra, 27 May 1891.

68. Ibid., p. 73: Hull to Governor, dd. Accra, 27 May 1891. Kumase informants, however, never substantiated this assumption during the course of field interviews, perhaps revealing a protreaty bias.

69. PRO, C.O. 879/38, African (West) 451: Griffith to Knutsford, dd. Accra, 8 May 1891.

70. NAG, Acc. No. 3011/56, M.P. 178/91: Van Dyke to Colonial Secretary, dd. Praso, 2 Aug. 1891, citing information from Saltpond traders just returned from Kumase. These Fante merchants further noted that rumors circulated throughout the metropolitan region in 1891 regarding the British intention to invade Asante.

71. Lewin, field-notes: interview with Yaw Safo, dd. Kumase, 28 Sept. 1970.

72. Ibid., interview with Akyereapem, dd. Kumase, 9 Aug. 1970.
73. *Further Correspondence*, C. 7917, 1896, p. 72: Hull to Governor, dd. Accra, 27 May 1891.
74. Ibid., p. 71: Kwaku Dua III to Governor, dd. Kumase, 7 May 1891.
75. Ibid., pp. 75–76: Hodgson to Knutsford, dd. Accra, 5 Oct. 1891.
76. Ibid., pp. 76–77: Hodgson to Knutsford, dd. Accra, 5 Oct. 1891.
77. Ibid., p. 48: Griffith to Asantehene, dd. Accra, 11 Mar. 1891.
78. Idem. See also Lewin, "Structure of Political Conflict," II, pp. 372–74: interview with Boaten Sapon, 12 Mar. 1971.
79. *Further Correspondence*, C. 7917, 1896, p. 48: Griffith to Asantehene, dd. Accra, 11 Mar. 1891.
80. *Further Correspondence*, C. 5615, 1888, p. 122: Barnett's report on Asante, received in Accra on 10 May 1888. See also *Further Correspondence*, C. 7917, 1896, pp. 59, 73: Hull to Governor, dd. Kumase, Accra, 3 Apr. and 27 May 1891.
81. Lewin, "Structure of Political Conflict," II, pp. 392–93: interview with Kokofuhene Osei Asibe III and Adu Buobi, 19 Mar. 1971.
82. *Further Correspondence*, C. 7917, 1896, p. 41: Hull to Governor, dd. Accra, 28 Jan. 1891, p. 47: Griffith to Asantehene, dd. Accra, 11 Mar. 1891, and p. 86: Hull to Acting Governor, dd. Manso, 14 Sept. 1893.
83. Ibid., pp. 86–87: Hull to Acting Governor, dd. Manso, 14 Sept. 1893.
84. Ibid., p. 89: Hull to Acting Governor, dd. Insuaim, 17 Sept. 1893, and Memorandum by Acting Governor, dd. 4 Sept. 1893.
85. Ibid., p. 92: Hodgson to Hull, dd. Accra, 22 Sept. 1893, and p. 91: Hodgson to Ferguson, dd. Accra, 22 Sept. 1893, instructing him "to start a system of espionage" with regard to Asante troop movements in the northeast.
86. Idem. NAG, ADM 11/1/1482, No. 2786: Kakari to Griffith, dd. Accra, 27 June 1894; PRO, C.O. 96/255, No. 5222: Griffith to Ripon, dd. Accra, 19 Feb. 1895, and C.O. 96/248, No. 17845: Griffith to Ripon, dd. Cape Coast, 14 Sept. 1894. Part of this money was to be used to pay the debts incurred by the Kokofu refugees resident in the Colony.
87. Lewin, "Structure of Political Conflict," II, pp. 149–50: interview with Kwadwo Afodo, 27 Aug. 1970. Atweneboanna's line has not occupied the kingship since this law was enacted. See *Gold Coast Chronicle*, 14 Sept. 1895, p. 2, for another such account of this trial.
88. *Further Correspondence*, C. 7917, 1896, p. 97: Hull to Acting Governor, dd. Insuaim, 28 Sept. 1893. See also pp. 70–71: Kwaku Dua III to Governor, dd. Kumase, 7 May 1891, and p. 87: Hull to Acting Governor, dd. Manso, 14 Sept. 1893.
89. Idem. See also p. 106: Vroom to Colonial Secretary, dd. Elmina, 2 Nov. 1893, and p. 108: Memorandum from Yaw Boakye to Vroom, dd. 22 Oct. 1893. Vroom talked with the Bekwaehene in Adosuwa near the capital of Bekwae.
90. The deposed Bekwaehene Osei Kwaku Abrebrease is remembered for his cruelty and his terroristic methods to augment his authority and power in the district. See Lewin, "Structure of Political Conflict," II, pp. 384–86: interview with Bekwaehene Osei Kwadwo II, Kwadwo Donko, and Kwabena Antwi, 19 Mar. 1971.
91. See Wilks, *Asante in Nineteenth Century*, pp. 310–16, citing information ob-

tained in interview conducted by T. A. Mustapha with the Hausa headman of Wankyi, dd. Wankyi, 1965.

92. *Further Correspondence*, C. 7917, 1896, pp. 136–37: Memorandum by Ferguson, dd. 9 Nov. 1893.

93. Ibid., p. 138: Memorandum by Ferguson, dd. 9 Nov. 1893, and p. 78: Griffith to Ripon, dd. Accra, 13 Dec. 1892.

94. See, e.g., Lewin, field-notes: interview with Domfe Kyere, 25 Apr. 1971.

95. PRO, C.O. 879/31, African (West) 384, pp. 1–3: Memorandum by Hemming on *Correspondence with German Government about Krepi and Anglo-German Claims*, dd. Colonial Office, 11 Dec. 1889.

96. Kimble, *Political History*, pp. 282–83.

97. *Further Correspondence*, C. 7917, 1896, p. 78: Griffith to Ripon, dd. 13 Dec. 1892, and see p. 80: Ripon to Griffith, dd. London, 25 Jan. 1893.

98. Wilks, *Asante in Nineteenth Century*, p. 302.

99. For a discussion of French colonial expansion in the northern Ivory Coast, see A. S. Kanya-Forstner, *The Conquest of the Western Sudan: A Study in French Military Imperialism* (Cambridge, 1969), pp. 153–55, and pp. 142–51, for the background to increased French activity in the area.

100. Freeman, *Travels and Life*, pp. 206–7, 297–301.

101. See, e.g., *Further Correspondence*, C. 3687, 1883, pp. 110–13, 119–21: Lonsdale's report on his mission to Asante and Gyaman, 1882, and p. 71: Moloney to Kimberley, dd. Accra, 19 Sept. 1882; *Further Correspondence*, C. 5357, 1888, pp. 62–63: Lonsdale to Administrator, dd. Denkyira, 10 June 1887; *Further Correspondence*, C. 5615, 1888, p. 33: Barnett to Governor, dd. Edwabin, 26 Feb. 1888; *Further Correspondence*, C. 7917, 1896, p. 151: Scott to Colonial Secretary, dd. Atebubu, 24 Dec. 1893, and p. 149: Hodgson to Ripon, dd. Accra, 9 Jan. 1894.

102. Ibid., pp. 137–38: Memorandum by Ferguson, dd. 9 Nov. 1893, and pp. 79–80: Nkoransahene Kofi Fa to Governor, dd. Nkomasa, 13 Oct. 1892.

103. Ibid., p. 95: Hodgson to Inspector-General, dd. Accra, 29 Sept. 1893, and p. 117: Ferguson to Hodgson, dd. Abetifi, 7 Nov. 1893.

104. Ibid., pp. 117–19: Ferguson to Hodgson, dd. Atebubu, 27 Oct. 1893, p. 127: Chiefs of Agogo to Scott, dd. 8 Nov. 1893, in Scott to Hodgson, dd. Abetifi, 8 Nov. 1893, and pp. 188–89: Ferguson to Hodgson, dd. Atebubu, 27 Oct. 1893.

105. Lewin, "Structure of Political Conflict," II, pp. 121–22: interview with Adu Gyamera, 10 Aug. 1970. For a similar account, see *Further Correspondence*, C. 7917, 1896, p. 88: Hull to Acting Governor, dd. Insuaim, 17 Sept. 1893, citing information from a rubber trader, George Apea, who maintained that "the Kumasis have suffered severely from sickness, famine, and from the ravages of a leopard or leopards," which would in part explain popular Asante belief regarding the relationship between the Nkoransahene Kofi Fa and the Kumase leopard.

106. *Further Correspondence*, C. 7917, 1896, p. 139: Memorandum by Ferguson, dd. 9 Nov. 1893.

107. Ibid., pp. 139–41: Memorandum by Ferguson, dd. 9 Nov. 1893.

108. Lewin, "Structure of Political Conflict," II, p. 327: interview with Hemanhene Kwabena Apawu, 8 Dec. 1970.

109. *Further Correspondence*, C. 7917, 1896, p. 93: Hodgson to Ripon, dd. Accra, 29 Sept. 1893, and p. 140: Memorandum by Ferguson, dd. 9 Nov. 1893. De-

spite the rejection of Kumase's initiatives in 1893, the central government's agents continued to work in Atebubu. In August 1895, e.g., the newly installed Atebubuhene Kofi Amoaku maintained that a Kumase official had been executed for allegedly poisoning his predecessor, the late Atebubuhene Kwabena Asante. See PRO, C.O. 879/43, African (West) 490: Maxwell to Chamberlain, dd. Accra, 5 Aug. 1895.

110. *Further Correspondence*, C. 7917, 1896, p. 140: Memorandum by Ferguson, dd. 9 Nov. 1893, and see p. 105: Vroom to Colonial Secretary, dd. Elmina, 2 Nov. 1893, and p. 107: Message from Kwaku Dua III to Acting Governor, transmitted by Vroom, dd. 19 Oct. 1893.

111. Ibid., p. 154: Ferguson to Adjutant of Expeditionary Force, dd. Atebubu, 25 Dec. 1893, and p. 149: Hodgson to Ripon, dd. Accra, 9 Jan. 1894; PRO, C.O. 879/50, African (West) 540, p. 10: Ferguson's 1892 Treaties in Memorandum on *Claims of Great Britain and France in Territories Adjacent to Gold Coast.*

112. Lewin, "Structure of Political Conflict," II, pp. 308–9, 428–29: interviews with Nkwantakesehene (of Kumase) Owusu Afriyie, 27 Nov. 1970; Anamenakohene Kwabena Dwoben II, 4 Apr. 1971.

113. *Further Correspondence*, C. 7917, 1896, p. 153: Scott to Colonial Secretary, dd. Atebubu, 25 Dec. 1893, and p. 163: Ferguson to Adjutant of Expeditionary Force, dd. Amantin, 16 Jan. 1894.

114. See, e.g., Lewin, field-notes: interview with al-Hajj Sulāyman, dd. Kumase, 29 May 1970.

115. *Further Correspondence*, C. 7917, 1896, p. 131: Hodgson to Ripon, received on 13 Jan. 1894, and p. 156: Hodgson to Inspector-General, dd. Accra, 10 Jan. 1894.

CHAPTER 8

1. *Further Correspondence*, C. 7917, 1896, pp. 93, 157: Hodgson to Ripon, dd. Accra, 29 Sept. 1893, 29 Jan. 1894; NAG, ADM 11/1/1482, No. 4353: Lenehan to Chief Medical Officer, dd. Bompata, in Chief Medical Officer to Acting Colonial Secretary, dd. Accra, 4 Oct. 1894.

2. *Further Correspondence*, C. 7917, 1896, p. 222: Notes on Political Situation of Asante, dd. Christiansborg, 13 Apr. 1894.

3. Ibid., p. 159: Hodgson to Ripon, dd. Accra, 12 Feb. 1894. See also p. 93: Hodgson to Ripon, dd. Accra, 29 Sept. 1893, p. 208: Griffith to Ripon, dd. Cape Coast, 20 Sept. 1894, and p. 163: Ferguson to Adjutant, Atebubu Expeditionary Force, dd. Amantin, 16 Jan. 1894.

4. A full investigation of the infrastructure of the Gold Coast Colony is necessary. Such a study would reveal the significance of the Colony's road and telegraph systems for the military take-over of Asante. Following the creation of the post of Inspector of Interior Roads in 1889, the Gold Coast administration inaugurated an extensive road modernization program extending throughout the Akyem region to Praso near the Pra River. Complementing this program was the growth of telegraph stations throughout the Colony, which reduced communication barriers and increased the efficiency of the British intelligence apparatus. In 1888 supervision of the telegraph was transferred from the Public Works Department to the Postal Department, and in 1890 the telegraph system was consolidated under its own head. Thus from 1890 onwards the Colony's telegraph system increased rapidly in the number of reporting stations and in

the total mileage of telegraph lines. See, e.g., *Despatch from Governor Griffith*, C. 7225, pp. 1–11, 56–57; PRO, C.O. 96/159, No. 446: Young to Derby, dd. Accra, 18 Sept. 1884, transmitting estimates for 1885; C.O. 96/211, No. 225: Griffith to Knutsford, dd. Accra, 22 Sept. 1890, transmitting report on telegraph department; C.O. 96/200, No. 68: Griffith to Knutsford, dd. Accra, 29 Mar. 1889, transmitting annual report on Gold Coast Post Office operations.

5. *Further Correspondence*, C. 7917, 1896, p. 96: Ferguson to Adjutant, Atebubu Expeditionary Force, dd. Mo, 9 Mar. 1894, pp. 196–97: Nkoransahene Kofi Fa to Scott, dd. Nkoransa, 14 Apr. 1894, and pp. 218–19: Ferguson to Governor, dd. Bombir, near Kintampo, 1 Mar. 1894.

6. Lewin, field-notes: interview with Adu Gyamera, dd. Kumase, 9 Sept. 1970. See also NAG, ADM 11/1/1482, No. 5534: Griffith to Knutsford, dd. Accra, 6 Dec. 1889, and No. 3693: Kokofuhene Osei Asibe and Yaw Atweneboanna to Colonial Secretary, dd. Accra, 23 Aug. 1894.

7. Lewin, "Structure of Political Conflict," II, pp. 251–53: interview with Bantamahene Owusu Amankwatia IV, dd. Bantama, 13 Oct. 1970.

8. See, e.g., *Further Correspondence*, C. 7917, 1896, p. 94: Hodgson to Asantehene, dd. Accra, 29 Sept. 1893, p. 95: Hodgson to Vroom, dd. 29 Sept. 1893, pp. 102, 128: Hodgson to Ripon, dd. Accra, 13, 22 Nov. 1893, p. 153: Scott to Colonial Secretary, dd. Atebubu, 25 Dec. 1893, and p. 160: Kwaku Dua III to Acting Governor, dd. Kumase, 25 Nov. 1893; PRO, C.O. 96/259, No. 287: Maxwell to Ripon, dd. Accra, 2 July 1895, citing information on Stewart's mission to Sehwi in June 1895.

9. Lewin, field-notes: interviews with Kwadwo Afodo, 1 June 1971; Omantihene Owusu Nkwantabisa, 3 June 1971.

10. Ibid., interviews with Kwabena Baako, 10 June 1971; Nana Opoku, 12 June 1971.

11. Kimble, *Political History*, pp. 284–85; Tordoff, *Ashanti under Prempehs*, pp. 55–56.

12. *Further Correspondence*, C. 7917, 1896, p. 159: Hodgson to Ripon, dd. Accra, 12 Feb. 1894, p. 203: Griffith to Ripon, dd. Accra, 10 Aug. 1894, p. 223: Memorandum by Vroom, dd. Elmina, 30 Apr. 1894, and p. 225: Memorandum by Griffith as to policy to be adopted towards Asante, dd. Accra, 25 Oct. 1894. See also pp. 145–46: Liverpool Chamber of Commerce to Roseberry, dd. Liverpool, 9 Jan. 1894, pp. 146–47: Glasgow Chamber of Commerce to Ripon, dd. Glasgow, 26 Jan. 1894, and p. 132: London Chamber of Commerce, dd. London, 13 Jan. 1894.

13. For a discussion since the Asantehene Mensa Bonsu's reign, see Lewin, "Structure of Political Conflict," I, pp. 77, 85–87, and field-notes: interview with Omantihene Owusu Nkwantabisa, 3 June 1971.

14. Most informants concur that the death penalty was sharply reduced. See, e.g., Lewin, field-notes: interviews with Kwabena Baako, 10 June 1971; Nana Opoku, 12 June 1971.

15. PRO, C.O. 879/43, African (West) 490, p. 59: Griffith to Colonial Office, dd. Ealing, 1 July 1895, citing information from Brew of Dunkwa and the Kyidomhene of Kumase, Kwame Boaten.

16. Lewin, "Structure of Political Conflict," II, p. 64: interview with I. K. Agyeman, 8 July 1970.

17. Ibid., pp. 170–71: interview with Kwadwo Bo, 1 Sept. 1970.

18. *Further Correspondence,* C. 7917, 1896, p. 255: Memorandum by Griffith, dd. Accra, 25 Oct. 1894, and p. 228: Asantes in Western Protectorate to Governor, dd. Cape Coast, 1 Oct. 1894.

19. Ibid., p. 166: Hodgson to Vroom, dd. Accra, 23 Feb. 1894, pp. 170–71: Hodgson to Ripon, dd. Accra, 5 Mar. 1894, and p. 224: Memorandum by Vroom, dd. Elmina, 30 Apr. 1894.

20. Ibid., p. 227: Memorandum by Griffith, dd. Accra, 25 Oct. 1894.

21. Ibid., p. 199: Ramseyer to Colonial Office, dd. Neuchatel, 10 Aug. 1894. See also p. 200: Perregaux to Ramseyer, dd. Abetifi, 25 June 1894.

22. *Further Correspondence,* C. 7917, 1896, p. 201: Kwaku Dua III to Governor, dd. Kumase, 28 June 1894, and p. 207: Extract from *The Gold Coast Methodist Times,* dd. 31 Aug. 1894, in Griffith to Ripon, dd. Cape Coast, 14 Sept. 1894.

23. Lewin, field-notes: interview with Nsumankwaahene Domfe Gyeabo III, 29 Apr. 1971.

24. See, e.g., PRO, C.O. 879/44, African (West) 500, p. 27: Maxwell to Chamberlain, dd. Accra, 19 Nov. 1895, and C.O. 879/43, African (West) 490, p. 59: Perregaux to Governor, dd. Abetifi, 17 May 1895, in Maxwell to Ripon, dd. Accra, 4 June 1895.

25. BMA, Basel: Haasis to Basel, dd. Abetifi, 19 Sept. 1893.

26. *Further Correspondence,* C. 7917, 1896, p. 158: Scott to Colonial Secretary, dd. Atebubu, 16 Jan. 1894.

27. PRO, C.O. 879/44, African (West) 500, p. 23: Maxwell to Chamberlain, dd. Accra, 14 Nov. 1895, citing Ramseyer's letter of 25 Oct. 1895 to Governor, and p. 49: Maxwell to Chamberlain, dd. Kumase, 20 Jan. 1896.

28. See, e.g., Lewin, field-notes: interviews with Domfe Kyere, 25 Apr. 1971; Kwadwo Afodo, 27 Apr. 1971.

29. Lewin, "Structure of Political Conflict," II, pp. 66–68, 76, 368: interviews with al-Hajj Sulāyman, 10, 21 July 1970; Domfe Kyere, 2 Jan. 1971.

30. *Further Correspondence,* C. 7917, p. 93: Hodgson to Ripon, dd. Accra, 29 Sept. 1893. PRO, C.O. 879/43, African (West) 490, p. 147: Stewart and Vroom's report on mission to Kumase, dd. Accra, 26 Oct. 1895, and C.O. 96/262, No. 22254: Maxwell to Chamberlain, dd. Cape Coast, 14 Nov. 1895, citing information from Yaw Baako, an Akyem rubber trader who was in Kumase on 10 Sept. 1895.

31. Lewin, "Structure of Political Conflict," II, pp. 44–45: interview with Kwadwo Donko, 13 June 1970.

32. Lewin, field-notes: interview with Domfe Kyere, 2 Jan. 1971. See also chapter 3 for a discussion of the activities of this new Asante commercial elite.

33. PRO, C.O. 879/43, African (West) 490, p. 65: Maxwell to Ripon, dd. Accra, 13 June 1895.

34. Lewin, "Structure of Political Conflict," II, pp. 386–394: interviews with Kokofuhene Osei Asibe III and Adu Buobi; Bekwaehene Osei Kwadwo II, Kwadwo Donko, and Kwabena Antwi, 19 Mar. 1971; Freeman, *Travels and Life,* pp. 368–69.

35. *Further Correspondence,* C. 7917, 1896, p. 201: Kwaku Dua III to Governor, dd. Kumase, 28 June 1894, and p. 207: Extract from *The Gold Coast Methodist Times,* dd. 31 Aug. 1894, in Griffith to Ripon, dd. Cape Coast, 14 Sept. 1894. See also pp. 181–82: Vroom to Governor, dd. Christiansborg, 24 Apr. 1894.

36. Ibid., p. 203: Griffith to Ripon, dd. Accra, 10 Aug. 1894, p. 204: Ennisson to Colonial Secretary, dd. Praso, 29 July 1894, p. 227: Asantes in Western Protectorate to Governor, dd. Cape Coast, 1 Oct. 1894, and p. 236: A. Owusu Ansa to Loy, dd. Axim, 7 Nov. 1894, in Griffith to Ripon, dd. Accra, 15 Nov. 1894.

37. See, e.g., Lewin, field-notes: interview with Domfe Kyere, 2 Jan. 1971.

38. *Further Correspondence*, C. 7917, 1896, p. 182: Vroom to Governor, dd. Christiansborg, 24 Apr. 1894.

39. See, e.g., Lewin, field-notes: interview with Kwadwo Afodo, 1 June 1971. See also PRO, C.O. 879/43, African (West) 490, p. 63: Maxwell to Ripon, dd. Accra, 13 June 1895, citing information from A. Owusu Ansa and Colony sources.

40. PRO, C.O. 96/260, No. 18264: Minutes on Maxwell to Chamberlain, dd. Cape Coast, 26 Sept. 1895.

41. Ibid., Minutes, cited above.

42. *Further Correspondence*, C. 7917, 1896, p. 203: Griffith to Ripon, dd. Accra, 10 Aug. 1894, p. 204: Ennisson to Colonial Secretary, dd. Praso, 29 July 1894, p. 227: Asantes in Western Protectorate to Governor, dd. Cape Coast, 1 Oct. 1894, and p. 236: A. Owusu Ansa to Loy, dd. Axim, 7 Nov. 1894, in Griffith to Ripon, dd. Accra, 15 Nov. 1894.

43. Ibid., p. 201: Kwaku Dua III to Governor, dd. Kumase, 28 June 1894.

44. Idem. See also p. 213: Loy to Colonial Secretary, dd. Axim, 17 Oct. 1894, in Griffith to Ripon, dd. Accra, 24 Oct. 1894, and p. 214: Griffith to Ripon, dd. Accra, 31 Oct. 1894; Lewin, "Structure of Political Conflict," II, p. 366: interview with Omantihene Owusu Nkwantabisa, 29 Dec. 1970. Kwado Tufo, the head of the Asantehene's gunners, was from the town of Kropo in metropolitan Asante.

45. *Further Correspondence*, C. 7917, 1896, p. 214: Griffith to Ripon, received 27 Nov. 1894.

46. Idem. See also p. 234: A. Owusu Ansa to Griffith, dd. Cape Coast, 17 Nov. 1894, pp. 238–39: Griffith to Ripon, dd. Cape Coast, 29 Nov. 1894, and PRO, C.O. 96/267, No. 15812: J. Owusu Ansa to Chamberlain, dd. Lennox Gardens, 5 Sept. 1895, in which Ansa maintained that the Asante embassy came to negotiate directly with the secretary of state for the colonies because the governor had made it impossible to convene new diplomatic talks in Accra. Ansa further stated that British officials on the Gold Coast while professing friendship to the Asante government had at the same time attempted to undermine the authority of Prempe's regime. Yet one functionary in the Colonial Office maintained on the issue of the Asante embassy's credentials: "the position is that the Queen cannot receive these persons. The King of Ashante is now only the head of the tribe, and does not hold a position which would entitle him to send 'ambassadors' to the Queen of England; neither are they the class of persons whom the Queen could be asked to receive." *Further Correspondence*, C. 7917, 1896, p. 237: Buxton to Labouchere, dd. Downing Street, 15 Dec. 1894.

47. For a discussion of the principal factors underlying the British decision to take over the Asante kingdom, see John D. Hargreaves, *Prelude to the Partition of West Africa* (London, 1963), pp. 316–49, and also see pp. 301–15; Boniface I. Obichere, *West African States and European Expansion, The Dahomey-Niger Hinterland, 1885–1898* (New Haven and London, 1971), pp. 123–93, passim; Tordoff, *Ashanti under Prempehs*, pp. 53–70.

48. NAG, Accra, ADM 1/9/4: Griffith to Herivel, dd. Accra, 7 May 1894. This development is discussed in detail by Wilks, "Dissidence in Asante Politics," in I. Abu-Lughod (ed.), *African Themes* (Evanston, 1975), pp. 55–63, and *Asante in Nineteenth Century*, pp. 636–37, 641–47.

49. Ibid., pp. 647–54, and see also pp. 655–62.

50. Tordoff, *Ashanti under Prempehs*, pp. 59–60; Ronald Robinson et al., *Africa and the Victorians: The Official Mind of Imperialism* (London, 1961), pp. 395, 403.

51. See, e.g., PRO, C.O. 879/41, African (West) 478, pp. 79–80, 117–21: Ferguson to Governor, dd. Nkoransa, Christiansborg, 22 Jan., 22 Feb. 1895, and C.O. 96/225, Nos. 19648, 18026: Griffith to Knutsford, dd. Accra, 2 Sept., 6 Aug. 1892, and minutes by Hemming, dd. 3 Oct., 27 Nov. 1892.

52. PRO, C.O. 96/270, Nos. 4814, 5770: Maxwell to Chamberlain, dd. Accra, 28 Jan., 20 Feb. 1896, and C.O. 879/38, African (West) 458, p. 31: Ferguson to Governor, dd. Bimbila, 29 Aug. 1892.

53. PRO, C.O. 879/45, African (West) 506, pp. 2–3: Maxwell to Chamberlain, dd. Cape Coast, 17 Dec. 1895; Lewin, "Structure of Political Conflict," II, p. 362: interview with Nana Opoku, 28 Dec. 1970. See also Wilks, *Asante in Nineteenth Century*, pp. 310–27, passim.

54. PRO, C.O. 96/259, No. 16297: Maxwell to Chamberlain, dd. Accra, 19 Aug. 1895.

55. Lewin, "Structure of Political Conflict," II, p. 161: interview with Kwadwo Afodo, 30 Aug. 1970, and see also p. 362: interview of 28 Dec. 1970, cited in note 53.

56. For accounts of the Almami Samori's career and resistance to the expansion of French imperialism in the Western Sudan, see Yves Person, "Guinea-Samori" (trans. J. White), in Michael Crowder (ed.), *West African Resistance* (London, 1971), pp. 111–43, and Kanya-Forstner, *Conquest of Western Sudan*, pp. 98–100, 175–76, 184–88, 251–53, 269–70.

57. PRO, C.O. 879/45, African (West) 506, p. 2: Maxwell to Chamberlain, dd. Cape Coast, 10 Dec. 1895, citing information from a Hausa trader, Sowete, who was present in Bonduku for the arrival of the Asantehene's envoys. See also C.O. 879/43, African (West) 490, p. 147: Report of Stewart and Vroom on their mission to Kumase, dd. Accra, 26 Oct. 1895, in Maxwell to Chamberlain, dd. Accra, 28 Oct. 1895, which reports on contacts between Prempe and Samori, and C.O. 879/49, African (West) 534, p. 48: Memorandum of interview held in Kumase, dd. Kumase, 16 Aug. 1897, in Maxwell to Chamberlain, dd. Kintampo, 4 Sept. 1897.

58. PRO, C.O. 879/43, African (West) 490, pp. 96–97: Maxwell to Kwaku Dua III, dd. Cape Coast, 23 Sept. 1895.

59. Ibid., pp. 97–98: Maxwell's instructions for Stewart and Vroom, dd. Cape Coast, 23 Sept. 1895, and Maxwell to Kwaku Dua III, dd. Cape Coast, 23 Sept. 1895.

60. PRO, C.O. 879/44, African (West) 500, p. 67: J. and A. Owusu Ansa and Asante ambassadors to Maxwell, dd. London, 27 Sept. 1895, and C.O. 96/261, No. 428: Maxwell to Chamberlain, dd. Cape Coast, 22 Oct. 1895, submitting Cade's documents on mining rights in Bekwae and Adanse.

61. NAG, ADM 11/1/1482, No. 1790: Belfield to Colonial Secretary, dd. Praso, 1 Jan. 1896, citing information from Dwaben envoys, and see PRO, C.O. 96/270, No. 2933: Maxwell to Chamberlain, dd. Cape Coast, 13 Jan. 1896, for Bekwae and Abodom treaties.

62. Lewin, field-notes: interview with Domfe Kyere, 8 Feb. 1971.
63. PRO, C.O. 96/261, No. 20787: Stewart and Vroom's report to Acting Colonial Secretary, dd. Cape Coast, 26 Oct. 1895, C.O. 879/44, African (West) 500, p. 11: Colonial Secretary to Ramseyer, dd. Accra, 7 Oct. 1895, and p. 13: Maxwell to Chamberlain, dd. Cape Coast, 23 Dec. 1895. The official explanation of J. Owusu Ansa's politics and diplomacy should be compared with his own testimony of British mistreatment in 1896. For his account, see C.O. 879/49, African (West) 534, pp. 25–27: Petition of J. and A. Owusu Ansa to the Queen of Great Britain, dd. London, Dec. 1896.
64. PRO, C.O. 879/43, African (West) 490, p. 147: Report of Stewart and Vroom, dd. Accra, 26 Oct. 1895.
65. Lewin, "Structure of Political Conflict," II, pp. 106–7: interview with Adu Gyamera, 6 Aug. 1970. Vroom—like H. Plange and G. E. Ferguson—had a long career in the service of European officials on the Gold Coast. Vroom was employed by the Dutch from 1864 to 1872 and commenced nineteen years of employment for the British government in 1872. He was appointed clerk of customs, subcollecter of customs in May 1874, served as interpreter for the Western Boundary Commission in Jan. 1892, and conducted special missions to Sehwi in Feb. 1893 and to Asante in Oct. 1893, Feb. 1894, and Oct. 1895. Vroom was Governor Maxwell's main interpreter in Kumase in Jan. 1896 and retired on 4 Feb. 1901. In his later years Hendrik Vroom remained a vehement Asantephobe. See PRO, C.O. 96/394, No. 42: Nathan to Chamberlain, dd. Accra, 24 Jan. 1902, reporting death of Vroom.
66. Lewin, "Structure of Political Conflict," II, pp. 148–49: interview with Kwadwo Afodo, 27 Aug. 1970.
67. PRO, C.O. 879/44, African (West) 500, p. 15: Proceedings at an interview granted to Asante messengers by the Governor, dd. Cape Coast, 18 Dec. 1895.
68. Idem. See also C.O. 879/44, African (West) 500, p. 33: Maxwell to Chamberlain, dd. Accra, 23 Nov. 1895, citing telegram from London to J. G. Halm, the Asante government's envoy at Cape Coast.
69. PRO, C.O. 879/44, African (West) 500, p. 15: Proceedings at an interview, dd. Cape Coast, 18 Dec. 1895.
70. Ibid., African (West) 500, pp. 187–88: Kwaku Dua III to Chamberlain, dd. Elmina, July 1896. For detailed accounts of the preparations and operations of the expeditionary force written from a British viewpoint, see R. S. S. Baden-Powell, The Downfall of Prempeh (London, 1896), pp. 43–172; B. Burleigh, Two Campaigns: Madagascar and Ashantee (London, 1896), pp. 412–555; G. C. Musgrove, To Kumassi with Scott (London, 1896), pp. 67–216.
71. Lewin, "Structure of Political Conflict," II, p. 154: interview with Kwadwo Afodo, 30 Aug. 1970.
72. PRO, C.O. 879/49, African (West) 534, p. 56: Hodgson to Chamberlain, dd. Accra, 18 May 1898; C.O. 879/44, African (West) 500, p. 11: Chamberlain to Maxwell, dd. London, 17 Jan. 1896, p. 50: Maxwell to Chamberlain, dd. Kumase, 20 Jan. 1896, and pp. 51–54: Notes of a Palaver held at Kumase on Monday, 20 Jan. 1896, with Asantehene and his principal chiefs and captains. For the standard British explanation of the proceedings, see Claridge, Gold Coast, II, pp. 411–16; Baden-Powell, Downfall of Prempeh, pp. 117–26; Tordoff, Ashanti under Prempehs, pp. 67–74.
73. Lewin, "Structure of Political Conflict," II, p. 150: interview with Kwadwo Afodo, 27 Aug. 1970.

74. Ibid., p. 367: interview with Domfe Kyere, 2 Jan. 1971.

75. Ibid., p. 151: interview of 27 Aug. 1970, cited in note 73. See also p. 213: interview with Kwabena Baako, 14 Sept. 1970.

76. PRO, C.O. 879/44, African (West) 500, p. 50: Maxwell to Chamberlain, dd. Kumase, 20 Jan. 1896. Tordoff, *Ashanti under Prempehs*, p. 69.

77. PRO, C.O. 879/44, African (West) 500, pp. 53–54: Notes on a Palaver held at Kumase. Several other Kumase councillors—such as the Amakomhene—were also arrested and taken to Elmina, but aged informants especially remembered and referred to these thirteen officeholders. See, e.g., Lewin, "Structure of Political Conflict," II, pp. 173, 223, 400: interviews with Amakomhene Mensa Yiadom II, 2 Sept. 1970; Kofi Afrane, 15 Sept. 1970; Domfe Kyere, 24 Mar. 1971.

78. Lewin, field-notes: interview with Omantihene Owusu Nkwantabisa, 18 Dec. 1970.

79. Lewin, "Structure of Political Conflict," II, pp. 213, 232–33: interview with Kwabena Baako, 14, 17 Sept. 1970.

80. Ibid., p. 108: interview with Adu Gyamera, 6 Aug. 1970.

81. Ibid., p. 238: interview with Yaw Safo, 25 Sept. 1970.

82. Ibid., p. 28: interview with Kwadwo Mosi, 8 June 1970.

83. Ibid., p. 223: interview with Kofi Afrane, 15 Sept. 1970.

84. Ibid., p. 393: interview with Kokofuhene Osei Asibe III and Adu Buobi, 19 Mar. 1971.

85. Ibid., p. 194: interview with Kwaku Anno, 4 Sept. 1970.

86. Ibid., p. 74: interview with al-Hajj Sulāyman, 10 July 1970. Kumase informants disagreed over the place Prempe was lodged following his arrest. Afodo, e.g., noted that the Asantehene stayed in a tent at Edwabrem. Yet, despite the difference in opinion, it was very significant that Prempe was not permitted to return to the palace, and most informants emphasized this aspect of the capture.

87. Ibid., p. 151: interview with Kwadwo Afodo, 27 Aug. 1970. Compare with Burleigh, *Two Campaigns*, pp. 528, 535. See Tordoff, "The Exile and Repatriation of Nana Prempeh I of Ashanti (1896–1924)," *THSG* 4 (1960), for further details from a strictly British viewpoint.

88. See chapters 3 and 7 for a discussion of this dimension.

89. Lewin, "Structure of Political Conflict," II, p. 15: interview with Boagyaahene Osei Akwasi, 2 June 1970.

90. Lewin, field-notes: interview with Omantihene Owusu Nkwantabisa, 18 Dec. 1970.

91. See, e.g., Lewin, "Structure of Political Conflict," II, pp. 386, 394: interviews with Kokofuhene Osei Asibe III and Adu Buobi; Bekwaehene Osei Kwadwo II, Kwadwo Donko, and Kwabena Antwi, 19 Mar. 1971; Freeman, *Travels and Life*, pp. 368–69.

92. PRO, C.O. 879/43, African (West) 490, p. 60: Griffith to Colonial Secretary, dd. Ealing, 1 July 1895.

93. PRO, C.O. 879/44, African (West) 500, pp. 74, 94–95, 97: Maxwell to Chamberlain, dd. Cape Coast, 28 Jan., 20 Feb. 1896.

94. Ibid., p. 96: Maxwell to Chamberlain, dd. Cape Coast, 20 Feb. 1896. See Tordoff, *Ashanti under Prempehs*, pp. 79, 83, for a discussion.

95. Lewin, "Structure of Political Conflict," II, p. 397: interview with Domfe Kyere, 29 Mar. 1971.

96. Ibid., p. 275: interview with Domfe Kyere, 30 Oct. 1970.

97. Ibid., p. 365: interview with Omantihene Owusu Nkwantabisa, 29 Dec. 1970.
98. On this theme the analogy to the French experience in the nineteenth and twentieth centuries is striking.
99. See, e.g., Lewin, "Structure of Political Conflict," II, pp. 37, 131, 191: interviews with Boagyaahene Osei Akwasi, 9 June 1970; Kwaku Anno, 4 Sept. 1970; Akyereapem, 11 Aug. 1970.
100. Ibid., pp. 455–56: interview with Domfe Kyere, 15 Apr. 1971. PRO, C.O. 879/44, African (West) 500, p. 96: Maxwell to Chamberlain, dd. Cape Coast, 20 Feb. 1896. Compare with Tordoff, *Ashanti under Prempehs*, pp. 83, 85, 105.
101. PRO, C.O. 879/44, African (West) 500, p. 96: Maxwell to Chamberlain, dd. Cape Coast, 20 Feb. 1896. See also Lewin, "Structure of Political Conflict," II, pp. 364–65: interview with Omantihene Owusu Nkwantabisa, 29 Dec. 1970.
102. Ibid., p. 456: interview with Domfe Kyere, 15 Apr. 1971.
103. Idem., and see p. 329: interview with Atwemahene Antwi Agyei IV, 11 Dec. 1970.
104. Idem., and see p. 306: interview with Toasehene Kofi Wusu, 27 Nov. 1970. Toasehene Kwame Afrifa is mistakenly referred to as the Atwemahene in most British accounts, and some Kumase informants often make a similar error.
105. The most prominent of these Prempean leaders in Kumase after 1896 were: the Adontenhene Gyamfi, Atwema Agogohene Osei Kwabena, Nkwantakesehene Yaw Asamoa, Fantehene Kwadwo Nkyidwo, Boamanhene Akoko, Anyinasehene Yaw Barima, Kronkohene Kwadwo Pan, Ampabamehene Kwabena Kwaku I, Baworohene Kwabena Adomako, Akumantihene Kwadwo Asare, Kwaasohene Kwadwo Nkatia, Kwamanhene Yaw Asiama, Atumpakahene Adu Bruwaa, Oyoko Bremanhene Kofi Myame, Banemuhene Otaa, Kwamohene Amoako Mensa, Nkraohene Kwabena Dua, Ahenkrohene Kofi Apea, Nkonsonhene Kofi Fofie, and Antoahene Kwaku Ware, who was succeeded by Oheneba Antoa Mensa in 1897. Lewin, "Structure of Political Conflict," II, pp. 244, 246, 247, 249, 263, 268, 278, 281, 285, 294, 296, 308, 319, 323, 331, 340, 344, 347, 348, 349, 353, 354: interviews with Hiahene Mensa Bonsu, Adumhene Asamoa Totoe II, Gyaasehene Opoku Mensa II, Atipinhene Osei Kwame, Nsumankwaahene Domfe Gyeabo III, Anantahene Apea Dankwa II, Adontenhene Agyeman Nkwantabisa II, 2, 9, 23, 30 Oct. 1970; Ankobeahene Poku-Dum, Fantehene Kwame Ti, Anyinasehene Akyampon Akwasi Ababio, Boamanhene Yeboa Asuama, Nkwantakesehene Owusu Afriyie II, 4, 6, 20, 27 Nov. 1970: Atwema Agoghene Owusu Afriyie I, Banmuhene Kofi Safo Ababio, Ahenkrohene Kwadwo Apea, Baworohene Yaw Owusu, Kronkohene Kwabena Amo, Antoahene Opoku Agyeman II, Kwamohene Owusu Agyman Boaten II, Kwaasohene Kwame Ntimoa Ababio, Akumantihene Kwabena Asare, Kwamanhene Kodua Debra II, 4, 6, 11, 16, 19, 20, 21 Dec. 1970. Antoa Mensa, who was to play a major role in the hostilities of 1900–1901, was a son of the Asantehene Kwaku Dua Panin, a nephew of Kwasi Gyambibi, and a cousin to the Asantehene Agyeman Prempe. See p. 84: interview with Samuel Prempe, 23 July 1970.
106. PRO, C.O. 879/49, African (West) 530, p. 42: Vroom's report, dd. Bekwae, 19 June 1897, in Maxwell to Chamberlain, dd. Accra, 14 July 1897, and see p. 39: Maxwell to Chamberlain, dd. Accra, 14 July 1897, and C.O. 879/44, African (West) 504, pp. 183–84: Hodgson to Chamberlain, dd. Accra, 5 Aug. 1896.
107. PRO, C.O. 879/49, African (West) 530, p. 42: Vroom's report, dd. 19 June 1897.

108. Ibid., p. 40: Vroom's report, dd. 19 June 1897.
109. Ibid., p. 42: Vroom's report, dd. 19 June 1897. See also Lewin, "Structure of Political Conflict," II, pp. 203–6, 213–15: interviews with Amakoo, 11 Sept. 1970; Kwabena Baako, 14 Sept. 1970.
110. Ibid., p. 455: interview with Domfe Kyere, 15 Apr. 1971.
111. Ibid., pp. 241, 244, 249, 251–53, 299–301, 333–34, 337–39: interviews with Akyempemhene Boakye Dankwa II, Hiahene Mensa Bonsu, 2 Oct. 1970; Atipinhene Osei Kwame, 9 Oct. 1970; Bantamahene Owusu Amankwatia IV, 13 Oct. 1970; Akuroponhene Kwasi Ansere, 20 Nov. 1970; Akrafohene Kwasi Mensa, 11 Dec. 1970; and Asokore Mamponhene Boakye Dankwa II, 15 Dec. 1970.
112. PRO, C.O. 879/49, African (West) 530, p. 43: Vroom's report, dd. 19 June 1897. See also C.O. 879/44, African (West) 500, p. 116: List of treaties with British government in Maxwell to Chamberlain, dd. Cape Coast, 22 Feb. 1896.
113. PRO, C.O. 879/49, African (West) 530, p. 43: Vroom's report, dd. 19 June 1897.
114. PRO, C.O. 879/49, African (West) 530, pp. 39–40: Vroom's report.
115. PRO, C.O. 879/44, African (West) 500, p. 116: Maxwell to Resident, dd. Cape Coast, 10 Feb. 1896.
116. Lewin, "Structure of Political Conflict," II, pp. 364–65: interview with Omantihene Owusu Nkwantabisa, 29 Dec. 1970.
117. See, e.g., PRO, C.O. 879/44, African (West) 500, p. 97: Maxwell to Chamberlain, dd. Cape Coast, 20 Feb. 1896.
118. For these observations, see Lewin, "Structure of Political Conflict," II, pp. 105–10, 128–29, 451–52: interviews with Adu Gyamera, Akyereapem, 6, 11 Aug. 1970; Domfe Kyere, 13 Apr. 1971.
119. See, e.g., ibid., pp. 76–77, 217–18: interviews with al-Hajj Sulāyman, 21 July 1970; Kwabena Baako, 14 Sept. 1970.
120. See, e.g., ibid., pp. 396–99: interview with Domfe Kyere, 21 Mar. 1971, who, like many aged Kumase informants, typifies the pro-Opoku Mensa position.
121. Ibid., pp. 396–99, interview of 21 Mar. 1971, and Lewin, field-notes: interview with Omantihene Owusu Nkwantabisa, dd. Kumase, 18 Dec. 1970. Following the Yaa Asantewaa War of Independence, Kofi Nti was appointed Dadiesoabahene by the British. Kwasi Adabo, another Kofi Kakari and Yaw Atweneboanna partisan, became Akyempemhene. Kwaku Nkatia was installed Manso Nkwantahene, and Kwabena Kokofu came to occupy the Saawua stool. For some of these officeholders after 1901, see NAG, Acc. No. 1248/57, No. 427: Rewards to Loyal Chiefs, in Resident to Acting Colonial Secretary, dd. Kumase, 13 Dec. 1901.
122. PRO, C.O. 879/44, African (West) 500, p. 98: Maxwell to Chamberlain, dd. Cape Coast, 20 Feb. 1896; C.O. 879/49, African (West) 530, p. 44: Vroom's report, dd. 19 June 1897.
123. BMA, Basel: Ramseyer to Basel, dd. Kumase, 19 Mar. 1896, 29 June, 30 Aug. 1897. See NAG, ADM 11/1/1775, Palaver Book: Fuller to Governor, dd. Kumase, 20 Feb. 1912, noting that the "uncompromising and distinctively antagonistic attitude of the missionaries toward mediatory measures" continued in the post-1900 era, a statement confirmed by most Asante informants living during the period.
124. PRO, C.O. 879/49, African (West) 530, p. 44: Vroom's report, dd. 19 June 1897.

125. Ibid., p. 43: Vroom's report, dd. 19 June 1897. See also BMA, Basel: Zellweger to Basel, dd. Kumase, 23 Mar. 1898, citing information from a Kumase catechist; Ramseyer to Basel, dd. Kumase, 28 Sept. 1898.

126. Lewin, field-notes: interviews with Issa Kilishi, 14 June, 27 Nov. 1970; Amina Wagadugu, 26 June 1970; Mai Kano, 28 June 1970; Malam Gariba, 28 Nov. 1970.

127. Ibid., interviews with Domfe Kyere, 25 Apr. 1971; al-Hajj Adamu Dagomba, 9 July 1970; Amina Wagadugu, 1 July 1970.

128. See, e.g., ibid., interviews with al-Hajj Sumalar, 23 July, 30 Dec. 1970; al-Hajj Sulāyman, 26 July 1970. In 1898 al-Hajj Sulāyman himself was "pawned" by his family to repay such a loan.

129. Lewin, "Structure of Political Conflict," II, pp. 122–24, 369–70, 425–26: interviews with Adu Gyamera, 10 Aug. 1970; Domfe Kyere, 2 Jan., 4 Apr. 1971. PRO, C.O. 96/292, No. 164: Hull to Colonial Secretary, dd. Takyiman, 14 Feb. 1897; C.O. 96/279, No. 25601: Maxwell to Chamberlain, dd. Cape Coast, 19 Nov. 1896, citing information from Pigott, the resident in Kumase; C.O. 96/290, No. 8155: Maxwell to Chamberlain, dd. Cape Coast, 15 Mar. 1897; C.O. 879/49, African (West) 530, p. 39: Vroom's report, dd. 19 June 1897.

130. PRO, C.O. 879/44, African (West) 500, p. 74: Maxwell to Chamberlain, dd. Kumase, 28 Jan. 1896. Lewin, "Structure of Political Conflict," II, pp. 63–64: interview with I. K. Agyeman, 8 July 1970.

131. Lewin, "Structure of Political Conflict," II, pp. 195–96, 451–52: interviews with Kwaku Anno, 4 Sept. 1970; Domfe Kyere, 13 Apr. 1971.

132. See, e.g., PRO, C.O. 879/44, African (West) 500, p. 166–67: Hodgson to Chamberlain, dd. Accra, 14 May 1896, and p. 75: Maxwell to Chamberlain, dd. Kumase, 28 Jan. 1896; C.O. 96/337, No. 2040: Stewart to Colonial Secretary, dd. Kumase, 28 Nov. 1898, in Low to Chamberlain, dd. Cape Coast, 6 Jan. 1899.

133. These tendencies had been growing since late 1895 when various Fante rubber traders were imprisoned by a number of Asante *krofo*, or citizens, in the environs of the capital. With the Council of Kumase's new policy of permitting limited immigration of northerners and Colony citizens into the metropolitan region, antiforeigner feelings arose much like in the war period of 1873–74. See, e.g., PRO, C.O. 96/259, No. 14209: Maxwell to Ripon, dd. Cape Coast, 19 July 1895.

134. Most Kumase informants stated that Atweneboanna had virtually no chance of becoming the Asantehene as he always lacked sufficient support among the members of the Council of Kumase. Furthermore, he was known at this time as a man of "weak character." Compare with PRO, C.O. 879/49, African (West) 530, p. 43: Vroom's report, dd. 19 June 1897. Even Governor Maxwell eventually lost interest in promoting Atweneboanna's candidacy. See, e.g., C.O. 879/44, African (West) 500, p. 75: Maxwell to Chamberlain, dd. Kumase, 28 Jan. 1896.

135. Lewin, "Structure of Political Conflict," II, p. 425: interview with Domfe Kyere, 4 Apr. 1971, and field-notes, 25 Apr. 1971.

136. Hodgson, who succeeded William Maxwell as governor at the end of 1897, made this demand without the knowledge or approval of officials in the Colonial Office. His policies, like those of his predecessors, Griffith and Maxwell, had been too frequently frustrated by the actions of authorities in Kumase; and thus his unsuccessful persuasions and threats over the past six years culminated in

this provocative, intensely unpopular demand. For a preliminary discussion of a subject that requires much more research, see Tordoff, *Ashanti under Prempehs*, pp. 98–101, and see p. 86 for a brief account of the efforts of the Kumase diplomats Yaw Boaten and Kwaku Fokuo to raise funds for Prempe's release. The Colonial Office, however, had already made the decision to deport Prempe and his councillors to Sierra Leone.

137. Lewin, "Structure of Political Conflict," II, p. 77: interview with al-Hajj Sulāyman, 21 July 1970.
138. Ibid., pp. 154–55: interview with Kwadwo Afodo, 30 Aug. 1970. See Tordoff, *Ashanti under Prempehs*, pp. 97–108, and Kimble, *Political History*, pp. 299–300, 315–20, for the standard British-based perspective on the immediate causes for the outbreak of military hostilities. The four and one-half month war is considered by several British primary accounts including C. H. Armitage and A. F. Montanaro, *The Ashanti Campaign of 1900* (London, 1901); Harold C. Biss, *The Relief of Kumasi* (London, 1901); and Lady Mary A. Hodgson, *The Siege of Kumassi* (London, 1901). I intend to prepare for publication a full discussion of Asante participants, strategy, and military organization in the confrontation. The Asante view of the war is yet another neglected theme in nineteenth-century Asante history.
139. For a detailed account of the horrors of the conflict written from a British perspective, see Claridge, *Gold Coast*, II, pp. 457–566.
140. Lewin, "Structure of Political Conflict," II, p. 124: interview with Adu Gyamera, 10 Aug. 1970.

GLOSSARY
OF MAIN ASANTE TWI TERMS

This glossary presents the principal Asante Twi terms that appear in the text. It has been constructed with the preferred Asante orthography, although for reasons of simplicity this practice has not been consistently followed in the text. Hence, the Asante Twi "ɔ" appears as "o" and the "ɛ" as "e" in personal and place names in the text. Further, this glossary has been alphabetized by omitting the initial vowel or initial nasal "m" and "n." Thus, for example, ɔman would appear under "m" and Asantehene under "s" below.

I am indebted to Ivor Wilks for his suggestions on the organization of this glossary.

B

ɔbaa-panin	the occupant of a female stool; usually refers to the queen mother of a stool other than that of Kumase.
abakomadwa	the stool occupied by the Kumase heir apparent; customarily supervised by the Nkonsonhene of Kumase.
aban	a building of stone; government.
abansifoɔ	Asante road guards; also known as akwansifoɔ, or highway police.
batani, pl. abatafoɔ	a trader, official or private; the Batahene of Kumase was responsible for the state trading activities.
ɔbayifoɔn, pl. abayifoɔ	witch and wizard.
bese fufuo	white kola.
bese kɔkɔɔ	red kola.
ɔbirɛmpɔn, pl. abonsamfoɔ	literally, "the satans"; refers to Asante politicoreligious cult.
ɔbonsamfoɔ, pl. abirɛmpon	literally, "big chief"; usually reserved for the heads of outlying districts of the state or senior Kumase officials.
brono, pl. abrono	ward and residential unit of an urban center or village.
Buabassa	title of the Gyaasehene of Kumase.
oburoni, pl. abrofoɔ	whiteman or European.
abusua, pl. mmusua	matriclan or matrilineage; the head of an abusua is abusua-panin, pl. abusua-mpaninfoɔ.

277

D

Adae — the festival for the ancestors occurring twice in every Asante month of forty-two days.

adamfo, — literally, "a friend."
pl. *nnamfo*

odekuro, — a lesser ranked chief; usually the head of a town or
pl. *adekurofoɔ* — village.

dommum, — a captive taken in times of war.
pl. *nnommum*

adɔmfo — an enemy in warfare.

ɔdɔnkɔ, — a person who is bought; usually a slave; unfree plan-
pl. *nnɔnkɔfoɔ* — tation laborer.

Adonten — the main body of an army; the Adontenhene of Kumase commanded the principal military division of the nation.

adumfoɔ — executioners serving under the Adumhene of Kumase; carry out death sentence.

dwa — an Asante stool, the symbol of office and hence political authority.

edwa — a market in an urban or rural locality.

Odwira — the most significant annual Asante festival, held both in Kumase and the outlying districts; has political and religious importance.

adwuma — the concept of work.

F

mfasoɔ — profit from capital or wealth.

fekuo — literally, a "grouping" of persons with something in common; used to refer to the main divisions or departments of government of officeholders in Kumase.

afena, — the sword of an officeholder.
pl. *mfena*

fotoɔ — the National Treasury; to be distinguished from the Sanaa, the Asantehene's Treasury.

G

agudeɛ dwa — a stool not created by the Asantehene which independently existed before the formation of the Asante kingdom; for example, Amakom, Tafo, and Kaase.

Gyaase — refers to the *fekuo* responsible for the maintenance of the Asantehene's royal household; led by the Gyaasehene.

Gyaasewa — the treasury organization under the jurisdiction of the Gyaasewahene of Kumase.

agyapadeɛ — the property of an Asante citizen or stranger.

278

H

ɔhene, pl. *ahene*	ruler, head, or leader of a polity, district, or organization.
ɔheneba, pl. *ahenemma*	the son of an ɔhene or chief; may refer to a prince of the Golden Stool.
ahenemmahene	the chief of the children of the chief.
ahenkwaa, pl. *nhenkwaa*	literally, "servant of a chief" or ɔhene; refers to the functionaries of central and local government; same as *asomfoɔ*.
ahensie	the enstoolment of a chief.
ahentuo	the deposition of a chief.
ohia	the concept of poverty; hence, *ohiani*, a poor person, and *ahiafoɔ*, the poor of Asante society.
ɔhoho, pl. *ahɔhoɔ*	a stranger to Asante society; usually refers to a noncitizen of the nation.
Ahwehwebaa	the second highest sword in the Asante state; various *ahene* swear the oath of allegiance to the Asantehene on this sword.
ɔhwesoni, pl. *nhwɛsofo*	literally, "caretakers of lands"; refers to administrative supervisors of outlying areas of the state; officeholders in ten Kumase *fekuo*.

K

akoa, pl. *nkoa*	literally, "a subject" of the Asantehene and thus a citizen of the Asante Nation.
ko	literally, "a battle"; hence *amanko*, or civil war.
akɔmfoɔ	the shrine priests who derive their power from sacred objects such as stones, rivers, or trees.
okonkoni, pl. *akonkofo*	a middleman in trade and commerce.
Kontihene	the military title of the Bantamahene of Kumase.
Kramo, pl. Nkramo	an Asante Muslim.
kroni, pl. *krofoɔ*	literally, "the children of the town"; usually refers to citizens of the state, as does *kroba*, pl. *kromma*.
kumaa	literally, "the younger."
kuro, pl. *nkuro*	a small town.
akuraa, pl. *nkuraa*	a village.
Akwamuhene	second-in-command of an army after the Kontihene; title held by the Asafohene of Kumase.
nkwankwaa	literally, "the young men"; refers to Asante commoners, men without office.
akwanmofoɔ	officials in the Public Works Department of Kumase responsible for maintaining roads and sanitation; serves under the Akwanmofoɔhene, the chief of this *ekuo* in the Gyaase Fekuo.

279

nkwansrafoɔ ——————————— highway police on the roads; also known as *abansifoɔ* and *akwansifoɔ*.

ɔkyeame, ——————————— linguist, secretary, spokesman, or adviser to the
   pl. *akyeame* Asantehene and his councillors; participated in decision-making, and member of Council of Kumase.

akyeremadefoɔ ——————————— court drummers in Kumase who were recruited for state trading, highway patrol, immigration duties, and other specialized civil functions.

M

mmamma ——————————— sons and grandsons of occupants holding civil or military appointive offices; to be distinguished from hereditary officeholders.

ɔman, ——————————— a situational and functional term referring to district,
   pl. *aman* territorial division, state, or nation, depending upon the context used; hence, Asanteman.

ɔmanhene, ——————————— the leader of a large, spatially compact district in the
   pl. *amanhene* metropolitan region; refers usually to the rulers of the five older *amantoɔ*: Bekwae, Dwaben, Kokofu, Mampon, and Nsuta.

Amansie ——————————— literally, "origin of nations"; refers to the southern region of metropolitan Asante, including the districts of Amoafo, Bekwae, Dadiase, Danyase, and Kokofu.

amantoɔ ——————————— the five largest and oldest territorial districts of the metropolitan region: Bekwae, Dwaben, Kokofu, Mampon, and Nsuta.

mmeranteɛ ——————————— literally, "young men"; see *aberanteɛ*.

N

Nifahene ——————————— the commander of the right wing of the Asante army.

P

ɔpaadini, ——————————— the carrier for a trader, chief, or governmental official.
   pl. *apaadifo*

panin ——————————— literally, "the older."

ɔpanin, ——————————— literally, an "elderly" or old person; refers to an office-
   pl. *mpaninfoɔ* holder of an important or lesser significance; can mean councillor.

mpaninie ——————————— the concept of office; to be distinguished from *amannuo*, or administration.

Mponpomsuo ——————————— variously spelled name of the senior sword of the Asante state; refers to the highest sword on which chiefs take the oath of allegiance to the Asantehene.

opooboni, ——————————— literally, "bully"; used to refer to extra-legal activities
   pl. *apoobofoɔ* of certain Asante officeholders or commoners; *apoobo* refers to the "act of bullying."

S

asafo	a unit or company organized for communal or military purposes; hence, *asafohene* or *asahene*, a military leader or commander.
Sanaa	the Asantehene's Treasury, headed by the Sanaahene.
Asantehemaa	the queen mother of Asante who nominates the Asantehene; selected from women of the royal Oyoko dynasty.
Asantehene	the head of the Asante Nation and a male member of the royal Oyoko dynasty.
Asanteman	literally, "the Asante Nation"; refers to the Asante Union in contrast to the Asante Nkabom, or Asante Confederacy.
Asantemanhyiamu	the highest council *de jure* in the Asante Nation, complementing the Council of Kumase, the state's second legislative and judicial body.
sekan	knife.
ɛsɛn, pl. nsɛniefoɔ	literally, "the people who wear the talisman and shoot for the Asantehene"; these courtiers and heralds frequently were recruited for diplomatic assignments and political negotiations.
asɛnii	a trial in court.
asɛniibea	a court of justice.
serekye	silk; often used to refer to a handsome person; hence, Kramo Serekye, the nickname of a prominent Asante Muslim leader in the 1890s.
sika	gold, money.
Sika Dwa	the Golden Stool of Asante.
asikadini, pl. asikadifo	a miner in the state-owned gold fields.
sika futuro	gold dust.
sikani, pl. asikafo or asikafoɔ	a person of wealth in the community; a "rich man."
sika mpɔ	gold nugget.
asoamfoɔ	the hammock-carriers or bearers of the Asantehene; reside in the village of Suame.
osokwani	a hornblower at the Asantehene's court; recruited for and appointed by the Asantehene for road patrol, immigration, and state trading assignments.
ɛsom	the concept of service.
nsuaeɛ	the act of swearing the oath of allegiance.
Nsumankwaahene	the head or chief of the Asantehene's scribes and physicians and of the Asante Muslim communities living in Kumase and its environs.

T

ntafoɔ	name given to people from the northern savanna hinterlands of the empire; hence, an ɔtani would be one such northerner; stranger to Asante.

ntahara ----------- a special horn in the palace.

ɛtoɔ ----------- tax, tribute, paid by citizens or subjects.

ntɔn ----------- association by patrifiliation.

atrankonnwafoɔ ----------- courtiers who give advice during legal cases; hence, an *atrankonnwani* always advises a ruler.

tu aban ----------- a military or other type of coup.

Atwema ----------- one of the four main geographic and dialectic regions of metropolitan Asante; usually refers to the rural hinterland of Kumase; to be distinguished from the other three regions of Amansie, Kwabre, and Sekyere.

W

awowa ----------- a pawn; person sold for a debt; unfree status.

awunyadie ----------- an estate tax.

wura ----------- literally, "lord"; refers to a superior officeholder in a *fekuo*, or *oman*, or the Asantehene.

Y

ayibuadie ----------- an inheritance tax.

Oyokoni,
   pl. Oyokofo ----------- a member of the Oyoko matriclan.

SOURCES

A. Documents

Public Record Office, London
C.O. 96 Series: Gold Coast, Original Correspondence, vols. 100–379.
National Archives of Ghana/Accra
 ADM 1/3 Series.
 ADM 1/5 Series.
 ADM 1/6 Series.
 ADM 1/7 Series.
 ADM 1/10 Series.
 ADM 1/11 Series.
 ADM 1/12 Series.
 ADM 11/1 Series, Secretary of Native Affairs files.
 Acc. No. Series [now catalogued in ADM 11/1 Series].
 SC 5/9, 53, 55, 56, 59 Series [Vroom papers].
National Archives of Ghana/Kumase
 D Series: Chief Commissioner of Asante files on Native Affairs.
Methodist Mission Archives, London
 Box Nos. 7–9: Original Correspondence files, 1868–1902 [includes Thomas R. Picot and William F. Somerville Correspondence; Reverend Benjamin Tregaskis–Owusu Ansa Correspondence; W. Terry Coppin's Journal of his mission to Kumase in 1885].
Basel Mission Archives, Switzerland
 Abetifi, Kyebi, Begoro, and Anum letters and missionary reports.
 F. Ramseyer letters and reports from Kumase, 1896–1905.
 Paul Jenkins, *Abstracts of Basel Mission Gold Coast Correspondence*, 1970.
Institute of African Studies, University of Ghana
 IAS/AS: Asante Stool Histories, recorded by J. Agyeman-Duah.
 IAS/CR: Asante Court Record Collection.
 IAS/JEK: Krakye Traditions, recorded by J. E. Kumah.

B. Official Printed Material

(i) Parliamentary Papers
 Further Correspondence Respecting the Ashantee Invasion (March, 1874):
 XLVI No. 1 (C. 890) 1
   No. 2 (C. 891) 254
   No. 3 (C. 892) 483
   No. 4 (C. 893) 755
   No. 5 (C. 894) 831
   No. 7 (C. 921) 921

No. 8 (C. 922)   943
No. 9 (C. 1006) 1045
Correspondence Relating to the Affairs of the Gold Coast, C. 1140 (February 1875), LII, 325.
Correspondence Relating to the Queen's Jurisdiction on the Gold Coast and the Abolition of Slavery within the Protectorate, C. 1139 (February 1875), LII, 277.
Further Correspondence Relating to the Abolition of Slavery on the Gold Coast, C. 1159 (February 1875), LII, 441.
Papers Relating to Her Majesty's Possessions in West Africa, C. 1343 (August 1875), LII, 779.
Papers Relating to Her Majesty's Possessions in West Africa, C. 1402 (February 1876), LII, 403.
Affairs of the Gold Coast and Threatened Ashanti Invasion, C. 3064 (August 1881), LXV, 443.
Further Correspondence Regarding Affairs of the Gold Coast, C. 3386 (August 1882), LXVI, 1.
Further Correspondence Regarding Affairs of the Gold Coast, C. 3687 (July 1883), XLVIII, 453.
Further Correspondence Regarding the Affairs of the Gold Coast, C. 4052 (June 1884), LVI, 283.
Further Correspondence Respecting the Affairs of the Gold Coast, C. 4477 (July 1885), LV, 519.
Further Correspondence Respecting the Affairs of the Gold Coast, C. 4906 (September 1886), XLVII, 233.
Further Correspondence Respecting the Affairs of the Gold Coast, C. 5357 (April 1888), LXXV, 109.
Further Correspondence Respecting the Affairs of the Gold Coast, C. 5615 (December 1888), LXXV, 203.
Despatch from Governor Sir W. Brandford Griffith, K.C.M.G. Forwarding a Memorial from Merchants, Agents, and Traders of the Gold Coast Colony, C. 7225 (November 1893), LVIII, 651.
Further Correspondence Relating to Affairs in Ashanti, C. 7917 (February 1896), LVIII, 455.
Further Correspondence Relative to Affairs in Ashanti, C. 7918 (February 1896), LVIII, 707.

(ii) Confidential Prints

African (West) No. 384	C.O. 879/31
Nos. 448, 458	C.O. 879/38
No. 462	C.O. 879/40
No. 478	C.O. 879/41
No. 490	C.O. 879/43
Nos. 500, 504	C.O. 879/44
Nos. 506–7	C.O. 879/45
Nos. 530, 534	C.O. 879/49
No. 540	C.O. 879/50
No. 549	C.O. 879/52
Nos. 562, 564	C.O. 879/54
No. 585	C.O. 879/58

No. 621   C.O. 879/62
No. 649   C.O. 879/67

(iii) Official Reports
Colonial Reports, Gold Coast, 1892–1900.
Colonial Reports, Asante, 1897–1899.

(iv) Treaties and Boundary Negotiations
Correspondence Relative to the Cession of the Dutch Settlements on the West Coast of Africa, C. 670 (February 1872).
Correspondence Respecting the Affairs of the Gambia and the Proposed Exchange with France of Possessions on the West Coast of Africa, C. 1409 (February 1876).
Collection of Treaties with Native Chiefs, etc., in West Africa (London, 1914), African (West) No. 1010.

C. NEWSPAPERS

The African Times, 1872–1898
The Gold Coast Chronicle, Accra, 1894–1901
The Gold Coast Times, Cape Coast, 1874–1885
The Gold Coast Methodist Times, Cape Coast, 1894
The Western Echo, Cape Coast, 1885–1888

D. SECONDARY WORKS

Adjaye, Joseph K. "Asabi Antwi and Oral Retrieval Mechanisms in Asante Diplomatic Practice." Asante Seminar '76, Bulletin No. 5 (1976), 26–28.

Agbodeka, Francis. African Politics and British Policy in the Gold Coast, 1868–1900. London: Longmans, 1971.

Agyeman, E. A. "Gyaman—Its Relations with Ashanti, 1720–1820." M.A. thesis, University of Ghana, 1965.

Ameyaw, Kwabena. "Kwahu—An Early Forest State." Ghana Notes and Queries 9 (1966), 39–45.

Anaman, Rev. J. B. The Gold Coast Guide. London: Christian Herald, second edition, 1902.

Arhin, Kwame. "The Financing of the Ashanti Expansion (1700–1820)." Africa 37 (1967), 283–91.

――――. "The Structure of Greater Ashanti (1700–1824)." The Journal of African African History 8 (1967), 65–85.

――――. "The Missionary Role on the Gold Coast and in Ashanti: Reverend F. A. Ramseyer and the British Take-over of Ashanti, 1869-1894." University of Ghana Institute of African Studies Research Review 4 (1968), 1–15.

――――. "The Development of Market Centres at Atebubu and Kintampo since 1874." Ph.D. thesis, University of London, 1969.

――――. "Ashanti and the North-East." University of Ghana Institute of African Studies Research Review, Supplement 2 (1970), 1–38.

――――. "Aspects of the Ashanti Northern Trade in the Nineteenth Century." Africa 40 (1970), 363–73.

――――. "Succession and Gold Mining at Manso-Nkwanta." University of Ghana Institute of African Studies Research Review 6 (1970), 101–9.

――――. "Strangers and Hosts: Study in the Political Organization and History of Atebubu Town." Transactions of the Historical Society of Ghana 12 (1971), 63–82.

Sources

————. "The Ashanti Rubber Trade with the Gold Coast in the Eighteen-Nineties." *Africa* 42 (1972), 32–43.

Armitage, C. H., and A. F. Montanaro. *The Ashanti Campaign of 1900.* London: Sands, 1901.

Arthur, John. *Brong Ahafo Handbook.* Accra: Graphic Press, 1961.

Baden-Powell, R. S. S. *The Downfall of Prempeh: A Diary of Life with the Native Levy in Ashanti, 1895–96.* London: Methuen, second edition, 1896.

Bevin, H. J. "The Gold Coast Economy about 1880." *Transactions of the Gold Coast and Togoland Historical Society* 3 (1956), 73–86.

————. "M. J. Bonnat: Trader and Mining Promoter." *The Economic Bulletin of Ghana* 4 (1960), 1–12.

Biss, Harold C. *The Relief of Kumasi.* London: Methuen, second edition, 1901.

Boahen, Adu. "Juaben and Kumasi Relations in the Nineteenth Century." Draft paper, Institute of African Studies, Legon, 1965.

————. "Politics in Ghana, 1800–1874," in *History of West Africa,* Volume 2, edited by J. F. A. Ajayi and Michael Crowder, 167–261. London: Longmans, 1974.

Boaten, Kwasi. "An Historical Geography of Northern Asante, 1702–1945." M.A. thesis, University of Ghana, 1969.

Bowdich, T. Edward. *Mission from Cape Coast Castle to Ashantee.* London: Frank Cass and Co., Ltd., third edition, 1966. (Original ed., London: John Murray, 1819).

Boyle, Frederick. *Through Fanteeland to Coomassie: A Diary of the Ashantee Expedition.* London: Chapman and Hall, 1874.

Brackenbury, Henry. *The Ashanti War; a Narrative.* Two volumes. London: William Blackwood and Sons, 1874.

———— and G. L. Huyshe. *Fanti and Ashanti.* London: William Blackwood and Sons, 1873.

Braimah, J. A., and J. R. Goody. *Salaga: The Struggle for Power.* London: Longmans, 1967.

Burleigh, Bennet. *Two Campaigns: Madagascar and Ashantee.* London: T. Fisher Unwin, 1896.

Burton, Richard F., and V. L. Cameron. *To the Gold Coast for Gold.* Two volumes. London: Chatto and Windus, 1883.

Busia, Kofi A. *The Position of the Chief in the Modern Political System of Ashanti.* London: Oxford University Press, 1951.

Casely Hayford, J. E. *Gold Coast Native Institutions.* London: Sweet and Maxwell, Ltd., 1903.

Christaller, J. G. *A Dictionary of the Asante and Fanti Language Called Tschi.* Basel: 1881.

————. "Eine Reise in den Hinterlandern von Togo." *Mitteilungen der Geographischen Gesellschaft für Thuringen* 8 (1889), 1–28.

Claridge, W. Walton. *A History of the Gold Coast and Ashanti.* Two volumes. London: Frank Cass and Co., Ltd., second edition, 1964. (Original ed., London: John Murray, 1915).

Collins, E. "The Panic Element in Nineteenth-Century British Relations with Ashanti." *Transactions of the Historical Society of Ghana* 5 (1962), 79–144.

Coombs, Douglas. *The Gold Coast, Britain, and the Netherlands, 1850–1870.* London: Oxford University Press, 1963.

Sources

De Graft-Johnson, J. C. "The Population of Ghana, 1846–1967." *Transactions of the Historical Society of Ghana* 10 (1969), 1–12.

Dickson, Kwamina B. "Trade Patterns in Ghana at the Beginning of the Eighteenth Century." *The Geographical Review* 56 (1966), 417–31.

——. *A Historical Geography of Ghana.* Cambridge: Cambridge University Press, 1971.

Djang, S. S. *The Sunlight Reference Almanac.* Aburi: 1936.

Dobson, George. "The River Volta, Gold Coast, West Africa." *The Journal of the Manchester Geographical Society* 8 (1892), 19–25.

Dumett, Raymond. "British Official Attitudes in Relation to Economic Development in the Gold Coast, 1874–1905." Ph.D. thesis, University of London, 1966.

——. "The Rubber Trade of the Gold Coast and Asante in the Nineteenth Century: African Innovation and Market Responsiveness." *The Journal of African History* 12 (1971), 79–101.

Dunn, John, and A. F. Robertson. *Dependence and Opportunity: Political Change in Ahafo.* Cambridge: Cambridge University Press, 1973.

Dupuis, Joseph. *Journal of a Residence in Ashantee.* London: Frank Cass and Co., Ltd., second edition, 1966. (Original ed., London: Henry Colburn, 1824.)

Ellis, A. B. *The Land of Fetish.* London: Chapman and Hall, 1883.

——. *The Tshi-Speaking Peoples of the Gold Coast of West Africa.* London: Chapman and Hall, 1887.

——. *A History of the Gold Coast of West Africa.* London: Chapman and Hall, 1893.

Evangelische Heidenbote. November 1875, No. 11, 81–84; May 1876, No. 12, 5–6, 33–34; April 1882, No. 4, 25–27; March 1892, No. 3, 17–19; June 1895, No. 6, 45–57; March 1897, No. 3, 19–22, 70.

Fage, J. D. "Slavery and the Slave Trade in the Context of West African History." *The Journal of African History* 10 (1969), 393–404.

Field, Margaret, J. *Akim-Kotoku, an Oman of the Gold Coast.* Accra: Crown Agents, 1948.

Fortes, M. "Ashanti Survey, 1945–46: An Experiment in Social Research." *Geographical Journal* 110 (1947), 149–79.

Freeman, Richard Austin. *Travels and Life in Ashanti and Jaman.* London: Frank Cass and Co., Ltd., 1898.

Freeman, Thomas Birch. *Journal of Various Visits to the Kingdoms of Ashanti, Aku, and Dahomi, in Western Africa.* London: John Mason, second edition, 1844.

Fuller, Sir Francis. *A Vanished Dynasty: Ashanti.* London: Frank Cass and Co., Ltd., second edition, 1968. (Original ed., London: John Murray, 1921.)

Fynn, J. K. *Asante and Its Neighbours, 1700–1807.* London: Longmans, 1971.

Goody, Jack. "Ashanti and the North-West." *University of Ghana Institute of African Studies Research Review,* Supplement 1 (1965), 1–110.

——. "Salaga in 1876." *Ghana Notes and Queries* 8 (1966), 1–5.

—— and C. Y. Boateng. "The History and Traditions of Nkoranza." *University of Ghana Institute of African Studies Research Review,* Supplement 1 (1965), 170–184.

Gould, Peter R. *The Development of the Transportation Pattern in Ghana.* Northwestern University Studies in Geography No. 5, Evanston: 1960.

Gros, J. *Voyages, Aventures et Captivité de J. Bonnat Chez les Achantis.* Paris: 1884.

Hagan, G. P. "Ashanti Bureaucracy: A Study of the Growth of Centralized Administration in Ashanti from the Time of Osei Tutu to the Time of Osei Tutu Kwamina Esibe Bonsu." *Transactions of the Historical Society of Ghana* 12 (1971), 43–62.

―――. "The Golden Stool and the Oaths to the King of Ashanti." *University of Ghana Institute of African Studies Research Review* 4 (1968), 1–33.

Hargreaves, John D. *Prelude to the Partition of West Africa.* London: Macmillan and Co., 1963.

Hay, Sir John D. *Ashanti and the Gold Coast.* London: Edward Stanford, 1874.

Henty, G. A. *The March to Coomassie.* London: Tinsley Brothers, 1874.

Hill, Polly. *Migrant Cocoa Farmers of Southern Ghana.* Cambridge: Cambridge University Press, 1963.

Hobbs, H. J. "History of Nkoranza." *The Gold Coast Review* 3 (1927), 117–22.

Hodgson, Lady Mary A. *The Siege of Kumassi.* London: C. Arthur Pearson, Ltd., second edition, 1901.

Hopkins, A. G. *An Economic History of West Africa.* London: Longmans, 1973.

Horton, Africanus B. *Letters on the Political Condition of the Gold Coast.* London: Frank Cass and Co., Ltd., second edition, 1970. (Original ed., 1870.)

Johnson, Marion (ed.). *Salaga Papers.* Two volumes. Legon: Institute of African Studies, 1965.

Johnson, Marion. "Ashanti East of the Volta." *Transactions of the Historical Society of Ghana* 7 (1966), 33–59.

―――. "M. Bonnat on the Volta." *Ghana Notes and Queries* 10 (1968), 4–17.

―――. "Kumasi, Juaben, and M. Bonnat." *Transactions of the Historical Society of Ghana* 12 (1971), 17–41.

Kanya-Forstner, A. S. *The Conquest of the Western Sudan: A Study in French Military Imperialism.* Cambridge: Cambridge University Press, 1969.

Kea, R. A. "Firearms and Warfare on the Gold and Slave Coasts from the Sixteenth to the Nineteenth Centuries." *The Journal of African History* 12 (1971), 185–213.

Kimble, David. *A Political History of Ghana: The Rise of Gold Coast Nationalism, 1850–1928.* Oxford: Clarendon Press, 1963.

Kirby, Captain Brandon. "A Journey into the Interior of Ashanti." *Proceedings of the Royal Geographical Society* 6 (1884), 447–52.

Klein, A. Norman. "West African Unfree Labor before and after the Rise of the Atlantic Slave Trade," in *Slavery in the New World*, edited by L. Foner and E. D. Genovese, 87–95. Englewood-Cliffs, N.J.: Prentice-Hall, Inc., 1969.

Kwamena-Poh, M. A. *Government and Politics in the Akuapem State, 1730–1850.* London: Longmans, 1973.

Kyerematen, A. A. Y. *Panoply of Ghana.* London : Longmans, 1964.

―――. "The Royal Stools of Ashanti." *Africa* 39 (1969), 1–10.

Lewin, Thomas J. *The English Involvement in Ashanti around 1900.* Kumase Project, Report No. 2. Legon: Institute of African Studies, University of Ghana, 1968.

―――. "The Structure of Political Conflict in Asante, 1875–1900." Two volumes. Ph.D. thesis, Northwestern University, 1974.

―――― and Dennis Fitzsimmons. "The Political Organization of Space in Asante: Part I." *Asante Seminar '76*, Bulletin No. 4 (1976), 25–33.

―――. "The Political Organization of Space in Asante: Part II." *Asante Seminar '76*, Bulletin No. 5 (1976), 15–21.

————. "The Political Organization of Space in Asante: Part III." *Asante Seminar* '76, Bulletin No. 6 (1976), 22–32.

Maurice, Sir John Frederick. *The Ashantee War, a Popular Narrative.* London: n.p., 1874.

McCaskie, Thomas C. "Innovational Eclecticism: The Asante Empire and Europe in the Nineteenth Century." *Comparative Studies in Society and History* 14 (1972), 30–45.

————. "The Paramountcy of the Asantehene Kwaku Dua (1834–1867): A Study in Asante Political Culture." Ph.D. thesis, University of Cambridge, 1974.

McIntyre, William D. "British Policy in West Africa: The Ashanti Expedition of 1873–4." *The Historical Journal* 5 (1962), 19–46.

————. *The Imperial Frontier in the Tropics, 1865–75.* London: Macmillan, 1967.

Metcalfe, G. E. *Maclean of the Gold Coast.* London: Oxford University Press, 1962.

————. *Great Britain and Ghana, Documents of Ghana History 1807–1957.* London: Thomas Nelson and Sons, Ltd., 1964.

Miles, John. "The Ashanti War of 1873–4: A Study in Ashanti Military Organization and Techniques." M.A. thesis, University of London, 1968.

Musgrove, George C. *To Kumassi with Scott.* London: Wightman and Co., 1896.

Myatt, Frederick. *The Golden Stool: Ashanti 1900.* London: William Kimber, 1966.

Obichere, Boniface I. *West African States and European Expansion, The Dahomey-Niger Hinterlands, 1885–1898.* New Haven and London: Yale University Press, 1971.

Ogg, David. *Europe of the Ancien Regime, 1715–1783.* New York: Harper and Row, 1965.

Perregaux, E. "A Few Notes on Kwahu, 'Quahoe,' a Territory on the Gold Coast Colony." *Journal of the Royal African Society* 2 (1903), 444–50.

Person, Yves. "Guinea-Samori" (trans. J. White), in *West African Resistance*, edited by Michael Crowder, 111–43. London: Hutchinson, 1971.

————. "The Atlantic Coast and the Southern Savannahs, 1800–1880," in *History of West Africa*, Volume 2, edited by J. F. A. Ajayi and Michael Crowder, 262–307. London: Longmans, 1974.

Priestley, M. "The Ashanti Question and the British: Eighteenth Century Origins." *The Journal of African History* 2 (1961), 35–59.

Ramseyer, F. A., and J. Kühne. *Four Years in Ashantee.* New York: Robert Carter and Brothers, 1875.

Rattray, R. S. *Ashanti.* Oxford: Clarendon Press, 1923.

————. *Religion and Art in Ashanti.* Oxford: Clarendon Press, 1927.

————. *Ashanti Law and Constitution.* Oxford: Clarendon Press, 1929.

Reade, W. Winwood. *The Story of the Ashantee Campaign.* London: Smith, Elder, and Co., 1874.

Reindorf, Rev. Carl Christian. *The History of the Gold Coast and Ashante.* Accra: Ghana Universities Press, 1966. (Original edition, n.d., prob. 1895.)

Rice, Jeffrey. "Cohort Groups in Asante, ca. 1870." *Asante Seminar* '75, Bulletin No. 3 (1975), 21–24.

Robertson, A. F., "Histories and Political Opposition in Ahafo, Ghana." *Africa* 43 (1973), 41–58.

Robinson, Ronald, John Gallagher, and Alice Denny. *Africa and the Victorians: The Official Mind of Imperialism.* London: Macmillan, 1961.

Salmon, Charles S. "British Policy in West Africa." *The Contemporary Review* 42 (1882), 878–93.

Semmel, Bernard. *The Rise of Free Trade Imperialism; Classical Political Economy: The Empire of Free Trade, and Imperialism, 1750–1850.* Cambridge: Cambridge University Press, 1970.

Stanley, Henry M. *Coomassie and Magdala, the Story of Two British Campaigns in Africa.* New York: Harper and Bros., 1874.

Steel, R. W. "The Population of Ashanti: A Geographical Analysis." *Geographical Journal* 112 (1948), 64–77.

Steiner, P. *Dark and Stormy Days at Kumassi, 1900.* London: S. W. Partridge and Co., 1901.

———. *Ein Besuch in Okwawu.* Basel: Basel Press, 1882.

Swithenbank, Michael. *Ashanti Fetish Houses.* Accra: Ghana Universities Press, 1969.

Szereszewski, R. *Structural Changes in the Economy of Ghana, 1891–1911.* London: Weidenfeld and Nicolson, 1965.

Thomas, Roger G. "Forced Labour in British West Africa: The Case of the Northern Territories of the Gold Coast, 1906–1927." *The Journal of African History* 14 (1973), 79–103.

Tordoff, William. "The Brong-Ahafo Region." *The Economic Bulletin of Ghana* 3 (1959), 2–18.

———. "The Exile and Repatriation of Nana Prempeh I of Ashanti (1896–1924)." *Transactions of the Historical Society of Ghana* 4 (1960), 33–58.

———. "A Note on Relations Between Samory and King Prempeh I of Ashanti." *Ghana Notes and Queries* 3 (1961), 5–7.

———. "Brandford Griffith's Offer of British Protection to Ashanti (1891)." *Transactions of the Historical Society of Ghana* 6 (1962), 31–49.

———. *Ashanti under the Prempehs, 1888–1935.* London: Oxford University Press, 1965.

———. "The Ashanti Confederacy." *The Journal of African History* 3 (1962), 399–417.

Triulzi, Alexandro. "The Asantehene-in-Council: Ashanti Politics under Colonial Rule, 1935–50." *Africa* 42 (1972), 98–111.

Walker, A. J. "The Kwahus." *The Gold Coast Review* 1 (1925), 15–28.

Walter, Eugene V. *Terror and Resistance, a Study of Political Violence.* New York: Oxford University Press, 1969.

Ward, W. E. F. *A History of Ghana.* London: George Allen and Unwin, fourth edition, 1967.

Weaver, Dolly. "Krachi Dente in Politics in the Late 19th Century." Draft paper, Department of History, University of Ghana, Legon, 1973.

Wilks, Ivor. *The Northern Factor in Ashanti History.* Legon: Institute of African Studies, University College of Ghana, 1961.

———. "A Medieval Trade-Route from the Niger to the Gulf of Guinea." *The Journal of African History* 3 (1962), 337–41.

———. "Aspects of Bureaucratization in Ashanti in the Nineteenth Century." *The Journal of African History* 7 (1966), 215–32.

———. "The Position of Muslims in Metropolitan Ashanti in the Early Nineteenth Century," in *Islam in Tropical Africa,* edited by I. M. Lewis, 318–41. London: Oxford University Press, 1966.

————. "Ashanti Government," in *West African Kingdoms in the Nineteenth Century*, edited by Daryll Forde and P. M. Kaberry, 206–238. London: Oxford University Press, 1967.

————. *Political Bi-Polarity in Nineteenth Century Asante*. Edinburgh: Ninth Melville J. Herskovits Memorial Lecture, 1970.

————. "Asante Policy towards the Hausa Trade in the Nineteenth Century," in *The Development of Indigenous Trade and Markets in West Africa*, edited by Claude Meillassoux, 124–41. London: Oxford University Press, 1971.

————. "The Mossi and Akan States, 1500–1800," in *History of West Africa*, Volume 1, edited by J. F. A. Ajayi and Michael Crowder, 344–86. London: Longmans, 1971.

————. *Asante in the Nineteenth Century: The Structure and Evolution of a Political Order*. Cambridge: Cambridge University Press, 1975.

————. "Dissidence in Asante Politics: Two Tracts from the Late Nineteenth Century," in *African Themes: Northwestern University Studies in Honor of Gwendolen M. Carter*, edited by I. Abu-Lughod, 47–63. Evanston: Northwestern University Press, 1975.

————. "Land, Labour, Capital and the Forest Kingdom of Asante: A Model of Early Change," in *Evolution of Social Systems*, edited by J. Friedman and M. Rowlands, 487–534. London: Duckworth, 1978.

————. "The Golden Stool and the Elephant's Tail: The Rise of the Asante Middle Class," in *Studies in Economic Anthropology*, edited by George Dalton. 1979, forthcoming.

Wood, Col. Evelyn. *The Ashanti Expedition of 1873–4*. London: W. Mitchell and Co., 1874.

E. ASANTE COLLECTIVE BIOGRAPHY PROJECT

Ongoing project and seminar at Northwestern University designed to provide a data resource center on nineteeth-century officeholders. Newsletters published with pre-code sheets on major figures and commentaries on the biographical profiles of individuals.

F. FIELD INTERVIEWS

Interviews are alphabetized according to the first letter of the informant's first name or the title of the office the informant occupies in the Asante political establishment. The arrangement depends upon the citation in the text and notes. The date on which the interview was conducted is given. Interviews with an * are found in my field-notes on public deposit, and all others are located in Lewin, "Structure of Political Conflict," II.

Adontenhene Agyeman Nkwantabisa III	30 Oct. 1970
Adu Gyamera	6, 10, 15, 17, 27 Aug., 9, 10, Sept. 1970; *9 Jan., *1, *16 Feb., *28 Apr. 1971
Adumhene Asamoa Totoe II	9 Oct. 1970
Agyei Maniampon Abrebrease (of Mampon)	14 Mar. 1971
Ahenkrohene Kwadwo Apea	11 Dec. 1970
Akosua Ama	2, 3, 4 June 1970
Akrafohene Kwasi Mensa	11 Dec. 1970
Akumantihene Kwabena Asare	21 Dec. 1970
Akuroponhene Kwasi Ansere	20 Nov. 1970

Akyawkromhene Owusu Akyaw	20 Dec. 1970
Akyeamehene Kwadwo Asabere	13 Oct. 1970
Akyempemhene Boakye Dankwa II	2 Oct. 1970
Akyereapem	7, *9, 11 Aug. 1970
al-Hajj Adamu Dagomba	*9 July 1970
al-Hajj Sulāyman	26, *27, 28, *29 May, 10, 21, *26 July 1970
al-Hajj Sumalar	*23 July, *30 Dec. 1970
Amakomhene Mensa Yiadom II	2 Sept. 1970
Amakoo	11, 17 Sept. 1970
Amina Wagadugu	*26 June, *1 July 1970
Ampabamehene Kwabena Kwaku II	17 Dec. 1970
Anamenakohene Kwabena Dwoben II	4 Apr. 1971
Anantahene Apea Dankwa II	23 Oct. 1970
Ankobeahene Poku-Dum	4 Nov. 1970
Antoahene Opoku Agyeman II	20 Dec. 1970
Anyinasehene Akyampon Akwasi Ababio	20 Nov. 1970
Asokore Mamponhene Boakye Dankwa II	15 Dec. 1970
Asokwahene Kofi Poku and his councillors	14 June 1970
Atipinhene Osei Kwame	9 Oct. 1970
Atumpakahene Okyerema Pon II	21 Dec. 1970
Atutuehene Opon Wadie	27 Nov. 1970
Atwema Agogohene Owusu Nkwantabisa	4 Dec. 1970
Atwemahene Antwi Agyei	11 Dec. 1970
Banemuhene Kofi Safo Ababio	6 Dec. 1970
Bantamahene Owusu Amankwatia IV	13, *14 Oct. 1970
Barehene Gyedu Kumanin II	4 Dec. 1970
Baworohene Yaw Wusu	16 Dec. 1970
Bekwaehene Osei Kwadwo II, Kwadwo Donko, and Kwabena Antwi	19 Mar. 1971
Boagyaahene Osei Akwasi	2, 9 June 1970
Boamanhene Yeboa Asuama	20 Nov. 1970
Boaten Sapon (of Dwaben)	12 Mar. 1971
Buokromhene Owusu Bempah	23 Oct. 1970
Dadiesoabahene Yaw Boaten	13 Nov. 1970
Domfe Kyere	30 Oct. 1970; *2, *6, *7 Jan., *6, *8, *9, *16, *18 Feb., 21, 24, 28 Mar. 4, *8, 7, 10, 13, 15, 17, *25, *28 Apr. 1971
Esianponhene Kwasi Anofi	21 Dec. 1970
Fantehene Kwame Twi	6 Nov. 1970
Fontomfromhene Tweneboa Kodua Ababio II	21 Dec. 1970
Gyaasehene Opoku Mensa II	9 Oct. 1970
Hemanhene Kwabena Apawa II	8 Dec. 1970
Hiahene Mensa Bonsu	2 Oct. 1970
I. K. Agyeman	16, *17, 22, 30 June, 8 July 1970; *6 Feb. 1971
Issa Kilishi	*14 June, *27 Nov. 1970
J. W. Opon	8 June 1970, 31 Mar. 1971
Kenyasehene Osei Kenyase	24 Nov. 1970

Kofi Afrane	15 Sept. 1970
Kokofuhene Osei Asibe III and Adu Buobi	19 Dec. 1970, 19, *20 Mar. 1971
Kronkohene Kwabena Amo	19 Dec. 1970
Kumawuhene Otuo Akyampon II	18 Apr. 1971
Kuntanasehene Kofi Boaten II	5 Apr. 1971
Kwabena Antwi	*20 Mar. 1971
Kwabena Baako	14, 17 Sept. 1970; *10 June 1971
Kwadwo Afodo	27, 30 Aug. 1970; *8 Jan., *6, 14 Feb., *27, *28 Apr., *1 June 1971
Kwadwo Bo	1, 3, 4 Sept. 1970; *14 Feb. 1971
Kwadwo Donko	13 June 1970
Kwadwo Mosi	8 June 1970
Kwasohene Kwame Ntiamoa Ababio	21 Dec. 1970
Kwaku Anno	4 Sept. 1970
Kwamanhene Kodua Debra II	21 Dec. 1970
Kwamohene Owusu Agyeman Boaten II	20 Dec. 1970
Kyidomhene Osei Yaw	16 Oct. 1970
Mai Kano	*28 June 1970
Malam Gariba	*28 Nov. 1970
Malam Haruna	29 May, 4, 5 Aug. 1970
Mamesenhene Akwasi Poku Ababio	6 Nov. 1970
Mamunatu	5, 30 Aug. 1970
Manwerehene Kwabena Boaten	16 Oct. 1970
Moses Kwasi Dzoto	31 Mar. 2 Apr. 1971
Nana Opoku	28 Dec. 1970; *12 June 1971
Nancy Adriana Taylor	11 June 1970
Nkonsonhene Owusu Premo	25, 30 Mar. 1971
Nkwantakesehene Owusu Afriyie II	27 Nov. 1970
Nsenehene Kwasi Adu	19 Mar. 1971
Nsumankwaahene Domfe Gyeabo III	23 Oct. 1970; *29 Apr. 1971
Obaapanin Ama Dapaa	16 Oct. 1970
Offumanhene Kwasi Dua	25 Mar. 1971
Okyeame Boakye Tenten	2 Apr. 1971
Okyeame Boakye Yam	1 Apr. 1971
Omantihene Owusu Nkwantabisa	4, *5, *18, 29 Dec. 1970; *4 Feb., *1 May 1971
Oyoko Bremanhene Kofi Amoako	13 Nov. 1970
Oyokohene Kofi Poku	16 Oct. 1970
Saamanhene Osei Kwaku II (Gyaasehene of Kumase)	23 Oct. 1970
Saawuahene Kwabena Edusei	22 Dec. 1970
Samuel Prempe	23 July 1970
Soaduhene Kanin Tini	11 Dec. 1970
Somihene Boakye Ansa	27 Nov. 1970
Tafohene Boadu Kwadwo II	13 Nov. 1970
Toasehene Kofi Wusu	27 Nov. 1970
Tredehene Nubin Asare II	27 Nov. 1970
Yaw Safo	25, *28 Sept. 1970; *9 Feb., 8 Apr. 1971
Yawkromhene Kwaku Ti II	8 Apr. 1971

INDEX

Abease: British treaty with, 178
Abene, 103
Abenehene. See Kwadwo Akuamoa II
Abetifi, 103; Basel mission station in, 104; British in, 177
Abetifihene. See Kofi Denkyi
Abodom: Bekwae alliance with, 100
Abodomhene. See Kwaku Dua
Abonkosu: Nsuta resettlement of, 137
Abontendomhene. See Saakode
Abontendomhene of Edweso. See Kwame Ntahara
Abuakwa (in Atwema), 29
Abu Bakr, 185
Accra: as part of British Protected Territory, 42; Dwaben alliance with, 89; and Manso secessionists, 75; as trade center, 12, 44, 50, 88, 106
Ada, 50, 106
Adae ceremonies, 15, 20
Adangme: as part of British Protected Territory, 42
Adankranya: Bekwae alliance with, 100
Adankranyahene. See Kwasi Pipim
Adanse, 33, 56; clash with Bekwae, 96–97, 99–102; fails to enlist British assistance, 102; attempt to enlist separatists, 102; solicits British assistance, 101; British influence in, 51; and British mediation, 52, 95; persistent Kumase influence in, 96; and ouster of Kumase government, 96; fluctuating relationship with Kumase, 93–95; growth of localism in, 86, 92, 96–97, 104; localists' reliance on British support, 93; Nkansa-Kotirko faction defeated in, 97; political instability of, 92; reorganization of, 92; trade interference with,

100; alliance with Wassa and Denkyira, 93
Adansehene, 92, 93. See also Kwaku Nkansa
Adanse refugees: return to Asante sought, 144, 145, 167–68; Agyeman Prempe and British positions on, 147; continued support of Yaw Atweneboanna, 125
Adontenhene: on Council of Kumase, 33. See also Kwame Frimpon
Adu Agyei (Nsutahene): and treaty with British, 207
Adu Bofo (Gyaasewahene): anti-missionary stance of, 67
Adu Buobi, 254 n. 26; Agyeman Prempe's arrest recalled by, 203
Adu Gyamera, 233 n. 34; Agyeman Prempe's arrest recalled by, 201–2; and account of British-Kumase meeting, 195
Adu Kofi (Anantahene): as adviser to Agyeman Prempe, 158; supports triumvirate, 211
Adu Kwaku (Mpatasehene), 75
Adum (ward), 19
Adumhene, 123; on Council of Kumase, 33. See also Asamoa Kwame, Kwabena Tooto
Adusei, 77
Adu Tire (Nsutahene), 112; overtures to Agyeman Prempe, 136; defeated at Bafoso, 126; flight of, 132; supports Yaw Atweneboanna, 116
Afra Kuma (Dwabenhemaa), 146
Afranewa, 212
Afua Kobi (Asantehemaa), 74, 82; and peace interest, 49
Agogo, 29, 137; British in, 177; British